ARCHITECT'S HANDBOOK
of Construction Detailing

SECOND EDITION

ARCHITECT'S HANDBOOK
of Construction Detailing

David Kent Ballast, FAIA, CSI

John Wiley & Sons, Inc.

Copyright © 2009 by John Wiley & Sons, Inc. All rights reserved.

Published by John Wiley & Sons, Inc., Hoboken, New Jersey.
Published simultaneously in Canada.

For general information about our other products and services, please contact our Customer Care Department within the United States at (800) 762-2974, outside the United States at (317) 572-3993 or fax (317) 572-4002.

Wiley also publishes its books in a variety of electronic formats. Some content that appears in print may not be available in electronic books. For more information about Wiley products, visit our web site at www.wiley.com.

Library of Congress Cataloging-in-Publication Data:

Ballast, David Kent.
    Architect's handbook of construction detailing / David Ballast. – 2nd ed.
        p.   cm.
    Includes bibliographical references and index.
    ISBN 978-0-470-38191-5 (cloth : alk. paper)
    1. Building–Details–Drawings.   I. Title.

    TH2031.B35 2009
    692'.2–dc22
                                                        2008047065
Printed in the United States of America.

10 9 8 7 6 5 4 3

CONTENTS

3 METAL DETAILS 143

4 WOOD DETAILS _____ 169

5 THERMAL AND MOISTURE PROTECTION DETAILS _____ 203

6 DOOR AND WINDOW DETAILS   297

7 FINISH DETAILS   347

LIST OF TABLES

PREFACE

While construction details can add to the style and aesthetic appeal of a building, they are useless unless they can successfully provide the basic functional requirements of satisfying the building's purpose, protecting against the elements, providing durable interior finishes, and making construction efficient and economical.

Most building problems and outright failures occur because of poorly designed or constructed details. Although detailing is vitally important for preventing problems, it is becoming a lost art at the same time that it is becoming more complex due to the proliferation of new materials and construction techniques, more stringent energy and sustainability requirements, and safety and security concerns. Architecture schools rarely provide students with the fundamental grounding in detailing and specifying or spend as much time on them as on design and other subjects. In architectural practice, final detailing is often left until the end of the design and documents phases, when time and money are limited, for their thorough development.

The *Architect's Handbook of Construction Detailing* provides architects, interior designers, contractors, students, and others involved with the construction industry with a convenient source of detailing and specification information on hundreds of commonly used details and materials.

Although no one book can provide all the details that are used in construction, the *Architect's Handbook of Construction Detailing* provides basic detail configurations that can be used as the basis for project-specific detail development. Because detailing is closely tied to specifying, this book also provides fundamental material data and information. The written information is coordinated with the illustrated details in a keynote format.

The current edition of this book updates and expands features in the first edition. Details have been revised to reflect new technologies and more stringent requirements for energy conservation. New sections have been added on concrete with insulation, autoclaved aerated concrete, glass fiber reinforced concrete panels, precast concrete with insulation, multistory wood framing, structural insulated panels, vegetated protected membrane roofing, weather barrier concepts, thermoplastic polyolefin roofing, fire-resistant glazing, proprietary gypsum wallboard slip joints, and laminate flooring.

The keynoting system has been updated from the previous Construction Specifications Institute's five-digit *MasterFormat*™ numbering system to the current six-digit system. All illustrations have been redrawn and industry standard references, including ASTM and ANSI standards, have been updated, as have the sources for information in the appendices.

As with the first edition, each detail section follows a similar format to make it easy to find information and relate it to the drawing. The details in the book may be used to help solve specific problems, as the basis for developing a master detail system, or as a reference for checking existing drawings and specifications. The book can also be used to develop and coordinate specifications with details.

ACKNOWLEDGMENTS

I would like to thank the many people who contributed to the making of this book. For the publisher John Wiley & Sons, Amanda Miller, vice president and publisher, and John Czarnecki, Assoc. AIA, senior editor, were instrumental in suggesting this new edition. Thanks also to the other fine people at John Wiley & Sons: Donna Conte, senior production editor; Sadie Abuhoff, editorial assistant; Helen Greenberg for copyediting; Figaro for design and page layout.

INTRODUCTION

What This Book Will Do for You

The *Architect's Handbook of Construction Detailing* presents ready-to-use information about critical building details to help you produce construction drawings, design and develop custom details, prepare specifications, and check existing drawings in your files. The details presented can be used directly for common construction situations. If modifications are necessary for unique project conditions, the data presented with each drawing tell you what can and cannot be changed to maintain the integrity of the detail.

The construction assemblies in this book have been selected to help you avoid problems in those areas where they are most likely to occur. Information presented in seven sections shows you how to detail such conditions as exterior cladding, roofing, doors, masonry, and many, many others so that you can prevent common mistakes that architects seem to repeat far too often. In addition to clearly drawn graphic details, accurate, to-the-point information is given to help you coordinate a detail with other parts of your design, specify materials, and develop your own layout if necessary.

A broad range of architectural details is covered, from concrete construction to finishes. Each drawing has an identifying number according to the Construction Specifications Institute's *MasterFormat* system, and all the pertinent materials used in the details are identified by the same numbering system. This makes it easy for you to produce drawings with time-saving keynoting, to coordinate the drawings and information with your specification system, and to supplement the details with your own data filing procedures. Most details have been drawn at three-inch scale. When another scale is used, it is shown at the bottom of the drawing.

Among the many other details, this *Handbook*

- Shows the recommended way to detail concrete joints. (See Sections 1-5, 1-6, and 1-7)
- Specifies the most common concrete construction tolerances. (See Sections 1-1, 1-2, 1-3, 1-11, and 1-13)
- Presents common methods of assembling precast wall panels. (See Sections 1-16, 1-17, and 1-19)
- Describes how to assemble brick veneer walls to avoid cracks and leaks. (See Sections 2-9 and 2-11)
- Compiles the many ways stone veneer should be attached to concrete and steel frames. (See Sections 2-22, 2-23, 2-25, 2-26, 2-27, 2-31 and 2-32)
- Provides the secrets to designing elegant stairways. (See Sections 3-10 through 3-13)
- Simplifies the methods of forming expansion joints. (See Sections 2-2 and 3-16)
- Shows how to fabricate glued-laminated beam and column connections. (See Section 4-10)
- Tells how to create sheet membrane waterproofing details. (See Sections 5-1 and 5-2)
- Organizes information on asphalt and fiberglass shingles. (See Section 5-9)
- Lays out the many variations of single-ply roofing. (See Sections 5-16 through 5-36)
- Explains the dos and don'ts of joint fillers and sealants. (See Section 5-38)
- Illustrates steel door frame assemblies and what is involved in their proper construction. (See Sections 6-1. 6-2, and 6-3)

- Describes how to detail a safety glass door. (See Section 6-8)
- Identifies the essential elements of steel, aluminum, and wood window detailing. (See Sections 6-16 through 6-19)
- Shows how fire-rated gypsum wallboard assemblies should be drawn. (See Sections 7-5 through 7-11)
- Illustrates the many ways to detail ceramic tile floors and walls. (See Sections 7-15 through 7-22)
- Gives guidance on detailing stone flooring. (See Sections 7-25 and 7-26)

The information presented about each detail in this book follows a similar format to make it easy to find precisely the data required for your research. The first part of each detail information package shows the detail itself, with materials identified by *MasterFormat* number and other critical components dimensioned or labeled with design guidelines. Each of the components identified on the drawing by keynote number refers you to requirements for those materials given in the text. This gives you an invaluable guide for coordinating your drawings and specifications.

The second part of the package consists of a brief description of the detail along with the limitations on using it. Then specific guidelines are presented to help you understand the critical points of construction and what must be considered in modifying the detail or developing your own. Next, points of coordination are listed to aid you in fitting the detail into the context of your design. Likely failure points are also outlined to alert you to common problems encountered in the design and construction of the detail. Finally, material and installation requirements for components of the detail are listed according to the keynote numbering system used in the detail.

All of the information is presented in concise, easy-to-follow lists and notations so that you do not have to waste time wading through lengthy text. Appendices provide the full title of ASTM and other industry standards referred to in the book as well as sources for additional information if you want to do more research.

The configuration of the details and accompanying data have been compiled from the most authoritative sources available. However, the material presented in this book should only be used as a supplement to normal, competent professional knowledge and judgment. This is because there are an unlimited number of variations of any basic detail to fit the requirements of a specific building project. In addition, factors outside the limits of a particular detail, such as structural loading, climate, and occupancy conditions, may impinge on the detail's performance or exact method of construction.

You may want to use the details in this book to help solve specific problems, as the basis for your office's own master detail system, or simply as a reference for checking existing drawings. If you have master details on a computer-aided drafting system or an automated specification writing system, you may want to review those data to see if modifications or corrections are warranted. Regardless of how you use this book, you will find it a time-saving reference that can minimize errors and improve the technical documentation of your projects.

HOW SI UNITS ARE USED IN THIS BOOK

This edition of the *Architect's Handbook of Construction Detailing* includes equivalent measurements, using the Système Internationale (SI), in the text and illustrations. However, the use of SI units for construction and book publishing in the United States is problematic. This is because the building construction industry in the United States (with the exception of federal construction) has generally not adopted the *metric system*, as it is commonly called. Equivalent measurements of customary U.S. units (also called *English* or *inch-pound units*) are usually given as soft conversions using standard conversion factors. This always results in a number with excessive significant digits. When construction is done using SI units, the building is designed and drawn according to hard conversions, where planning dimensions and building products are based on a metric module from the beginning. For example, studs are spaced 400 mm on center to accommodate panel products that are manufactured in standard 1200 mm widths.

During the transition to SI units in the United States, code-writing bodies, federal laws (such as the Americans with Disabilities Act [ADA]), product manufacturers, trade associations, and other construction-related industries typically still use the customary U.S. system and make soft conversions to develop SI equivalents. Some manufacturers produce the same product using both measuring systems. Although there are industry standards for developing SI equivalents, there is no consistency for rounding off when conversions are made. For example, the *International Building Code* (IBC) shows a 152 mm equivalent when a 6 in. dimension is required. The *ADA Accessibility Guidelines* shows a 150 mm equivalent for the same dimension.

For the purposes of this book, the following conventions have been adopted.

Throughout this book, the customary U.S. measurements are given first and the SI equivalents follow in parentheses. In the text, the unit suffixes for both systems, such as *ft* or *mm*, are shown. In the illustrations, the number values and U.S. unit suffixes are given first (*in., ft,* etc.) and the SI value after them in parentheses but *without* the unit if the number is in millimeters but *with* the unit if it is in meters or some other unit except millimeters. This follows standard construction practice for SI units on architectural drawings; a number is understood to be in millimeters unless some other unit is given. The exception to this convention occurs when a number is based on an international standard or product. In this case, the primary measurement is given first in SI units with the U.S. equivalent in parentheses. The unit suffix is shown for *both* in the text as well as in the illustrations to avoid confusion.

When there is a ratio or some combination of units where it might be confusing, unit suffixes are used for all numbers—for example, 6 mm/3 m.

When a standards-writing organization or a trade association gives dual units for a particular measurement, those numbers are used exactly as they come from the source. For example, one group might use 6.4 mm as the equivalent for 1/4 in., while another organization might use 6 mm.

When an SI conversion is used by a code agency, such as the IBC or published in another regulation, such as the *ADA Accessibility Guidelines* (ADAAG), the SI equivalents used by the issuing agency are printed in this book. For example, the IBC uses a 152 mm equivalent when a 6 in. dimension is required, while the ADAAG gives a 150 mm equivalent for the same dimension.

If a specific conversion is not otherwise given by a trade association or standards-writing organization, when converted values are rounded, the SI equivalent is rounded to the nearest millimeter for numbers under a few inches unless the dimension is very small (as for small tolerances like $1/16$ in.), in which case a more precise decimal equivalent is given.

For dimensions over a few inches, the SI equivalent is rounded to the nearest 5 mm and to the nearest 10 mm for numbers over a few feet. When the dimension exceeds several feet, the number is rounded to the nearest 100 mm.

Abbreviations

AAC	autoclaved aerated concrete
ACI	American Concrete Institute
AISC	American Institute of Steel Construction
AWI	Architectural Woodwork Institute
CFC	chlorofluorocarbon
ECH	epichlorohydrin
EN	European Norms
EPA	Environmental Protection Agency
EIFS	exterior insulation and finish system
EPDM	ethylene propylene diene monomer
EPS	expanded polystyrene board
FMG	Factory Mutual Global (class ratings)
FMRG	Factory Mutual Research Corporation
GFRC	glass fiber reinforced concrete
HCFC	hydrochloro-fluorocarbon
HFC	hydrofluorocarbon
HVAC	heating, ventilation, air conditioning
LEED	Leadership in Energy and Environmental Design
NFPA	National Fire Protection Association
NRC	noise reduction coefficient
NTMA	National Terrazzo and Mosaic Association
OSB	oriented strand board
PB	polymer based
PET	polyethylene terephthalate
PM	polymer modified
PVC	polyvinyl chloride
SBR	styrene butadiene rubber
SIP	structural insulated panel
STC	Sound Transmission Class
TPO	thermoplastic polyolefin
UL	Underwriters Laboratories
VOC	volatile organic compound
w.g.	water gage
XPS	extended polystyrene board

ARCHITECT'S HANDBOOK
of Construction Detailing

CHAPTER 1

CONCRETE DETAILS

1-1 CONCRETE SLAB-ON-GRADE TOLERANCES

Description

Because no building can be perfectly level, plumb, and straight, there are certain acceptable tolerances for various types of construction, which have become industry standards. These tolerances give architects, engineers, and contractors allowable variations from given dimensions and elevations. Knowing these tolerances is important in detailing because allowances must be made for variations from idealized dimensions when several materials are connected, when clearances are required, or when appearance is critical. This section and Sections 1-2, 1-3, 1-11, 1-13, 1-22, and 1-23 give some of the industry standard tolerances regarding concrete construction.

Slabs-on-grade (as well as elevated slabs) are subject to two tolerances. One is the overall tolerance above and below the specified elevation, and the other is the flatness and levelness of the floor finish. Flatness is the degree to which the surface approximates a plane. Levelness is the degree to which the surface parallels the horizontal plane.

Limitations of Use

- These tolerances are for slabs-on-grade as specified by the American Concrete Institute (ACI). See Section 1-2 for tolerances of other slab surfaces.
- The tolerances given can also be used to specify sloped surfaces.
- Verify the size of temperature reinforcement, the concrete strength, and the size and spacing of rebars (if any) with a structural engineer.

Detailing Considerations

- Do not specify a tolerance higher than that actually required for the project because higher finish tolerances generally cost more to achieve. For example, a moderately flat floor ($\pm^3/_8$ in. in 10 ft [10 mm in 3 m]) is generally sufficient for carpet or an exterior walk.
- Verify the slab thickness required for the project. A 4 in. (100 mm) slab is the minimum thickness allowable and is used for residential and lightly loaded commercial floors subject to foot traffic. A 5 in. (127 mm) thickness is required for light industrial and

1

commercial floors where there is foot traffic and pneumatic wheeled traffic. Floors with heavy loads require thicker slabs and special reinforcing.

Coordination Required

- In order to maintain the specified level of the slab, proper compaction and subgrade preparation must be specified and maintained during construction. Soil and fill under slabs should be compacted to 95 percent of standard Proctor density.
- Locate joints according to the information given in Sections 1-5, 1-6, and 1-7.
- Vapor barriers should be used under slabs to prevent moisture migration into the slab, to prevent shrinkage cracks, and to provide a barrier to radon penetration. However, in order to prevent plastic and drying shrinkage caused by differential water loss between the top and bottom of the slab, the slab must be properly cured following ACI recommendations.
- Reinforcing and concrete strength should be selected based on the service requirements of the slab. Generally, lightly loaded slabs require a minimum compressive concrete strength of 3500 psi (24,000 kPa), while light industrial and commercial slabs require a compressive strength of 4000 psi (27,500 kPa).

Allowable Tolerances

Level alignment tolerance is shown in Fig. 1-1(a). This means that over the entire surface of a concrete slab, all points must fall within an envelope $3/4$ in. (19 mm) above or below the theoretical elevation plane.

Random traffic floor finish tolerances may be specified either by the traditional 10 ft (3 m) straightedge method, shown in Fig. 1-1(b), or by the F-number system. For a complete discussion of the F-number system refer to ACI 302.1R–89, *Guide for Concrete Floor and Slab Construction*, and ACI Compilation No. 9, *Concrete Floor Flatness and Levelness*.

If the 10 ft (3 m) straightedge method is used, there are three floor classifications: conventional, moderately flat, and flat. In order for a surface to meet the requirements of one of these three classifications, a minimum of 0.01 times the area of the floor measured in ft^2 (0.1 times the area in m^2) must be taken. Ninety percent of the samples must be within the first column shown in Fig. 1-1(b), and 100 percent of the samples must fall within the second column in Fig. 1-1(b). The orientation of the straightedge must be parallel, perpendicular, or at a 45 degree angle to the longest construction joint bounding the test surface. ACI 117, *Specifications for Tolerances for Concrete Construction and Materials and Commentary*, details the other requirements for taking the samples.

The F-number system, diagrammed in Fig. 1-1(c), is a statistical method used to measure and specify both the local flatness of a floor within adjacent 12 in. (300 mm) intervals (the F_F number) and the local levelness of a floor (the F_L number) over a 10 ft (3.05 m) distance. The higher the F_F or F_L number, the flatter or more level the floor. To determine if a floor falls within the tolerances of a particular F_F and F_L number measurements must be taken according to the procedure set forth in ASTM E1155-87. In most cases, a sophisticated instrument must be used that can take the measurements and perform the calculations necessary for determining the F numbers. Although there is no direct correlation, an F_F50 roughly corresponds to a $1/8$ in. (3.2 mm) gap under a 10 ft (3.05 m) straightedge. An F_F25 roughly corresponds to a $1/4$ in. (6 mm) gap under a 10 ft (3.05 m) straightedge.

Figure 1-1 Concrete slabs-on-grade tolerances 03 05 03

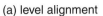

(a) level alignment

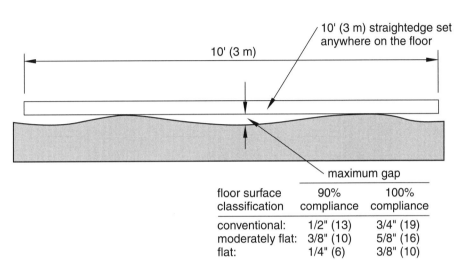

floor surface classification	maximum gap 90% compliance	100% compliance
conventional:	1/2" (13)	3/4" (19)
moderately flat:	3/8" (10)	5/8" (16)
flat:	1/4" (6)	3/8" (10)

(b) 10-ft straightedge method

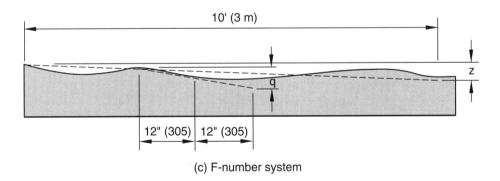

(c) F-number system

For slabs-on-grade the F-number system works well. However, to determine the F numbers, measurements must be taken within 72 hours of floor installation and, for suspended slabs, before shoring and forms are removed. Therefore, for suspended slabs, the specified levelness of a floor may be compromised when the floor deflects when the shoring is removed and loads are applied.

ACI 117 gives requirements for five classes of floors that can be specified: conventional, moderately flat, flat, very flat, and superflat. In order to meet the requirements for whatever class of floor is specified, the procedures of ASTM E1155 must be followed and the test results must meet certain overall flatness (SOF_F) values and specified overall levelness (SOF_L) values. In addition, minimum local values for flatness and levelness must also be achieved. These are $3/5$ of the SOF_F and SOF_L values. For example, a "conventional" floor must have an SOF_F of

20 and an SOF_L of 15, while a superflat floor must have an SOF_F of 60 and an SOF_L of 40. Refer to ACI 117 for detailed requirements.

1-2 CAST-IN-PLACE CONCRETE SECTIONAL TOLERANCES

Description

Figure 1-2 shows dimensional tolerances for cast-in-place concrete elements. It includes elevation tolerances as well as cross-sectional tolerances for elements such as columns, beams, walls, and slabs.

Figure 1-2 Cast-in-place concrete sectional tolerances 03 05 04

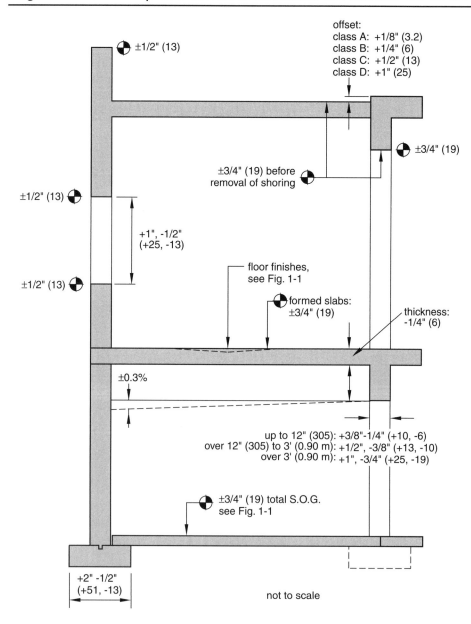

offset:
class A: +1/8" (3.2)
class B: +1/4" (6)
class C: +1/2" (13)
class D: +1" (25)

±1/2" (13)

±3/4" (19)

±3/4" (19) before removal of shoring

±1/2" (13)

+1", -1/2" (+25, -13)

floor finishes, see Fig. 1-1

±1/2" (13)

formed slabs: ±3/4" (19)

thickness: -1/4" (6)

±0.3%

up to 12" (305): +3/8"-1/4" (+10, -6)
over 12" (305) to 3' (0.90 m): +1/2", -3/8" (+13, -10)
over 3' (0.90 m): +1", -3/4" (+25, -19)

±3/4" (19) total S.O.G. see Fig. 1-1

+2" -1/2" (+51, -13)

not to scale

Limitations of Use

- The tolerances shown in this drawing should be used with judgment as a range of acceptability and an estimate of likely variation from true measurements, not as a basis for rejection of work.
- Floor tolerance measurements must be made within 72 hours after the concrete is finished and before the shoring is removed.
- For additional tolerances, refer to ACI 117.
- If smaller tolerances are required, they should be clearly indicated in the contract documents and discussed with the contractor prior to construction.

Detailing Considerations

- In some cases tolerances may accumulate, resulting in a wider variation from true measurement than that due to individual tolerances alone.
- In general, higher accuracy requires a higher construction cost.
- A floor poured over metal decking will generally deflect significantly. If deflection must be limited, extra support or more rigid decking may be needed.

Coordination Required

- If other materials are being used with or attached to the concrete, the expected tolerances of the other materials must be known so that allowance can be made for both.
- Benchmarks and control points should be agreed on by the contractor and architect prior to construction and should be maintained throughout construction.
- Refer to Sections 1-11 and 1-13 for tolerances of precast concrete.

Allowable Tolerances

The various sectional tolerances are shown diagrammatically in Fig. 1-2. The level alignment tolerance of $\pm^1/_2$ in. (13 mm) for lintels, sills, and parapets also applies to horizontal grooves and other lines exposed to view. Offsets listed as Class A, B, C, and D are for adjacent pieces of formwork facing material. Note that the level alignment of the top surface of formed slabs and other formed surfaces is measured *before* the removal of shoring. There is no requirement for slabs on structural steel or precast concrete. The tolerance for the top of a wall is $\pm^3/_4$ in. (19).

For slabs-on-grade, the tolerance is $-^3/_8$ in. (-10 mm) for the average of all samples and $-^3/_4$ in. (-19 mm) for an individual sample. The minimum number of samples that must be taken is one per 10,000 ft^2 (929 m^2).

1-3   CAST-IN-PLACE CONCRETE PLAN TOLERANCES

Description

Figure 1-3 complements Fig. 1-2 and illustrates allowable variations from lateral dimensions for various concrete elements such as columns, piers, walls, and openings. The tolerances

Figure 1-3 Cast-in-place concrete plan tolerances 03 05 05

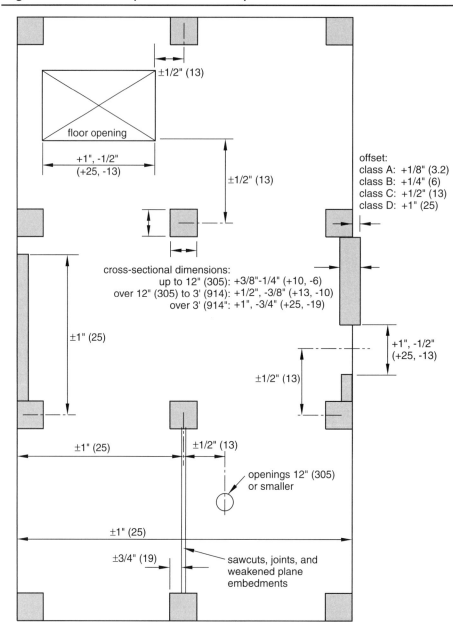

not to scale

shown in Fig. 1-3 are based on recommendations of the ACI. In some cases, the tolerances may conflict with individual ACI documents. In these cases, the tolerances required should be specified in the contract documents.

Limitations of Use

- The tolerances shown in Fig. 1-3 should be used with judgment as a range of acceptability and an estimate of likely variation from true measurements, not as a basis for rejection of work.

- If smaller tolerances are required, they should be clearly indicated in the contract documents and discussed with the contractor prior to construction.
- For additional tolerances, refer to ACI 117.

Detailing Considerations

- In some cases tolerances may accumulate, resulting in a wider variation from true measurement than that due to individual tolerances alone.
- Generally speaking, higher accuracy requires a higher construction cost.
- Details should provide sufficient clearance for the tolerances shown as well as for attached materials.

Coordination Required

- If other materials are being used with or attached to the concrete construction, the expected tolerances of the other materials must be known so that allowance can be made for both.
- Benchmarks and control points should be agreed on by the contractor and architect prior to construction and should be maintained throughout construction.
- Refer to Sections 1-11 and 1-13 for tolerances of precast concrete.

1-4   WATERSTOPS

Description

A waterstop is a premolded sealant used across concrete joints to stop the passage of water under hydrostatic pressure. There are dozens of different styles and sizes of waterstops made from several types of materials to suit particular situations. Waterstops are made for two basic types of joints: working and nonworking. Working joints are those where significant movement is expected; nonworking joints are those where little or no movement is expected.

Figure 1-4 shows two typical types of joints. A centerbulb waterstop is shown in the working joint in Fig. 1-4(a), which allows movement both parallel and perpendicular to the plane of the concrete. For a nonworking joint, as shown in Fig. 1-4(b), a dumbbell or flat, serrated waterstop can be used. The dumbbell shape shown here holds the waterstop in place and provides a longer path for water to travel across the joint, improving its watertightness. If a great deal of movement is expected, a U-shaped, tear-web center section can be selected, as shown in Fig. 1-4(c)

Limitations of Use

- The details included here show only two of the many styles of waterstops available for various applications. Refer to manufacturers' literature for specific recommendations on material and configuration of a waterstop.

Detailing Considerations

- Most waterstops are either 6 in. (152 mm) or 9 in. (229 mm) wide; some are available up to 12 in. (305 mm).

Figure 1-4 Waterstops 03 15 13

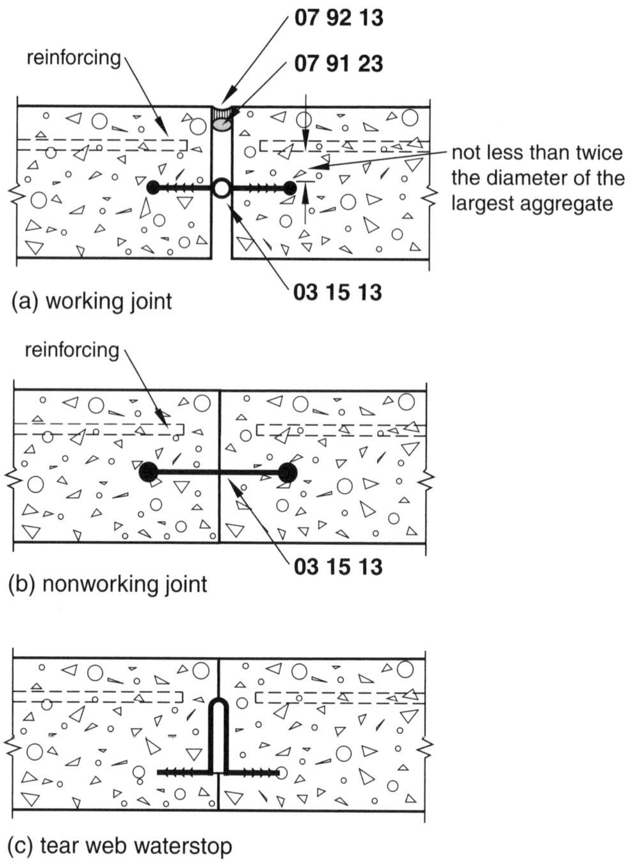

(a) working joint

(b) nonworking joint

(c) tear web waterstop

- Select the type and shape of waterstop based on the requirements of the joint, either working or nonworking.

Likely Failure Points

- Splitting of the joint due to the use of an incorrect type of waterstop for the movement expected
- Leaking due to honeycombing near the seal caused by displacement of the waterstop during placing and consolidation of the concrete
- Leaking caused by incomplete or improper splicing
- Leaking caused by contamination of the waterstop by form coatings

Materials

03 15 13 WATERSTOP

Waterstops for general construction are typically made from polyvinyl chloride (PVC), styrene butadiene rubber (SBR), and neoprene. Other materials are available, including metal, which are resistant to certain types of chemicals or which are more appropriate for special uses.

PVC can be easily spliced, while other materials require the use of preformed fittings for angles or the use of skilled workers to make the correct fittings and splices.

The width of the waterstop should not be greater than the thickness of the wall.

07 91 23 BACKER ROD

Closed cell polyethylene foam, with the diameter at least 25 percent greater than the joint width.

07 92 13 SEALANT

Materials

Polysulfide, polyurethane, or silicone, ASTM C920, are the most common types used. Sealant may either be Type S or M (one part or multicomponent), Grade P or NS (pourable or nonsag), and Class 25.

Sealant must be compatible with the type of joint filler used.

Execution

Sealant depth equal to the width of the joint up to $1/2$ in. (13 mm), with a minimum depth of $1/4$ in. (6 mm).

Sealant depth $1/2$ in. (13 mm) for joint widths from $1/2$ in. to 1 in. (13 mm to 25 mm).

For sealants with a ±25 percent movement capability, the joint width should be four times the expected movement of the joint.

Sealant should not bond to the joint filler.

1-5   SLAB-ON-GRADE CONTROL JOINT

Description

Figure 1–5 shows one of the three types of joints used in concrete slabs-on-grade. Control joints, also called *contraction joints*, are used to induce cracking in preselected locations when the slab shortens due to drying, shrinking, and temperature changes. For lightly loaded slabs, a minimum thickness of 4 in. (102 mm) is required. For most light industrial and commercial work, slab thicknesses of 5 in. or 6 in. (127 mm or 152 mm) are recommended, depending on the loading conditions. Industrial floors may require even thicker slabs.

Limitations of Use

- The detail shown is for lightly loaded and moderately loaded interior and exterior slabs. Heavy-duty industrial floors, street pavements, and other heavily loaded slabs require special considerations for reinforcement, design thickness, and joint construction.
- Verify the size and spacing of rebars, if required, with a structural engineer.

Detailing Considerations

- Control joints may be formed by sawcutting shortly after the slab hardens (as shown in Fig. 1-5), by hand tooling, or by using preformed plastic or metal strips pressed into the fresh concrete.

Figure 1-5 Slab-on-grade control joint   03 30 07

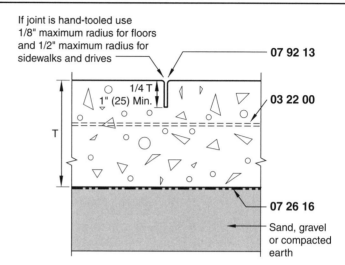

- For interior slabs, control joints should be placed 15 ft to 20 ft (4.6 m to 6.1 m) apart in both directions. Slab sections formed with control joints should be square or nearly square. For sidewalks or driveways control joints should be spaced at intervals approximately equal to the width of the slab, but walks or drives wider than about 12 ft (3.6 m) should have an intermediate control joint in the center. If control joints will be visible in the completed construction, their location should be planned to coincide with lines of other building elements, such as column centerlines and other joints.
- Isolation and construction joints can also serve as control joints.
- Vapor barriers should be used under slabs to prevent moisture migration into the slab, to prevent shrinkage cracks, and to provide a barrier to radon penetration. However, in order to prevent plastic and drying shrinkage caused by differential water loss between the top and bottom of the slab, the slab must be properly cured following ACI recommendations.
- Seal control joints to prevent spalling of the concrete.

Coordination Required

- Select a vapor barrier and granular fill under the slab to satisfy the requirements of the project. In most cases, a gravel subbase should be placed under the slab to provide drainage.
- Reinforcing and concrete strength should be selected based on service requirements of the slab.
- The subgrade should be compacted to 95 percent of standard Proctor density prior to placing the subbase.

Likely Failure Points

- Cracking of the slab in undesirable locations if control joints are placed farther apart than 20 ft (6.1 m) or if sections of the slab are elongated (length-to-width ratio greater than 1.5) or are L-shaped

- Cracking of the slab if control joint grooves are not deep enough
- Random cracking before sawing of control joints usually means that the sawing was delayed too long

Materials

03 22 00 WELDED WIRE REINFORCEMENT

6 × 6 —W1.4 × 1.4 (152 × 152 –MW9 × MW9), minimum or as required by the structural requirements of the job.

Place welded wire reinforcement in the top one-third of the slab.

If fabric is carried through control joints, cut every other wire to ensure that the cracking will occur at the joint.

Reinforcement is often not used where frequent control joints are used.

Welded wire reinforcement should extend to about 2 in. (51 mm) from the edge of the slab but no more than 6 in. (152 mm) from the edges.

07 26 16 VAPOR BARRIER

6 mil (0.15 mm) polyethylene.

Permeance of less than 0.3 perm (17 ng/s•m^2•Pa) determined in accordance with ASTM E96.

Barrier should not be punctured during construction activities.

Edges should be lapped a minimum of 6 in. (152 mm) and taped and should be carefully fitted around openings.

07 92 13 SEALANT

Materials

Polysulfide, polyurethane, or silicone, ASTM C920, are the most common types used. Sealant may be either Type S or M (one part or multicomponent), Grade P or NS (pourable or nonsag), and Class 25.

Sealant must be compatible with the type of joint filler used.

Use epoxy resin when support is needed for small, hard-wheeled traffic.

Execution

Sealant depth equal to the width of the joint up to $^1/_2$ in. (13 mm), with a minimum depth of $^1/_4$ in. (6 mm).

Sealant depth $^1/_2$ in. (13 mm) for joint widths from $^1/_2$ in. to 1 in. (13 mm to 25 mm).

For sealants with a ±25 percent movement capability, the joint width should be four times the expected movement of the joint.

Sealant should not bond to the joint filler.

Thoroughly clean the joint of dirt and debris prior to application of the sealant.

Figure 1-6 Slab-on-grade isolation joint 03 30 08

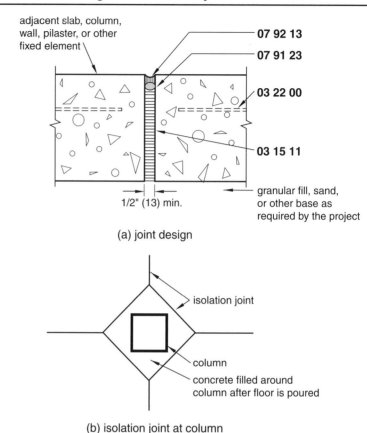

(a) joint design

(b) isolation joint at column

1-6 SLAB-ON-GRADE ISOLATION JOINT

Description

Figure 1-6(a) shows one of the three types of joints used in concrete slabs-on-grade. Isolation joints, also called *expansion joints*, are used to structurally separate the slab from other building elements to accommodate differential movement. They are usually located at footings, columns, walls, machinery bases, and other points of restraint such as pipes, stairways, and similar fixed structural elements. Figure 1-6(b) shows the general configuration when an isolation joint is located at a column.

For lightly loaded slabs, a minimum thickness of 4 in. (102 mm) is required. For most commercial work, slab thicknesses of 5 in. (127 mm) or 6 in. (152 mm) are recommended, depending on the loading conditions. Industrial floors may require even thicker slabs.

Limitations of Use

- The detail shown here is for lightly loaded and moderately loaded interior and exterior slabs. Heavy-duty industrial floors, street pavements, and other heavily loaded slabs require special considerations for reinforcement, design thickness, and joint construction.
- If required, verify the size and spacing of rebars with a structural engineer.

Detailing Considerations

- Isolation joint fillers must extend the full thickness of the joint.
- The width of isolation joints should be sized to accommodate the expected movement of the slab, allowing for about a 50 percent maximum compression of the joint. In most cases, a $1/2$ in. (13 mm) joint is adequate, but wider joints may be needed for large slabs or extreme conditions.
- In certain noncritical locations such as garage floors, protected exterior slab/foundation intersections, and similar conditions, the sealant and backer rod may be omitted, with the joint filler placed flush with the top of the slab.
- Vapor barriers should be used under slabs to prevent moisture migration into the slab, to prevent shrinkage cracks, and to provide a barrier to radon penetration. However, in order to prevent plastic and drying shrinkage caused by differential water loss between the top and bottom of the slab, the slab must be properly cured following ACI recommendations.
- A bond breaker should be used with isolation joints if the joint filler does not serve this purpose.

Coordination Required

- Select a vapor barrier and granular fill under the slab to satisfy the requirements of the project. In most cases, a gravel subbase should be placed under the slab to provide drainage.
- Reinforcing and concrete strength should be selected based on service requirements of the slab.
- The subgrade should be compacted to 95 percent of standard Proctor density prior to placing the subbase.

Likely Failure Points

- Cracking of the slab near walls or columns if proper isolation joints are not formed
- Cracking near the isolation joint if the joint filler is displaced during construction
- Slab settlement if the ground under the slab is not compacted to the proper density

Materials

03 22 00 WELDED WIRE REINFORCEMENT

6 × 6—W1.4 × 1.4 (152 × 152 –MW9 × MW9), minimum or as required by the structural requirements of the job.

Place welded wire reinforcement in the top one-third of the slab.

Reinforcement is often not used where frequent control joints are used.

Welded wire reinforcement should extend to about 2 in. (51 mm) from the edge of the slab but no more than 6 in. (152 mm) from the edges.

03 15 11 EXPANSION JOINT FILLER

Compressible joint fillers may be bituminous-impregnated fiberboard or glass fiber or one of several other types of joint fillers. In some situations, the joint filler may be used alone without a sealant.

07 91 23 BACKER ROD

Closed cell polyethylene foam, with the diameter at least 25 percent greater than the joint width.

07 92 13 SEALANT

Materials

Polysulfide, polyurethane, or silicone, ASTM C920, are the most common types used. Sealant may be either Type S or M (one part or multicomponent), Grade P or NS (pourable or nonsag), and Class 25.

Sealant must be compatible with the type of joint filler used.

Execution

Sealant depth equal to the width of the joint up to 1/2 in. (13 mm), with a minimum depth of 1/4 in. (6 mm).

Sealant depth 1/2 in. (13 mm) for joint widths from 1/2 in. to 1 in. (13 mm to 25 mm).

For sealants with a ±25 percent movement capability, the joint width should be four times the expected movement of the joint.

Sealant should not bond to the joint filler.

Thoroughly clean the joint of dirt and debris prior to application of sealant.

1-7 SLAB-ON-GRADE CONSTRUCTION JOINT

Description

Figure 1-7 shows two variations of a construction joint. Construction joints provide stopping points for construction activities. A construction joint may also serve as a control or isolation joint. Construction joints can be formed with separate wood strips placed on the form after the first pour to form the keyway or prefabricated forms made specifically for this purpose may be used.

For lightly loaded slabs, a minimum thickness of 4 in. (102 mm) is required. For most commercial work, slab thicknesses of 5 in. (127 mm) or 6 in. (152 mm) are recommended, depending on the loading conditions.

Limitations of Use

- The details shown here are for lightly loaded and moderately loaded interior and exterior slabs. Heavy-duty industrial floors, street pavements, and other heavily loaded slabs require special considerations for reinforcement, design thickness, and joint construction.
- Verify the size and spacing of dowels, if required, with a structural engineer.
- Butt-type construction joints (those without reinforcing dowels, or keyed joints) should be limited to lightly loaded slabs 4 in. (102 mm) thick.

Detailing Considerations

- Construction joints should not be placed closer than 5 ft (1525 mm) to any other parallel joint.

Figure 1-7 Slab-on-grade construction joint 03 30 09

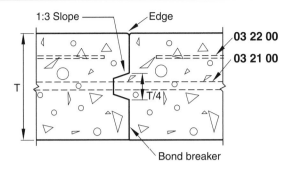

(a) construction joint with keyway

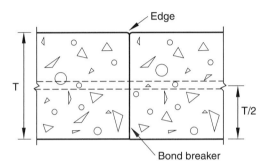

(b) construction joint without keyway

- A bond breaker must be used with construction joints.
- Vapor barriers should be used under slabs to prevent moisture migration into the slab, to prevent shrinkage cracks, and to provide a barrier to radon penetration. However, in order to prevent plastic and drying shrinkage caused by differential water loss between the top and bottom of the slab, the slab must be properly cured following ACI recommendations.
- The top of the joint should be given a slight radius edge to avoid spalling of the concrete.

Coordination Required

- Select a vapor barrier and granular fill under the slab to satisfy the requirements of the project. In most cases, a gravel subbase should be placed under the slab to provide drainage.
- Reinforcing and concrete strength should be selected based on service requirements of the slab.
- The subgrade should be compacted to 95 percent of standard Proctor density prior to placing the subbase.

Likely Failure Points

- Cracking caused by misaligned dowels in construction joints
- Cracking due to omission of the bond breaker on the joint or one end of the dowel
- Slab settlement if the ground under the slab is not compacted to the proper density

Materials

03 21 00 REINFORCING DOWELS

Materials

Use reinforcing dowels in construction joints for heavily loaded floors and where wheeled traffic is present.

#6 (#1) rebar for slabs 5 in. (127 mm) to 6 in. (152 mm) deep.

#8 (#25) rebar for slabs 7 in. (178 mm) to 8 in. (203 mm) deep.

Minimum 16 in. (406 mm) long dowels for 5 in. (127 mm) to 6 in. (152 mm) slabs; minimum 18 in. (457 mm) dowels for 7 in. (178 mm) to 8 in. (203 mm) slabs.

Execution

Space 12 in. (305 mm) on center.

A dowel extending into the second pour must be coated with bond breaker.

Align and support dowels during pouring.

03 22 00 WELDED WIRE REINFORCEMENT

6 × 6—W1.4 × 1.4 (152 × 152 –MW9 × MW9), minimum or as required by the structural requirements of the job.

Place welded wire reinforcement in the top one-third of the slab.

Temperature reinforcement is often not used where frequent control joints are used.

Welded wire reinforcement should extend to about 2 in. (51 mm) from the edge of the slab but no more than 6 in. (152 mm) from the edges.

1-8   CAST-IN-PLACE CONCRETE WALL WITH INSULATION

Description

Figure 1-8 shows two basic methods of detailing a cast-in-place wall to include insulation and interior finish. Figure 1-8(a) shows the use of stud framing to provide a space for insulation as well as the substrate for the interior finish. Figure 1-8(b) illustrates the application of rigid insulation directly to the concrete, with the finish being applied to smaller framing. As an alternative, Z-shaped furring strips can be attached to the concrete. However, furring attached directly to the concrete creates a thermal bridge and reduces the overall R-value slightly. Depending on the building use, separate framing is useful to provide space for additional insulation as well as space for electrical service and plumbing pipes. In both cases a window jamb is shown, but the door framing is similar.

One of the detailing problems with cast-in-place concrete is accommodating construction tolerances, both for the opening size and for the window or door, which is usually steel or aluminum. ACI tolerances allow for an opening to be oversize by 1 in. (25 mm) or undersized by $1/2$ in. (13 mm). This means that at each jamb, the edge of the concrete opening may be larger by $1/2$ in. (13 mm) or smaller by $1/4$ in. (6 mm). Tolerances for steel door frames at each jamb are $1/16$ in. (1.6 mm) larger or $3/64$ in. (1.2 mm) smaller than their listed dimension. To allow for tolerances and a workable sealant joint, the design dimension of the concrete

Figure 1-8 Cast-in-place concrete wall with insulation 03 30 53

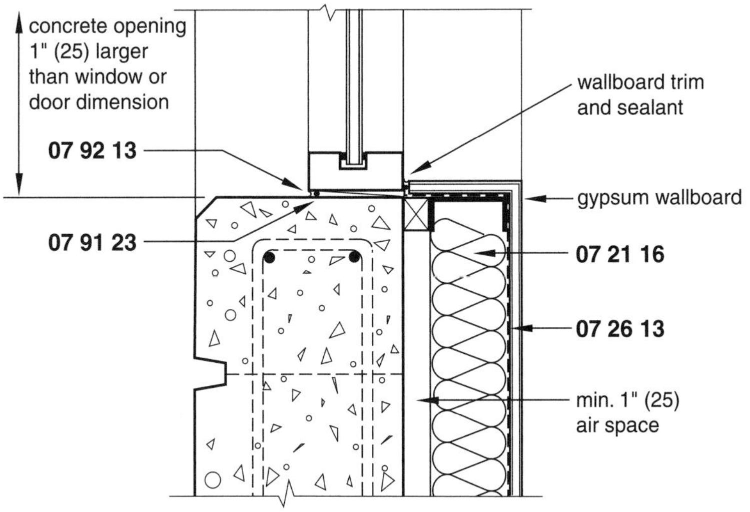

concrete opening
1" (25) larger
than window or
door dimension

07 92 13

07 91 23

wallboard trim
and sealant

gypsum wallboard

07 21 16

07 26 13

min. 1" (25)
air space

(a) stud framing with batt insulation

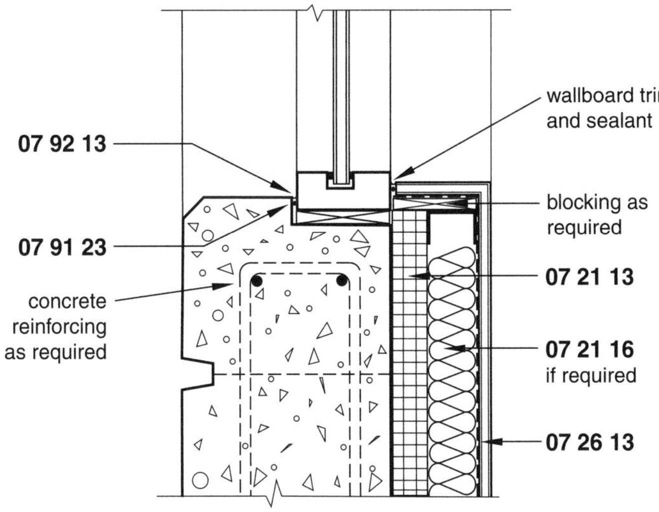

07 92 13

07 91 23

concrete
reinforcing
as required

wallboard trim
and sealant

blocking as
required

07 21 13

07 21 16
if required

07 26 13

(b) direct application of insulation

opening shown in Fig. 1–8(a) should be 1 in. (25 mm) wider than the width of the door or window frame ($\frac{1}{2}$ in. [13 mm] at each jamb). This allows the concrete to be undersized and the frame to be oversized while still allowing sufficient space for sealant.

Figure 1–8(b) illustrates the use of a notch in the concrete to account for construction tolerance issues. In this case, variations in opening size or frame size can be accommodated with blocking in the notch and covered with interior finish or trim. Although notching the concrete increases the formwork costs slightly, it accommodates tolerances and maintains a uniform joint width for sealant.

Limitations of Use

- These details do not include requirements for the concrete wall. Refer to Section 1-9 and ACI requirements for formwork, concrete composition, and reinforcement.

Detailing Considerations

- Maintain an air space of at least 1 in. (25 mm) between the inside face of the concrete and the batt insulation to minimize thermal bridging through the studs and avoid possible wetting of the insulation from any moisture that might penetrate the concrete wall.
- If joints in the concrete are well sealed, the concrete will act as an air barrier. Joints between the roof and floor structure should be well sealed to maintain the continuity of the air barrier. Refer to Section 5-5 for more information on air barriers.
- Verify the need for a vapor retarder and its location. Place it as shown on the warm side of the insulation in a cool or cold climate. Refer to Section 5-5 for more information on vapor retarders.
- Window sills should be detailed with flashing (including end dams) to drain any moisture to the outside.
- Maximum furring or stud spacing is 24 in. (610 mm) on center.
- Precast concrete insulated panels can also be used in lieu of cast concrete. This construction eliminates thermal bridging and provides an extra layer of insulation.
- Foam insulation must be covered with a code-approved thermal barrier. This is a minimum 1/2 in. (13 mm) layer of gypsum wallboard.
- Refer to Section 1-9 for information on architectural concrete.

Likely Failure Points

- Degradation of foam plastic insulation if a compatible adhesive is not used
- Degradation of batt insulation if subjected to moisture
- Air leakage due to an inadequate seal between concrete and framing
- Moisture penetration due to lack of an adequate seal between vapor retarder and framing

Materials

07 21 16 BATT INSULATION

Fiberglass, ASTM C665, Type I or Type II (unfaced or faced).

Mineral fiber, ASTM C553.

Apply in the thicknesses required for thermal resistance.

07 21 13 BOARD INSULATION

Materials

Polyisocyanurate foam board, ASTM C591.

Extruded polystyrene, ASTM C578.

Apply in the thicknesses required for thermal resistance.

Verify compatibility with the adhesive used.

Execution

If mastic is applied, use a full adhesive bed or grid of adhesive.

Insulation may be installed with metal or plastic stick clips placed in a grid pattern. Follow manufacturers' recommendations for spacing. Metal clips provide a minor thermal bridge.

07 26 13 Vapor retarder

4 mil (0.1 mm) polyethylene film, 0.08 maximum perm rating.

07 92 13 Elastomeric joint sealant

Materials

Solvent-based acrylic, ASTM C834.

Acrylic latex may also be used.

One-part polyurethane, ASTM C920, Type S, Grade NS, Class 25 or 50, as required.

One-part silicone, ASTM C920, Type S, Grade NS, Class 25 or 50, as required.

Execution

Sealant depth equal to the width of the joint up to $1/2$ in. (13 mm), with a minimum depth of $1/4$ in. (6 mm).

See Section 5-38 for methods of sizing joints.

07 91 23 Backer rod

Closed cell foam, ASTM D1056, Type 2.

25 percent to 33 percent larger than joint width.

1-9 ARCHITECTURAL CONCRETE

Description

Architectural concrete is exposed concrete that is intended to act as a finished surface either on the interior or exterior of a structure. Special attention is required in detailing and specifying architectural concrete to ensure that the final appearance has minimal color and texture variation and minimal surface defects when viewed from a distance of 20 ft (6.1 m).

Although there are many considerations in achieving a quality architectural concrete surface, including concrete mix, curing, and finishing procedures, Fig. 1-9 illustrates some of the primary considerations for detailing openings, joints, formwork, and reinforcement placement.

Limitations of Use

- Refer to ACI 303R for additional recommendations concerning concrete mix, requirements for forms, curing, and methods of treating and finishing the concrete surface.

Detailing Considerations

- Best results are obtained when large areas of concrete are constructed with textured forms or have textured finishes.
- Joint layout should be designed to divide large concrete surfaces into manageable sections for construction.
- Horizontal control joints may be needed at the top and bottom of openings in walls.

Figure 1-9 Architectural concrete 03 33 00

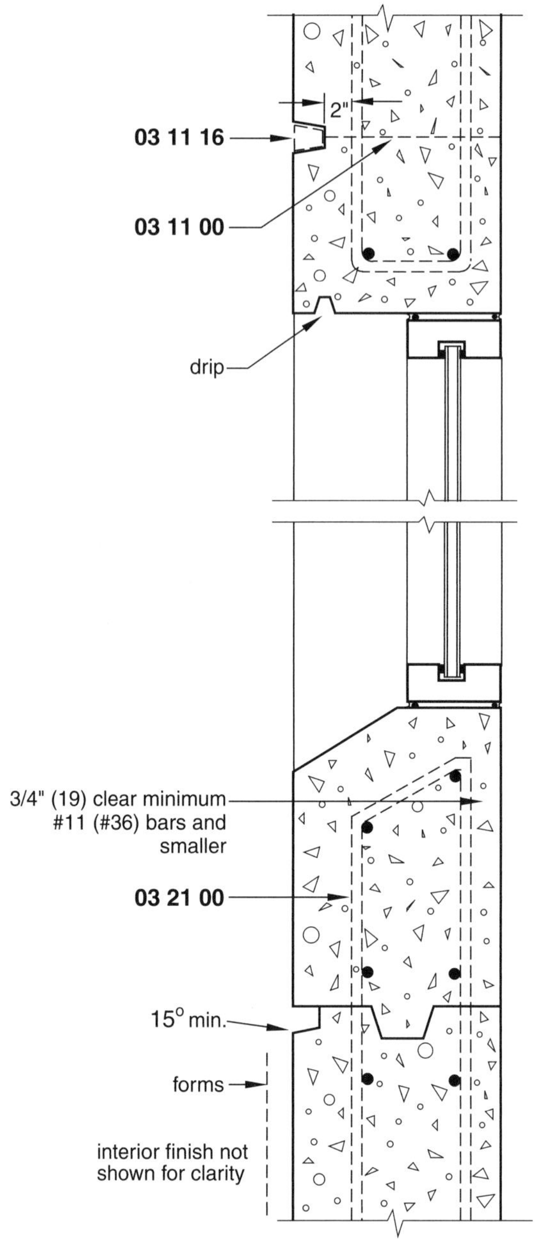

03 11 16

03 11 00

2"

drip

3/4" (19) clear minimum
#11 (#36) bars and
smaller

03 21 00

15° min.

forms

interior finish not
shown for clarity

- Common vertical cracking in walls can be concealed with vertical rustication joints at the midspan of bays unless other vertical joints are provided.
- In long walls, vertical cracking can be controlled by providing construction joints not more than 20 ft (6.1 m) on center or by placing deep, narrow rustication strips on both sides of the wall to induce cracking. The depth of this type of joint should be 1.5 times the maximum aggregate size.
- Sills and similar horizontal surfaces should be sloped to encourage washing of airborne dirt from the concrete by rainwater. Smooth surfaces should have a minimum slope of 1:12, while extremely textured surfaces may have a slope of up to 1:1. Parapets should slope away from the face of the concrete.

- Recommended joint depths are ³/₄ in. (19 mm) for small rustication or pattern grooves and 1¹/₂ in. (38 mm) for control joints and panel divisions.
- Generally, avoid right and acute angle corners because of the difficulty of form removal without potential damage during construction. Use chamfer strips on right angle corners. Wood chamfer strips should have a minimum face width of 1 in. (25 mm) and be spliced only at concrete joints.
- Drips should be cast into all horizontal offsets and placed as near to the exterior surface as possible but not closer than 1¹/₂ in. (38 mm).
- Refer to Section 1-8 for information on insulation and interior finish details.

Coordination Required

- Joint locations must also meet the structural requirements of the wall.
- Regions of flexural tension in beams and other elements should be identified with the help of the structural engineer so that the depths of rustication strips can be kept to a minimum. The increased concrete cover over reinforcing due to the strips can cause any cracks that occur to be wider than they normally would be with less concrete cover.

Likely Failure Points

- Defects on the surface caused by leakage from form joints
- Form joints must be made grout-tight. This can be done by using low-slump concrete, using various types of liners, using pressure-sensitive rubber gaskets, or caulking and using a lumber batten backing.

Materials

03 21 00 REINFORCING STEEL

The clear distance between forms and reinforcing bars should be 2 in. (51 mm), 1.25 times the bar size, or 1.5 times the maximum aggregate size, whichever is largest. This is done to minimize the chance of rust stains and to facilitate the placement of the concrete. If part of the concrete will be removed after removal of forms, additional coverage should be provided.

The clear distance between bars should be 2 in. (51 mm), 1.25 times the bar diameter, or 1.75 times the maximum aggregate size, whichever is largest.

Horizontal reinforcing in walls should be 1.5 times the ACI 318 minimum to minimize the width of cracks.

Horizontal reinforcing crossing construction joints or control joints formed by deep rustication strips should not exceed one-half of the horizontal reinforcement elsewhere in the wall.

Tie wire, chairs, spacers, and bolsters should be stainless steel.

03 11 16 RUSTICATION STRIP

Wooden strips used for rustication joints should have a width at least equal to their depth. Metal strips should have a minimum width of ³/₄ in. (38 mm).

Strips used to form joints should be angled at least 15 degrees to allow for removal. End joints of insert strips should be mitered and tightly fitted.

03 11 00 FORM TIE

Various types of form ties can be selected, depending on the appearance desired. Cones are available that will form a hole up to 2 in. (51 mm) deep and about 1 in. (25 mm) in diameter. Cones from he-bolt form ties leave a hole 1 in. to 2 in. (25 mm to 51 mm) in diameter. Cones from she-bolt form ties leave a hole $3/4$ in. to $1^1/2$ in. (19 mm to 38 mm) in diameter, depending on the strength category of the tie. Snap ties will result in holes about $1/4$ in. (6 mm) in diameter and about 1 in. (25 mm) deep but leave a rough appearance and are usually not used for architectural concrete.

Tie holes may be patched or left as cast for architectural effect.

1-10   PRECAST CONCRETE SPANDREL WITH INSULATION

Description

Figure 1-10 illustrates a common method of detailing a precast concrete panel on a cast-in-place concrete structural frame. Details for precast panels on a steel frame are similar. While this detail indicates panel attachment to concrete structural columns at either end of the panel, panels may also be attached at the floor line, as shown in Figs. 1-19 and 1-20. For a full discussion of precast concrete design, refer to *Architectural Precast Concrete*, published by the Precast/Prestressed Concrete Institute.

Limitations of Use

- This detail shows a cladding panel not intended to support any additional gravity loads other than its own weight, wind, seismic forces, and the load of the window system.
- This detail illustrates the use of an open precast frame for the window unit. That is, the four sides of the window opening are separate precast units. Closed window openings are entirely contained in one panel and are generally more economical than open designs.
- Because there are many possible variations in panel configuration and attachment methods, this detail shows only one possible method of detailing. Specific project details must be based on the structural requirements of the building, climate, types of windows used, interior finish requirement, exterior panel appearance, and the preferred methods of casting by the local precaster.

Detailing Considerations

- Locate the window frame a minimum of 2 in. (51 mm) from the face of the precast panel to avoid water dripping from the panel across the window.
- Precast panel connections should provide for adjustability in three dimensions.
- Panel connections should allow for a concrete beam and slab tolerance of $\pm 3/4$ in. (38 mm), a horizontal location of beam edge tolerance of ± 1 in. (25 mm), and a precast panel tolerance of $+1/4$ in. (6 mm).

Figure 1-10 Precast concrete spandrel with insulation 03 40 01

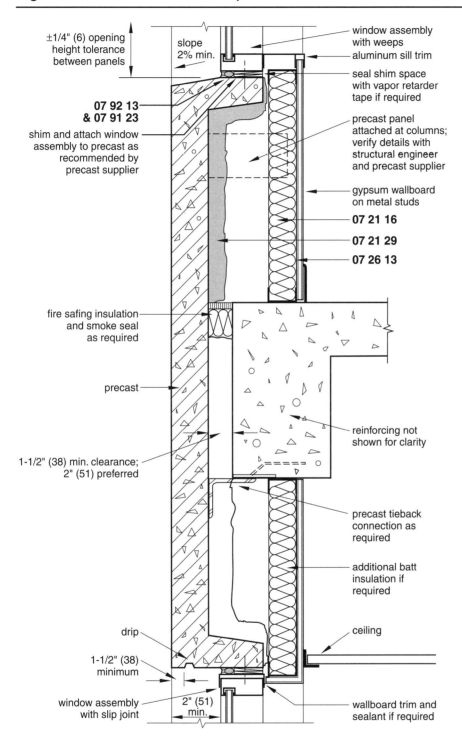

±1/4" (6) opening height tolerance between panels

slope 2% min.

window assembly with weeps

aluminum sill trim

seal shim space with vapor retarder tape if required

07 92 13 & 07 91 23
shim and attach window assembly to precast as recommended by precast supplier

precast panel attached at columns; verify details with structural engineer and precast supplier

gypsum wallboard on metal studs

07 21 16

07 21 29

07 26 13

fire safing insulation and smoke seal as required

precast

reinforcing not shown for clarity

1-1/2" (38) min. clearance; 2" (51) preferred

precast tieback connection as required

additional batt insulation if required

drip

ceiling

1-1/2" (38) minimum

window assembly with slip joint

2" (51) min.

wallboard trim and sealant if required

- If a rough texture is specified for the precast panel, specify the extent of the texturing to provide for a smooth surface where window framing and sealant are installed. Hold the concrete texturing at least 1/2 in. (13 mm) from the interface of the precast and the window frame.
- Provide flashing with end dams under the window sill if required.

- Verify the need for a vapor retarder based on climate and building use.
- If spray polyurethane foam is used, a thermal barrier may be required by the local building code. A ½ in. (13 mm) layer of gypsum wallboard is usually sufficient for this purpose.

Coordination Required

- Develop panel sizes and connection methods with the structural engineer to minimize deflection and movement of each panel and to avoid conflicts between connections and interior finish requirements.
- Coordinate with the precast supplier to determine the most economical configuration for panels, proper draft for casting (see Section 1-15), attachment methods, erection sequencing, and other aspects of panel manufacturing.
- Consider window washing methods when recessing windows deeply into precast units.
- Use stainless steel, galvanized steel, or plastic for trim, inserts, flashing, and other items incorporated into the precast. Other materials require separation with dielectric materials.

Materials

07 21 16 BATT INSULATION

Fiberglass, ASTM C665, Type I or Type II (unfaced or faced).

Mineral fiber, ASTM C553.

Apply in thicknesses as required for thermal resistance.

07 21 20 SPRAYED INSULATION

Closed cell polyurethane foam, ASTM C1029.

Open cell Icynene foam.

07 26 13 VAPOR RETARDER

ASTM C1136.

4 mil (0.1 mm) polyethylene film, 0.08 (4.6 ng/s • m^2 • Pa) maximum perm rating.

07 91 23 BACKER ROD

Closed cell foam, ASTM D1056, Type 2.

25 percent to 33 percent larger than joint width.

07 92 13 SEALANT

Materials

Solvent-based acrylic, ASTM C834.

Acrylic latex may also be used.

One-part polyurethane, ASTM C920, Type S, Grade NS, Class 25 or 50, as required.

One-part silicone, ASTM C920, Type S, Grade NS, Class 25 or 50, as required.

Execution

Sealant depth equal to the width of the joint up to $1/2$ in. (13 mm), with a minimum depth of $1/4$ in. (6 mm).

See Section 5-38 for methods of sizing joints.

1-11   PRECAST CONCRETE BEAM AND DOUBLE TEE TOLERANCES

Description

Figure 1-11 gives some of the primary size tolerances of two types of precast concrete structural elements. As with cast-in-place concrete, knowing these tolerances is important for developing connection details between structural components and for detailing other building materials that may use the concrete structure as a substrate. During construction, one surface is usually designated as the primary control surface, the location of which is controlled during erection.

Limitations of Use

- These guidelines are generally considered standard in the industry. If closer tolerances are required, they should be clearly indicated on the drawings and specifications.
- These tolerances are for components whose appearance is not critical. See Section 1-13 for architectural precast tolerances.

Detailing Considerations

- In general, fabrication and erection costs are proportional to the level of tolerance required. Tolerances higher than industry standard should not be specified unless they are absolutely necessary.
- Tolerances may be cumulative between two elements or between a structural element and another building component that has its own tolerance.
- Erection tolerance from the theoretical building grid is $\pm 1/2$ in. (13 mm).
- Horizontal alignment tolerance for beams is $\pm 1/4$ in. (6 mm) for architectural edges where appearance is important and $\pm 1/2$ in. (13 mm) for visually noncritical edges.
- Horizontal end alignment tolerance for double tees is ± 1 in. (25 mm).
- The erection tolerances of the primary control surface are not additive to the product tolerances shown in Fig. 1-11. See Section 1-23 for more information on precast erection tolerances.

Coordination Required

- Required tolerances for each project should be included in the specifications so that there is no misunderstanding. Reference should be made to industry standard publications, such as ACI 117, or specific tolerances should be itemized, especially if they deviate from normal trade practices.

Figure 1-11 Precast beam and double tee tolerances 04 41 00

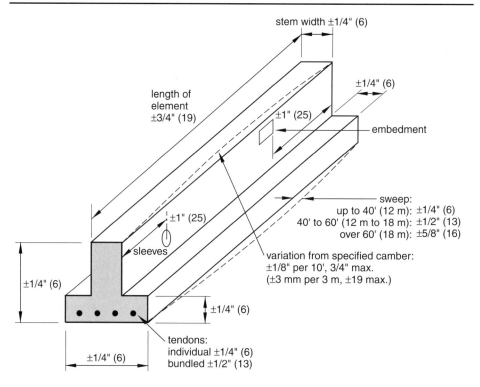

stem width ±1/4" (6)

±1/4" (6)

length of
element
±3/4" (19)

±1" (25)

embedment

sweep:
up to 40' (12 m): ±1/4" (6)
40' to 60' (12 m to 18 m): ±1/2" (13)
over 60' (18 m): ±5/8" (16)

±1" (25)

sleeves

variation from specified camber:
±1/8" per 10', 3/4" max.
(±3 mm per 3 m, ±19 max.)

±1/4" (6)

±1/4" (6)

tendons:
individual ±1/4" (6)
bundled ±1/2" (13)

±1/4" (6)

(a) precast concrete beam

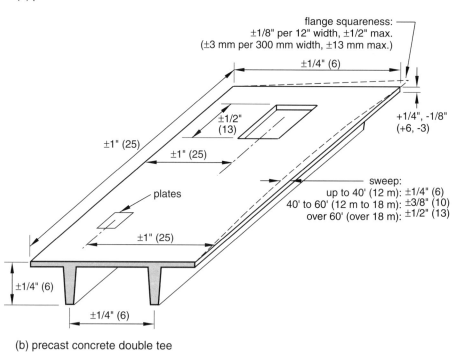

flange squareness:
±1/8" per 12" width, ±1/2" max.
(±3 mm per 300 mm width, ±13 mm max.)

±1/4" (6)

±1/2"
(13)

+1/4", -1/8"
(+6, -3)

±1" (25)

±1" (25)

sweep:
up to 40' (12 m): ±1/4" (6)
40' to 60' (12 m to 18 m): ±3/8" (10)
over 60' (over 18 m): ±1/2" (13)

plates

±1" (25)

±1/4" (6)

±1/4" (6)

(b) precast concrete double tee

1-12 AUTOCLAVED AERATED CONCRETE PANELS

Description

Autoclaved aerated concrete (AAC) is a concrete-like material made with portland cement, lime, water, silica sand or recycled fly ash, and an expanding agent, such as aluminum powder. When combined and poured into molds, the aluminum reacts with the lime and cement to form microscopic hydrogen bubbles, expanding the mixture by about five times its original volume. Once the mixture has partially hardened, it is cut to size and steam-cured in a pressurized autoclave.

ACC is typically formed into blocks or panels for use as exterior walls, floors, and roofs and interior partitions. Blocks are typically 8 in. by 8 in. by 24 in. (200 mm by 200 mm by 600 mm), and panels are available in thicknesses from 2 in. to 15 in. (50 mm to 375 mm), 24 in. (600 mm) wide, and up to 20 ft (6000 mm) long. Bond beams and other specialized shapes are also available. The size availability of all products depends on the manufacturer. ACC is formed to varying densities, depending on the strength required. Compressive strengths of 290 psi (2.0 Mpa), 580 psi (4.0 Mpa), and 870 psi (6.0 Mpa) are available.

Because of its structural qualities and limitations, ACC is typically used as a bearing material for residential or commercial low- to mid-rise buildings, but it can be used as nonstructural cladding for buildings of any height, especially when its qualities of fire resistance, light weight, thermal mass, and sound insulation are desired. Figure 1-12 shows one possible use of an ACC panel product in a load-bearing application.

ACC provides many advantages as a building material. It is structurally sound, lightweight (about 20 to 50 lbm/ft^3 or 400 to 800 kg/m^3), easily cut in the field, fire resistant, dimensionally stable, functions as a thermal mass, and is thermally and acoustically insulating. In addition, it has many sustainable benefits. ACC is made of plentiful raw materials, and some products use recycled fly ash instead of sand. The product does not produce indoor air quality problems, nor are pollutants produced in its manufacture. ADD can be reused or ground up for use in other products at the end of a building's life cycle. The most problematic part of manufacturing is the use of energy in the autoclaving and drying process.

Panels are assembled on a thin mortar bed on the foundation with anchoring as recommended by the manufacturer. Panels used for walls can be oriented vertically or horizontally, while floor and roof panels are laid flat. Additional reinforcing bars or straps are used as required by the structural needs of the building and to anchor other building materials to the ACC. Refer to Section 2-15 for information on AAC unit masonry.

Because of its closed-cell formation, ACC is lightweight and can be cut with common power or hand tools. Shapes, reveals, signage, and other effects can also be carved or routed into the material. The R-value of ACC is approximately 1.25 hr-ft^2-°F/Btu per inch (8.66 RSI/m), depending on the density, with the added benefit of having thermal mass, which can increase its effective R-value, especially in warmer climates. Because the product is uniform throughout, there is no thermal bridging due to studs or other framing.

More information can be obtained from individual manufacturers and from the Autoclaved Aerated Concrete Products Association.

Limitations of Use

- Currently, there are only a few ACC manufacturing plants in the United States, all located in Texas, Arizona, Florida, and Georgia. Although ACC is lightweight, its shipping costs may be excessive for delivery to northern locations.

Figure 1-12 Autoclaved aerated concrete panels 04 22 23.1

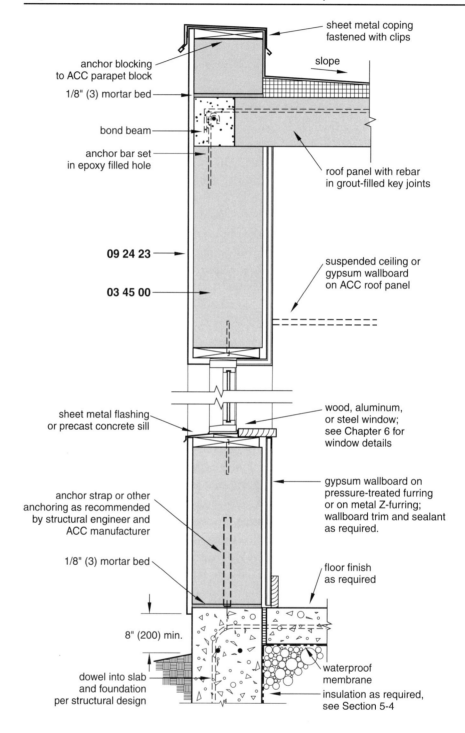

anchor blocking
to ACC parapet block

1/8" (3) mortar bed

bond beam

anchor bar set
in epoxy filled hole

09 24 23

03 45 00

sheet metal coping
fastened with clips

slope

roof panel with rebar
in grout-filled key joints

suspended ceiling or
gypsum wallboard
on ACC roof panel

sheet metal flashing
or precast concrete sill

wood, aluminum,
or steel window;
see Chapter 6 for
window details

anchor strap or other
anchoring as recommended
by structural engineer and
ACC manufacturer

gypsum wallboard on
pressure-treated furring
or on metal Z-furring;
wallboard trim and sealant
as required.

1/8" (3) mortar bed

floor finish
as required

8" (200) min.

dowel into slab
and foundation
per structural design

waterproof
membrane

insulation as required,
see Section 5-4

- Because construction with ACC is relatively new in the United States, it may be difficult to find skilled contractors and workers.
- Additional time may be required for the ACC to dry thoroughly to stabilize at its long-term moisture content of 4 percent to 8 percent. In some climates or where construction schedules are short, dehumidifiers may be required to hasten the drying process. Exterior finishes should be vapor permeable, and vapor barriers on the interior

should be limited when possible. Verify specific applications and construction details with the manufacturer.

- Blocking applied and attached to the ACC should be pressure treated.

Detailing Considerations

- Building with ACC is specific to each manufacturer. Consult with the manufacturer for materials recommended for mortar, grout, anchoring, miscellaneous fasteners, and other accessories.
- Roofs may be constructed of ACC panels, wood trusses, or other structural material as recommended by the engineer and as required by the design of the building. If ACC panels are used for a flat structural roof, use tapered insulation to provide drainage.
- Details of window and door openings may vary slightly, depending on the type of frame used. Wood frames should include a rough buck attached to the ACC. Aluminum frames may be attached directly. Verify suggested attachment of frames with the ACC manufacturer.
- Figure 1-12 shows a wood frame with a sheet metal sill and flashing on rough wood framing. A precast concrete sill may also be used; however, flashing should be installed under the concrete sill.

Coordination Required

- Verify all structural requirements with the structural engineer and manufacturer.
- Exterior finish should be vapor-permeable, polymer-modified stucco. Brick and other cladding may also be used.
- When wall and roof panels are used together, an airtight envelope is created. If possible, the building should be allowed to dry for several months before enclosing it. Alternately, the heating, ventilating, and air-conditioning (HVAC) system can be used to dehumidify the air.
- Interior wall finishes for ACC panel products are commonly mineral-based plaster applied about 1/8 in. (3 mm) thick or gypsum wallboard placed on pressure-treated furring strips. Metal furring can also be used if additional space is required for insulation or electrical services.
- Interior wall tile can be applied using a thin-set mortar or organic adhesive over a portland cement or gypsum-based base coat applied to the ACC.
- As adjacent floor panels are well aligned, floor finishes such as carpet, resilient tile or sheet goods, ceramic tile, and linoleum can be placed directly over the ACC. However, in some cases, it may be necessary to apply a topping, such as gypsum, over the ACC to provide a smooth subsurface for finish materials.

Materials

03 45 00 AUTOCLAVED AERATED CONCRETE PANEL

ASTM C1452.

Strength class ACC 2.0, ACC 4.0, or ACC 6.0 as required.

Foundation attachment and reinforcing as required by the structural engineer and manufacturer.

09 24 23 STUCCO

Portland cement, polymer-modified stucco.

Apply according to ASTM C926 or as recommended by the ACC manufacturer.

1-13 ARCHITECTURAL PRECAST CONCRETE PANEL TOLERANCES

Description

Figure 1-13 shows some of the manufacturing tolerances for precast panels commonly used as exterior cladding. These tolerances are some of the most common ones with which architects

Figure 1-13 Architectural precast panel tolerances 03 45 13

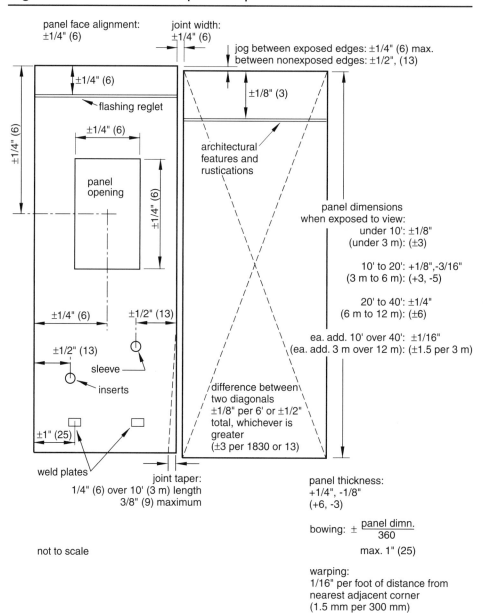

panel face alignment: ±1/4" (6)

joint width: ±1/4" (6)

jog between exposed edges: ±1/4" (6) max. between nonexposed edges: ±1/2", (13)

±1/4" (6)

±1/4" (6)

flashing reglet

±1/8" (3)

±1/4" (6)

±1/4" (6)

panel opening

architectural features and rustications

panel dimensions when exposed to view:
under 10': ±1/8" (under 3 m): (±3)

10' to 20': +1/8",-3/16" (3 m to 6 m): (+3, -5)

20' to 40': ±1/4" (6 m to 12 m): (±6)

ea. add. 10' over 40': ±1/16" (ea. add. 3 m over 12 m): (±1.5 per 3 m)

±1/4" (6)

±1/2" (13)

±1/2" (13)

sleeve

inserts

difference between two diagonals ±1/8" per 6' or ±1/2" total, whichever is greater (±3 per 1830 or 13)

±1" (25)

weld plates

joint taper:
1/4" (6) over 10' (3 m) length
3/8" (9) maximum

panel thickness:
+1/4", -1/8"
(+6, -3)

bowing: $\pm \dfrac{\text{panel dimn.}}{360}$

max. 1" (25)

warping:
1/16" per foot of distance from nearest adjacent corner
(1.5 mm per 300 mm)

not to scale

are concerned. They can serve as a guideline for developing details of panel connections and for coordination of details with other materials. Manufacturing tolerances must be coordinated with erection tolerances and tolerances for other building systems. During construction, one surface is usually designated as the primary control surface, the location of which is controlled during erection. The product tolerances given in this section are *not* additive to the erection tolerances of the primary control surfaces. However, product tolerances are additive to secondary control surface erection tolerances. Refer to *Tolerance Manual for Precast and Prestressed Concrete Construction* (MNL-135), published by the Precast/Prestressed Concrete Institute, for more information.

Limitations of Use

- These tolerances apply to architectural panels, spandrels, and column covers.
- These guidelines are generally considered standard in the industry. If closer tolerances are required, they should be clearly indicated on the drawings and specifications. Requirements for closer tolerances should be reviewed with the precaster to determine the cost and scheduling consequences of tighter tolerances.

Detailing Considerations

- Sufficient clearance between precast units and the structural frame should be provided to allow for the erection of the precast without having to alter its physical dimensions or deviate from detailed structural connections.
- In some cases, allowable tolerances for steel or concrete framing in tall buildings may require that attachment of precast elements follow the frame up the height of the building without being in a true plane.
- Details should be developed so that architectural precast elements overlap cast-in-place framing. This conceals any differential tolerances in the two materials.
- Bowing is an overall out-of-plane condition in which the corners of the panels may be in the same plane but the portion between the corners is out of plane. Warping, on the other hand, is an out-of-plane condition in which the corners do not fall in the same plane. Both conditions can affect the alignment and appearance of panels. The difference between diagonals applies to major openings as well as to the panel itself.
- The likelihood of bowing or warping is decreased if the panel contains ribs or other design features that provide additional stiffness.
- In some instances, the higher cost of tooling required for close tolerances may be offset by the use of a highly repetitive panel product.

Coordination Required

- Required tolerances for each project should be included in the specifications so that there is no misunderstanding. Reference should be made to industry standard publications, such as ACI 117, the AISC *Code of Standard Practices,* and the *Tolerance Manual for Precast and Prestressed Concrete Construction* or specific tolerances should be itemized, especially if they deviate from normal trade practices.

1-14 ARCHITECTURAL PRECAST PANEL SIZE AND CONFIGURATION

Description

Figure 1-14 illustrates some of the considerations for determining the size, general configuration, and typical detailing requirements for non-load-bearing architectural precast concrete

Figure 1-14 Architectural precast panel size and configuration 03 45 14

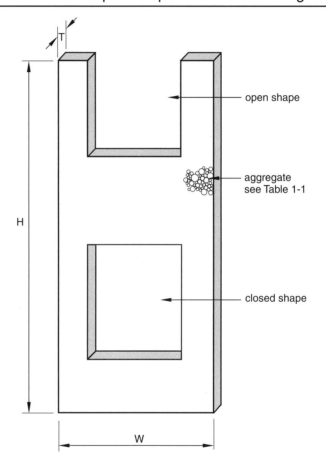

(a) precast size and configuration considerations

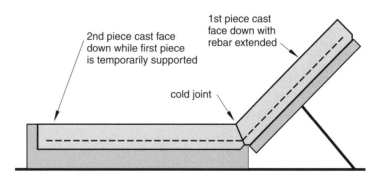

(b) sequential precasting

panels. These types of panels are used for window walls, column and beam covers, spandrel panels, mullions, and similar applications. Figure 1-14(a) illustrates a panel cast in one operation. For more complex shapes, panels can be fabricated in two or more castings, as shown in Fig. 1-14(b). Because there are so many possible variations of precast panels, this section only outlines some of the general requirements.

Limitations of Use

- Non-load-bearing panels only resist forces resulting from transfer of wind and seismic loads and transfer of the panel's own weight to the structure.
- Special connections, which allow pronounced lateral movement, are required in high seismic areas.

Detailing Considerations

- Closed shapes are easier to handle than open shapes due to their inherent rigidity. Open shapes may require more reinforcing, temporary braces during transportation and erection, and thicker castings.
- Precast panels should be made as large as possible to minimize shipping and erection costs. Large panels also minimize the number of joints, which must be sealed in the field. The maximum size of panels is usually determined by the limitations of the precasting plant, transportation, and clearances at the job site for access and erection.
- Although minimum panel thickness depends on many factors, such as the minimum cover required over reinforcing, the following guidelines for slenderness ratios are useful for preliminary design decisions. The slenderness ratio is the panel thickness, T, divided by the unsupported length when the panel is in its final position.
  - Flat panels that are not prestressed: 1/20 to 1/50.
  - Flat panels that are prestressed: 1/30 to 1/60.
- Connections of adjacent panels should be designed to minimize deviation in casting and erection tolerances.
- Provide adequate clearances between the structure and the panel to allow access for making adjustments and connections.
- Panel shapes should be designed to minimize the number of joints.
- When possible, a single spandrel panel should be used in lieu of several smaller panels. The connections should be made at the column lines to minimize deflection of the floor slab and to reduce the size of or eliminate the need for an edge beam.
- Connections should be designed to allow for lateral translation and frame shortening. See Section 1-19.

Coordination Required

- The optimum panel size for a project can best be determined with close coordination between the architect, the engineer, and the precast fabricator.
- Maximum panel size may depend on the available room on site for truck access and crane capacity and location.
- The optimum panel size may be controlled by the local highway load limits and the maximum truck size. Although regulations vary by state, standard flatbed trucks can carry loads 8 ft (2440 mm) wide by 8 ft (2440 mm) high by 45 ft (13.7 m) long without a special permit. With other types of trucks and permits, the size can be increased to

Table 1-1 Concrete Aggregate Visibility

Aggregate size, in in. (mm)	Distance at which texture is visible, in ft. (m)
1/4–1/2 (6–13)	20–30 (6.1–9.1)
1/2–1 (13–25)	30–75 (9.1–22.9)
1–2 (25–51)	75–125 (22.9–38.1)
2–3 (51–76)	125–175 (38.1–53.3)

accommodate panels from 10 to 12 ft (3050 mm to 3660 mm) wide. The typical load limit is 20 tons (18,140 kg). Exact requirement for each geographic area should be determined early in the design process.

- One of the criteria for determining aggregate size is the desired appearance of the finished concrete. For textured surfaces to be apparent, the size of the aggregate used depends on the typical distance from which the concrete will be viewed. Table 1-1 gives the recommended aggregate size for various viewing distances. Note that this is based on a single-color aggregate. A full-size mock-up should be constructed before the final aggregate size is specified.

- Detailing of the panels may require provisions for window-washing equipment.

- Expected frame shortening must be calculated to establish the actual elevations required for fabricating the panels.

Likely Failure Points

- Unequal deflection between adjacent panels because they are supported on portions of the building structure that have differing stiffnesses

- Bowing and cracking of the panel caused by thermal gradients and rigid restraint on all four edges

1-15 ARCHITECTURAL PRECAST CONCRETE FORMING

Description

This section gives general guidelines for developing precast details based on the limitations and requirements of the precast forming process. Although an enormous range of shapes, details, and finishes is possible with precast concrete, economic considerations usually require the designer to limit the number and complexity of individual shapes.

The greatest economy is achieved with the use of an envelope mold, as shown in Fig. 1-15(a). With this type of mold, all surfaces and sides remain in place during casting and stripping. However, the normally high tooling costs for envelope molds require high reuse to make them economical. Other types of molds, such as the one shown in Fig. 1-15(b), require one or more pieces to be removed before the concrete is stripped. This makes complex shapes possible but increases the cost and time required for forming. In addition, there is an increased chance of misalignment when the removable sections are reinstalled for the next casting.

Limitations of Use

- Because of the many variables in selecting the optimum forming method, consult with local precasters early in the design process.

Figure 1-15 Architectural precast concrete forming 03 45 15

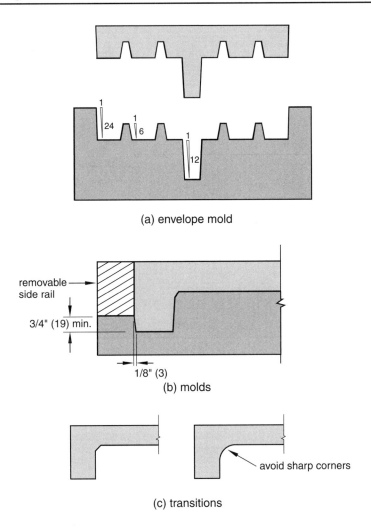

(a) envelope mold

(b) molds

(c) transitions

- Envelope molds do not allow lifting hooks to be installed in the sides of a panel.
- Figure 1-15(a) illustrates one-piece forming. Individual units may be formed from two or more castings with cold joints, as shown in Fig. 1-14(b). In addition, molds may be rotated during casting to obtain a uniform surface finish on multifaceted units.
- Negative drafts are possible but require removable form pieces.

Detailing Considerations

- The greatest economy is achieved by limiting the number of molds that must be made and by reusing the same master mold as many times as possible. However, several different configurations can be made from one master mold by the use of blockouts and bulkheads.
- The draft, or slope, of side pieces on a panel should be designed within the minimum limitations shown in Fig. 1-15(a). Side forms should have a 1:24 draft, panel projections a 1:12 draft, and false joints, ribs, and reveals a 1:6 draft. Removable side pieces such as the one shown in Fig. 1-15(b) allow flat edges to be formed and conceal any leakage that may occur by locating it away from the visible face of the panel.

- Avoid the use of thin or fragile edge pieces.
- Whenever possible, design chamfered or rounded edges, as shown in Fig. 1-15(c), to minimize the possibility of edge damage and to conceal slight misalignment between panels.
- Design gradual transitions from one mass of concrete to another.

1-16   ARCHITECTURAL PRECAST CORNERS

Description

Figure 1–16 illustrates two common methods for forming outside corners with adjacent precast concrete and for providing for adjustment at corner points. The primary considerations in designing corners are to avoid special corner molds whenever possible, providing for corners that minimize chipping, allowing for alignment of the panels, and providing the proper joint width for sealants.

Figure 1-16 Architectural precast corners 03 45 16

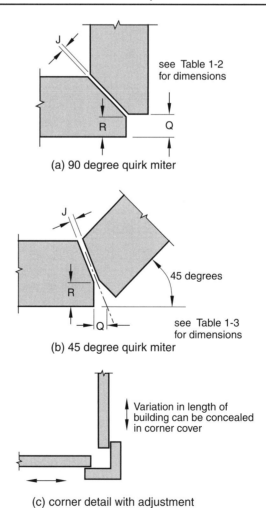

(a) 90 degree quirk miter

(b) 45 degree quirk miter

(c) corner detail with adjustment

Table 1-2 Recommended Dimensions of 90 Degree Quirk Miters, in. (mm)				
	Quirk, Q		Return, R	
Joint, J	in.	mm	in.	mm
3/4 (19)	1 1/4	32	3/4	19
	1 1/2	38	1	25
	1 3/4	44	1 1/4	32
	2	51	1 1/2	38
1 (25)	1 1/2	38	1 3/16	21
	1 3/4	44	1 1/16	27
	2	51	1 5/16	33

Detailing Considerations

- Whenever possible, edges should be chamfered or rounded to minimize the possibility of edge damage and to conceal slight misalignment between panels. The optimum size of a radius depends on the size of the aggregate, the mold materials, and the production techniques used.
- When the aggregate size exceeds 1 in. (25 mm), it should be stopped at a demarcation joint (see Fig. 1-17) and a smooth outside corner made with a 1/4 in. to 1/2 in. (6 mm to 13 mm) radius.
- If possible, outside corners should be formed from the same type of panels used for the walls. This avoids the need to make a special mold just for the corners.
- Forty-five and ninety degree corners should be formed with a quirk miter, as shown in Fig. 1-16(a and b). Quirk returns should not be less than 3/4 in. (19 mm) or 1.5 times the maximum size of the aggregate. The sizes of quirks and returns based on joint widths as recommended by the Precast/Prestressed Concrete Institute are given in Tables 1-2 and 1-3.
- To avoid alignment problems with mitered corners, a separate corner piece may be cast or the miter connection assembled in the shop and shipped to the site in one piece.

Coordination Required

- Detail corner pieces to accommodate erection tolerances.
- Size and locate joints to accommodate building movement as well as fabrication and erection tolerances. The proper type of sealant must be selected to fit the joint and allow for expected movement. See Section 1-17.

Table 1-3 Recommended Dimensions of 45 Degree Quirk Miters, in. (mm)		
Joint width, J in in. (mm)	Quirk, Q, in in. (mm)	Return, R, in in. (mm)
3/4 (19)	3/4 (19)	13/16 (21)
	7/8 (22)	1 1/16 (27)
1 (25)	7/8 (22)	13/16 (21)
	1 (25)	1 1/16 (27)

Figure 1-17 Architectural precast joints 03 45 17

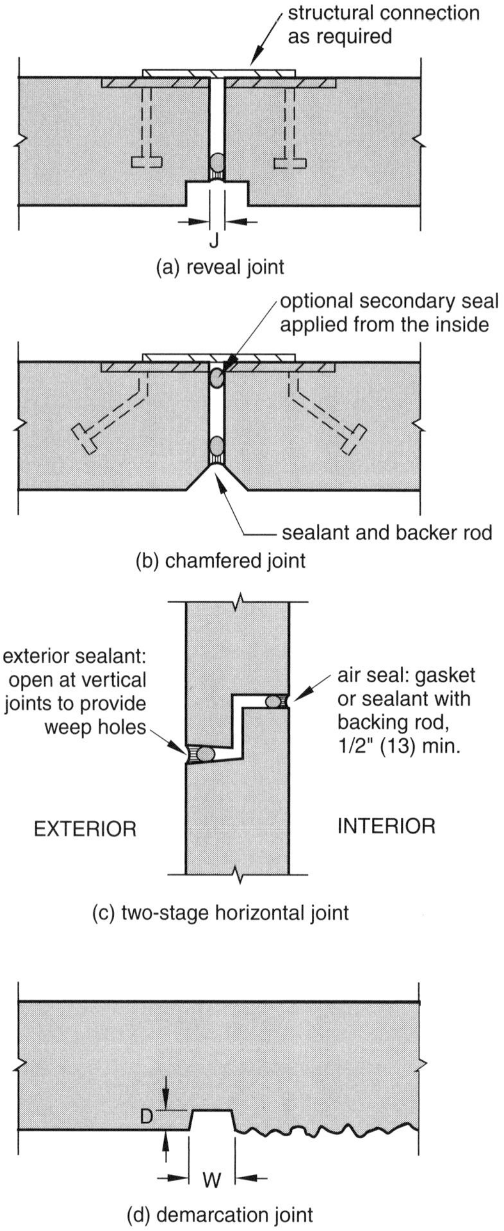

structural connection
as required

(a) reveal joint

optional secondary seal
applied from the inside

sealant and backer rod

(b) chamfered joint

exterior sealant:
open at vertical
joints to provide
weep holes

air seal: gasket
or sealant with
backing rod,
1/2" (13) min.

EXTERIOR

INTERIOR

(c) two-stage horizontal joint

(d) demarcation joint

- Accommodation for variations in the overall length of the building frame and casting tolerances may be taken up with the corner pieces or with joints between panels. Some types of corner designs do not allow any tolerances to be made up at the corner. See Fig 1-16(c).

Likely Failure Points

- Misalignment of mitered corners due to normal fabrication and erection tolerances
- Cracks caused by sharp transitions between areas of unequal mass

1-17 ARCHITECTURAL PRECAST JOINTS

Description

Like other types of construction, joints in precast concrete components are required to join several pieces together, to allow for fabrication and erection tolerances, and to accommodate movement caused by temperature changes, moisture, structural loading, and deflection.

The most common type of precast joint is a one-stage joint field molded with elastomeric sealants. See Fig. 1-17(a and b). Two-stage joints, as shown in Fig. 1-17(c), are sometimes used in areas subject to severe weather. Two-stage joints are detailed to provide a vented cavity behind the exposed concrete. The cavity equalizes pressure between the outside and the inside and allows any water that penetrates the outer surface to drain back to the outside before it penetrates the interior seal.

Limitations of Use

- The guidelines given here are for one-stage joints only.
- Good inspection and maintenance are required for one-stage joints to ensure that the weathertightness of the joint is maintained throughout the life of the building.
- This detail does not include major building movement joints or preformed compression sealants or gaskets.

Detailing Considerations

- The number of joints should be kept to a minimum whenever possible.
- Joints should be located at the maximum panel thickness.
- Joints should be recessed with a reveal or chamfer, as shown in Fig. 1-7(a and b). This not only minimizes the appearance of slightly nonaligned panels but also provides a channel for rain runoff.
- A second seal is often applied behind the exposed seal. This seal can be applied from the outside or the inside. However, the cavity created should be vented and drained to the outside, just as with a two-stage joint.
- Avoid joints in forward-sloping surfaces such as under window sills.
- Joints should be aligned vertically and horizontally instead of being staggered.
- For demarcation joints, as shown in Fig. 1-17(d), the minimum depth of the joint, D, should be at least 1.5 times the aggregate size. The width, W, should be greater than the depth and equal to a standard dimensional lumber size, such as $3/4$ in. or $1\frac{1}{2}$ in. (19 mm or 38 mm).
- Joint width should be determined by the expected movement of the joint, the movement capability of the sealant, fabrication tolerances, and the appearance desired. Generally, precast joints should never be less than $1/2$ in. (13 mm). Most joints are between $1/2$ in. (13 mm) and $3/4$ in. (19 mm) wide. Unless otherwise specified by the manufacturer, the depth of the joint depends on the width according to the following guidelines:
  - Sealant depth should be equal to the width of the joint up to $1/2$ in. (13 mm) with a minimum depth of $1/4$ in. (6 mm).
  - For joints $1/2$ in. to 1 in. (13 mm to 25 mm) wide, the sealant depth should be one-half of the width.

- For joints wider than 1 in. (25 mm), the sealant depth should be $1/2$ in. (13 mm) maximum.
- Joint width can be calculated using the procedures given in Section 5-38.

Coordination Required

- Joints must accommodate thermal movement, structural deflections, creep, and building drift.
- Sealants must be compatible with the expected movement of the joint. Proper preparation and priming of the joint are required for a good installation.
- Backer rod sizes should be selected so that, when installed, they are compressed 30 percent to 50 percent.
- Because sealants must be applied over relatively smooth surfaces, panel finishes, especially on inside corners, must be detailed to provide an appropriate base for the sealant.

Likely Failure Points

- Water leakage caused by pressure differentials between the inside and outside of a single-stage joint
- Dirt accumulation in joints due to slow-curing sealants
- Sealant failure when joints are staggered, causing possible shear forces to be induced in the sealant

Materials

- Nonstaining elastomeric joint sealants should be specified. For precast concrete, either one- or two-component polysulfides, polyurethanes, or silicones are used.
- Refer to Section 5-38 for sealant types and recommendations.

1-18 ARCHITECTURAL PRECAST WEATHERING DETAILS

Description

Weathering is the change in appearance of a building component over time caused by the effects of the environment. One of the most common effects of weathering on architectural precast units is the staining of accumulated, water-washed dirt on surfaces, creating an undesirable appearance.

The effects of weathering are complex because of the many variables involved. Weathering can be affected by the texture and orientation of precast surfaces, local climatic conditions, the type of dirt and pollution in the air, and the amount and location of glass, among other factors. This section outlines only a few of the many considerations useful for developing architectural precast sections that will weather well. See Fig. 1-18.

Detailing Considerations

- If possible, water runoff should be directed away from the building with overhangs, drips, and other treatments. Drips should be provided at soffits and under any horizontal

Figure 1-18 Architectural precast weathering details 03 45 18

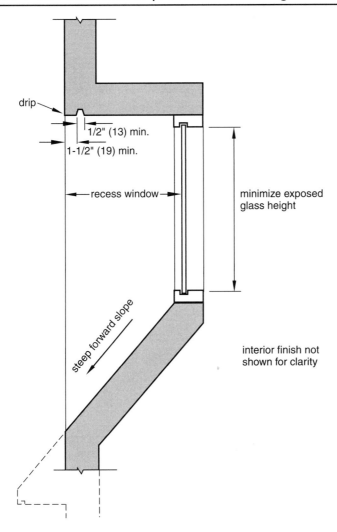

drip

1/2" (13) min.

1-1/2" (19) min.

recess window

minimize exposed
glass height

steep forward slope

interior finish not
shown for clarity

projections. Drips may be stopped short of the sides of recessed areas by about 1 in. or 2 in. (25 mm to 51 mm) to avoid water concentrations at the sides of the recess.

- Sloped surfaces should be smooth, with a steep angle to encourage natural washing.
- Windows should be recessed when possible and protected from runoff from vertical surfaces above to avoid staining and streaking on the glass. Water flow on a window tends to concentrate toward the edges, so provisions should be made to collect this water and direct it away from the building or disperse it.
- When windows are flush or nearly flush with the vertical concrete surface, the precast should be textured or have projections such as vertical ribs to disperse the water flow and conceal any staining.
- Because vertical surfaces and elements such as projecting fins can concentrate water, the intersection of vertical and horizontal surfaces should be given special attention. As shown in the detail, this may take the form of drips over vertical surfaces. Avoid stopping vertical joints flush with a solid panel face.

- Special consideration should be given to runoff under windows because wind-driven water will run off the glass faster than on adjacent concrete surfaces, resulting in differential staining.

Coordination Required

- To minimize the visibility of weathering, precast concrete units should have a gray or dark color and either a rough texture or a polished or honed surface.
- Sealing the concrete may lessen the effects of weathering by reducing absorption of the concrete and by increasing natural washing of the surfaces.
- If window framing is flush with the concrete surface, drips may be built into the window head rather than in the precast panel.

1-19 ARCHITECTURAL PRECAST PANEL CONNECTIONS

Description

Figure 1-19 illustrates some of the basic principles for designing non-load-bearing precast panel connections to a structural frame. Because there are so many possible connection details to meet the requirements of a specific project, this section only gives general guidelines for preliminary design. In most cases, the final connection design will depend on several variables in addition to the preferences of the precast fabricator.

Limitations of Use

- Detailed engineering design is required for panel reinforcement as well as for individual connector design.
- Special engineering design is required in high seismic areas.

Detailing Considerations

- Only two points of bearing should be designed into the panel support system. These are best located on only one structural level at the bottom of the panel, as shown in Fig. 1-19, but they may be located at the top of the panel or at the intermediate floor. One bearing point should have a rigid connection, and the other should allow for lateral movement. Other tie-back connections should allow for movement vertically and laterally.
- Panel connections should provide for at least 1 in. (25 mm) of vertical adjustments and 2 in. (51 mm) of horizontal adjustments to accommodate manufacturing and erection tolerances of both the panel and the building frame. Slotted holes, oversized weld plates, leveling bolts, shims, and similar devices can provide for these adjustments. Clearances and shim space, as shown in Fig. 1-19, should also be provided.
- Tie-back connections may be made with bolted connections, weld plates, or rods.
- Connections should be standardized as much as possible throughout the building.
- Connection locations must allow room for accessibility during erection.

Figure 1-19 Architectural precast panel connections 03 45 19

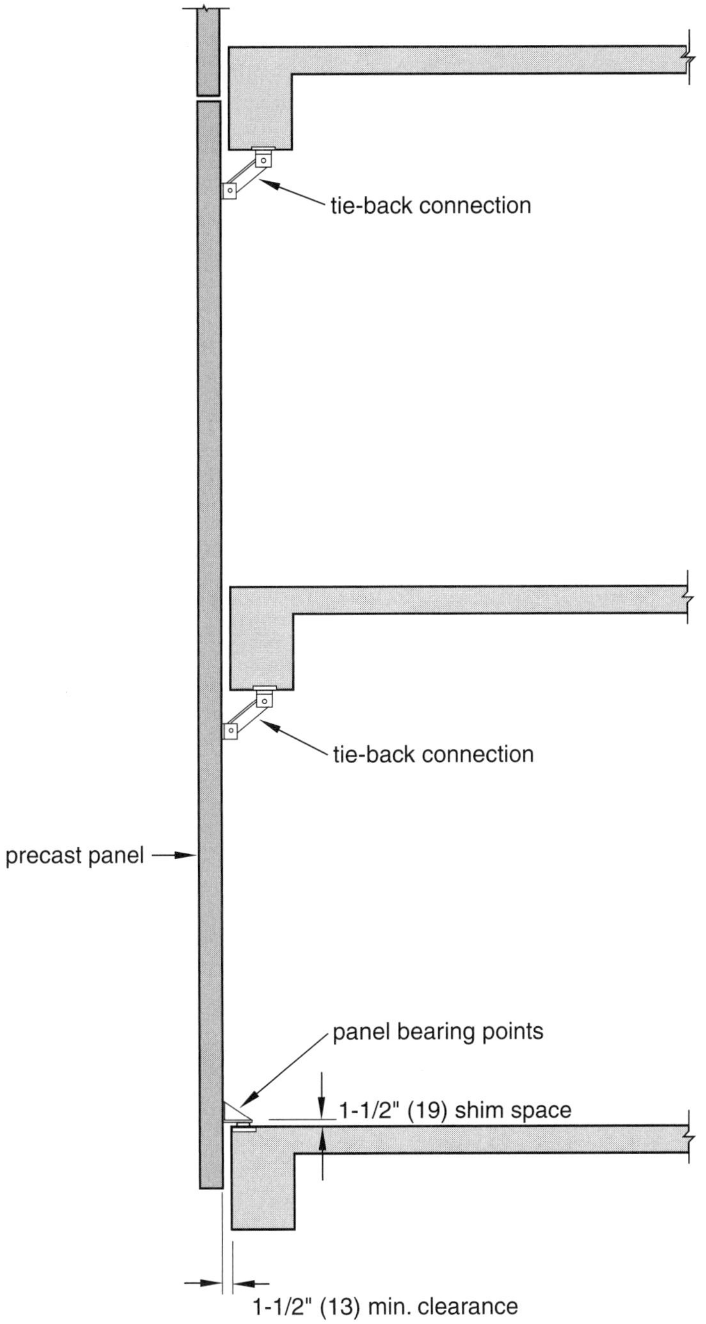

tie-back connection

tie-back connection

precast panel →

panel bearing points

1-1/2" (19) shim space

1-1/2" (13) min. clearance

Coordination Required

- Because panels spanning two or more floors should not be supported on alternate floors, one floor should be designed by the structural engineer to carry the gravity load of all the panels adjacent to that floor.

Likely Failure Points

- Cracking of the panel if a sufficient number of points of connection do not allow for movement

▪ Cracking or other damage to the panel caused by differential movement of the supporting structure if the panel is supported at more than one level

1-20 ARCHITECTURAL PRECAST SPANDREL PANELS

Description

Figure 1-20 illustrates some of the construction requirements that should be considered in developing details for non-load-bearing spandrel panels. As with precast panel connections, there are many possible configurations and connection details for spandrel panels. Therefore, Fig. 1-20 only gives a few of the general requirements that are helpful for the preliminary design. A concrete structural frame is indicated, but panels can just as easily be attached to a steel frame. See Fig. 1-10 for another type of spandrel panel.

Figure 1-20 Architectural precast spandrel panels 03 45 20

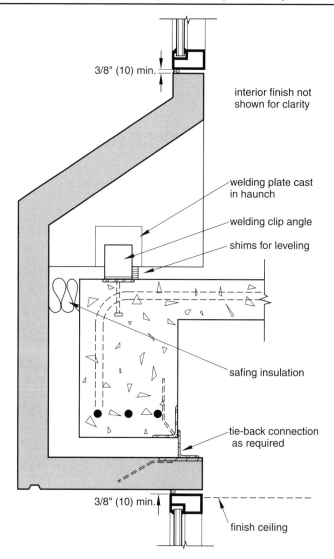

3/8" (10) min.

interior finish not
shown for clarity

welding plate cast
in haunch

welding clip angle

shims for leveling

safing insulation

tie-back connection
as required

3/8" (10) min.

finish ceiling

Limitations of Use

- This detail shows the use of non-load-bearing spandrel panels only.
- Detailed engineering design and review with the precast fabricator are required prior to developing details for a specific project.
- Special engineering design is required in high seismic areas.

Detailing Considerations

- If possible, spandrel panels should be cast in one piece to span between columns and should be attached to the columns as close to their centerlines as possible. This avoids possible differential movement between the floor structure and the panel. Figure 1-20 shows a typical bearing connection made at the floor line instead of at the column.
- Two bearing points are preferred, one rigid and one allowing for lateral displacement to accommodate temperature changes and frame movement.
- Avoid supporting spandrel panels on cantilevered beams or floor slabs.
- Connections should be standardized as much as possible throughout the building.
- Design connection locations to allow room for accessibility during erection.

Coordination Required

- Provisions must be made for the placement and anchoring of window frames. Generally, a $3/8$ in. (10 mm) minimum shim space should be provided between the precast unit and the window frame.
- In cold climates, provisions for installing insulation must be considered.
- Safing insulation is required between the fire-rated structure and the back of the panel.
- Complex spandrel panel shapes may create problems with erection inside the line of crane cables. The precast fabricator and erector should be consulted.

1-21 ARCHITECTURAL PRECAST PARAPET

Description

Figure 1-21 shows some of the detail requirements for roofing at a precast concrete parapet. Although cap flashing over the top of the parapet may be used, most designers prefer not to expose a strip of metal along the top edge. However, if coping is not used, the horizontal panel joints on top of the parapet must be given careful consideration. In addition, this detail illustrates the use of surface-applied counterflashing rather than a recessed flashing reglet cast into the panel because it is difficult to achieve close enough tolerances so that the cast-in reglets match up at adjacent panels.

Limitations of Use

- This detail shows only one general method of describing a single-ply roof. The exact details of the precast panel must be coordinated with the type of roofing used.
- This detail does not address the use of gravel stops.

Figure 1-21 Architectural precast parapet 03 45 21

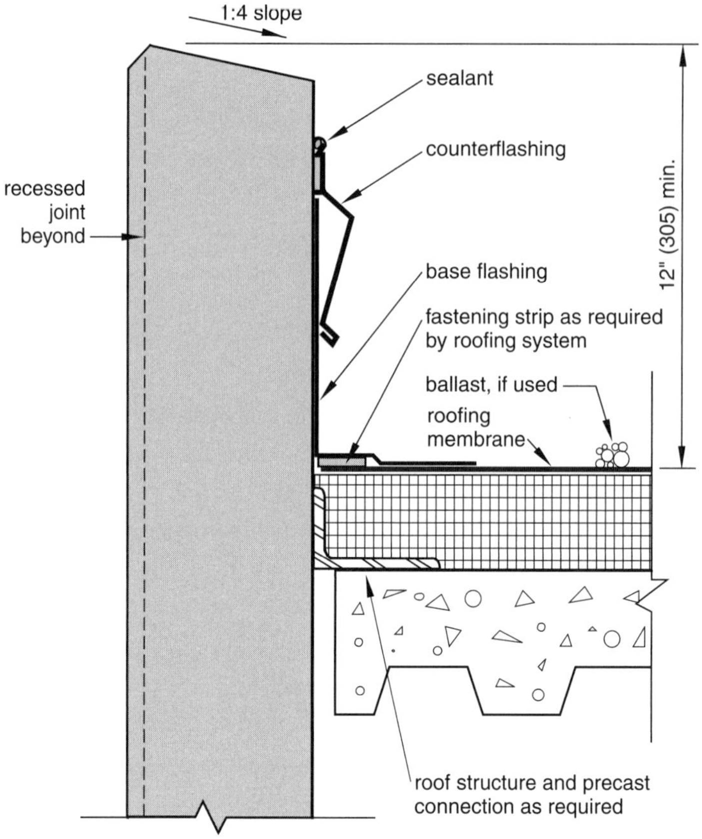

1:4 slope

sealant

counterflashing

recessed joint beyond

12" (305) min.

base flashing

fastening strip as required by roofing system

ballast, if used

roofing membrane

roof structure and precast connection as required

(a) typical parapet detail

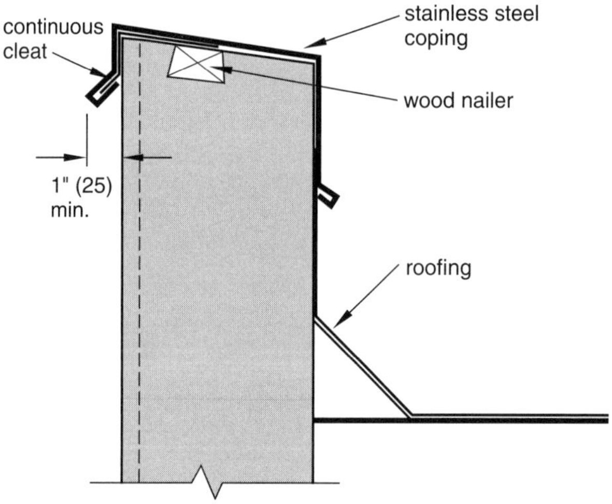

continuous cleat

stainless steel coping

wood nailer

1" (25) min.

roofing

(b) alternate detail with coping

Detailing Considerations

- The top of the parapet should be sloped toward the roof to prevent runoff over the face of the precast panel.
- The parapet should be a minimum of 12 in. (305 mm) high to prevent water from being blown over the edge of the parapet. However, this minimum dimension may need to

be increased based on the minimum distances from roof surface to counterflashing demanded by the specific type of roofing system used. See Chapter 5 for roofing details.

- Metal counterflashing must not be attached to the roofing membrane. Metal should not be used for base flashing.
- Surface-applied counterflashing should be attached to the concrete panel with slotted anchor holes.
- Provide slip joints between adjacent pieces of counterflashing (and cap flashing, if used) to allow for panel movement.
- If cap flashing is used over the parapet, the drip edge on the face of the panel should extend at least 1 in. (25 mm) from the panel's face. The top of the wall may also be capped with a stone or cast stone coping.
- Provide expansion space between the edge of the roof and the precast panel if large movements are expected. See Figs. 5-17, 5-22, and 5-27.
- The side of the panel to receive single-ply roofing must have a smooth trowel finish.

Coordination Required

- Specific types of roofing systems will require modifications to the schematic arrangement shown in this detail.
- Some flashing materials, such as copper, may cause staining on precast concrete.
- Built-up and modified bitumen roofing require cant strips.
- Flashing reglets normally have an installation tolerance of $\pm 1/4$ in. (6 mm). However, for roof flashing, the dimension from the top of the panel to the reglet should be held to $\pm 1/8$ in. (3 mm).
- Exposed concrete surfaces on the back of the parapet should be waterproofed.
- Flashing installation should be periodically inspected. Regular maintenance is required to prevent leakage.

Likely Failure Points

- Splitting or tearing of the roofing membrane if cap flashing or counterflashing is fixed to the roofing
- Water leakage caused by sealant failure at the horizontal joints along the top edge of the parapet
- Buckling or failure of counterflashing if adequate slip joints are not provided

1-22 CAST-IN-PLACE/PRECAST CONNECTION

Description

Figure 1-22 illustrates one of many ways to attach a precast panel to a cast-in-place concrete frame and to attach a precast column to a cast-in-place foundation. Because both systems have relatively large tolerances, connection detailing must accommodate the worst expected combination of tolerances while still providing for erection clearances and minimizing erection time.

Figure 1-22 Cast-in-place/precast connection 03 45 90

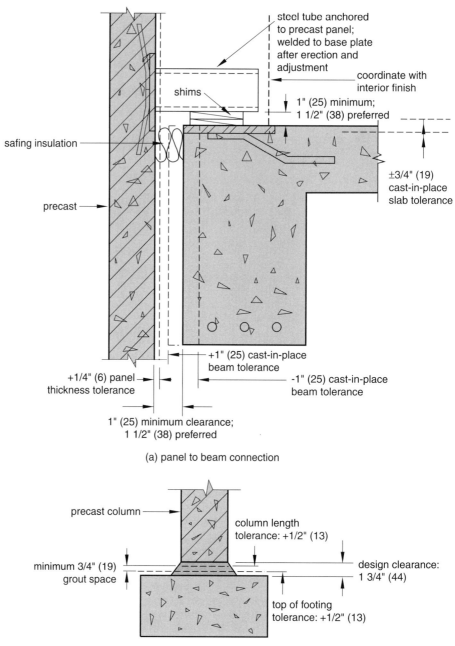

(a) panel to beam connection

(b) column to footing connection

Figure 1-22(a) shows a steel tube welded to a plate cast into the panel. Other steel shapes, such as angles and channels, can be cast into the panel to provide a connection. Vertical adjustment can be made with shims or with leveling bolts.

The recommended lateral design clearance is 1½ in. (38 mm). This allows the beam to be out by the maximum of 1 in. (25 mm) and the panel thickness to be over by the allowable ¼ in. (6 mm).

Figure 1-22(b) shows the design clearance required to accommodate tolerances for both cast-in-place footings and precast columns. The footing height must be designed to accommodate possible variations in the length of the column and placement tolerances of the footing while providing for sufficient clearance for grouting under the base plate cast onto the bottom of the column. In most cases, the elevation of the haunch used to support beams or panels is the primary control surface and may determine the clearance between the bottom of the column and the top of the footing.

Limitations of Use

- Figure 1-22 shows only one possible method of attachment. The structural engineer and the precast manufacturer should be consulted to determine the most appropriate connection method.
- This detail shows a gravity connection. For large panels, tieback connections are also required, as shown in Fig. 1-19.
- The specific connection method must be coordinated with the interior finish and mechanical system so that the steel support and any piping are concealed.

Detailing Considerations

- For horizontal alignment of several panels within a cast-in-place structural bay, the vertical joints are typically used to accommodate tolerance problems, with each joint accommodating a portion of the total expected tolerance. Procedures for determining joint width are given in Section 5-38.
- Connections should be designed to be made on the top of the concrete frame so that access is not required between the back of the panel and the face of the beam.
- To minimize costs, the connections should be designed to minimize the time the panel must be held in place with a crane while adjustments and fastenings are made.
- If the cast-in-place beam and floor structure are large enough, a blockout may be used to keep the top of the steel connection below the level of the floor to minimize conflicts with interior finishes.

Likely Failure Points

- Failure of the connection due to eccentric loading when excessive tolerances are encountered.

1-23 PRECAST FLOOR/BEAM ERECTION TOLERANCES

Description

The tolerances shown in Fig. 1-23 are recommended tolerances rather than strict standards for floor and roof members. They are reasonable variations that can be expected in most situations. However, because precast erection is subject to many variables and because some situations are visually more critical than others, tolerances should be reviewed with the precast supplier prior to finalizing specifications. To minimize costs, the tolerances described in this section can be increased where the members will be covered with other finish material or in structures where visual appearance is not critical.

Figure 1-23 Precast floor/beam erection tolerances 03 45 91

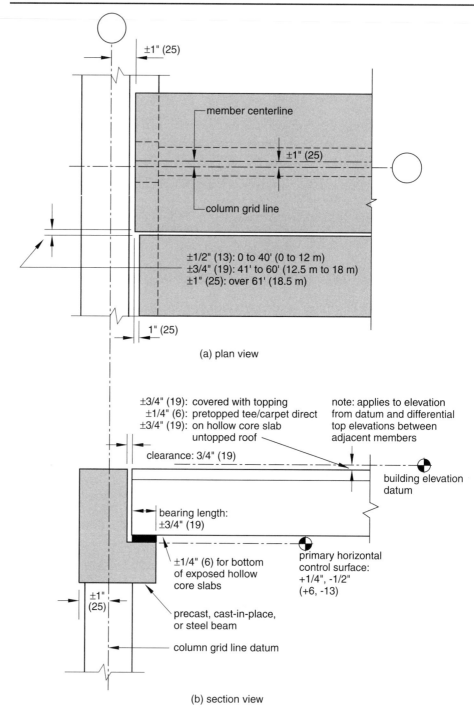

±1" (25)

member centerline

±1" (25)

column grid line

±1/2" (13): 0 to 40' (0 to 12 m)
±3/4" (19): 41' to 60' (12.5 m to 18 m)
±1" (25): over 61' (18.5 m)

1" (25)

(a) plan view

±3/4" (19): covered with topping
±1/4" (6): pretopped tee/carpet direct
±3/4" (19): on hollow core slab
            untopped roof

note: applies to elevation
from datum and differential
top elevations between
adjacent members

clearance: 3/4" (19)

building elevation
datum

bearing length:
±3/4" (19)

±1/4" (6) for bottom
of exposed hollow
core slabs

primary horizontal
control surface:
+1/4", -1/2"
(+6, -13)

±1"
(25)

precast, cast-in-place,
or steel beam

column grid line datum

(b) section view

Limitations of Use

- This section includes only some of the tolerances for precast elements. For a complete listing, refer to *Tolerance Manual for Precast and Prestressed Concrete Construction*, published by the Precast/Prestressed Concrete Institute.

Detailing Considerations

- The erection tolerances shown in this section apply to precast elements attached to other precast elements, to cast-in-place concrete or masonry, and to steel members.
- The erection tolerances shown in this section must be coordinated with manufacturing tolerances and tolerances for other building systems to which the precast system is connected. The erection tolerances are based on the primary control surfaces, which are the surfaces that are controlled during erection. The erection tolerances are *not* additive to any product tolerances. However, erection tolerances are additive to the product tolerances for secondary control surfaces.
- When a precast beam is placed on a steel column, the 1 in. (25 mm) horizontal location tolerance still applies, but it is measured from the centerline of the steel.

1-24   GLASS FIBER REINFORCED CONCRETE PANELS

Description

Glass fiber reinforced concrete (GFRC) is a product manufactured with a cement/aggregate slurry reinforced with alkali-resistant glass fibers. GFRC panels are typically used for exterior cladding, column covers, and interior finish panels. They can be manufactured with or without a face mix of conventional concrete with decorative aggregates. When a face mix is used, GFRC panels have the same appearance as standard precast concrete panels. Because of their light weight, GFRC components are easier and less expensive to transport and install than precast concrete and can be manufactured in a wide variety of shapes and sizes.

GFRC panels are normally $1/2$ in. to $5/8$ in. (13 mm to 16 mm) thick, not including any exposed aggregate or veneer finish, if used. The panels are normally attached to a stiffening assembly of metal studs, structural tubes, or integral ribs made by spraying over rib formers. The framework is then attached to the building structure. The panel frame provides support for window framing, interior finish, and other finish elements. As long as sufficient clearance and adequate adjustable fasteners are provided, GFRC panels can be installed to fairly tight tolerances.

Figure 1-24 illustrates a typical GFRC spandrel panel connection to the building structure. Most GFRC installations are specific to the manufacturer producing them. Exact panel formulations, framing, connection details, and other aspects of the project must be verified with the manufacturer.

Limitations of Use

- This section includes only some of the requirements and tolerances for GFRC. For a complete listing, refer to *Recommended Practice for Glass Fiber Reinforced Concrete Panels*, published by the Precast/Prestressed Concrete Institute.
- Verify exact details with the manufacturer.
- This detail does not show provisions for seismic anchoring.

Figure 1-24 Glass fiber reinforced concrete panels 03 49 00

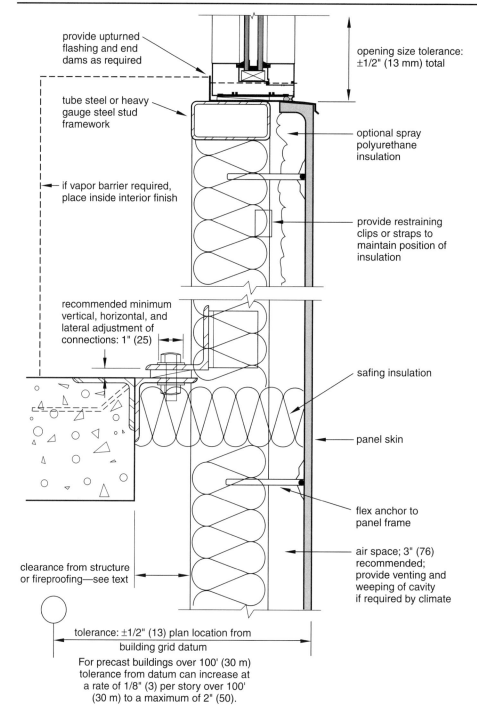

provide upturned flashing and end dams as required

tube steel or heavy gauge steel stud framework

if vapor barrier required, place inside interior finish

recommended minimum vertical, horizontal, and lateral adjustment of connections: 1" (25)

clearance from structure or fireproofing—see text

opening size tolerance: ±1/2" (13 mm) total

optional spray polyurethane insulation

provide restraining clips or straps to maintain position of insulation

safing insulation

panel skin

flex anchor to panel frame

air space; 3" (76) recommended; provide venting and weeping of cavity if required by climate

tolerance: ±1/2" (13) plan location from building grid datum

For precast buildings over 100' (30 m) tolerance from datum can increase at a rate of 1/8" (3) per story over 100' (30 m) to a maximum of 2" (50).

Detailing Considerations

- GFRC panels should be attached to the building structure at only two bearing points on one level. Flexible tie-back connections must be provided at another level to stabilize the panel and accommodate wind and seismic loads.

- Window framing should be attached to the panel frame only. Joints should be designed to allow the GFRC skin to expand or contract $1/8$ in. per 10 ft (3 mm per 3 m) due to thermal and moisture effects.
- Required joint widths should be calculated using the procedures given in Section 5-38. The minimum recommended joint width for GFRC panels is $3/4$ in. (19 mm) for field panels and 1 in. (25 mm) for corners. The minimum recommended panel edge return for sealant application is $1^1/2$ in. (38 mm), with 2 in. (51 mm) preferred.
- Verify fire safing details and specifications with local codes and fire rating requirements of the floor assembly.
- Maintain a 2 in. (51 mm) clearance between the GFRC panel and cast-in-place concrete.
- Maintain a $1^1/2$ in. (38 mm) clearance between the GFRC panel and steel fireproofing or precast structure.
- Maintain a 3 in. (76 mm) clearance between GFRC covers and columns.
- If an air space is provided between the GFRC panel and insulation and the cavity is properly ventilated, the assembly becomes a rain screen system. If spray-on insulation is applied to the back of the panel, the assembly becomes a barrier system. Refer to Section 5-5.

Coordination Required

- Coordinate the window layout with joint and structural locations so that openings are least affected by structural movement. Windows are best located entirely within one panel.
- A dew point analysis should be done to determine the amount of insulation required and whether a vapor retarder is required. See Section 5-5 for more information on weather barrier concepts.
- An adhesion test should be done to determine the compatibility of the sealant with the GFRC surface.

Likely Failure Points

- Staining of the panel due to improper application of sealant primer
- Cracking of the panel skin due to restraint by the window frame

CHAPTER 2

MASONRY DETAILS

2-1 VERTICAL CONCRETE MASONRY EXPANSION JOINT

Description

A vertical concrete masonry expansion joint, as shown in Fig. 2-1, is used to accommodate horizontal movement caused by shrinkage and thermal expansion and contraction.

This detail is used in commercial construction where steel or concrete columns support the floor and ceiling structure or where the masonry is used as a load-bearing wall. See Fig. 2-2 for vertical expansion joints in brick. See Fig. 2-3 for expansion joints in load-bearing composite walls.

Limitations of Use

- This detail is for concrete masonry exterior walls.
- This detail does not include horizontal expansion joints.
- This detail does not include reinforcing for seismic loads.

Detailing Considerations

- Through-wall building expansion joints must be provided to accommodate differential structural movement, settling, and movement caused by seismic activity.
- Shear lugs should be used to transfer lateral wind loads from one side of the joint to the other. Joint-stabilizing anchors can also be used.
- Joint reinforcement must be discontinuous at expansion joints.
- Joint reinforcement is generally spaced at every other bed joint.

Coordination Required

- Locate expansion joints at points of least bending moment or at supports.
- Expansion joints should be located at changes in wall height or thickness; at pilasters, recesses, and chases; at one side of all wall openings; and at wall intersections.

Figure 2-1 Vertical concrete masonry control joint 04 05 23.1

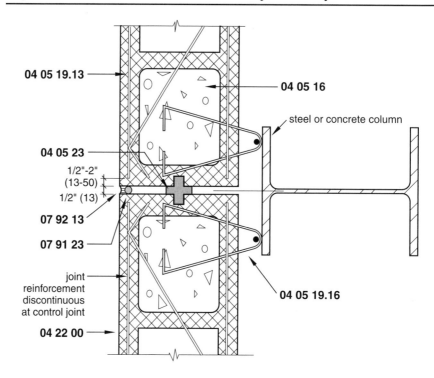

04 05 19.13

04 05 16

steel or concrete column

04 05 23

1/2"-2"
(13-50)

1/2" (13)

07 92 13

07 91 23

joint
reinforcement
discontinuous
at control joint

04 22 00

04 05 19.16

- Also locate expansion joints at movement joints in foundations and floors, below movement joints in roofs, and below floors that bear on a wall.
- Expansion joints should be designed to provide masonry panels that are as square as possible. The ratio of length to height (aspect ratio) should be as close to 1 as practical, but not more than 3.
- Joint reinforcement and bond beams must not be placed across the expansion joint.
- Mortar accelerators containing calcium chloride should not be used with reinforcing anchors and ties.
- One rule of thumb for spacing expansion joints is $1\frac{1}{2}$ times the wall height or 25 ft (7.6 m) maximum. Other spacing guidelines are given in Table 2-1.

Table 2-1   Maximum Horizontal Spacing of Vertical Control Joints in Exterior Concrete Masonry Walls, in ft (m)

Maximum annual relative humidity	Vertical spacing of bed joint reinforcement, in. (mm)	Spacing of control joints, ft (m); Type of masonry	
		Type I	Type II
Greater than 75%	None	12 (3.66)	6 (1.83)
	16 (406)	18 (5.49)	10 (3.05)
	8 (203)	24 (7.32)	14 (4.27)
Between 50% and 75%	None	18 (5.49)	12 (3.66)
	16 (406)	24 (7.32)	16 (4.88)
	8 (203)	30 (9.14)	20 (6.10)
Less than 50%	None	24 (7.32)	18 (5.49)
	16 (406)	30 (9.14)	22 (6.71)
	8 (203)	36 (10.97)	26 (7.92)

Source: Masonry Structural Design for Buildings, TM 5-809-3, Department of the Army, Navy, and Air Force, August 1982.

Likely Failure Points

- Joint cracking if horizontal reinforcement is continued across joint or mortar used in joint

Materials

04 05 16 MASONRY GROUTING

Fine or coarse grout, ASTM C476.

Ultimate compressive strength (28 days) of at least 2500 psi (17,237 kPa).

04 05 19.13 JOINT REINFORCEMENT

Materials

Fabricated from hard tempered, cold drawn steel wire, ASTM A951.

If reinforcement carries horizontal loads, reinforcement should be the deformed type.

Minimum W1.7 (MW11) but not more than one-half the thickness of the bed joint.

Two-wire, truss type.

Class 3, ASTM A641 for partially embedded joint reinforcement.

Use ties conforming to ASTM A153, Class B-2, in very corrosive environments (1.50 oz/ft^2 [458 g/m^2] of wire) or use stainless steel ties conforming to ASTM A167.

Size of horizontal reinforcement determined by structural requirements of the wall.

Execution

Ends of joint reinforcement should be placed $\frac{1}{2}$ in. to 2 in. (13 mm to 51 mm) from expansion joint and should not be continuous through expansion joints.

Lap joint reinforcement should be 6 in. (152 mm) elsewhere in wall.

Place 16 in. (400 mm) on center vertically and under the top course of masonry.

Place extra reinforcement in the first two bed joints above and below openings and extend 24 in. (600 mm) beyond the opening.

Center reinforcement with longitudinal wires centered over each face shell.

Lay reinforcement on bare masonry; then place mortar and slightly wiggle wire to get some mortar under the reinforcement.

04 05 19.16 MASONRY ANCHORS

Vertically adjustable, type to suit support.

Fabricated from hard tempered, cold drawn steel wire, ASTM A82.

Optional: stainless steel, 18-8, Type 302/304, cold rolled, annealed, ASTM A240.

Spaced 16 in. (400 mm) on center.

04 05 23 SHEAR LUG

Used to transfer lateral wind loads from one side of the joint to the other.

Made of polyvinyl chloride (PVC), ASTM D2287, or hard rubber.

Joint-stabilizing anchors may be used in lieu of shear lugs.

04 22 00 CONCRETE UNIT MASONRY

Materials

ASTM C90, Grade N.

Type 1, moisture-controlled, and Type 2, non-moisture-controlled, are available, but Type 1 is subject to less shrinkage and is best used in arid climates.

Sash block used to accept shear lug.

07 91 23 BACKER RODS

Closed cell polyethylene foam, with the diameter at least 25 percent greater than the joint width.

07 92 13 ELASTOMERIC JOINT SEALANT

Materials

One-part polysulfide, polyurethane, or silicone, ASTM C920, Type S, Grade NS, Class 25 or 50.

Execution

Sealant depth equal to the width of the joint up to $\frac{1}{2}$ in. (13 mm), with a minimum depth of $\frac{1}{4}$ in. (6 mm).

Sealant depth $\frac{1}{2}$ in. (13 mm) for joint widths from $\frac{1}{2}$ in. to 1 in. (13 mm to 25 mm).

For sealants with a ±25 percent movement capability, the joint width should be four times the expected movement of the joint.

Proper priming and backer rods are required.

2-2 VERTICAL BRICK EXPANSION JOINT

Description

Figure 2-2 illustrates an expansion joint that is required to accommodate expansion and contraction caused by temperature changes, moisture absorption, shrinkage, creep, deformation under load, and relative movement between the structure and the brick.

Limitations of Use

- This detail does not include horizontal control joints. See Section 2-11.
- This detail does not include reinforcing for seismic loads.

Detailing Considerations

- Vertical expansion joints should be installed at concrete or concrete masonry control joints, at offsets, at changes in wall height, junctions, and corners, at parapets using about one-half of the spacing used in the wall below, and at one side of any opening.

Figure 2-2 Vertical brick expansion joint 04 05 23.2

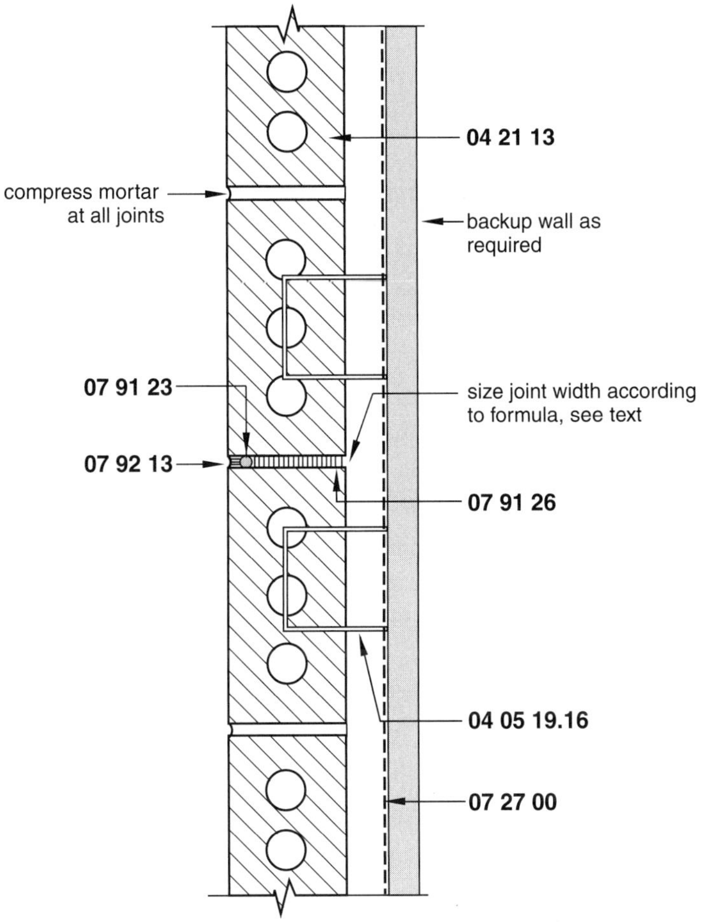

- Spacing of vertical expansion joints in long runs of brick walls can be calculated based on the width of the expansion joint, the sealant movement capabilities, and the total extent of movement caused by temperature and moisture. As a general rule, the total movement of brick can be estimated by multiplying the length of the brickwork by 0.0009. The Brick Industry Association recommends the following formula for determining the spacing of joints:

$$S = \frac{w_j e_j}{0.009} \qquad \text{(eq. 2-1)}$$

where

S = spacing between expansion joints, in. (mm).

w_j = width of expansion joint, in. (mm). Refer to the following section on how to determine the width of expansion joints.

e_j = percent extensibility of the expansion joint material in percent (e.g., 25 for 25 percent).

The number 0.009 is an approximation of the amount of change based on moisture expansion and thermal expansion, assuming a 100°F (38°C) temperature change. However, this temperature change assumption is low in many climatic regions. See Section 2-11 for an explanation of how this is derived.

As a rule of thumb, vertical expansion joints should also be located about every 15 ft to 30 ft (4.6 m to 9.1 m) in long runs of wall.

- Through-wall building expansion joints must be provided to accommodate differential structural movement, settling, and movement caused by seismic activity.
- Reinforcement must be discontinuous at the expansion joint.

Sizing Vertical Expansion Joints in Brick Masonry

Expansion joints in brick masonry can be sized according to the following formula:

$$w = \frac{[k_e + k_t(\Delta T)]L}{S} + T \qquad \text{(eq. 2-2)}$$

where

w = the total expected movement of the brick area in in. (mm).
k_e = coefficient of moisture expansion of brick in in./in. (mm/mm).
k_t = coefficient of thermal expansion of brick in in./in./°F (mm/mm/°C).
ΔT = the temperature range to which the brickwork is subject.
L = length of the brick segment being considered in in. (mm).
S = sealant movement capacity, expressed as a decimal; that is, ±25 percent would be entered as 0.25.
T = tolerance of the brick and installation in in. (mm). A conservative value of $\frac{1}{4}$ in. (6 mm) may be used.

In addition to adding the effects of tolerances, the expected movement of the building frame may also be added to the total movement calculated for expansion the temperature change.

The coefficient of moisture expansion is 5×10^{-4} in./in. (3×10^{-4} mm/mm).

The coefficient of thermal expansion is 4×10^{-6} in./in./°F (7.2×10^{-6} mm/mm/°C).

The temperature range depends on the climate, wall orientation, brick color, and brick type. In many cases, the surface temperature of the brick may be significantly higher than the ambient air temperature. A value of 100°F (38°C) is often used, but a value of 140°F (60°C) is conservative in climates with wide variations in winter and summer temperatures.

In most cases, sealant movement capability is a minimum of 25 percent, but a sealant with a 50 percent movement capability is recommended. Lower movement capability will result in closer spacing of joints.

Brick tolerances are subject to both manufacturing and installation tolerances. Manufacturing tolerances are minor and can usually be accommodated by varying the head joints slightly as the wall is laid. The out-of-plumb tolerance for expansion joints and other conspicuous lines is ±$\frac{1}{4}$ in. in any story or 20 ft (±6.4 mm in 6 m) and ±$\frac{1}{2}$ in. in 40 ft or more (±12.7 mm in 12 m). If tighter tolerances are needed to minimize the width of the joint, these tolerances must be specified in the contract documents.

Assuming a 100°F (38°C) temperature difference and a 50 percent sealant movement capability, Table 2-2 shows joint widths for various joint spacings.

Coordination Required

- Horizontal expansion joints must also be provided when the building height exceeds three stories (about 30 ft [9.1 m]) or when a brick wythe is supported on a shelf angle or the brick is used within the structural frame. See Section 2-11.

Table 2-2 Recommended Brick Joint Widths Based on Joint Spacing

Joint spacing, ft (m)	Anticipated expansion, in. (mm)	Joint width, in. (mm)
10 (3)	$^1/_8$ (3)	$^3/_8$ (6)
15 (4.5)	$^3/_{16}$ (5)	$^3/_8$ (10)
20 (6.1)	$^1/_4$ (6)	$^1/_2$ (13)
25 (7.6)	$^5/_{16}$ (8)	$^5/_8$ (16)

Note: Based on 100°F (38°C) temperature range and using a Class 50 sealant. Tolerances not included.

- Select brick grades according to exterior exposure and soil contact.
- Mortar accelerators containing calcium chloride should not be used when mortar may come in contact with reinforcing anchors and ties.

Likely Failure Points

- Joint cracking if horizontal reinforcement is continued across the joint or if mortar is used in the joint

Materials

04 05 19.16 MASONRY ANCHORS

Vertically adjustable, type to suit the support.

Fabricated from hard tempered, cold drawn steel wire, ASTM A82.

Optional: stainless steel, 18-8, Type 302/304, cold rolled, annealed, ASTM A240.

Spaced 16 in. (400 mm) on center or as required by the building code.

04 21 13 BRICK MASONRY

Materials

Grade SW or MW as required by the geographical location.

Hollow facing brick, ASTM C652, or solid facing brick, ASTM C216.

07 27 00 AIR BARRIER

Nonwoven, spun-bonded olefin sheet membrane, liquid-applied membrane, or self-adhering membrane, ASTM E1677.

Vapor-permeable or vapor-impermeable as required by local climatic conditions.

Install according to the manufacturer's instructions.

Refer to Section 5-5 for more information.

07 91 23 BACKER ROD

Closed cell polyethylene foam, with the diameter at least 25 percent greater than the joint width.

07 91 26 COMPRESSIBLE JOINT FILLER

Closed cell material, preformed compressible filler, or copper sheet.

Should compress to 30 percent to 50 percent of the original thickness.

07 92 13 ELASTOMERIC JOINT SEALANT

Materials

One-part polysulfide, polyurethane, or silicone, ASTM C920, Type S, Grade NS, Class 25 or 50.

Execution

Sealant depth equal to the width of the joint up to $\frac{1}{2}$ in. (13 mm), with a minimum depth of $\frac{1}{4}$ in. (6 mm).

Sealant depth $\frac{1}{2}$ in. (13 mm) for joint widths from $\frac{1}{2}$ in. to 1 in. (13 mm to 25 mm).

For sealants with a ±25 percent movement capability, the joint width should be four times the expected movement of the joint.

Proper priming and backer rods required.

2-3 VERTICAL MASONRY EXPANSION JOINT IN COMPOSITE WALL

Description

A vertical expansion joint in a composite wall, as shown in Fig. 2-3, is used to accommodate differential movement between the two materials caused by shrinkage and thermal expansion and contraction as well as by expansion of the brick caused by water absorption.

This detail is used in commercial and residential construction where the masonry is used as a load-bearing wall. See Section 2-2 for a discussion of vertical brick expansion joints.

Limitations of Use

- This detail is for exterior masonry walls.
- This detail does not include horizontal expansion joints.
- This detail does not include reinforcing for seismic loads.
- Figure 2-3 does not show insulation on the outside of the block wall. Additional rigid board insulation can provide an additional R-value as well as a smooth surface to apply an air barrier. Loose fill insulation may also be placed in the concrete masonry units.

Detailing Considerations

- Expansion joints should be installed in the brick wythe wherever expansion joints are installed in the block wythe. They should also be installed at changes in wall thickness or height, at one side of any opening, and at pilasters, recesses, chases, and returns.
- Through-wall building expansion joints must be provided to accommodate differential structural movement, settling, and movement caused by seismic activity. Generally, spacing of concrete block expansion joints should not exceed 40 ft (12.2 m).
- Insulation placed in the cavity can increase the differential movement.

Figure 2-3 Vertical expansion joint in composite walls 04 05 23.3

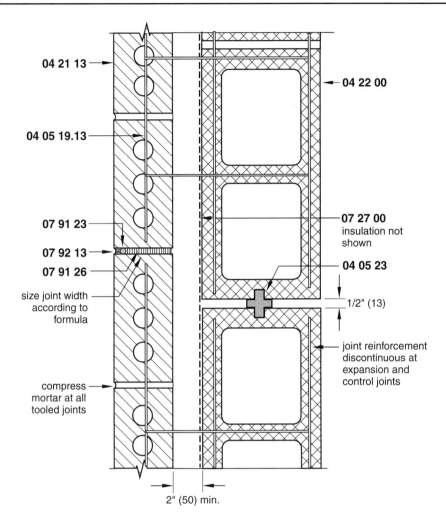

04 21 13

04 05 19.13

07 91 23

07 92 13

07 91 26

size joint width according to formula

compress mortar at all tooled joints

2" (50) min.

04 22 00

07 27 00 insulation not shown

04 05 23

1/2" (13)

joint reinforcement discontinuous at expansion and control joints

- Shear lugs should be used to transfer lateral wind loads from one side of the joint to the other. Joint-stabilizing anchors can also be used.
- Joint reinforcement must be discontinuous at the joint.
- Joint reinforcement is generally spaced at every other bed joint.
- If rigid insulation is used in the cavity, 2 in. (50 mm) of air space should be provided in addition to the insulation thickness.

Coordination Required

- Locate expansion joints at points of least bending moment or at supports.
- Expansion joints should be located at changes in wall height or thickness; at pilasters, recesses, and chases; at one side of all wall openings; and at wall intersections. See Sections 2-1 and 2-2 for additional recommendations.
- See Section 2-2 for guidelines on sizing joints in brick.
- Select brick grades according to the soil and the exterior exposure.
- Mortar accelerators containing calcium chloride should not be used when mortar may come in contact with reinforcing anchors and ties.

Likely Failure Points

- Cracking of either wythe due to stress built up when the two materials are not allowed to move separately
- Brick expands and the concrete block may shrink

Materials

04 05 23 SHEAR LUG

Used to transfer lateral wind loads from one side of the joint to the other.

Made of PVC, ASTM D2287, or hard rubber.

Joint-stabilizing anchors may be used in lieu of shear lugs.

04 05 19.13 JOINT REINFORCEMENT

Materials

Fabricated from hard tempered, cold drawn steel wire, ASTM A951.

If reinforcement carries horizontal loads, reinforcement should be the deformed type.

Minimum W1.7 (MW11), but not more than one-half of the thickness of the bed joint.

Two-wire, truss type.

Class 3, ASTM A641 for partially embedded joint reinforcement.

Use ties conforming to ASTM A153, Class B-2, in very corrosive environments (1.50 oz/ft^2 [458 g/m^2] of wire) or use stainless steel ties conforming to ASTM A167.

The size of horizontal reinforcement is determined by the structural requirements of the wall.

Execution

Ends of joint reinforcement should be placed $\frac{1}{2}$ in. to 2 in. (13 mm to 51 mm) from the expansion joint and should not be continuous through expansion joints.

Lap joint reinforcement should be 6 in. (152 mm) elsewhere in wall.

Place 16 in. (400 mm) on center vertically and under the top course of masonry.

Place extra reinforcement in the first two bed joints above and below openings and extend 24 in. (600 mm) beyond the opening.

Center reinforcement with longitudinal wires centered over each face shell.

Lay reinforcement on bare masonry; then place mortar and slightly wiggle wire to get some mortar under the reinforcement.

04 21 13 BRICK MASONRY

Materials

Grade SW or MW as required by the geographical location.

Hollow facing brick, ASTM C652, or solid facing brick, ASTM C216.

04 22 00 CONCRETE UNIT MASONRY

Materials

ASTM C90, Grade N.

Type 1, moisture-controlled, and Type 2, non-moisture-controlled, are available, but Type 1 is subject to less shrinkage and is best used in arid climates.

Sash block is used to accept shear lug.

07 27 00 AIR BARRIER

Nonwoven, spun-bonded olefin sheet membrane, liquid-applied membrane, or self-adhering membrane, ASTM E1677.

Vapor-permeable or vapor-impermeable as required by local climatic conditions.

Install according to the manufacturer's instructions.

Refer to Section 5-5 for more information.

07 91 23 BACKER ROD

Closed cell polyethylene foam, with the diameter at least 25 percent greater than the joint width.

07 91 26 COMPRESSIBLE JOINT FILLER

Closed cell material, preformed compressible filler, or copper sheet.

Should compress to 30 percent to 50 percent of the original thickness.

07 92 13 ELASTOMERIC JOINT SEALANT

Materials

One-part polysulfide, polyurethane, or silicone, ASTM C920, Type S, Grade NS, Class 25 or 50.

Execution

Sealant depth equal to the width of the joint up to $\frac{1}{2}$ in. (13 mm), with a minimum depth of $\frac{1}{4}$ in. (6 mm).

Sealant depth $\frac{1}{2}$ in. (13 mm) for joint widths from $\frac{1}{2}$ in. to 1 in. (13 mm to 25 mm).

For sealants with a ±25 percent movement capability, the joint width should be four times the expected movement of the joint.

Proper priming and backer rods are required.

2-4 BRICK/MASONRY CAVITY WALL AT GRADE

Description

Figure 2-4 illustrates one type of multiwythe, masonry-bearing wall construction that uses brick as the exterior veneer and concrete masonry as the load-bearing backup wythe. It is a drainage wall system in that any water that penetrates the exterior brick wythe through wind-driven rain, capillary action, or small cracks drains down to flashing and weep holes, where it drains to the outside before it can penetrate the interior wythe.

This system can be used as a bearing wall system supporting wood joists, steel joists, or precast concrete cored slabs, or as a non-load-bearing system with a poured-in-place concrete, precast concrete, or steel frame.

Figure 2-4 Brick/masonry cavity wall at grade 04 21 10.1

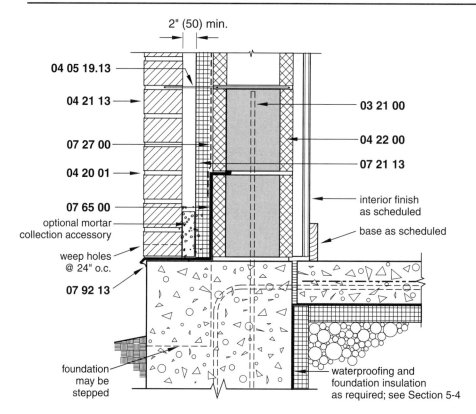

2" (50) min.

04 05 19.13

04 21 13 → 03 21 00

07 27 00 → 04 22 00

04 20 01 → 07 21 13

07 65 00 → interior finish as scheduled
optional mortar collection accessory

base as scheduled

weep holes @ 24" o.c.

07 92 13

foundation may be stepped

waterproofing and foundation insulation as required; see Section 5-4

Limitations of Use

- This detail and Sections 2-5 and 2-6 illustrate a low- to medium-rise building. For higher buildings, shelf angle supports with horizontal expansion joints, such as the one shown in Fig. 2-11, must be used. The height of this type of brick wall bearing directly on the foundation should not exceed 25 ft (7.6 m) or as required by the local building code.
- Requirements for grouting and reinforcing the concrete masonry cores should be verified with a structural engineer to meet the specific gravity and seismic loading requirements of the job.

Detailing Considerations

- Insulation can be placed either on the inside face of the concrete masonry wythe or in the cavity. If it is placed in the cavity, an additional 2 in. (50 mm), minimum, of air space should be provided between the brick and the insulation. In addition, poured or foam insulation can be placed in the cavities of the concrete masonry.
- Base flashing must be located above ground level.
- Where flashing is not continuous, the ends of the flashing must be turned up several inches into the head joint to form a dam.
- Insulation placed in the cavity can increase the differential movement between the block and the brick.
- In addition to an open head joint for weep holes, various types of manufactured items are available to provide drainage of water accumulating in the cavity. To keep mortar

out of the cavity, a premanufactured mesh or other mortar-management accessory may be used at the base of the wall.

Coordination Required

- The expected shortening of the concrete or steel frame should be calculated if these structural systems are used.
- Provide proper vertical control and expansion joints. See Section 2-3.
- Select brick grades according to the soil and the exterior exposure.
- Mortar accelerators containing calcium chloride should not be used when mortar may come in contact with reinforcing anchors and ties.

Likely Failure Points

- Cracking of either wythe due to stress built up when the two materials are not allowed to move separately
- Water leakage if flashing is not extended beyond the brick with a formed drip

Materials

03 21 00 REINFORCING STEEL

ASTM A615, Grade 60.

#3 bars (#10) or as required by the structural design.

Place in fully grouted concrete masonry unit cells.

04 05 19.13 JOINT REINFORCEMENT

Materials

Fabricated from hard tempered, cold drawn steel wire, ASTM A951.

If reinforcement carries horizontal loads, reinforcement should be the deformed type.

Minimum W1.7 (MW11), but not more than one-half the thickness of the bed joint.

Three-wire, ladder-type, or two-wire type with tab ties. Do not use truss-type reinforcement. Use adjustable ties if substantial differential vertical movement is expected or if bed joints of brick do not align with concrete masonry units.

Class 3, ASTM A641, for partially embedded joint reinforcement.

Use ties conforming to ASTM A153, Class B-2, where ties cross cavities or in very corrosive environments (1.50 oz/ft^2 [458 g/m^2] of wire) or use stainless steel ties conforming to ASTM A167.

The size of horizontal reinforcement is determined by the structural requirements of the wall.

Execution

Lap joint reinforcement 6 in. (152 mm).

Place 16 in. (400 mm) on center vertically and under the top course of masonry.

Place extra reinforcement in the first two bed joints above and below openings and extend 24 in. (600 mm) beyond the opening.

Center reinforcement with longitudinal wires centered over each face shell.

Lay reinforcement on bare masonry; then place mortar and slightly wiggle wire to get some mortar under the reinforcement.

04 20 01 MORTAR

Materials

Portland cement–lime, ASTM C270.

Type M, N, or S, depending on the loads, brick used, and climate. Do not use mortar that is stronger in compression than is required by the structural requirements of the job.

Execution

Fill all mortar joints completely.

Keep all air spaces and expansion joints clear of mortar.

Tool joint with vee or concave profile.

04 21 13 BRICK MASONRY

Materials

Grade SW or MW as required by geographical location.

Hollow facing brick: ASTM C652.

Solid facing brick: ASTM C216.

04 22 00 CONCRETE UNIT MASONRY

Materials

ASTM C90, Grade N.

Type 1, moisture-controlled, and Type 2, non-moisture-controlled, are available, but Type 1 is subject to less shrinkage and is best used in arid climates.

07 21 13 BUILDING INSULATION

Rigid insulation or batt insulation is placed between furring or metal studs on the inside wall.

Loose insulation or rigid insulation specially manufactured for placement in the cells of the concrete block may be used to provide additional insulation.

Rigid insulation may be placed in the cavity, but an additional 2 in. (50 mm), minimum, of air space should be provided between the brick and insulation.

07 27 00 AIR BARRIER

Nonwoven, spun-bonded olefin sheet membrane, liquid-applied membrane, or self-adhering membrane, ASTM E1677.

Vapor-permeable or vapor-impermeable as required by local climatic conditions.

Lap over flashing and seal as recommended by the manufacturer.

Install according to manufacturer's instructions.

Refer to Section 5-5 for more information.

07 65 00 FLASHING

Materials

Flashing may be rigid copper or stainless steel, semiflexible composites of copper and other materials, or flexible membranes, such as peel-and-stick products.

Copper, ASTM B370, cold rolled, hard tempered, 10–20 oz (0.0135 in. [0.343 mm] to 0.0270 in. [0.686 mm]).

Stainless steel, ASTM A167, type 304 with 2D or 2B finish, 0.0187 in. (0.475 mm).

Copper composites, 5 oz (0.0068 in. [0.1715 mm]), laminated between fiberglass fabric or asphaltic material. Other proprietary products are also available.

Flexible membranes, 40 mil (1 mm) self-adhering rubberized asphalt, 40 mil ethylene propylene diene monomer (EPDM), or 40 mil composite of rubberized asphalt and cross-laminated polyethylene.

Must not be subject to ultraviolet degradation.

Must not be subject to deterioration in contact with alkaline masonry mortars or sealants.

Do not use asphalt-impregnated felt, aluminum, or lead flashing.

Execution

Extend flashing beyond exterior of brick at least $1/4$ in. (6 mm) and turn down at a 45 degree angle to form a drip.

Lap flashing a minimum of 6 in. (152 mm).

If flashing spans the open cavity at an angle, provide some type of support such as a mortar wash, plastic supports, or insulation cut at the same angle as the flashing.

Secure the flashing inside the cavity by tucking it into a bed joint, as shown in Fig. 2-4, or by securing it with a termination bar, the top of which should be sealed.

Use edge dams at openings.

07 92 13 ELASTOMERIC JOINT SEALANT

Materials

One-part polysulfide, polyurethane, or silicone, ASTM C920, Type S, Grade NS, Class 25 or 50.

2-5   BRICK/MASONRY CAVITY WALL AT SPANDREL

Description

Figure 2-5 illustrates one type of multiwythe masonry bearing wall construction that uses brick as the exterior veneer and concrete masonry as the load-bearing backup wythe. It is a drainage wall system in that any water that penetrates the exterior brick wythe through wind-driven rain, capillary action, or small cracks drains down to flashing and weep holes, where it drains to the outside before it can penetrate the interior wythe.

Figure 2-5 Brick/masonry cavity wall at spandrel 4 21 10.2

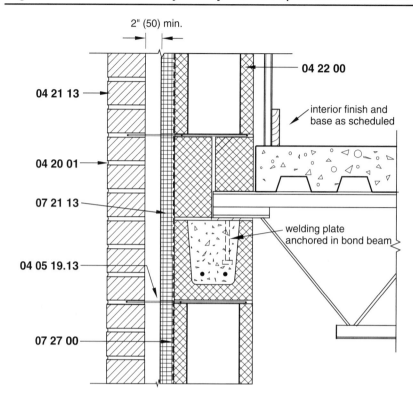

This system can be used as a bearing wall system supporting wood joists, precast concrete cored slabs, or, as shown here, steel joists. It can also be used as a non-load-bearing system with a poured-in-place concrete, precast concrete, or steel frame.

Limitations of Use

- This detail and Sections 2-4 and 2-6 illustrate a low- to medium-rise building. For higher buildings, shelf angle supports with horizontal expansion joints, such as the one shown in Fig. 2-11, must be used. The maximum height of the brick bearing directly on the foundation in this type of cavity wall should not exceed 25 ft (7.6 m) or as required by the local building code.
- Requirements for grouting and reinforcing the concrete masonry cores should be verified with a structural engineer to meet the specific gravity and seismic loading requirements of the job.
- The bearing details of the floor structure on the concrete masonry should be verified with a structural engineer.

Detailing Considerations

- Insulation can be placed either on the inside face of the concrete masonry wythe or in the cavity. If it is placed in the cavity, an additional 2 in. (50 mm), minimum, of air space should be provided between the brick and the insulation. In addition, poured or foam insulation can be placed in the cavities of the concrete masonry.
- Locate joint reinforcement below the bond beam and one course above the bond beam.
- Insulation placed in the cavity can increase the differential movement.

Coordination Required

- The expected shortening of the concrete or steel frame, if used, should be calculated. Horizontal expansion joints must be used to allow the frame to shorten independently of the frame.
- Provide proper vertical control and expansion joints. See Section 2-3.
- Mortar accelerators containing calcium chloride should not be used when the mortar may come in contact with reinforcing anchors and ties.

Likely Failure Points

- Cracking of either wythe due to stress built up when the two materials are not allowed to move separately
- Uplift of masonry placed directly on joists or precast slabs as the floor structure deflects

Materials

See Section 2-4 for material requirements.

2-6 BRICK/MASONRY CAVITY WALL AT ROOF/PARAPET

Description

Figure 2-6 shows the termination of the multiwythe bearing wall shown in Figs. 2-4 and 2-5 using a parapet rather than a simple gravel stop.

Parapets are classified as low or high. Low parapets are those extending 15 in. (381 mm) or less above the roof deck, while high parapets are those extending more than 15 in. (381 mm) above the deck to a maximum height three times the thickness of the parapet. If a low parapet is used, the counterflashing should extend into the joint below the coping and should also serve as the through-wall flashing.

For low parapets, a double-wythe brick parapet may be used instead of the triple-wythe construction shown in Fig. 2-6.

Limitations of Use

- Requirements for grouting and reinforcing the concrete masonry cores should be verified with a structural engineer to meet the specific gravity and seismic loading requirements of the job.
- The bearing details of the floor structure on the concrete masonry should be verified with a structural engineer.

Detailing Considerations

- Both sides of a parapet wall should be constructed of the same material to minimize differential movement caused by weather and temperature acting on dissimilar materials.
- Copings should be of precast concrete, stone, or terra cotta. These materials have coefficients of thermal expansion similar to that of brick and will move about the same

Figure 2-6 Brick/masonry cavity wall at roof/parapet 04 21 10.3

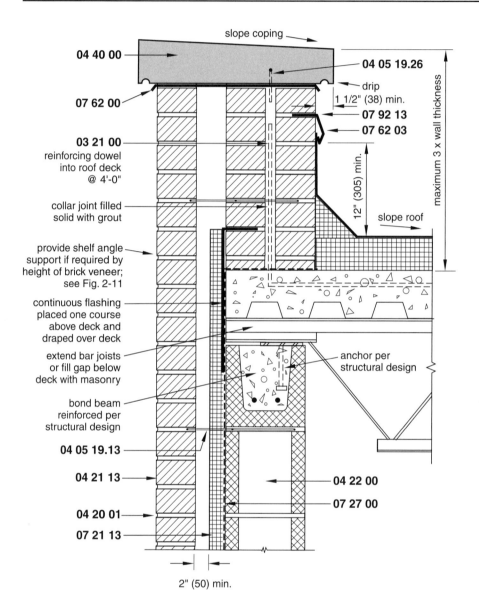

amount as the wall below. Avoid metal copings because of the difference in thermal movement between metal and brick. Also, avoid brick copings because the numerous joints tend to crack and leak.

- Rake the joints of the coping and seal with elastomeric sealant.
- Keep the height of the parapet to a minimum.
- The cavity should continue into the parapet.
- Locate joint reinforcement below the bond beam and one course above the bond beam.
- Locate expansion joints in the coping to coincide with the wall expansion and control joints and add an extra expansion joint between those placed in the wall below.
- To minimize thermal bridging, extend the cavity insulation up beyond the roof insulation.

Coordination Required

- Expansion joints should be placed near the building corners to avoid displacement of the parapet. Provide twice as many control joints in the parapet as in the wall below.
- Provide proper vertical control and expansion joints. See Fig. 2-3.
- Mortar accelerators containing calcium chloride should not be used when the mortar may come in contact with reinforcing anchors and ties.
- Locate movement joints in counterflashing at the same point as the soft joints in the coping.
- Provide vents in the upper part of brick veneer to ventilate air if the wall is designed as a pressure-equalized rain screen.

Likely Failure Points

- Cracking along the parapet if both brick and concrete masonry are used instead of all brick
- Leaks caused by using brick or metal copings or by omitting through-wall flashing
- Displacement of the parapet due to exposure of both sides to the weather without adequate provisions for movement

Materials

See Section 2-4 for material requirements in addition to the following.

04 05 19.26 MASONRY COPING ANCHOR

Stainless steel 304.

Seal hole where anchor penetrates flashing.

04 40 00 STONE COPING

Materials

Precast concrete, stone, or terra cotta.

Pitch toward the roof.

Project the drip edge at least $1\frac{1}{2}$ in. (38 mm) beyond the face of the wall and have a continuous drip.

Execution

Install with a mortar joint at one end and a soft joint at the other end. The soft joint should be a sealant over a compressible backer rod.

When installing the coping, set it on noncompressible shims of a thickness equal to the joint width and then spread the bed joint of mortar and place the coping. When the mortar has set, remove the shims and tuckpoint the void.

07 62 00 COUNTERFLASHING

Materials

Flashing may be rigid copper or stainless steel, semiflexible composites of copper and other materials, or flexible membranes, such as peel-and-stick products.

Copper, ASTM B370, cold rolled hard tempered, 10–20 oz (0.0135 in. [0.343 mm] to 0.0270 in. [0.686 mm]).

Stainless steel, ASTM A167, type 304 with 2D or 2B finish, 0.0187 in. (0.475 mm).

Copper composites, 5 oz (0.0068 in. [0.1715 mm]), laminated between fiberglass fabric or asphaltic material. Other proprietary products are also available.

Flexible membranes, 40 mil (1 mm) self-adhering rubberized asphalt, 40 mil EPDM, or 40 mil composite of rubberized asphalt and cross-laminated polyethylene.

Must not be subject to ultraviolet degradation.

Must not be subject to deterioration in contact with alkaline masonry mortars or sealants.

Do not use asphalt-impregnated felt, aluminum, or lead flashing.

Execution

Extend flashing beyond the exterior of the brick at least $\frac{1}{4}$ in. (6 mm) and turn it down at a 45 degree angle to form a drip.

Lap flashing a minimum of 6 in. (152 mm).

Embed the edge completely in the mortar joint.

Rake the mortar joint where flashing is installed and seal it continuously.

07 92 13 ELASTOMERIC JOINT SEALANT

Materials

One-part polysulfide, polyurethane, or silicone, ASTM C920, Type S, Grade NS, Class 25 or 50.

Oil-based calking should not be used.

Execution

In the soft joints of the coping, the sealant depth should be equal to the width of the joint up to $\frac{1}{2}$ in. (13 mm), with a minimum depth of $\frac{1}{4}$ in. (6 mm).

Proper priming and backer rods are required.

2-7 MASONRY GROUTED WALL

Description

Figure 2-7 shows a double-wythe wall designed so that both wythes act as a unit as a load-bearing wall. The space between the wythes, called the *collar joint*, is reinforced and completely filled with grout. The size and spacing of the reinforcing depend on the structural requirements of the job. If reinforcing between the wythes is not needed, the wall may be constructed as a composite wall without a collar joint. In this case, all the reinforcing is placed in the cavities of the block wythe.

For resistance to water penetration, this type of wall is considered a barrier wall. Any water that penetrates the outer wythe is stopped by the filled collar joint; it then flows back out of the system.

Figure 2-7 Masonry grouted wall 4 21 10.4

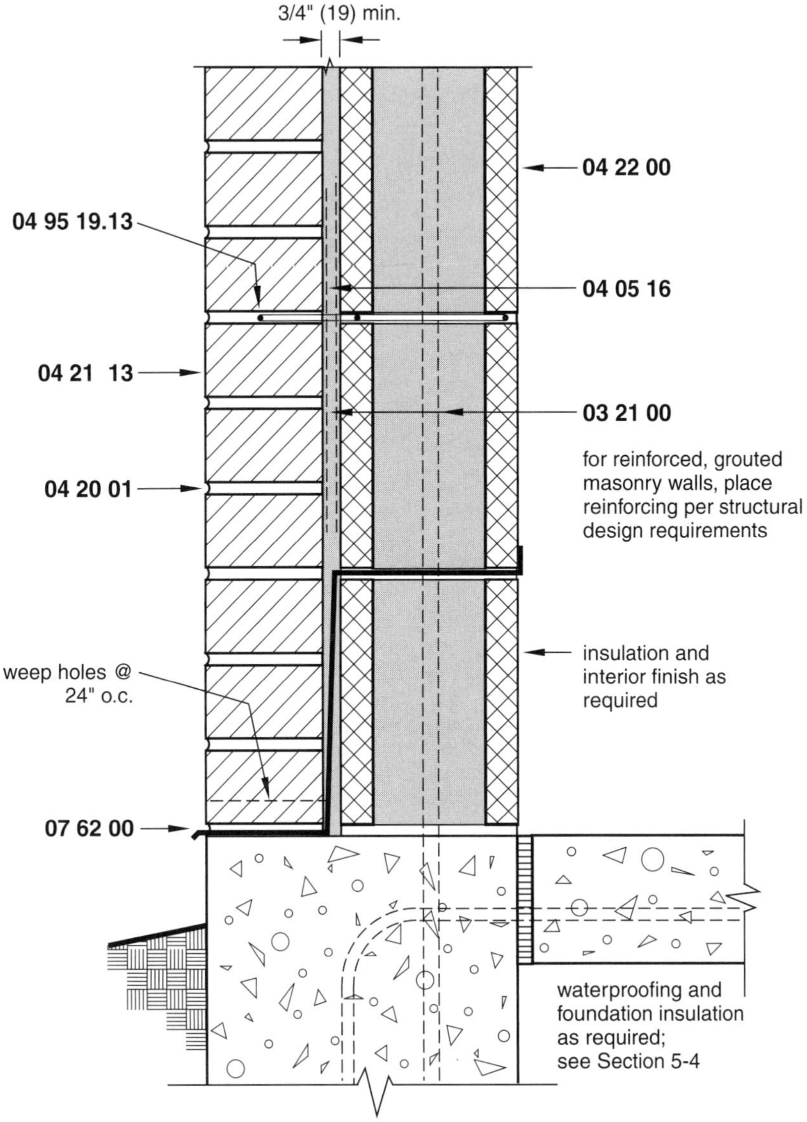

3/4" (19) min.

04 95 19.13

04 21 13

04 20 01

weep holes @
24" o.c.

07 62 00

04 22 00

04 05 16

03 21 00

for reinforced, grouted
masonry walls, place
reinforcing per structural
design requirements

insulation and
interior finish as
required

waterproofing and
foundation insulation
as required;
see Section 5-4

Limitations of Use

- An additional thickness of material is required for insulation and interior finish.
- Reinforcing must be verified with a structural engineer.

Detailing Considerations

- Provide flashing at the base course, above openings, and at the roof line, as with other masonry walls.
- For composite walls, a minimum collar joint width of $\frac{3}{4}$ in. (19 mm) is required with fine grout and a low pour height so that the joint can be completely filled with grout as each course of masonry is laid.
- The foundation may be stepped at the outside face to minimize the amount of concrete visible above grade.

Coordination Required

- Expansion and control joints should be located and designed as shown in Fig. 2-3.

Likely Failure Points

- Water leakage due to incomplete filling of the collar joint (Placing mortar in the joint with a trowel as the wythes are laid does not result in a completely filled joint.)

Materials

03 21 00 Reinforcing steel

ASTM A615, Grade 60.

Extend vertical bars into the foundation as required by the structural design.

Place in fully grouted concrete masonry unit cells.

04 05 16 Masonry grouting

Fine grout, ASTM C476.

Ultimate compressive strength (28 days) of at least 2,500 psi (17,237 kPa).

04 05 19.13 Joint reinforcement

Materials

Fabricated from hard tempered, cold drawn steel wire, ASTM A951.

If reinforcement carries horizontal loads, reinforcement should be the deformed type.

Minimum W1.7 (MW11), but not more than one-half the thickness of the bed joint.

Class 3, ASTM A641, for partially embedded joint reinforcement.

Use ties conforming to ASTM A153, Class B-2, in very corrosive environments (1.50 oz/ft^2 [458 g/m^2] of wire) or use stainless steel ties conforming to ASTM A167.

The size of horizontal reinforcement is determined by the structural requirements of the wall.

Execution

Lap joint reinforcement 6 in. (152 mm).

Place 16 in. (400 mm) on center vertically and under the top course of masonry.

Place extra reinforcement in the first two bed joints above and below openings and extend it 24 in. (600 mm) beyond the opening.

Center reinforcement with longitudinal wires centered over each face shell.

Lay reinforcement on bare masonry; then place mortar and slightly wiggle the wire to get some mortar under the reinforcement.

04 20 01 Mortar

Materials

Portland cement-lime, ASTM C270.

Type M, N, or S, depending on the loads, brick used, and climate. Do not use mortar that is stronger in compression than is required by the structural requirements of the job.

Admixtures and additives for workability are not recommended.

Execution

Fill all mortar joints completely.

Keep all expansion joints clear of mortar.

Tool joint with vee or concave profile.

04 21 13 BRICK MASONRY

Materials

Grade SW or MW as required by geographical location.

Hollow facing brick: ASTM C652.

Solid facing brick: ASTM C216.

Execution

Brick with more than a 30 g/min • 30 in.^{2} (30 g/min • 194 cm^2) initial rate of absorption must be wetted and permitted to dry prior to laying.

04 22 00 CONCRETE UNIT MASONRY

Materials

ASTM C90, Grade N.

Type 1, moisture-controlled, and Type 2, non-moisture-controlled, are available, but Type 1 is subject to less shrinkage and is best used in arid climates.

07 65 00 FLASHING

Materials

Flashing may be rigid copper or stainless steel, semiflexible composites of copper and other materials, or flexible membranes, such as peel-and-stick products.

Copper, ASTM B370, cold rolled, hard tempered, 10–20 oz (0.0135 in. [0.343 mm] to 0.0270 in. [0.686 mm]).

Stainless steel, ASTM A167, type 304 with 2D or 2B finish, 0.0187 in. (0.475 mm).

Copper composites, 5 oz (0.0068 in. [0.1715 mm]), laminated between fiberglass fabric or asphaltic material. Other proprietary products are also available.

Flexible membranes, 40 mil (1 mm) self-adhering rubberized asphalt, 40 mil EPDM, or 40 mil composite of rubberized asphalt and cross-laminated polyethylene.

Must not be subject to ultraviolet degradation.

Must not be subject to deterioration in contact with alkaline masonry mortars or sealants.

Do not use asphalt-impregnated felt, aluminum, or lead flashing.

Execution

Extend flashing beyond the exterior of the brick at least $^1/_4$ in. (6 mm) and turn it down at a 45 degree angle to form a drip.

Lap flashing a minimum of 6 in. (152 mm).

Secure the flashing inside the cavity by tucking it into a bed joint.

Use edge dams at openings.

2-8   BRICK VENEER, WOOD STUDS

Description

A brick veneer wall, as shown in Fig. 2-8, consists of a single wythe of brick used for the purpose of ornamentation, protection, or insulation. The masonry is non-load-bearing and is attached to a suitable backup wall with an air space between. Wood framing may be used as a low-cost method of building brick veneer walls, but this type of construction is usually limited to residential and light commercial structures.

Limitations of Use

- This detail does not include provisions for seismic design.
- The veneer can carry no loads other than its own weight, the dead load of the veneer above, and its proportionate share of the lateral load.

Figure 2-8 Brick veneer, wood studs 04 21 13.1

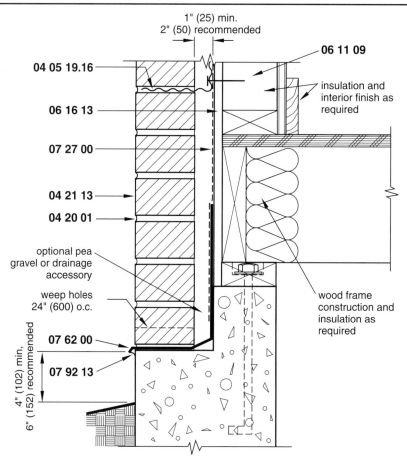

- Brick veneer walls over wood studs are generally limited to a maximum height of 30 ft (9144 mm). Local building codes may vary.

Detailing Considerations

- For most residential and small commercial structures, provisions for horizontal and lateral movement due to thermal and moisture expansion are generally not needed. However, for long, uninterrupted walls, vertical joints may be required.
- Windows should be attached either to the brick veneer or the backup wall, but not both.
- A minimum air space of at least 1 in. (25 mm) is required between the brick and the sheathing.
- Additional insulation may be provided by adding rigid board insulation outside of the studs.
- Use concave or vee mortar joints to prevent water penetration.
- In addition to an open head joint for weep holes, various types of manufactured items are available to provide drainage of water accumulating in the cavity. To keep mortar out of the cavity, a premanufactured mesh or other mortar-management accessory may be used at the base of the wall.
- Provide continuous flashing around corners. Premanufactured pieces are available for this purpose.
- To account for tolerances in foundation construction, the brick may be detailed to overhang the foundation by $\frac{1}{4}$ in. to $\frac{1}{2}$ in. (6 mm to 13 mm).

Coordination Required

- The width of the foundation should be at least as wide as the total wall assembly.
- Provide wood studs 16 in. (400 mm) on center.
- Provide a vapor barrier on the warm side of the insulation, if required.
- Detail the total wall height and the height of openings to coordinate with the modular brick dimension.
- Plan grading to allow for clearance between the ground and weep holes.

Likely Failure Points

- Insufficient weep holes or blocked weep holes preventing the escape of moisture inside the wall
- Corrosion of ties due to blockage of the air space by mortar droppings
- Cracking of brick due to foundation settlement or lack of expansion joints in long, uninterrupted walls

Materials

04 05 19.16 MASONRY TIES

Materials

Corrugated metal ties, minimum 22 gage (0.0312 in. [0.79 mm]), $\frac{7}{8}$ in. (22 mm) wide, 6 in. (152 mm) long.

Hot-dip galvanized, ASTM A153, Class B-3.

Execution

Embed a minimum of 2 in. (50 mm) in the brick wythe.

Secure to studs through sheathing with corrosion-resistant nails penetrating a minimum of $1\frac{1}{2}$ in. (38 mm).

Provide one tie for each 1.77 ft^2 (0.16 m^2) of wall area.

Maximum vertical and horizontal spacing of 16 in. (400 mm)

Install additional ties approximately 8 in. (200 mm) on center at jambs and near edges.

04 20 01 MORTAR

Materials

Portland cement-lime, ASTM C270.

Type N normally used.

Type M recommended where brick is in contact with earth.

Type S recommended where a high degree of flexural resistance is required.

Admixtures and additives for workability are not recommended.

Execution

Fill all mortar joints completely.

Keep all air spaces and expansion joints clear of mortar.

Tool joint with vee or concave profile.

04 21 13 BRICK MASONRY

Materials

Grade SW or MW as required by the geographical location. Grade SW is recommended for use in freezing climates.

Hollow facing brick: ASTM C652.

Solid facing brick: ASTM C216.

Building brick: ASTM C62.

Do not use salvaged brick.

Execution

Brick with more than a 30 g/min • 30 in.^{2} (30 g/min • 194 cm^2) initial rate of absorption must be wetted prior to laying.

06 11 09 WOOD STUD

Minimum 2 in. × 4 in. (51 mm × 102 mm) nominal size.

Maximum spacing of 16 in. (400 mm) on center.

06 16 13 INSULATING SHEATHING

Minimum $\frac{1}{2}$ in. (13 mm) thickness. Thicker insulation may be used as required by the climate.

Standard plywood or particleboard sheathing may be substituted with building paper over.

If insulating sheathing is used, provide plywood at corners or use other suitable lateral bracing.

If insulating or asphalt-impregnated sheathing is used, an air infiltration barrier may be applied over the sheathing.

07 27 00 AIR BARRIER

Nonwoven, spun-bonded olefin sheet membrane, liquid-applied membrane, or self-adhering membrane, ASTM E1677.

Vapor-permeable or vapor-impermeable as required by local climatic conditions.

Lap over flashing and seal as recommended by the manufacturer.

Install according to the manufacturer's instructions.

Refer to Section 5-5 for more information.

07 62 00 FLASHING

Materials

Flashing may be rigid copper or stainless steel, semiflexible composites of copper and other materials, or flexible membranes, such as peel-and-stick products.

Copper, ASTM B370, cold rolled hard tempered, 10–20 oz (0.0135 in. [0.343 mm] to 0.0270 in. [0.686 mm]).

Stainless steel, ASTM A167, type 304 with 2D or 2B finish, 0.0187 in. (0.475 mm).

Copper composites, 5 oz (0.0068 in. [0.1715 mm]), laminated between fiberglass fabric or asphaltic material. Other proprietary products are also available.

Flexible membranes, 40 mil (1 mm) self-adhering rubberized asphalt, 40 mil EPDM, or 40 mil composite of rubberized asphalt and cross-laminated polyethylene.

Must not be subject to ultraviolet degradation.

Must not be subject to deterioration in contact with alkaline masonry mortars or sealants.

Do not use asphalt-impregnated felt, aluminum, or lead flashing.

Execution

Extend flashing beyond the exterior of the brick at least $\frac{1}{4}$ in. (6 mm) and turn it down at a 45 degree angle to form a drip.

Lap flashing a minimum of 6 in. (152 mm) and seal it with mastic.

Provide flashing above doors and above and below windows and other openings.

Make dams at the ends of flashing over and under openings by turning up several inches into the head joint of the brick.

If veneer continues below flashing at the base of the wall, the cavity between the veneer and the backup wall should be grouted to the height of the flashing.

07 92 13 ELASTOMERIC JOINT SEALANT

Materials

One-part polysulfide, polyurethane, or silicone, ASTM C920, Type S, Grade NS, Class 25 or 50.

2-9   BRICK VENEER, STEEL STUD BACKING WALL

Description

A brick veneer wall, as shown in Fig. 2-9, is an exterior wall consisting of an outer wythe of brick separated from a backup wall by an air space and connected to it with metal ties, but not so bonded as to intentionally exert common action under load.

This detail is used in commercial multistory construction where spans are greater than 8 ft (2440 mm) and the use of residential brick veneer over wood studs does not apply. In most cases, the structural frame of the building is a steel or concrete system and the metal stud backup is a non-load-bearing wall. The backup wall must be designed to resist wind and seismic loads transferred from the brick.

There has been considerable controversy concerning the advisability of using brick veneer on steel studs. Reported failures have included corrosion of screws used to attach the masonry ties to the studs, degradation of sheathing caused by moisture, and cracking of brick caused

Figure 2-9 Brick veneer, steel stud panel walls   04 21 13.2

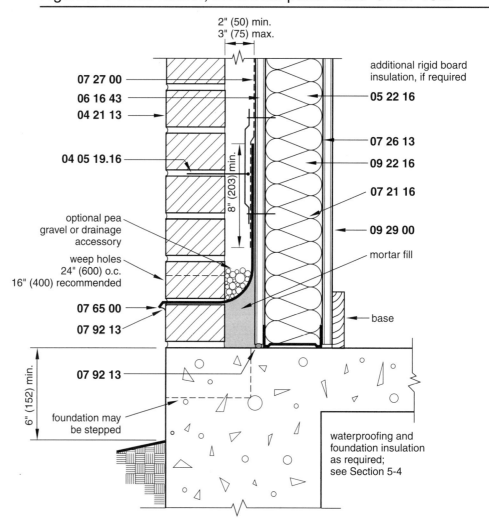

by inadequate stiffness of the stud wall. Most of these problems can be alleviated with proper detailing, installation, and supervision of construction.

Limitations of Use

- This detail does not include provisions for seismic design.
- The structural frame should be steel or reinforced concrete.
- The brick must not be subject to an axial load other than its own weight.
- Allowable flexural tensile stresses commonly used in structural design standards for masonry should not be used.
- Under lateral load, the deflection of both the veneer and the backup must be equal.

Detailing Considerations

- Movement of the structural frame must be considered and provided for, including deflection, thermal movement, and elastic shortening due to imposed loads. Concrete frames should also be analyzed for movement due to creep.
- The steel stud system must be designed to accommodate deflection of the structural frame to avoid bowing and transfer of deflection to the brick veneer.
- Closed-cell rigid insulation may be placed outside of the studs to provide additional insulation and to prevent thermal bridging through the metal studs. See Section 2-10 for optional detailing.
- The air barrier membrane should be continuous onto the foundation.
- The steel stud wall should have a maximum deflection of L/600. Some design tables and recommendations suggest a deflection of L/360, but this may result in wider cracks in the brick under full service load.
- Steel studs should be located a minimum of 6 in. (152 mm) above grade.
- Sheathing must be applied to both sides of the stud wall.
- In addition to an open head joint for weep holes, various types of manufactured items are available to provide drainage of water that accumulates in the cavity. If wick or tube weeps are used, they should be spaced a maximum of 16 in. (406 mm) on center. Wicks should be at least 16 in. (406 mm) long and extend through the brick and onto the back of the brick. To keep mortar out of the cavity, a premanufactured mesh or other mortar-management accessory may be used at the base of the wall.
- Additional vents may be placed along the top of the air cavity to help vent moisture and create a pressure-equalized air space.
- The entire structure must be analyzed to determine potential movement and optimum location of movement joints.
- Vertical and horizontal joints for individual brick panels must accommodate moisture and thermal movement of the brick. Vertical joints must be of compressible material to allow movement without concentrated stresses. See Section 2-2 for the design of vertical control joints.
- Horizontal joint reinforcing is not required in most cases, but will improve the continuity, tensile capacity, and toughness at corners, offsets, and intersecting walls.
- Flashing should be lapped at the ends and corners and sealed with mastic.
- Continue flashing across vertical expansion joints. At building expansion joints, the flashing should be turned up to form an end dam.

- Pea gravel may be placed above the flashing to prevent mortar droppings from blocking the weep holes. Various types of propriety mortar-management accessories are also available.
- In extreme climates, a condensation analysis should be done to determine the need for a vapor barrier.
- Windows should be attached either to the brick veneer or the backup wall, but not both.
- Parapet walls should be avoided unless absolutely required. If used, parapet walls should consist of brick, not steel studs. All vertical expansion joints should be carried through parapet walls.

Coordination Required

- Structural design of the building frame to minimize deflection and movement.
- Provide a vapor barrier on the warm side of the insulation, if required.
- Provide attachment of doors and windows to the backup wall separate from the veneer.

Likely Failure Points

- Insufficient control joints and expansion joints
- Top of the wall not allowed to move laterally with the control joint under the shelf angle
- Brick cracking due to insufficient stiffness of the steel stud backup wall
- Blocking of the air space caused by mortar droppings in air spaces less than 2 in. (51 mm) wide
- Corrosion of metal ties due to use of improper types or water migration across mortar droppings in the air space
- Lack of, or improper installation of, flashing and weep holes

Materials

04 05 19.16 MASONRY ANCHORS

Materials

Two-piece, vertically adjustable.

Hot-dip galvanized, ASTM C153, Class B-3.

Minimum W1.7 (9 gage, MW11).

No mechanical play in excess of 0.05 in. (1.27 mm).

No deformation over 0.05 in. (1.27 mm) for 100 lb (445 N) load in either tension or compression.

Flat, corrugated ties must not be used.

To avoid possible corrosion of screws attaching the ties to the steel studs, screwless anchors may be used.

Execution

Embed a minimum of 2 in. (51 mm) into brick wythe.

Secure to studs through sheathing.

One tie for each 2 ft^2 (0.2 m^2) of wall area.

Maximum vertical spacing of 18 in. (457 mm).

Maximum horizontal spacing of 32 in. (813 mm).

Install additional ties approximately 8 in. (203 mm) on center at jambs and near edges.

If screwless anchors are used, seal penetrations in the sheathing.

04 20 01 MORTAR

Materials

Portland cement-lime, ASTM C270.

Type N recommended for expected wind loads less than 25 psf (1200 Pa).

Type S recommended for expected wind loads over 25 psf (1200 Pa).

Admixtures and additives for workability not recommended.

Execution

Fill all mortar joints completely.

Keep all air spaces and expansion joints clear of mortar.

Tool joint with vee or concave profile.

04 21 13 BRICK MASONRY

Materials

Grade SW.

Hollow brick: ASTM C652.

Facing brick: ASTM C216.

Limit brick height to 4 in. (100 mm).

Execution

Brick with more than 30 g/min • 30 in.^{2} (30 g/min • 194 cm^2) initial rate of absorption must be wetted and permitted to dry prior to laying.

06 16 43 GYPSUM SHEATHING

Materials

Fiberglass mat–faced gypsum board (ASTM C1177) or gypsum fiber panels (ASTM C1278).

A $\frac{1}{2}$ in. (13 mm) minimum fiberglass mat–faced gypsum board is recommended.

Execution

ASTM C1280.

Seal joints with self-adhering tape as approved by the sheathing manufacturer.

07 27 00 AIR BARRIER

Nonwoven, spun-bonded olefin sheet membrane, liquid-applied membrane, or self-adhering membrane, ASTM E1677.

Vapor-permeable or vapor-impermeable as required by local climatic conditions.

Install according to the manufacturer's instructions.

Refer to Section 5-5 for more information.

07 26 13 VAPOR RETARDER

ASTM C1136.

4 mil (0.1 mm) polyethylene film, 0.1 maximum perm rating.

07 21 16 BLANKET INSULATION

Full batt insulation or as required by the project.

07 65 00 FLASHING

Materials

Flashing may be rigid copper or stainless steel, semiflexible composites of copper and other materials, or flexible membranes, such as peel-and-stick products.

Copper, ASTM B370, cold rolled hard tempered, 10–20 oz (0.0135 in. [0.343 mm] to 0.0270 in. [0.686 mm]).

Stainless steel, ASTM A167, type 304 with 2D or 2B finish, 0.0187 in. (0.475 mm).

Copper composites, 5 oz (0.0068 in. [0.1715 mm]), laminated between fiberglass fabric or asphaltic material. Other proprietary products are also available.

Flexible membranes, 40 mil (1 mm) self-adhering rubberized asphalt, 40 mil EPDM, or 40 mil composite of rubberized asphalt and cross-laminated polyethylene.

Must not be subject to ultraviolet degradation.

Must not be subject to deterioration in contact with alkaline masonry mortars or sealants.

Do not use asphalt-impregnated felt, aluminum, or lead flashing.

Execution

Extend flashing beyond the exterior of the brick at least $\frac{1}{4}$ in. (6 mm) and turn it down at a 45 degree angle to form a drip.

Extend flashing at least 8 in. (203 mm) vertically up the backing.

Lap flashing a minimum of 6 in. (152 mm) and seal with mastic.

Install flashing a minimum of 6 in. (122 mm) above grade.

Use edge dams at openings.

09 22 16 NONSTRUCTURAL METAL FRAMING

Materials

Minimum 18 gage (0.043 in. [1.09 mm]), zinc-coated, ASTM A653/A 653M, Grade G90/Z275.

Sized for maximum deflection, under full wind load, of L/600.

Execution

Horizontal bracing at midheight recommended.

Studs at openings designed to transfer loads of the tributary area within deflection criteria.

No field welding.

Make dams at the ends of flashing over and under openings by turning up several inches into the head joint of the brick.

Provide slip joints at the tops of studs to prevent vertical load transfer from the structure.

07 92 13 ELASTOMERIC JOINT SEALANT

Materials

One-part polysulfide, polyurethane, or silicone, ASTM C920, Type S, Grade NS, Class 25 or 50.

Oil-based calking should not be used.

09 29 00 GYPSUM WALLBOARD

ASTM C1396.

Some type of sheathing must be attached to both sides of studs.

Other types of interior sheathing may be used to satisfy the finish requirements of the job.

2-10 BRICK VENEER, STEEL STUD BACKUP WALL AT OPENING

Description

Figure 2-10 illustrates a typical window head section in a brick veneer wall designed as a punched opening, that is, one with brick on either side using a loose lintel to support the brick above. This configuration presumes that the brick will be supported at each floor line with shelf angles, as shown in Fig. 2-11. Figure 2-10 is slightly different from Figs. 2-9 and 2-11 in that a continuous layer of insulation is applied over the sheathing. This is the preferred detail because it adds insulation to the wall assembly, eliminates thermal breaks, and protects the air/vapor barrier applied to the outside of the sheathing.

Limitations of Use

- This detail does not include provisions for seismic design. Additional joint reinforcing is required in certain seismic zones.
- This design is for isolated openings with brick surrounding all four sides. Walls with continuous ribbon window openings must be detailed differently.
- The brick must not be subject to an axial load other than its own weight.
- Under lateral load, the deflection of both the veneer and the backup must be equal.

Detailing Considerations

- Provide a vapor barrier on the inside of the stud wall if required by the climate or the building use.
- Pea gravel may be placed above the flashing to prevent mortar droppings from blocking the weep holes. Various types of proprietary mortar-management accessories are also available.

Figure 2-10 Brick veneer, steel stud backup at opening 04 21 13.3

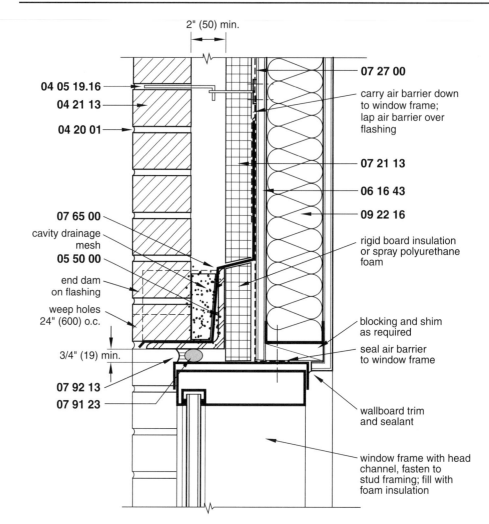

2" (50) min.

04 05 19.16
04 21 13
04 20 01

07 65 00
cavity drainage mesh
05 50 00
end dam on flashing
weep holes 24" (600) o.c.

3/4" (19) min.

07 92 13
07 91 23

07 27 00
carry air barrier down to window frame; lap air barrier over flashing

07 21 13
06 16 43
09 22 16

rigid board insulation or spray polyurethane foam

blocking and shim as required
seal air barrier to window frame

wallboard trim and sealant

window frame with head channel, fasten to stud framing; fill with foam insulation

- Either spray polyurethane foam or a rigid insulation board may be used below the flashing.
- The exact horizontal position of the steel lintel will vary slightly from that shown in Fig. 2-10, depending on the size of the angle used, the type of cavity drainage product used, and how far back from the face of the brick the flashing drip is placed. Lintels must support a minimum of two-thirds of the brick wythe thickness.

Coordination Required

- The air barrier should be continuous across the joint between the sheathing and the window. Follow the manufacturer's recommendations for sealing joints.
- Window framing with a thermal break should be specified to minimize heat transfer.
- The air barrier or another water-resistant barrier applied over the sheathing should be lapped a minimum of 6 in. (152 mm).
- Screws used to fasten anchors to studs should be corrosion-resistant, with polymer or zinc coatings, or should be the stainless steel, minimum No. 10 self-tapping type. If

stainless steel screws are used with carbon steel anchors, neoprene or EPDM washers should be used to prevent galvanic corrosion.

Likely Failure Points

See Sections 2-9 and 2.11 for common failure points.

Materials

04 05 19.16 MASONRY ANCHORS

Materials

Two-piece, vertically adjustable.

Hot-dip galvanized, ASTM C153, Class B-3.

Minimum W1.7 (9 gage, MW11).

No mechanical play in excess of 0.05 in. (1.27 mm).

No deformation over 0.05 in. (1.27 mm) for a 100 lb (445 N) load in either tension or compression.

Flat, corrugated ties must not be used.

To avoid possible corrosion of screws attaching the ties to the steel studs, screwless anchors may be used.

Execution

Embed a minimum of 2 in. (51 mm) in the brick wythe.

Secure to studs through sheathing.

One tie for each 2 ft^2 (0.2 m^2) of wall area. Minimum one tie for each 2⅔ ft^2 (0.25 m^2) if allowed by code.

Maximum vertical spacing of 18 in. (457 mm).

Maximum horizontal spacing of 32 in. (813 mm).

Install additional ties approximately 8 in. (203 mm) on center at jambs and near edges.

If screwless anchors are used, seal penetrations in the sheathing.

04 20 01 MORTAR

See Section 2-9 for material requirements.

04 21 13 BRICK MASONRY

See Section 2-9 for material requirements.

05 50 00 STEEL SHELF ANGLE

Materials

ASTM A36; galvanized steel recommended.

Maximum deflection l/600, but not to exceed 0.3 in. (7.6 mm).

A 5 in. × 5 in. × ⅜ in. (127 mm × 127 mm × 10 mm) angle is commonly used, but should have a minimum bearing of two-thirds the thickness of the brick wythe.

06 16 43 SHEATHING

Materials

Fiberglass mat–faced gypsum board (ASTM C1177) or gypsum fiber panels (ASTM C1278).

A $\frac{1}{2}$ in. (13 mm) minimum fiberglass mat–faced gypsum board is recommended.

Execution

ASTM C1280.

Seal joints with self-adhering tape as approved by the sheathing manufacturer.

07 21 13 BUILDING BOARD INSULATION

Materials

Extruded polystyrene, ASTM C578.

Polyisocyanurate foam board, ASTM C591 and ASTM C1289.

Thickness as required for the total R-value needed. Generally, $1\frac{1}{2}$ in. (38 mm) is used in colder climates.

Execution

Install in accordance with the manufacturer's instructions.

At least 30 percent of the area of the board must be adhered using the manufacturer's recommended adhesive.

Some building codes may require full adhesion if insulation is applied over paper-faced gypsum sheathing.

Boards must be tightly butted with cracks over $\frac{1}{16}$ in. (1.6 mm) filled with slivers of insulation.

07 27 00 AIR BARRIER

Nonwoven, spun-bonded olefin sheet membrane, liquid-applied membrane, or self-adhering membrane, ASTM E1677.

Vapor-permeable or vapor-impermeable as required by local climatic conditions.

Install according to the manufacturer's instructions.

Glass-mat gypsum sheathing with joints and screws taped may be used in lieu of an air barrier. Additional sealing may be required between the sheathing and other openings.

Refer to Section 5-5 for more information.

07 65 00 FLASHING

Materials

Flashing may be rigid copper or stainless steel, semiflexible composites of copper and other materials, or flexible membranes, such as peel-and-stick products.

Copper, ASTM B370, cold rolled hard tempered, 10–20 oz (0.0135 in. [0.343 mm] to 0.0270 in. [0.686 mm]).

Stainless steel, ASTM A167, type 304 with 2D or 2B finish, 0.0187 in. (0.475 mm).

Copper composites, 5 oz (0.0068 in. [0.1715 mm]), laminated between fiberglass fabric or asphaltic material. Other proprietary products are also available.

Flexible membranes, 40 mil (1 mm) self-adhering rubberized asphalt, 40 mil EPDM, or 40 mil composite of rubberized asphalt and cross-laminated polyethylene.

Must not be subject to ultraviolet degradation.

Must not be subject to deterioration in contact with alkaline masonry mortars or sealants.

Do not use asphalt-impregnated felt, aluminum, or lead flashing.

Execution

Extend flashing beyond angle at least $1/4$ in. (6 mm) and turn down at a 45 degree angle to form a drip.

Lap flashing a minimum of 6 in. (152 mm) and seal with mastic.

Use edge dams at openings.

07 91 23 BACKER RODS

Closed cell polyethylene foam, with the diameter at least 25 percent greater than the joint width.

07 92 13 ELASTOMERIC JOINT SEALANT

Materials

One-part polysulfide, polyurethane, or silicone, ASTM C920, Type S, Grade NS, Class 25 or 50.

Execution

Sealant depth equal to the width of the joint up to $1/2$ in. (13 mm), with a minimum depth of $1/4$ in. (6 mm).

Sealant depth $1/2$ in. (13 mm) for joint widths from $1/2$ in. to 1 in. (13 mm to 25 mm).

For sealants with a ±25 percent movement capability, the joint width should be four times the expected movement of the joint.

Proper priming and backer rods required.

09 22 16 NONSTRUCTURAL METAL FRAMING

Materials

Minimum 18 gage (0.043 in. [1.09 mm]), zinc-coated, ASTM A653/A 653M, Grade G90/Z275.

Sized for maximum deflection, under full wind load, of L/600.

See Section 2-9 for other requirements.

2-11   BRICK ON SHELF ANGLE

Description

A shelf angle is a structural steel member used to transfer the dead load of a brick wythe to the building frame. It is also used to provide a horizontal expansion joint, which allows the brick to expand vertically and accommodates frame shortening.

Figure 2-11 Brick on shelf angle 04 21 13.4

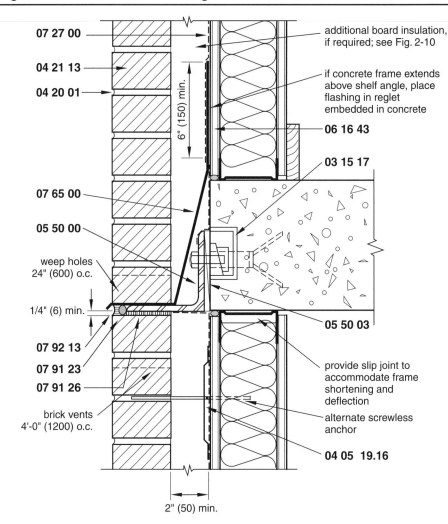

07 27 00

04 21 13

04 20 01

6" (150) min.

07 65 00

05 50 00

weep holes
24" (600) o.c.

1/4" (6) min.

07 92 13

07 91 23

07 91 26

brick vents
4'-0" (1200) o.c.

2" (50) min.

additional board insulation,
if required; see Fig. 2-10

if concrete frame extends
above shelf angle, place
flashing in reglet
embedded in concrete

06 16 43

03 15 17

05 50 03

provide slip joint to
accommodate frame
shortening and
deflection

alternate screwless
anchor

04 05 19.16

Shelf angles are usually not required on buildings of three stories or less (30 ft [9.14 m]) if the masonry can bear directly on the foundation and it is properly anchored to the backup wall.

The number of horizontal shelf angles should be kept to a minimum, but usually they are installed at every floor or at every other floor. Spacing wider than every floor requires structural analysis and an increase in the expansion joint width to accommodate increased movement. Figure 2-11 shows the shelf angle attached to a concrete structural frame with an insert. The angle can also be bolted or welded to a steel frame, as shown in Fig. 2-12.

Limitations of Use

- The size and thickness of the shelf angle and the spacing of the connections to the structural frame must be sized to limit deflection to L/600 but not to exceed 0.3 in. (7.6 mm).
- Provisions for seismic design are not shown in this detail.
- Angle size must be sufficient to fully support the brick while allowing for shimming and maintaining the cavity width.

- Figure 2-11 does not show a layer of rigid insulation on the outside of the sheathing, as is commonly used in some climates. See Fig. 2-10.

Detailing Considerations

- Shimming is usually required to compensate for the difference in tolerances between the structural frame and the veneer construction. Shims should extend the full height of the vertical leg of the shelf angle to avoid rotation of the angle under load. Total shimming thickness should not exceed 1 in. (25 mm).
- Holes for the shelf angle connections should be slotted either horizontally or vertically to allow for adjustment. The direction of slotting depends on the type of adjustment available with the concrete insert. If the insert provides for vertical adjustment, the shelf angle holes should be slotted horizontally.
- The width of the expansion joint should be sized to accommodate the expected movement of the frame and the brick, as described in the following section. A minimum of $\frac{1}{4}$ in. (6 mm) below the shelf angle is recommended. A lipped brick profile may be used to minimize the difference between normal bed joints and horizontal expansion joints. However, using a lipped brick makes it difficult to form and place rigid flashing. If flexible flashing is used, a sheet metal drip edge should be used.
- Continue flashing across vertical expansion joints. At building expansion joints, the flashing should be turned up to form an end dam.
- If the exposed edge of the flashing is objectionable, the brick (or several courses of bricks) may be projected slightly to form a belt course. If this is done, install a mortar wash above the projected brick.
- Pea gravel may be placed above the flashing to prevent mortar droppings from blocking the weep holes. Various types of proprietary mortar-management accessories are also available.
- A minimum $\frac{1}{16}$ in. (2 mm) gap should be provided between adjacent shelf angles to allow for their expansion due to temperature changes. A space of $\frac{1}{4}$ in. in 20 ft (6 mm in 6 m) between shelf angles is generally enough to provide for thermal expansion.
- Shelf angles do not need to be interrupted at vertical expansion joints.
- Flashing should be lapped at the ends and at corners and sealed with mastic.

Sizing Horizontal Expansion Joints in Brick Masonry

Brick masonry will move based on thermal expansion and contraction, irreversible moisture expansion, and creep. The following formula can be used to calculate these effects:

$$w = [k_e + k_c + k_t(\Delta T)]L \qquad \text{(eq. 2-3)}$$

where

w = the total expected movement of the brick area in in. (mm).
k_e = coefficient of moisture expansion of brick in in./in. (mm/mm).
k_c = creep in in./in. per psi (mm/mm per MPa).
k_t = coefficient of thermal expansion of brick in in./in./°F (mm/mm/°C).
ΔT = the temperature range to which the brickwork is subjected. Of course, this depends on the climate, wall orientation, brick color, and brick type. In many

cases, the surface temperature of the brick may be significantly higher than the ambient air temperature. A value of 100°F (38°C) is often used, but a value of 140°F (60°C) is conservative in climates with wide variations in winter and summer temperatures.

L = length of the wall under consideration in in. (mm).

The coefficient of moisture expansion is 5×10^{-4} in./in. (3×10^{-4} mm/mm).

The creep value is 7×10^{-8} in./in. per psi (1×10^{-5} mm/mm per MPa). However, for brick, this value is negligible and is generally not used to calculate horizontal expansion joints.

The coefficient of thermal expansion is 4×10^{-6} in./in./°F (7.2×10^{-6} mm/mm/°C).

Coordination Required

- The structural design of the building frame should minimize deflection and movement.
- Refer to Figs. 2-12 and 3-5 for masonry supports on steel-framed buildings.
- Standard masonry coursing should be used to locate the shelf angle.

Likely Failure Points

- Cracking or spalling of the brick due to rotation of the steel angle because of improper shimming or use of washers for shims instead of full-height shims
- Cracking of the brick due to an expansion joint that is too narrow
- Leaking of the wall due to missing flashing or improper installation of the flashing, such as holding the edge of the flashing behind the face of the brick

Materials

03 15 17 CONCRETE INSERT

Should provide for vertical or horizontal adjustment.

Tack the weld bolt to the shelf angle when adjustment is complete.

The insert must be oriented correctly and be perfectly level.

A wedge-type insert may not be appropriate for seismic loading.

Place compressible material over the bolt head to prevent the anchor bolt from puncturing the flashing.

04 05 19.16 MASONRY ANCHORS

See Section 2-10 for anchor requirements.

04 20 01 MORTAR

Materials

Portland cement-lime, ASTM C270.

Type N for expected wind loads less than 25 psf (1200 Pa).

Type S for expected wind loads over 25 psf (1200 Pa).

Admixtures and additives for workability not recommended.

Execution

Fill all mortar joints completely.

Keep all air spaces and expansion joints clear of mortar.

Tool joint with vee or concave profile.

04 21 13 BRICK MASONRY

Materials

Grade SW or MW as required by the geographical location.

Hollow facing brick: ASTM C652.

Solid facing brick: ASTM C216.

Building brick: ASTM C62.

Execution

Brick with more than a 30 g/min • 30 in.^{2} (30 g/min • 194 cm^2) initial rate of absorption must be wetted and permitted to dry prior to laying.

05 50 00 STEEL SHELF ANGLE

Materials

ASTM A36; galvanized steel recommended.

Maximum deflection L/600, but not to exceed 0.3 in. (7.6 mm).

A 5 in. × 5 in. × $^3/_8$ in. (127 mm × 127 mm × 10 mm) angle is commonly used.

Execution

Use at every story or every other story to support brick.

Provide vertically or horizontally slotted holes as required for adjustment, depending on the type of adjustment provided by the concrete insert.

Locate the bolt hole near the top of the angle.

Use a series of short lengths to allow for alignment and provide a minimum $^1/_{16}$ in. (2 mm) gap between ends of angles or $^1/_4$ in. in 20 ft (6 mm in 6 m).

05 50 03 STEEL SHIMS

Galvanized steel full length of angle.

Spot weld together after adjustment.

Maximum shim depth of 1 in. (25 mm).

06 16 43 SHEATHING

See Section 2-10 for sheathing requirements.

07 21 13 BUILDING BOARD INSULATION

Materials

Extruded polystyrene, ASTM C578.

Polyisocyanurate foam board, ASTM C591 and ASTM C1289.

Thickness as required for the total R-value needed. Generally, $1\frac{1}{2}$ in. (38 mm) is used in colder climates.

Execution

Install in accordance with manufacturers' instructions.

At least 30 percent of the area of the board must be adhered using the manufacturer's recommended adhesive.

Some building codes may require full adhesion if insulation is applied over paper-faced gypsum sheathing.

Boards must be tightly butted with cracks over $\frac{1}{16}$ in. (1.6 mm) filled with slivers of insulation.

07 27 00 AIR BARRIER

Nonwoven, spun-bonded olefin sheet membrane, liquid-applied membrane, or self-adhering membrane, ASTM E1677.

Vapor-permeable or vapor-impermeable as required by local climatic conditions.

Install according to the manufacturer's instructions.

Refer to Section 5-5 for more information.

07 65 00 FLASHING

See Section 2-10 for flashing requirements.

09 91 23 BACKER RODS

Closed cell polyethylene foam, with the diameter at least 25 percent greater than the joint width.

07 91 26 COMPRESSIBLE JOINT FILLER

Closed cell material, preformed compressible filler, or copper sheet.

Should compress to 30 percent to 50 percent of the original thickness.

Keep the joint totally free of mortar.

07 92 13 ELASTOMERIC JOINT SEALANT

See Section 2-10 for sealant requirements.

2-12   SHELF ANGLE ON STEEL FRAMING

Description

Figure 2-12 illustrates one method of providing support for brick veneer when a steel frame structural system is used. Shelf angles to support the brick may also be located at the floor line, similar to Fig. 2-11, or just below the steel frame, as shown in Fig. 3-5. The shelf angle may be supported with appropriately sized structural steel studs or with other types of structural steel framing attached to the primary beam with lateral bracing to adequately

Figure 2-12 Shelf angle on steel framing 04 21 13.5

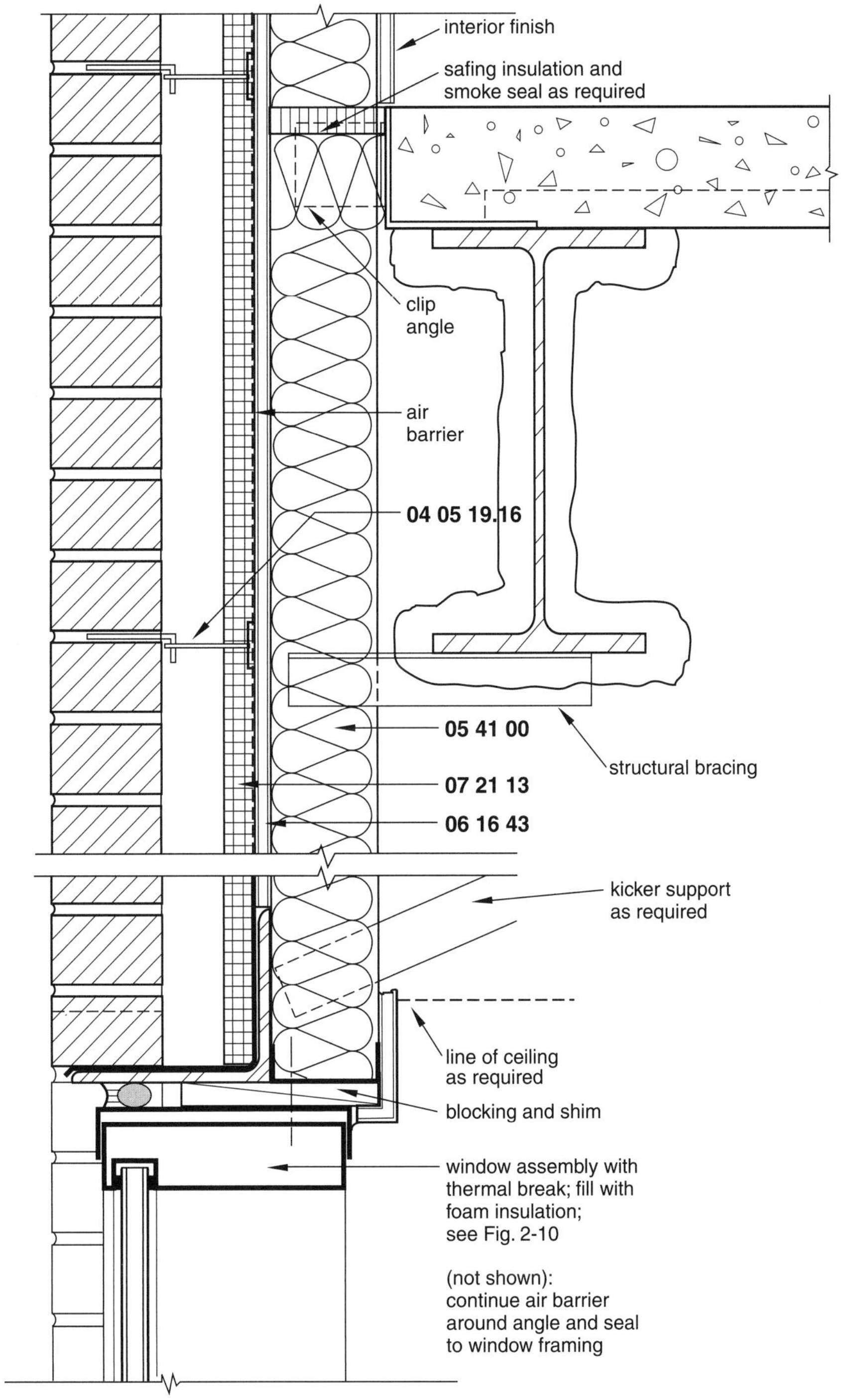

interior finish

safing insulation and
smoke seal as required

clip
angle

air
barrier

04 05 19.16

05 41 00

07 21 13

06 16 43

structural bracing

kicker support
as required

line of ceiling
as required

blocking and shim

window assembly with
thermal break; fill with
foam insulation;
see Fig. 2-10

(not shown):
continue air barrier
around angle and seal
to window framing

support the shelf angle. This detail is appropriate for continuous ribbon windows and allows easy accommodation of frame construction tolerances.

Limitations of Use

Refer to Sections 2-9, 2-10, and 2-11 for limitations of use.

Detailing Considerations

- The position of the edge of the concrete floor may be extended farther toward the exterior to eliminate the need for safing insulation.
- The steel angles and frame must be sized to prevent excessive rotation of the shelf angle.
- A minimum air cavity of 2 in. (51 mm) should be maintained behind the brick.
- The configurations of the weep holes, flashing, and sealant are identical to those of Fig. 2-10.

Coordination Required

- Batt and rigid insulation thickness should be determined by the required R-value of the entire wall assembly.
- If diagonal bracing is used for the lower portion of the steel stud framing, a mechanical system layout must be considered.
- The ceiling type and configuration must be coordinated with any diagonal bracing used.

Likely Failure Points

- Cracking of brick joints due to inadequate sizing of the stud backup wall and bracing.
- See Sections 2-9 and 2-11 for other likely failure points.

Materials

04 05 19.16 MASONRY ANCHORS

See Section 2-10 for anchor requirements.

05 41 00 STRUCTURAL METAL FRAMING

Materials

12 gage (0.097 in. [2.46 mm]), 14 gage (0.068 in. [1.73 mm]), 16 gage (0.054 in. [1.37 mm]), or 18 gage (0.043 in. [1.09 mm]) as required by structural requirements.

Zinc-coated, ASTM A653/A 653M, Grade G90/Z275.

Sized for maximum deflection, under full wind load, of L/600.

Brace as required by masonry panel size and lateral loading.

06 16 43 GYPSUM SHEATHING

Materials

Fiberglass mat–faced gypsum board (ASTM C1177) or gypsum fiber panels (ASTM C1278).

A $\frac{1}{2}$ in. (13 mm) minimum fiberglass mat–faced gypsum board is recommended.

Execution

ASTM C1280.

Seal joints with self-adhering tape as approved by the sheathing manufacturer.

07 21 13 BUILDING BOARD INSULATION

Materials

Extruded polystyrene, ASTM C578.

Polyisocyanurate foam board, ASTM C591 and ASTM C1289.

Thickness as required for the total R-value needed. To minimize the total space required between the back of the masonry and the steel framing and therefore the size of the shelf angle, a $\frac{3}{4}$ in. (19 mm) or 1 in. (25 mm) board is used.

Execution

Install in accordance with manufacturers' instructions.

2-13   INTERIOR MASONRY BEARING PARTITION

Description

Figure 2-13 shows the use of a single-wythe concrete masonry partition to support a floor or roof slab on open web steel joists. Double-wythe composite and reinforced walls may also be used.

This type of bearing partition is easy to construct, is relatively inexpensive, and provides good fire and acoustical control. It may be left unfinished, covered directly with gypsum wallboard, or furred out to provide space for electrical services.

Limitations of Use

- Anchorage and reinforcing are shown diagrammatically only. The exact configuration of reinforcing, partition thickness, and grouting must be designed by a qualified engineer to meet the particular project requirements.
- Provisions for seismic loads must be determined by the engineering design.

Detailing Considerations

- Correct width and reinforcing of the partition to support loads.
- The space required for electrical and other services may affect the type and thickness of the finish applied over the partition.
- Control joints may be required in long walls.

Coordination Required

- Fire resistance requirements of wall and floor/roof assemblies may affect the thickness and type of the floor/roof system used.
- Standard masonry coursing should be used to achieve desired finished floor heights.

Likely Failure Points

- Cracking in long, uninterrupted walls due to concrete masonry shrinkage

Figure 2-13 Interior masonry bearing partition 04 22 01

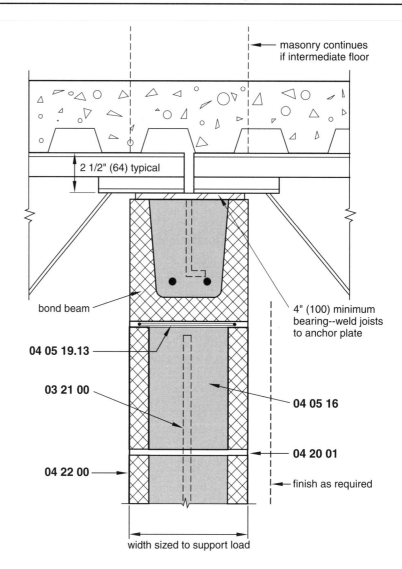

masonry continues
if intermediate floor

2 1/2" (64) typical

bond beam

04 05 19.13

03 21 00

04 22 00

4" (100) minimum
bearing--weld joists
to anchor plate

04 05 16

04 20 01

finish as required

width sized to support load

Materials

03 21 00 REINFORCING STEEL

ASTM A615/A 615M, Grade 40 or 60, as required by the engineering design.

04 05 16 MASONRY GROUTING

Fine or coarse grout, ASTM C476.

Ultimate compressive strength (28 days) of at least 2500 psi (17,240 kPa).

Remove debris and mortar droppings from cores prior to grouting.

04 05 19.13 JOINT REINFORCEMENT

Materials

Fabricated from hard tempered, cold drawn steel wire, ASTM A951.

If reinforcement carries horizontal loads, reinforcement should be the deformed type.

Minimum W1.7 (MW11), but not more than one-half the thickness of the bed joint.

Two-wire, truss type.

Class 3, ASTM A641, for partially embedded joint reinforcement.

Use ties conforming to ASTM A641, Class 3, for completely embedded joint reinforcement (0.80 oz/ft^2 [244 g/m^2] zinc).

Size of horizontal reinforcement determined by structural requirements of the wall.

Execution

Lap joint reinforcement 6 in. (152 mm).

Place 16 in. (400 mm) on center vertically and under the top course of masonry.

Place extra reinforcement in the first two bed joints above and below openings and extend 24 in. (600 mm) beyond the openings.

Center reinforcement with longitudinal wires centered over each face shell.

04 20 01 MORTAR

Materials

Portland cement-lime, ASTM C270.

Type N is the most common for normal loads on interior partitions. Type M may be required for unusually high loads.

Admixtures and additives for workability are not recommended.

Execution

Fill all mortar joints completely.

04 22 00 CONCRETE UNIT MASONRY

ASTM C90, Grade N.

Type 1, moisture-controlled, and Type 2, non-moisture-controlled, are available, but Type 1 is subject to less shrinkage and is best used in arid climates.

2-14 WOOD JOISTS ON INTERIOR MASONRY BEARING PARTITION

Description

Figure 2-14 illustrates a common method of supporting a wood floor system on both sides of an interior masonry bearing partition. Various proprietary types of joist anchors may be used in addition to the one shown. The extent of reinforcing and grouting should be verified by a structural engineer, depending on the loads carried. However, full grouting may be desired for acoustical control even if it is not required for structural reasons.

Detailing Considerations

- In most cases, the wall will need to be furred out for electrical and plumbing services.
- The ceiling may be framed directly on the joists or suspended.

Figure 2-14 Wood joists on interior masonry bearing partition 04 22 02

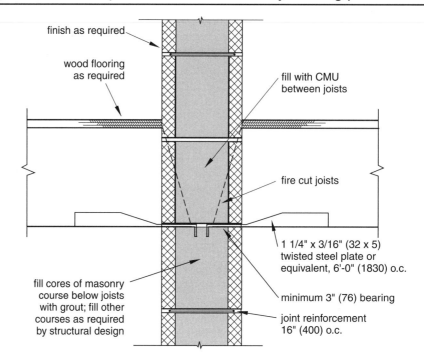

finish as required

wood flooring as required

fill with CMU between joists

fire cut joists

1 1/4" x 3/16" (32 x 5) twisted steel plate or equivalent, 6'-0" (1830) o.c.

minimum 3" (76) bearing

fill cores of masonry course below joists with grout; fill other courses as required by structural design

joint reinforcement 16" (400) o.c.

- The finished floor level should be determined by standard masonry coursing sizes and the required depth of the floor structure.

Materials

Refer to Section 2-13 for material requirements.

2-15   AUTOCLAVED AERATED CONCRETE MASONRY

Description

Figure 2-15 illustrates a common method of constructing an exterior wall with autoclaved aerated concrete (AAC) masonry to support a wood-framed roof. Many of the detailing requirements are similar to those of AAC panels. Refer to Section 1-12 for other information on AAC.

Standard AAC blocks are 8 in. × 8 in. × 24 in. long (200 mm × 200 mm × 610 mm), but other sizes are available, depending on the manufacturer's standards. Other thicknesses range from 4 in. to 16 in. (100 mm to 400 mm). The blocks can be easily cut with hand or common power tools. ACC masonry units are laid using a polymer-modified, thin-set mortar with $\frac{1}{16}$ in. (1.5 mm) joints. If walls need to be reinforced, cores are cut through the blocks and rebar and grout are placed in the cores.

Limitations of Use

Refer to Section 1-12 for limitations of use.

Figure 2-15 Autoclaved aerated concrete masonry 04 22 26

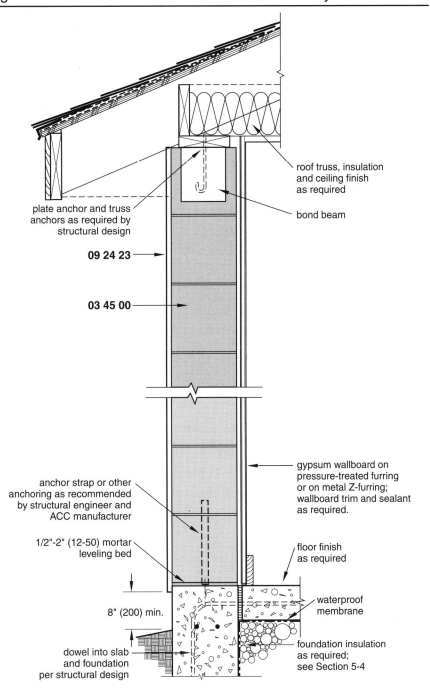

plate anchor and truss
anchors as required by
structural design

09 24 23

03 45 00

anchor strap or other
anchoring as recommended
by structural engineer and
ACC manufacturer

1/2"-2" (12-50) mortar
leveling bed

8" (200) min.

dowel into slab
and foundation
per structural design

roof truss, insulation
and ceiling finish
as required

bond beam

gypsum wallboard on
pressure-treated furring
or on metal Z-furring;
wallboard trim and sealant
as required.

floor finish
as required

waterproof
membrane

foundation insulation
as required;
see Section 5-4

Detailing Considerations

- Many of the detailing requirements for AAC are product specific. Verify individual details with the manufacturer.
- Roofs may be constructed of ACC panels, wood trusses, or other structural material as recommended by the engineer and as required by the design of the building. If ACC panels are used for a flat structural roof, use tapered insulation to provide drainage.

- Details of window and door openings may vary slightly, depending on the type of frame used. Wood frames should include a rough buck attached to the ACC. Aluminum frames may be attached directly. Verify suggested attachment of frames with the ACC manufacturer.

Coordination Required

- The first coat of interior plaster should be a gypsum-based product applied approximately $1/4$ in. (6 mm) thick. A second coat should be applied to smooth and even out the surface.
- Alternately, gypsum wallboard may be applied to pressure-treated furring strips or light-gage metal furring.
- Interior wall tile can be applied using a thin-set mortar or organic adhesive over a portland cement or gypsum-based base coat applied to the ACC.
- Verify all structural requirements with the structural engineer and manufacturer.
- Exterior finish should be vapor-permeable, polymer-modified stucco. Brick and other cladding may also be used.
- Interior wall tile can be applied using a thin-set mortar or organic adhesive over a portland cement or gypsum-based base coat applied to the ACC.

Materials

03 45 00 AUTOCLAVED AERATED CONCRETE MASONRY

ASTM C1452.

Strength class ACC 2.0, ACC 4.0, or ACC 6.0 as required.

Foundation attachment and reinforcing as required by the structural engineer and manufacturer.

09 24 23 STUCCO

Portland cement, polymer-modified stucco.

Apply according to ASTM C926 or as recommended by the ACC manufacturer.

2-16 REINFORCED CONCRETE MASONRY WALL AT GRADE

Description

Figure 2-16 illustrates a single-wythe concrete masonry unit bearing wall with no exterior finish other than a water-repellant coating. However, this wall can be used with adhered or anchored veneer, or with a brick outer wythe, as shown in Fig. 2-4, to form a cavity wall.

Limitations of Use

- This detail should not be used where a finished exterior appearance is important unless decorative block is used.

Figure 2-16 Reinforced concrete masonry wall at grade 04 22 23.1

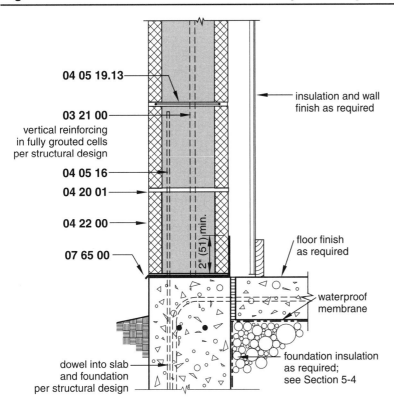

- **04 05 19.13**
- **03 21 00** vertical reinforcing in fully grouted cells per structural design
- **04 05 16**
- **04 20 01**
- **04 22 00**
- **07 65 00**

2" (51) min.

insulation and wall finish as required

floor finish as required

waterproof membrane

dowel into slab and foundation per structural design

foundation insulation as required; see Section 5-4

- Reinforcing should be verified with a structural engineer to meet specific job requirements.
- This construction (and that shown in Figs. 2–17 and 2–18) is considered a barrier wall, which relies on the mass of the wall and the integrity of construction to prevent water entry. If it is critical to maintain a dry interior, a cavity similar to that shown in Fig. 2–4 may be used, with concrete masonry being substituted for brick.

Detailing Considerations

- The wall should be doweled into the foundation according to the structural engineer's recommendations.
- If the wall is not fully grouted, the empty cells can be filled with insulation.
- Provide a vapor barrier on the warm side of the insulation if required by climatic and interior conditions.

Coordination Required

- Expansion joints should be located and detailed as shown in Section 2-1.
- Wall openings should be based on standard coursing measurements.
- Intersecting bearing walls should be provided with an expansion joint and tied together with strap anchors spaced a maximum of 48 in. (1220 mm) vertically.
- Select the type and thickness of insulation based on the required R-value of the wall assembly.

Likely Failure Points

- Water leakage caused by inadequate sealing of the exterior face or microcracking of the mortar joints
- Cracking of the wall if sufficient control joints are not provided

Materials

03 21 00 REINFORCING STEEL

ASTM A615, Grade 60.

Extend vertical bars into the foundation as required by the structural design.

04 05 16 MASONRY GROUTING

Fine or coarse grout, ASTM C476.

Ultimate compressive strength (28 days) of at least 2500 psi (17,237 kPa).

Use fine grout when openings are less than 2 in. (51 mm) in the least dimension.

04 05 19.13 JOINT REINFORCEMENT

Materials

Fabricated from hard tempered, cold drawn steel wire, ASTM A951/A 951M.

If reinforcement carries horizontal loads, reinforcement should be the deformed type.

Two-wire, truss type, minimum W1.7 (MW11), but not more than one-half the thickness of the bed joint.

Hot-dip galvanized, ASTM A153, Class B-3.

Execution

Ends of joint reinforcement should be placed ½ in. to 2 in. (13 mm to 51 mm) from the expansion joint and should not be continuous through control joints.

Lap joint reinforcement 6 in. (152 mm) elsewhere in the wall.

Place 16 in. (400 mm) on center vertically and under the top course of masonry.

Place extra reinforcement in the first two bed joints above and below openings and extend it 24 in. (600 mm) beyond the opening.

Center reinforcement with longitudinal wires centered over each face shell.

Lay reinforcement on bare masonry; then place mortar and slightly wiggle wire to get some mortar under the reinforcement.

04 20 01 MORTAR

Materials

Portland cement-lime, ASTM C270.

Type M, N, or S, depending on loads, masonry used, and climate. Do not use mortar that is stronger in compression than is required by the structural requirements of the job.

Admixtures and additives for workability are not recommended.

Execution

Fill all mortar joints completely.

Keep all expansion joints clear of mortar.

Tool exterior-facing joint with vee or concave profile.

04 22 00 CONCRETE UNIT MASONRY

Materials

ASTM C90, Grade N.

Type 1, moisture-controlled, and Type 2, non-moisture-controlled, are available, but Type 1 is subject to less shrinkage and is best used in arid climates.

07 65 00 FLASHING

Materials

Flashing may be rigid copper or stainless steel, semiflexible composites of copper and other materials, or flexible membranes, such as peel-and-stick products.

Copper, ASTM B370, cold rolled hard tempered, 10–20 oz (0.0135 in. [0.343 mm] to 0.0270 in. [0.686 mm]).

Stainless steel, ASTM A167, type 304 with 2D or 2B finish, 0.0187 in. (0.475 mm).

Copper composites, 5 oz (0.0068 in. [0.1715 mm]), laminated between fiberglass fabric or asphaltic material. Other proprietary products are also available.

Flexible membranes, 40 mil (1 mm) self-adhering rubberized asphalt, 40 mil EPDM, or 40 mil composite of rubberized asphalt and cross-laminated polyethylene.

Must not be subject to ultraviolet degradation.

Must not be subject to deterioration in contact with alkaline masonry mortars or sealants.

Do not use asphalt-impregnated felt, aluminum, or lead flashing.

Execution

Extend flashing beyond exterior of block at least $\frac{1}{4}$ in. (6 mm) and turn down at a 45 degree angle to form a drip.

Lap flashing a minimum of 6 in. (152 mm) and seal with mastic.

Use edge dams at openings.

2-17   REINFORCED CONCRETE MASONRY WALL AT FLOOR

Description

Figure 2-17 is similar to Fig. 2-16, showing the continuation of reinforced concrete masonry at an intermediate floor line. Although an open-web steel joist system with a concrete deck is shown, a similar detail may be used with wood or concrete floor systems. Wood joists may bear on half the masonry if they are firecut and tied to the masonry wall with anchor plates.

Figure 2-17 Reinforced concrete masonry wall at floor 04 22 23.2

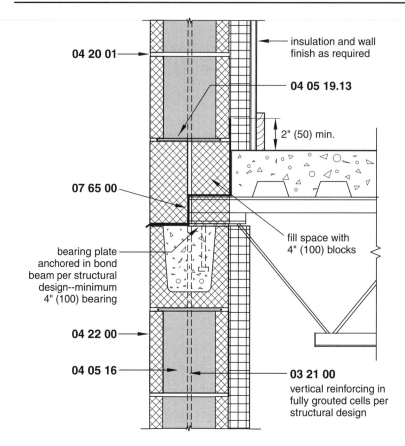

04 20 01

insulation and wall finish as required

04 05 19.13

2" (50) min.

07 65 00

fill space with 4" (100) blocks

bearing plate anchored in bond beam per structural design--minimum 4" (100) bearing

04 22 00

04 05 16

03 21 00
vertical reinforcing in fully grouted cells per structural design

Concrete floors require anchorage to the wall with reinforcing bars of a size and spacing determined by the structural requirements of the job.

Limitations of Use

- Reinforcing should be verified with a structural engineer.

Detailing Considerations

- Steel joists should have a minimum of 4 in. (102 mm) of bearing.
- Bridging perpendicular to the direction of the joists may be anchored to the wall by welding to steel angles bolted to fully grouted cells.
- For shear wall design, the edge of the roof deck parallel to the direction of the joists may be supported with a steel angle bolted to fully grouted cells.

Coordination Required

- Floor lines and window openings should be determined by the masonry coursing.

Materials

See Section 2-16 for material requirements.

Figure 2-18 Reinforced concrete masonry wall at parapet 04 22 23.3

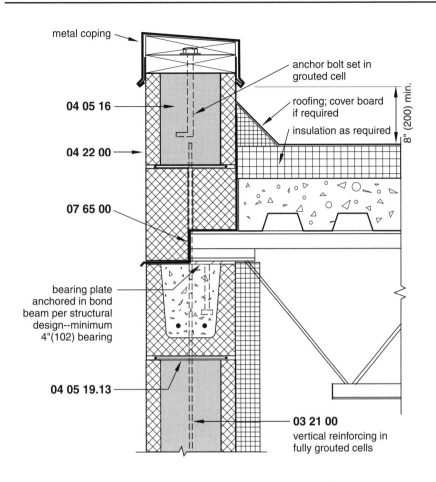

metal coping

04 05 16

04 22 00

07 65 00

bearing plate
anchored in bond
beam per structural
design--minimum
4"(102) bearing

04 05 19.13

anchor bolt set in
grouted cell

roofing; cover board
if required

insulation as required

8" (200) min.

03 21 00
vertical reinforcing in
fully grouted cells

2-18   REINFORCED CONCRETE MASONRY WALL AT PARAPET

Description

Figure 2-18 illustrates a parapet termination of the masonry wall shown in Figs. 2-16 and 2-17. A flat roof is indicated, but a sloped roof may be used as long as proper drainage is provided. With this detail, a slope of at least $\frac{1}{4}$ in./ft (20 mm/m) should be provided. A low parapet is shown, but a high parapet (over 15 in. [381 mm] from the top of the structural deck) may be used.

Limitations of Use

- Reinforcing should be verified with a structural engineer.

Detailing Considerations

- If stone coping is used instead of metal coping, provide through-wall flashing in the joint below the coping.

- Spandrel flashing should extend as far up as the height of the cant strip.
- Slip joints in the metal coping should be provided where masonry control joints occur and at intermediate points as required by the coping material.

Coordination Required

- Roofing should extend under coping or cap flashing a minimum of 4 in. (100 mm).

Materials

See Section 2-16 for material requirements.

2-19   GLASS BLOCK WALL AT SILL AND HEAD

Description

Figure 2-19 shows a standard method of anchoring a glass block wall at the sill and head. Figure 2-20 illustrates typical jamb and intermediate support conditions.

Limitations of Use

- The maximum size for panels and support spacing is given in Table 2-3.
- Verify seismic requirements of the local building code.

Detailing Considerations

- Deflection of floors, beams, and other members supporting glass block must not exceed L/600.
- Structural and other members above glass block panels must not deflect enough to transmit any load to the panel.
- Use special blocks to form 90 degree angles and include panel reinforcing into the corner block.

Coordination Required

- The width and height of openings with allowance for expansion space should be an even multiple of the size of the glass block used.
- Determine the expected deflection of the structure above the wall.

Likely Failure Points

- Cracking of the wall due to insufficient allowance for deflection of the structure or expansion of the glass block

Figure 2-19 Glass block wall at sill and head 04 23 13.1

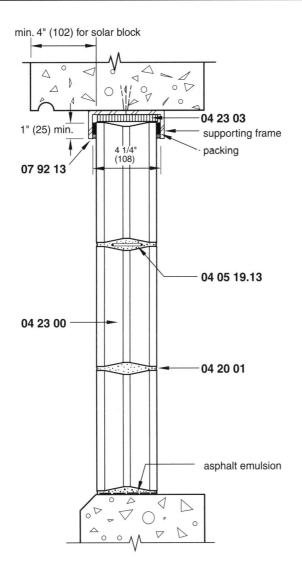

min. 4" (102) for solar block

04 23 03

1" (25) min.

07 92 13

4 1/4"
(108)

supporting frame

packing

04 05 19.13

04 23 00

04 20 01

asphalt emulsion

Table 2-3   Maximum Glass Block Panel Sizes Based on *International Building Code* Limitations

Glass masonry unit type	Interior Walls			Exterior Walls		
	Area, ft² (m²)	Height, ft (mm)	Width, ft (mm)	Area, ft² (m²)	Height, ft (mm)	Width, ft (mm)
Standard units	250 (23.2)	20 (6096)	25 (7620)	144ᵃ (13.4)	20 (6096)	25 (7620)
Thin units	150 (13.9)	20 (6096)	25 (7620)	85ᵇ (7.9)	10 (3048)	15 (4572)
Solid units	100 (9.3)	—	—	100 (9.3)	—	—

ᵃWhen design wind pressure is 20 psf (958 N/m²). Panel areas can be increased or decreased based of different wind pressures according to a graph in the *International Building Code*.
ᵇThin units for exterior applications cannot be used where design wind pressure exceeds 20 psf (958 N/m²).
Source: Based on 2006 *International Building Code* requirements.

Materials

04 05 19.13 JOINT REINFORCEMENT

Materials

Fabricated from hard tempered, cold drawn steel wire, ASTM A951.

Not less than two parallel longitudinal wires.

Minimum W1.7 (MW11), with welded cross wires of size W1.7 (MW11).

Execution

Locate horizontal reinforcement 16 in. (406 mm) on center.

Lap joint reinforcement at least 6 in. (152 mm).

Place reinforcement in the first bed joints above and below openings.

04 20 01 MORTAR

Materials

ASTM C270.

Type N for interior work, Type S for exterior walls.

Type 1 portland cement, ASTM C150. White portland cement may be used.

Lime with a high calcium content or pressure-hydrated dolomitic lime conforming to ASTM C207 for Type S lime.

Sand conforming to ASTM C144 with all grain sizes passing through a No. 12 sieve. Avoid the use of sands containing iron compounds with solar reflective glass block.

Accelerators or antifreeze compounds should not be used.

Execution

Fill all mortar joints completely.

Keep all expansion joints clear of mortar.

Tool joint with vee or concave profile.

04 23 00 GLASS UNIT MASONRY

Standard units must be at least $3\frac{7}{8}$ in. (98 mm) thick.

Thin units must be at least $3\frac{1}{8}$ in. (79 mm) thick for hollow units and 3 in. (76 mm) thick for solid units.

Based on a wedge-shaped head joint $\frac{1}{8}$ in. (3 mm) on the inside and $\frac{5}{8}$ in. (16 mm) on the outside, the dimensions given in Table 2-4 are the minimum radii for curved walls using glass block.

Table 2-4 Minimum Radii of Curved Glass Block Walls	
Block size	Minimum radius inside, in. (mm)
4 in. (100)	32 (813)
6 in. (150)	$48\frac{1}{2}$ (1232)
8 in. (200)	65 (1651)
12 in. (300)	$98\frac{1}{2}$ (2502)

04 23 03 EXPANSION STRIP

Materials

$\frac{3}{8}$ in. (10 mm) minimum resilient filler of polyethylene foam (black or white) or glass fiber.

Expansion joint must be entirely free of mortar.

07 92 13 ELASTOMERIC JOINT SEALANT

Materials

One part polysulfide or polyurethane, ASTM C920, Type S, Grade NS, Class 25 or 50.

Execution

Sealant depth equal to the width of the joint up to $\frac{1}{2}$ in. (13 mm), with a minimum depth of $\frac{1}{4}$ in. (6 mm).

Sealant depth $\frac{1}{2}$ in. (13 mm) for joint widths from $\frac{1}{2}$ in. to 1 in. (13 mm to 25 mm).

For sealants with a ± 25 percent movement capability, the joint width should be four times the expected movement of the joint.

Oil-based caulking should not be used.

Proper priming and backer rods are required.

2-20 GLASS BLOCK WALL AT JAMB AND VERTICAL JOINT

Description

Figure 2-20 shows standard methods of installing and anchoring glass block at the jambs and at intermediate vertical joints. Figure 2-20(a) illustrates the most common methods of jamb details, while Fig. 2-20(b) shows how an intermediate stiffener can be provided inside the block to maintain the width of the vertical mortar joint.

The intermediate stiffeners shown in these details are used to subdivide large expanses of glass block into individual panels whose area, height, and width fall within the required building code limitations shown in Table 2-3. Although a T-shaped stiffener is shown, a variety of structural shapes may be used. The vertical stiffener may be separate from the wall, as shown in Fig. 2-20(b), as long as sufficient anchorage between the stiffener and the glass block is provided.

Limitations of Use

- Verify seismic requirements of the local building code.

Detailing Considerations

- Intermediate vertical stiffeners should be located to provide the maximum allowable unbraced wall area as required by the building code. These areas are summarized in Table 2-3.
- Intermediate vertical stiffeners are also required at every change of direction in a multicurved wall and at every location where a curve joins a straight section.

Figure 2-20 Glass block wall at jamb and vertical joint 04 23 13.2

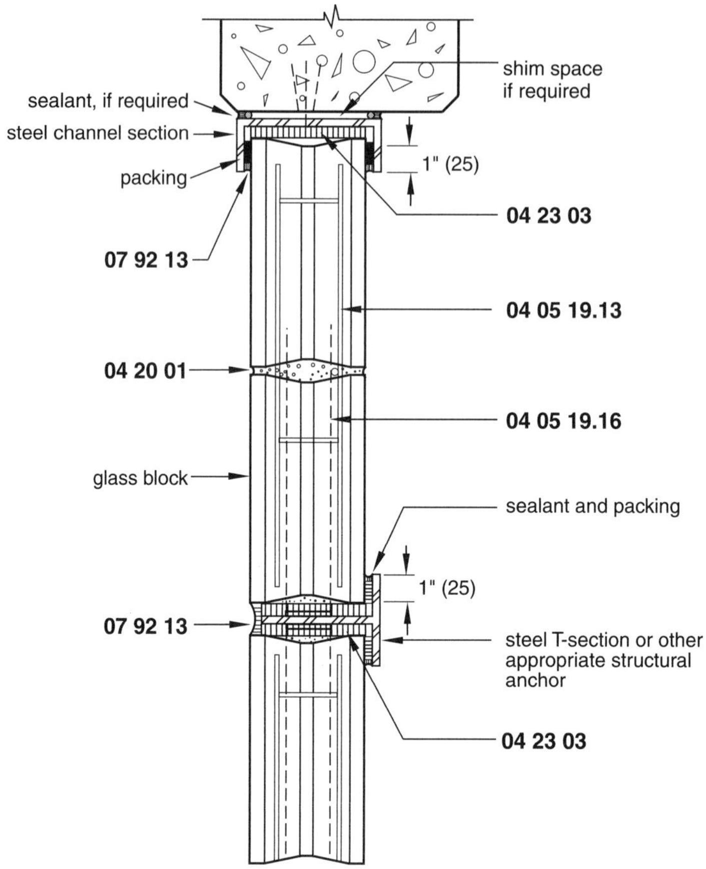

sealant, if required

steel channel section

packing

07 92 13

04 20 01

glass block

07 92 13

shim space
if required

1" (25)

04 23 03

04 05 19.13

04 05 19.16

sealant and packing

1" (25)

steel T-section or other
appropriate structural
anchor

04 23 03

(a) standard jamb details

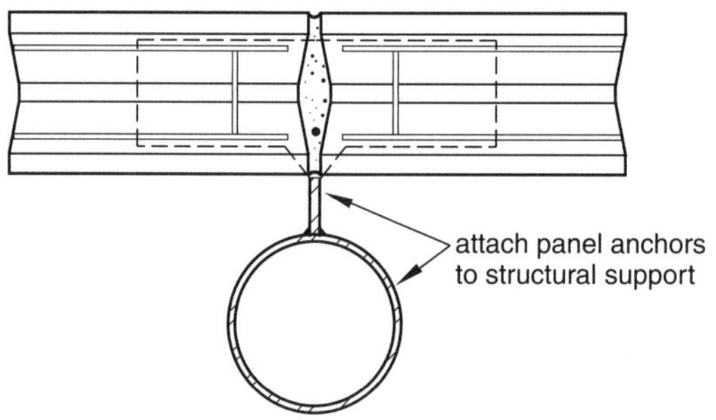

attach panel anchors
to structural support

(b) intermediate stiffener

Coordination Required

- The width and height of opening with allowance for expansion space should be an even multiple of the size of the glass block used.

Likely Failure Points

- Cracking or failure of the wall due to inadequate bracing or vertical support.

Materials

Refer to Section 2-19 for other material requirements.

04 05 19.16 PANEL ANCHOR

Materials

20 gage (0.0375 in. [0.953 mm]) galvanized, perforated steel strips $1\frac{3}{4}$ in. by 24 in. (44 mm by 610 mm).

Execution

Place panel anchors 16 in. (406 mm) on center vertically.

Extend panel anchors 10 in. (254 mm) into the adjacent construction.

2-21   GLASS BLOCK WALL—ALTERNATE DETAILS

Description

Figure 2-21 shows one method of setting glass block flush with the surrounding steel frame and eliminating vertical mullions. This is done by reinforcing both horizontally and vertically with the use of panel anchors rigidly attached to the bottom and top framing members. With proper detailing, this method can accommodate seismic movement.

Limitations of Use

- This type of detail may not be allowed by local building departments.
- Larger reinforcing may require a minimum mortar joint of $\frac{3}{8}$ in. (10 mm).

Detailing Considerations

- The glass block can be supported on angles attached to the building structure so that the wall can continue uninterrupted across floor lines.
- Joints comprised of compressible filler and sealant are located at the jambs and at every eighth vertical course.

Materials

Refer to Section 2-19 for other material requirements.

04 05 19.16 PANEL ANCHOR

Materials

20 gage (0.0375 in. [0.953 mm]) galvanized, perforated steel strips $1\frac{3}{4}$ in. (44 mm) wide.

Execution

Anchors are embedded in mortar joints and rigidly attached to the supporting frame at the top and bottom.

Figure 2-21 Glass block wall--alternate details 04 23 13.4

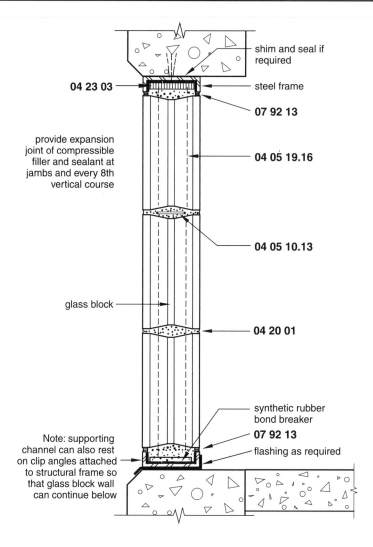

04 23 03

provide expansion
joint of compressible
filler and sealant at
jambs and every 8th
vertical course

glass block

Note: supporting
channel can also rest
on clip angles attached
to structural frame so
that glass block wall
can continue below

shim and seal if
required

steel frame

07 92 13

04 05 19.16

04 05 10.13

04 20 01

synthetic rubber
bond breaker

07 92 13

flashing as required

2-22 ANCHORED STONE VENEER WITH CONCRETE MASONRY UNIT BACKUP AT GRADE

Description

Figure 2-22 illustrates one method of attaching stone to a concrete masonry backup wall. It is used for stone veneer ranging from 2 in. (51 mm) to 10 in. (254 mm) thick and is used when the size and thickness of stone exceed the limitations for adhered veneer. The space between the back of the stone and the backup wall may either be fully grouted or left as a cavity, as shown in Fig. 2-22.

Limitations of Use

- The veneer cannot support any load other than its own weight and the vertical dead load of the veneer above. The backing wall must be designed for lateral forces.

Figure 2-22 Anchored stone veneer with CMU backup at grade 04 42 13.1

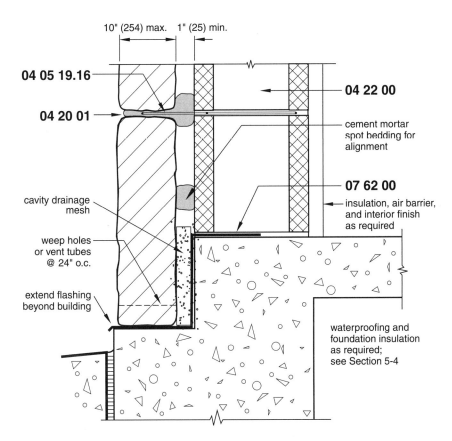

- Anchored veneer for buildings in seismic design categories C, D, E, and F must conform to the relevant requirements of ACI 530/ASCE5/TMS 402.
- Anchored veneer and attachments must be designed to resist a horizontal force equal to twice the weight of the veneer.

Detailing Considerations

- Various alternative anchoring methods between the stone and the backup wall may be used in lieu of the basic *International Building Code* requirements. Verify with local code requirements and manufacturers' specifications.
- Differential movement of the structural frame due to deflection, shrinkage, creep, and temperature changes must be considered.
- The entire structure must be analyzed to determine the potential movement and optimum location of control joints, depending on the type of stone veneer used, the backup wall, and the structural frame. See Table 2-5 for coefficients of thermal expansion for various building materials.
- The base of the stone and the flashing should be placed above grade.

Coordination Required

- Control joints should be located at changes in wall height or thickness; at pilasters, recesses, and chases; at one side of all wall openings; and at wall intersections.

Table 2-5   Average Coefficients of Thermal Expansion of Building Materials

	Rate of expansion	
Material	In. per in. per °F × 10^{-6}	mm/mm per °C × 10^{-6}
Masonry		
Brick	4.0	7.2
Concrete block (dense)	5.2	9.4
Concrete block (expanded shale)	4.3	7.7
Concrete (gravel aggregate)	5.5	9.9
Concrete (lightweight)	4.3	7.7
Plaster (gypsum)	6.6	11.9
Plaster (portland cement)	9.2	16.7
Stone		
Granite	4.4	7.9
Limestone	2.8	5.0
Marble	3.7–7.3	6.7–13.1
Metal		
Aluminum	13.2	23.8
Brass	10.4	18.7
Bronze	10.1	18.1
Cast iron	5.9	10.6
Copper	9.4	16.9
Lead	15.9	28.6
Stainless steel	9.6	17.3
Structural steel	6.7	12.1
Wood, parallel to grain		
Fir	2.1	3.8
Pine	3.0	5.4
Oak	2.7	4.9
Wood, perpendicular to grain		
Fir	32.0	57.6
Pine	19.0	34.2
Oak	30.0	54.0
Glass	5.0	9.0

Note: Multiply in./in./°F by 1.8 to get mm/mm/°C.

- Insulation may be placed in the cells of the block or applied to the inside face.
- Coursing of the stone should match that of the concrete block unless adjustable anchors are used.

Likely Failure Points

- Water leakage if the cavity is not kept clean of excess mortar
- Cracking of the veneer or mortar joints if differential movement between the structure and the stone is not accommodated

Materials

04 05 19.16 MASONRY ANCHOR TIES

Materials

Hot-dip galvanized, ASTM C153, Class B-3.

Minimum 0.1055 in. (2.68 mm) wire (or approved equal) threaded through anchor tie loops in masonry backup wall.

Legs of ties into stone veneer a minimum of 15 in. (381 mm) long, with the last 2 in. (51 mm) of each wire leg bent at a right angle and embedded in stone mortar.

Two-piece, vertically adjustable ties may be used if approved by the local building code.

Execution

One tie in the masonry backup wall for each 2 ft^2 (0.2 m^2) of wall area, maximum.

Maximum horizontal spacing 16 in. (406 mm).

Spot bedding at tie 1 in. (51 mm) minimum thickness must completely surround ties.

Install additional ties approximately 8 in. (200 mm) on center at jambs and near edges.

04 20 01 MORTAR

Materials

Portland cement–lime, ASTM C270.

One part portland cement, $\frac{1}{4}$ to $\frac{1}{2}$ part hydrated lime, and sand equal to three times the sum of the cementitious material.

Portland cement: ASTM C150, Type I or Type II, low alkali.

Hydrated line: ASTM C207.

Sand: ASTM C144, except that not less than 5 percent shall pass a No. 100 sieve.

Admixtures and additives for workability are not recommended.

Execution

Fill all mortar joints completely.

Keep all air spaces and expansion joints clear of mortar except for spot bedding.

Cover veneer ties completely with mortar.

Tool all joints completely.

04 22 00 CONCRETE MASONRY UNIT

Materials

ASTM C90, Grade N.

Type 1, moisture-controlled, and Type 2, non-moisture-controlled, are available, but Type 1 is subject to less shrinkage and is best used in arid climates.

07 62 00 FLASHING

Materials

Flashing may be rigid copper or stainless steel, semiflexible composites of copper and other materials, or flexible membranes, such as peel-and-stick products.

Copper, ASTM B370, cold rolled hard tempered, 10–20 oz (0.0135 in. [0.343 mm] to 0.0270 in. [0.686 mm]).

Stainless steel, ASTM A167, type 304 with 2D or 2B finish, 0.0187 in. (0.475 mm).

Copper composites, 5 oz (0.0068 in. [0.1715 mm]), laminated between fiberglass fabric or asphaltic material. Other proprietary products are also available.

Flexible membranes, 40 mil (1 mm) self-adhering rubberized asphalt, 40 mil EPDM, or 40 mil composite of rubberized asphalt and cross-laminated polyethylene.

Must not be subject to ultraviolet degradation.

Must not be subject to deterioration in contact with alkaline masonry mortars or sealants.

Do not use asphalt-impregnated felt, aluminum, or lead flashing.

Execution

Extend flashing beyond the exterior of the stone at least $\frac{1}{4}$ in. (6 mm) and turn it down at a 45 degree angle to form a drip.

Lap flashing a minimum of 6 in. (152 mm) and seal with mastic.

Secure the flashing inside the cavity by tucking into a bed joint, as shown in Fig. 2-22, or by securing it with a termination bar, the top of which should be sealed.

Use edge dams at openings.

Install flashing a minimum of 6 in. (122 mm) above grade.

2-23 ANCHORED STONE VENEER WITH CONCRETE MASONRY UNIT BACKUP AT SPANDREL

Description

Figure 2-23 is similar to Fig. 2-22, showing anchorage at the floor line. It is used when the dead load of the stone must be transferred to the structural frame rather than being carried directly to the foundation. It is used for stone veneer from 2 in. (51 mm) to 10 in. (254 mm) thick. Anchored veneer for buildings in seismic design categories C, D, E, and F must conform to the relevant requirements of ACI 530/ASCE5/TMS 402.

Limitations of Use

For limitations of use, see Section 2-22.

Detailing Considerations

- The size of the expansion joint below the shelf angle must accommodate the expected movement of the stone and the structural frame.

Coordination Required

- The angle must be sized to support the load above and to extend to within about $\frac{1}{2}$ in. (13 mm) of the exterior face of the stone.
- For other coordination requirements, see Section 2-22.

Likely Failure Points

- Breaking or tearing of the flashing if it is rubbed against the head of the anchor bolt
- Cracking of veneer or mortar joints if the expansion joint is not sized properly

Materials

Refer to Section 2-22 for other material requirements.

Figure 2-23 Anchored stone veneer with CMU backup at spandrel 04 42 13.2

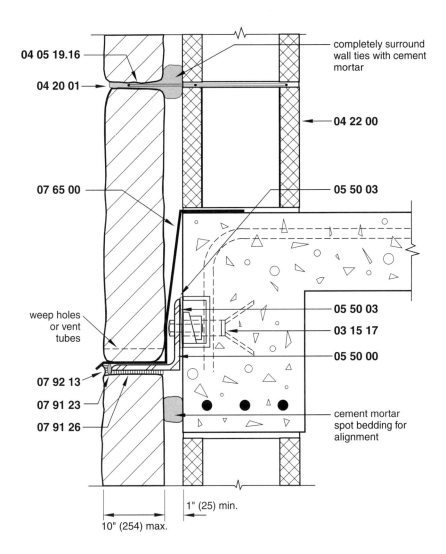

04 05 19.16

04 20 01

completely surround
wall ties with cement
mortar

04 22 00

07 65 00

05 50 03

weep holes
or vent
tubes

05 50 03

03 15 17

05 50 00

07 92 13

07 91 23

07 91 26

cement mortar
spot bedding for
alignment

1" (25) min.

10" (254) max.

03 15 17 CONCRETE INSERT

The insert should provide for horizontal or vertical adjustment, depending on whether the holes in the shelf angle are vertically or horizontally slotted.

The insert must be oriented correctly and be perfectly level.

A wedge-type insert may not be appropriate for seismic loading.

Place compressible material over the bolt head to prevent the anchor bolt from puncturing the flashing.

05 50 00 STEEL SHELF ANGLE

Materials

ASTM A36.

Maximum deflection l/600, but not to exceed 0.3 in. (7.6 mm).

Galvanized steel or stainless steel recommended.

Execution

Provide vertically or horizontally slotted holes as required for adjustment, depending on the type of adjustment provided by the concrete insert.

Locate the bolt hole near the top of the angle.

Use a series of short lengths to allow for alignment and provide a minimum $\frac{1}{16}$ in. (2 mm) gap between the ends of angles or $\frac{1}{4}$ in. in 20 ft (6 mm in 6 m).

05 50 03 STEEL SHIMS

Galvanized steel full length of angle.

Spot weld together after adjustment.

Maximum shim depth of 1 in. (51 mm).

07 91 23 BACKER ROD

Closed cell polyethylene foam, with the diameter at least 25 percent greater than the joint width.

07 91 26 COMPRESSIBLE JOINT FILLER

Closed cell material, preformed compressible filler, or copper sheet.

Should compress to 30 percent to 50 percent of the original thickness.

Keep the joint totally free of mortar.

07 92 13 ELASTOMERIC JOINT SEALANT

Materials

One-part polysulfide, polyurethane, or silicone, ASTM C920, Type S, Grade NS, Class 25 or 50.

Execution

Sealant depth equal to the width of the joint up to $\frac{1}{2}$ in. (13 mm), with a minimum depth of $\frac{1}{4}$ in. (6 mm).

Sealant depth $\frac{1}{2}$ in. (13 mm) for joint widths from $\frac{1}{2}$ in. to 1 in. (13 mm to 25 mm).

For sealants with a ±25 percent movement capability, the joint width should be four times the expected movement of the joint.

Proper priming and backer rods required.

2-24 ANCHORED STONE VENEER WITH CONCRETE MASONRY UNIT BACKUP AT PARAPET

Description

Figure 2-24 illustrates a parapet termination of the anchored stone veneer wall shown in Figs. 2-22 and 2-23. A flat roof is indicated, but a sloped roof may be used as long as proper drainage is provided. Because parapets are one of the most troublesome details with masonry construction, careful detailing and supervision of construction are required to avoid problems.

Figure 2-24 Anchored stone veneer with CMU backup at parapet 04 42 13.3

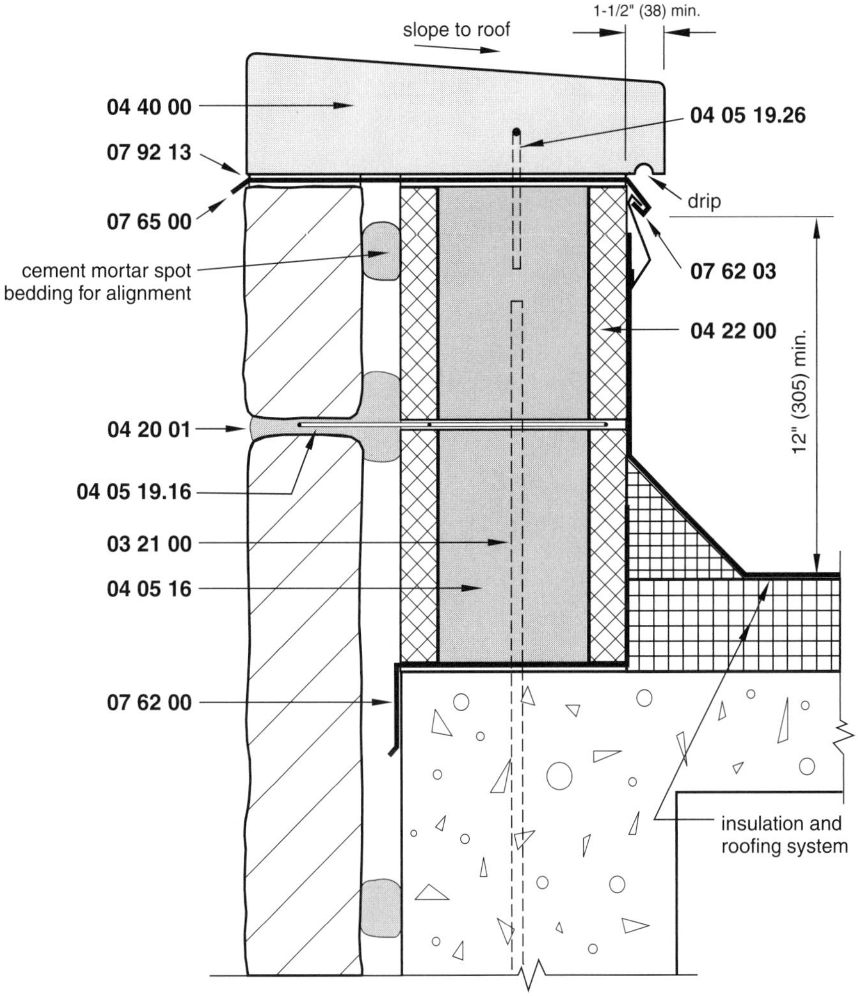

Limitations of Use

- Requirements for grouting and reinforcing the concrete masonry cores should be verified with a structural engineer to meet the gravity and seismic loading requirements of the job.
- For other limitations, see Section 2-22.

Detailing Considerations

- Copings should be of precast concrete, stone, or terra cotta. These materials have coefficients of thermal expansion similar to that of the stone wall and will move about the same amount as the wall below. Avoid metal copings because of the difference in thermal movement.
- Keep the height of the parapet to a minimum.
- The cavity and expansion joints should continue up through the parapet.
- Locate control joints in the coping to coincide with the wall control joints.

Coordination Required

- Provide proper vertical control joints in the concrete masonry wall. See Fig. 2-3.
- Locate movement joints in counterflashing at the same point as the soft joints in the coping.
- Locate expansion joints near the corners of the building.

Likely Failure Points

- Leaks caused by using metal copings and by omitting through-wall flashing
- Cracking of veneer or mortar joints if differential movement between the structure and the stone is not accommodated

Materials

Refer to Section 2-22 for other material requirements.

03 21 00 REINFORCING STEEL

ASTM A615, Grade 60.

#3 (#10) bars to anchor parapet to structure.

Seal hole where rebar penetrates flashing.

04 05 16 MASONRY GROUTING

Fine or coarse grout, ASTM C476.

04 05 19.26 MASONRY COPING ANCHOR

Stainless steel 304.

Seal the hole where the anchor penetrates the flashing.

04 40 00 STONE COPING

Materials

Precast concrete, stone, or terra cotta.

Pitch toward roof.

Project the drip edge at least $1\frac{1}{2}$ in. (38 mm) beyond the face of the wall and have a continuous drip.

Execution

Install with a mortar joint at one end and a soft joint at the other end. The soft joint should be a sealant over a compressible backer rod.

When installing the coping, set it on noncompressible shims of a thickness equal to the joint width and then spread the bed joint of mortar and place the coping. When the mortar has set, remove the shims and tuckpoint the void.

07 65 00 FLASHING

See Section 2-22.

Locate through-wall flashing in the mortar bed immediately below the coping.

Extend flashing at the roof deck below the level of the deck and up as high as the top of the cant strip.

07 62 03 COUNTERFLASHING

Materials

Flashing may be rigid copper or stainless steel, semiflexible composites of copper and other materials.

Copper, ASTM B370, cold rolled hard tempered, 10–20 oz (0.0135 in. [0.343 mm] to 0.0270 in. [0.686 mm]).

Stainless steel, ASTM A167, type 304 with 2D or 2B finish, 0.0187 in. (0.475 mm).

Copper composites, 5 oz (0.0068 in. [0.1715 mm]), laminated between fiberglass fabric or asphaltic material. Other proprietary products are also available.

Must not be subject to ultraviolet degradation.

Must not be subject to deterioration in contact with alkaline masonry mortars or sealants.

Do not use asphalt-impregnated felt, aluminum, or lead flashing.

Execution

Extend flashing beyond the exterior of masonry at least $\frac{1}{4}$ in. (6 mm) and turn it down at a 45 degree angle to form a drip.

Lap flashing a minimum of 6 in. (152 mm).

Embed the edge completely in the mortar joint.

Rake the mortar joint where flashing is installed and seal continuously.

07 92 13 ELASTOMERIC JOINT SEALANT

Materials

One-part polysulfide, polyurethane, or silicone, ASTM C920, Type S, Grade NS, Class 25 or 50.

Oil-based calking should not be used.

Execution

Sealant depth equal to the width of the joint up to $\frac{1}{2}$ in. (13 mm), with a minimum depth of $\frac{1}{4}$ in. (6 mm).

2-25   EXTERIOR STONE VENEER AT BASE

Description

For many buildings with stone veneer, a standard hand-set method of placing stone is used. Figure 2-25 is one of a series of three that shows one method of anchoring a thin veneer to a concrete structural frame with masonry backup walls. Typical anchoring conditions at an intermediate floor and parapet are shown in Figs. 2-26 and 2-27.

Figures 2-25, 2-26, and 2-27 show only one typical method for a hand-set application. There are many variations, depending on such variables as the size and thickness of the stone

Figure 2-25 Exterior stone veneer at base 04 42 13.4

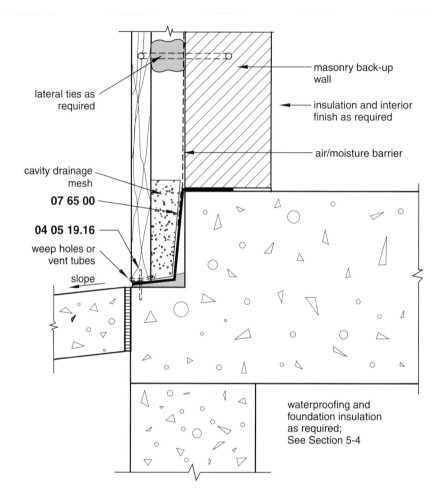

lateral ties as required

masonry back-up wall

insulation and interior finish as required

air/moisture barrier

cavity drainage mesh
07 65 00

04 05 19.16
weep holes or vent tubes

slope

waterproofing and foundation insulation as required; See Section 5-4

used, the type of backup wall, the size and configuration of the building, and the anchoring techniques preferred by the stone-setting contractor. Shop drawings will detail the exact method proposed by the contractor.

The traditional method of setting stone is more labor-intensive than other, recently developed methods and is usually most appropriate for small buildings or those with a great deal of variation in the stone detailing. Other systems that use prefabricated sections include steel truss–framed panels, stick-framed panels, and precast concrete/stone panels. With these systems, individual stone pieces are anchored to some type of backup structure, which is then attached to the building frame. One of these systems is shown in Fig. 2-31.

Limitations of Use

- The stone cannot support any load other than its own weight and the vertical dead load of the veneer above.
- Anchored veneer for buildings in seismic design categories C, D, E, and F must conform to the relevant requirements of ACI 530/ASCE5/TMS 402.
- Noncombustible, noncorrosive lintels must be used over all openings, and deflection cannot exceed 1/600 of the span under the full load of the veneer.

Detailing Considerations

- Minimum stone thicknesses are usually $\frac{3}{4}$ in. (19 mm) for single-story construction and $1\frac{1}{4}$ in. (32 mm) for multistory construction. However, stone thicknesses will vary, depending on the type and strength of the stone, the anticipated loads, the type of surface finish, the method of anchorage, and local building code requirements. The final decision on what thickness of stone should be used in critical situations should be based on laboratory tests on the type of stone and finish selected and the recommendations of the stone-setting contractor.

- Expansion joints must be provided to accommodate building and thermal movement as well as deflection of the structural frame. Additionally, on concrete frame buildings, concrete creep must be anticipated.

- The number and spacing of stone anchors are generally determined by the strength of the stone and the imposed wind loads on the panel.

- The stone veneer and its attachments must be designed to resist a horizontal force equal to twice the weight of the stone. See Table 2-6 for stone weights.

- Provisions must be made for adjustable erection connections to provide for building tolerances.

- An air/moisture barrier should be provided outside of the backup wall. In some cases, a liquid-applied barrier may be easier to apply around angles, anchors, and other components of the wall. See Section 5-5 for more information.

Coordination Required

- Polished finishes should not be used on marble for exterior applications. Weathering and pollution will quickly erode a polished finish.

- Chemical treatment of the final stone finish may be desirable to minimize permeability and attack by atmospheric pollution.

Table 2-6 Weights of Building Stone		
Stone type	Required min. weight, pcf (kg/m³)[a]	High weight, pcf (kg/m³)
Granite	160 (2560)	190 (3040)
Marble		
Calcite	162 (2592)	
Dolomite	175 (2800)	184 (2944)
Serpentine	168 (2688)	175 (2800)
Travertine	144 (2304)	160 (2560)
Limestone		
Low density	110 (1760)	135 (2160)
Medium density	136 (2176)	160 (2560)
High density	161 (2576)	185 (2960)
Sandstone		
Sandstone	140 (2240)	
Quartzitic sandstone	150 (2400)	
Quartzite	160 (2560)	170 (2720)

[a] Minimum weights as defined in ASTM specifications for the various building stones.

Likely Failure Points

- Cracking or breaking of stone that has been reduced in thickness by flame finishing, bush hammering, or other finishing methods (These types of finishes reduce the thickness of the stone and therefore its strength and resistance to weathering.)
- Spalling of stone adjacent to walkways where chloride de-icing salts are used
- Cracking of panels caused by concentrated stresses where leveling devices have been left in place
- Buckling of the veneer if provisions are not made for vertical movement such as frame shortening or structural movement
- Water leakage caused by improperly designed or installed waterproofing and weeps
- Spalling of the stone caused by freeze/thaw cycles of moisture trapped in the stone by water repellents

Materials

04 05 19.16 MASONRY ANCHOR

Dowel pin or inverted cramp anchor.

16 gage (0.0625 in. [1.588 mm]), mill galvanized, ASTM A653/A 653M, G90.

Optional: stainless steel, 18-8, Type 302/304, cold rolled, annealed, ASTM A240/A 240M.

07 65 00 FLASHING

Materials

Flashing may be rigid copper or stainless steel, semiflexible composites of copper and other materials, or flexible membranes, such as peel-and-stick products.

Copper, ASTM B370, cold rolled hard tempered, 10–20 oz (0.0135 in. [0.343 mm] to 0.0270 in. [0.686 mm]).

Stainless steel, ASTM A167, type 304 with 2D or 2B finish, 0.0187 in. (0.475 mm).

Copper composites, 5 oz (0.0068 in. [0.1715 mm]), laminated between fiberglass fabric or asphaltic material. Other proprietary products are also available.

Flexible membranes, 40 mil (1 mm) self-adhering rubberized asphalt, 40 mil EPDM, or 40 mil composite of rubberized asphalt and cross-laminated polyethylene.

Must not be subject to ultraviolet degradation.

Must not be subject to deterioration in contact with alkaline masonry mortars or sealants.

Do not use asphalt-impregnated felt, aluminum, or lead flashing.

Do not use copper or aluminum with limestone.

Execution

Extend flashing to the face of the stone or extend it ¼ in. (6 mm) outside the face of the stone and turn it down at a 45 degree angle to form a drip if the bottom of the stone is above the level of the horizontal slab.

Lap flashing a minimum of 6 in. (152 mm).

Figure 2-26 Exterior stone veneer at spandrel 04 42 13.5

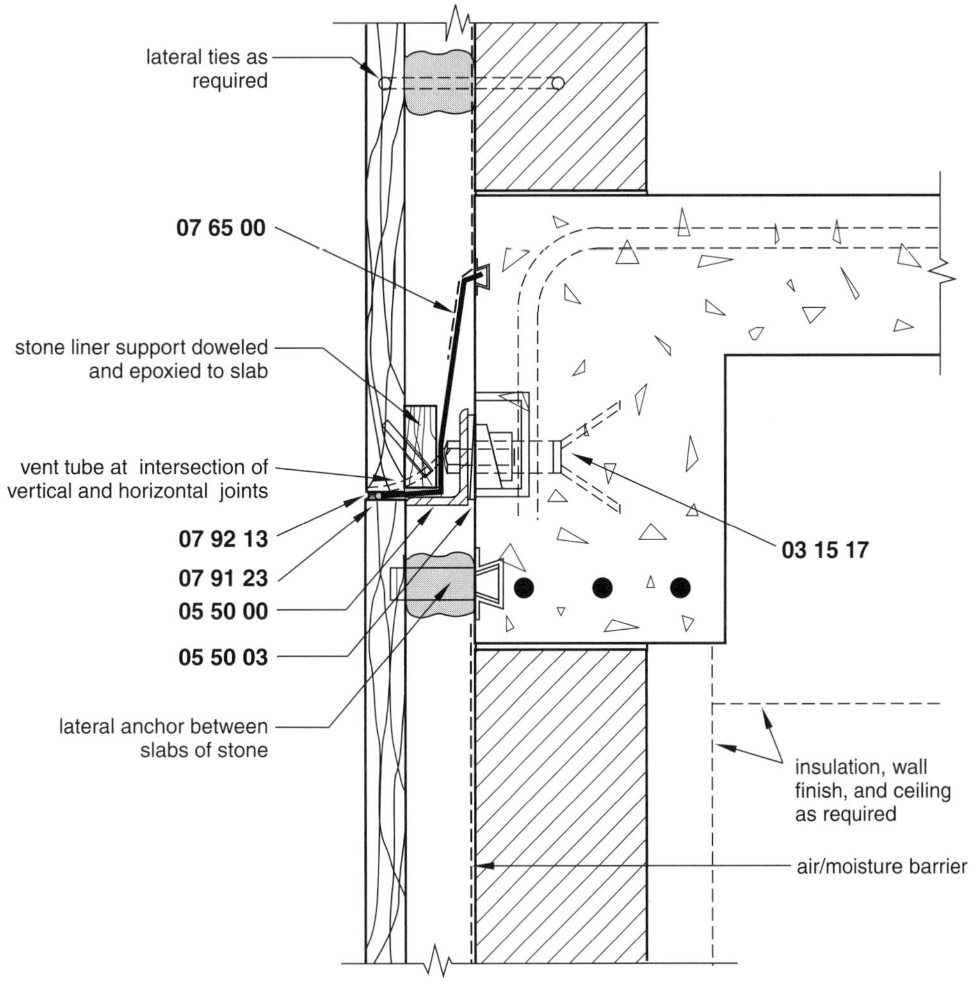

Labels in figure:
- lateral ties as required
- 07 65 00
- stone liner support doweled and epoxied to slab
- vent tube at intersection of vertical and horizontal joints
- 07 92 13
- 07 91 23
- 05 50 00
- 05 50 03
- lateral anchor between slabs of stone
- 03 15 17
- insulation, wall finish, and ceiling as required
- air/moisture barrier

2-26 EXTERIOR STONE VENEER AT SPANDREL

Description

Figure 2-26 is a continuation of Fig. 2-25, showing a typical horizontal support. This may occur at each floor line or under each stone panel. Refer to Fig. 2-25 for limitations of use, coordination required, and other detailing considerations. Shelf angles should be provided above all openings, at each floor line, and at intervals of no more than 12 ft (3.66 m) vertically above the first 25 ft (7.62 m) above grade.

Materials

03 15 17 CONCRETE INSERT

Should provide for vertical or horizontal adjustment.

Tack the weld bolt to the shelf angle when the adjustment is complete.

The insert must be oriented correctly and be perfectly level.

A wedge-type insert may not be appropriate for seismic loading.

Place compressible material over the bolt head to prevent the anchor bolt from puncturing the flashing.

05 50 00 STEEL SHELF ANGLE

Materials

ASTM A36; galvanized steel recommended.

Maximum deflection l/600, but not to exceed 0.3 in. (7.6 mm).

Execution

Use at every story or every other story to support the stone.

Provide vertically or horizontally slotted holes as required for adjustment, depending on the type of adjustment provided by the concrete insert.

Locate the bolt hole near the top of the angle.

Use a series of short lengths to allow for alignment and provide a minimum $\frac{1}{16}$ in. (2 mm) gap between ends of angles or $\frac{1}{4}$ in. in 20 ft (6 mm in 6 m).

05 50 03 SHIM

Galvanized steel full length of angle.

Spot weld together after adjustment.

Maximum shim depth of 1 in. (25 mm).

07 65 00 FLASHING

See Section 2-25.

07 91 23 BACKER ROD

Closed cell polyethylene foam, with the diameter at least 25 percent greater than the joint width.

07 92 13 ELASTOMERIC JOINT SEALANT

Polysulfide, polyurethane, or silicone, ASTM C920, Type S, Grade NS, Class 25 or 50.

Refer to Section 2-32 for requirements of joint design.

2-27   EXTERIOR STONE VENEER AT PARAPET

Description

Figure 2-27 is a continuation of Figs. 2-25 and 2-26, illustrating a common termination condition at the roofline. See Section 2-25 for limitation of use.

Figure 2-27 Exterior stone veneer at parapet 04 42 13.6

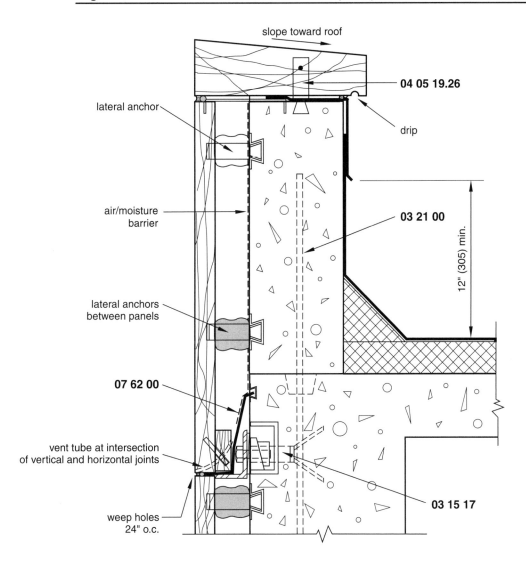

slope toward roof

04 05 19.26

lateral anchor

drip

air/moisture
barrier

03 21 00

12" (305) min.

lateral anchors
between panels

07 62 00

vent tube at intersection
of vertical and horizontal joints

03 15 17

weep holes
24" o.c.

Detailing Considerations

- The parapet may be either masonry or concrete, as shown in this detail.
- Copings should be stone, precast concrete, or terra cotta. These materials have coefficients of thermal expansion similar to that of the stone and will move about the same amount as the veneer below. Avoid metal copings unless adequate provisions are made for thermal expansion and contraction.
- See Section 2-25 for other detailing considerations.

Coordination Required

- Provide proper vertical control joints in masonry walls and continue the joint through the parapet and coping.
- Locate movement joints in the counterflashing to coincide with soft joints in coping.
- See Section 2-25 for other coordination requirements.

Likely Failure Points

- Breaking or tearing of the flashing if it is rubbed against the head of the anchor bolt
- Water leakage through coping if adequate provisions for movement are not made

Materials

See Sections 2-25 and 2-26 for other material requirements.

03 21 00 REINFORCING STEEL

ASTM A615, Grade 60.

#3 (#10) bars to anchor parapet to roof slab.

04 05 19.26 MASONRY COPING ANCHOR

Stainless steel 304.

Seal the hole where the anchor penetrates the flashing.

2-28   CUT STONE ON CONCRETE BACKUP WALL

Description

Figure 2-28 is one type of anchored veneer system in which the stone is secured to the backup wall with mechanical fasteners.

Figure 2-28 Cut stone on concrete backup wall 04 42 13.7

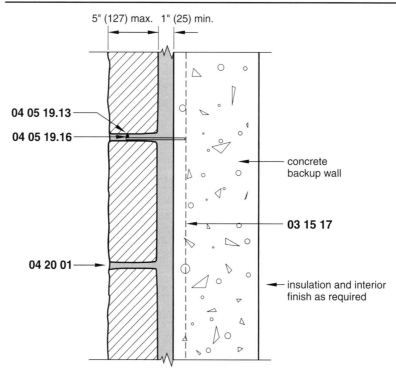

5" (127) max.   1" (25) min.

04 05 19.13

04 05 19.16

04 20 01

concrete backup wall

03 15 17

insulation and interior finish as required

Limitations of Use

- The stone cannot support any load other than its own weight and the vertical dead load of the veneer above.
- Anchored veneer for buildings in seismic design categories C, D, E, and F must conform to the relevant requirements of ACI 530/ASCE5/TMS 402.

Detailing Considerations

- Noncombustible, noncorrosive lintels must be used over all openings, and deflection cannot exceed 1/600 of the span under the full load of the veneer.

Coordination Required

- Provide allowances for differential movement between the stone and the backup wall and for movement caused by shrinkage, creep, and deflection of the concrete.
- Anchored veneer must be designed to resist a horizontal force equal to twice the weight of the veneer.

Materials

03 15 17 DOVETAIL ANCHOR

Anchors spaced a maximum of 24 in. (610 mm) apart horizontally.

04 05 19.16 MASONRY TIES

Fabricated from hard tempered, cold drawn steel wire, ASTM A82.

Optional: stainless steel, 18-8, Type 302/304, cold rolled, annealed, ASTM A240.

One tie for each 2 ft^2 (0.2 m^2) of wall area with 24 in. (610 mm) maximum horizontal spacing.

Verify additional requirements based on the seismic design category.

04 05 19.13 JOINT REINFORCEMENT

Fabricated from hard tempered, cold drawn steel wire, ASTM A951.

If reinforcement carries horizontal loads, reinforcement should be the deformed type.

Minimum W1.7 (MW11).

Class 3, ASTM A641 for partially embedded joint reinforcement.

Use ties conforming to ASTM A153, Class B-2, in very corrosive environments (1.50 oz/ft^2 [458 g/m^2] of wire) or use stainless steel ties conforming to ASTM A167.

Size of horizontal reinforcement determined by structural requirements of the wall.

Butt joints permitted.

04 20 01 MORTAR

Portland cement-lime, ASTM C270, Type S.

Admixtures and additives for workability are not recommended.

Use solid fill or spot-bed at anchors for alignment.

Figure 2-29 Interior stone veneer 4 42 16.1

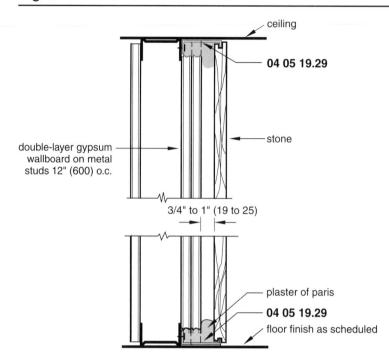

2-29 INTERIOR STONE VENEER

Description

Figure 2-29 illustrates a typical installation of standard-thickness stone on a gypsum wallboard partition. Where anchors are required, holes are cut in the gypsum board and filled with plaster of Paris spots. A similar method is used to apply stone to masonry or concrete backup walls.

Limitations of Use

- This detail is appropriate only for use with single lengths of stone, normally standard ceiling height. When large spaces are being finished or two or more pieces of stone are used, an intermediate, horizontal support angle must be used to carry the gravity load of the panel above.
- Verify spacing of anchors with the local building code.

Detailing Considerations

- An uneven floor may require cutting the bottom edge of the stone to align with the floor or a special base detail may be required.
- The stone should bear no load other than its own weight.

Coordination Required

- Verify the level of the floor.
- Verify requirements for anchoring in fire-rated partitions.
- Electrical boxes, switches, and other wall-mounted items must be set to be flush with the finished wall surface.

Likely Failure Points

- Crushing of the stone or failure of anchors if one piece of stone bears directly on a piece below

Materials

04 05 19.29 WIRE TIES

Noncorrosive ties, such as stainless steel, brass, or copper, spaced 24 in. (610 mm) on center or as required by the local building code.

Minimum #8 gage or $\frac{1}{8}$ in. (3.2 mm).

Wire ties should be embedded in plaster of Paris spots.

2-30   INTERIOR STONE VENEER AT VERTICAL JOINT

Description

Figure 2-30 shows a typical vertical joint of the installation shown in Fig. 2-29. Although this detail shows the joint coinciding with a stud, joints may occur anywhere in the wall.

Limitations of Use

- Anchors along the vertical edges should be placed 24 in. (610 mm) on center, but local building codes may require closer spacing.

Figure 2-30 Interior stone veneer at vertical joint 04 42 16.2

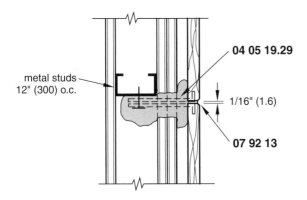

Detailing Considerations

- Consider the alignment of joints in the wall with those in the floor or ceiling.
- Eliminate or minimize the number of penetrations in the stone for such things as light switches, thermostats, and electrical outlets.

Coordination Required

- Verify requirements for anchoring in fire-rated partitions.
- Electrical boxes, switches, and other wall-mounted items must be set to be flush with the finished wall surface.

Likely Failure Points

- Chipping of the stone if the exposed edges are not beveled or eased
- Staining of the stone if the correct type of sealant or mortar is not used

Materials

04 05 19.29 WIRE TIES

Noncorrosive ties, such as stainless steel, brass, or copper, spaced 24 in. (610 mm) on center or as required by the local building code.

Minimum #8 gage or $\frac{1}{8}$ in. (3.2 mm).

Wire ties should be embedded in plaster of Paris spots and securely fastened to the stud or the wall. The ends of the ties should be set in holes drilled into the edges of the stone.

07 92 13 ELASTOMERIC JOINT SEALANT

Nonstaining white cement or sealant.

2-31 EXTERIOR STONE ON STEEL TRUSS FRAME

Description

In lieu of the traditional hand-set stone installation shown in Figs. 2-25, 2-26, and 2-27, pieces of stone can be attached to a supporting framework in the shop or on site and attached to the building in a large prefabricated section. Figure 2-31 shows one of the common methods for doing this. The stone is attached to a steel framework with stainless steel anchors set in epoxy in the back of the stone. The entire assembly is then lifted into place and secured to the building's structural system.

This method of stone installation is often used on high-rise buildings because the panels can easily be lifted into place and attached to the building frame from the inside. In most situations, the panels span one structural bay and are secured at the column lines so that the gravity load can be taken directly by the columns. For long spans intermediate supports may be required, as shown in this detail.

Figure 2-31 Exterior stone on steel truss frame 04 42 23

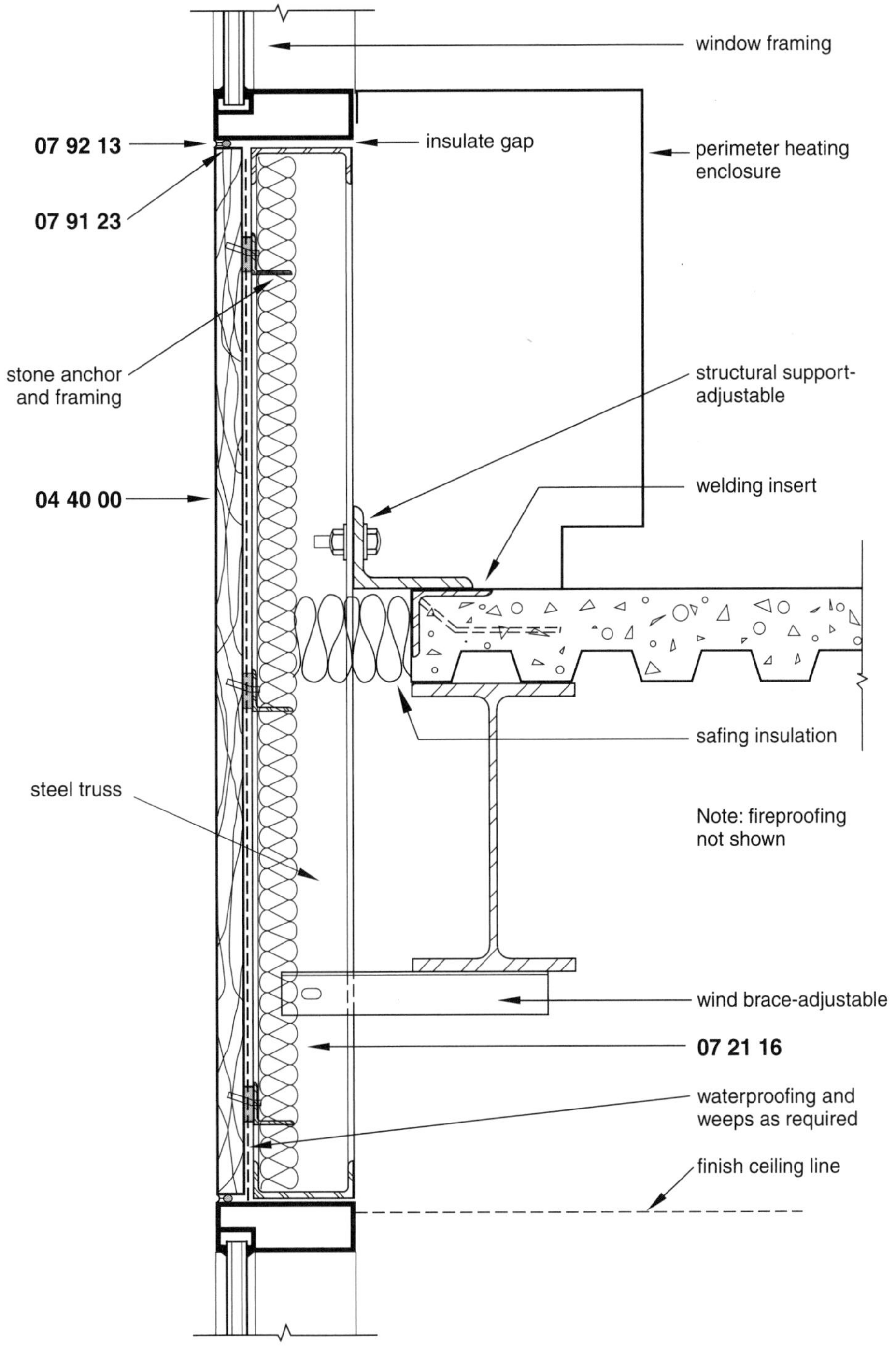

- window framing
- 07 92 13
- 07 91 23
- insulate gap
- perimeter heating enclosure
- stone anchor and framing
- structural support-adjustable
- 04 40 00
- welding insert
- steel truss
- safing insulation
- Note: fireproofing not shown
- wind brace-adjustable
- 07 21 16
- waterproofing and weeps as required
- finish ceiling line

Limitations of Use

- Steel truss frame systems are most economical for high-volume projects with facades that have repetitive elements and fairly simple configurations.
- This system requires stone with a minimum thickness of $1\frac{1}{4}$ in. (32 mm), although a minimum thickness of $1\frac{1}{2}$ in. (38 mm) is preferred. Thicker panels may be required.

- The stone veneer cannot support any load other than its own weight, the wind load, and the vertical dead load of any veneer immediately above it.
- The deflection of horizontal supports cannot exceed 1/600 of the span under the full load of the veneer.
- Connections and panel joints must accommodate relative movement between stories caused by wind and seismic forces as required by the applicable building code.

Detailing Considerations

- The number and spacing of stone anchors are generally determined by the strength of the stone and the imposed wind loads on the panel.
- The requirements for waterproofing, flashing, and weeps behind the stone must be reviewed and incorporated into the design.
- The stone veneer and its attachments must be designed to resist a horizontal force equal to twice the weight of the stone. See Table 2-6 for stone weights.
- Horizontal supports, attachments, and other structural framing for the stone must be made of noncombustible, corrosion-resistant materials.
- Provisions must be made for adjustable erection connections to provide for building tolerances.
- Provisions must be made for accommodating thermal movement, deformation, differential movement, and structural frame movement. Some of these problems can be minimized by attaching the steel truss frame only at columns or other compressive members to carry gravity loads.
- Insulation may be installed prior to panel placement.
- Wind bracing is required near the bottom of the panels.

Coordination Required

- Flashing and weeps may need to be incorporated into the design of the window framing system.
- The expected construction tolerances of the structural system being used must be determined to design an appropriate connection system.
- For large projects, a full-size mock-up should be constructed.

Likely Failure Points

- Buckling of the veneer if provisions are not made for vertical movement such as frame shortening or structural movement
- Cracking or breaking off of the stone veneer caused by inadequate provisions for lateral movement of the building
- Buckling of the veneer due to undersized joints or installation of sealant during cold weather
- Water leakage caused by improperly designed or installed waterproofing and weeps
- Spalling of the stone caused by freeze/thaw cycles of moisture trapped in the stone by water repellents

Materials

04 40 00 STONE

Granite (ASTM C615), marble (ASTM C503), or limestone (ASTM C568).

Minimum $1\frac{1}{4}$ in. (32 mm) thick; $1\frac{1}{2}$ in. (38 mm) minimum thickness recommended.

Exterior corners should have a quirk miter.

Provide drips where required.

Provide sloped surfaces on the top of exposed horizontal pieces of stone.

07 21 16 BLANKET INSULATION

Full batt insulation or as required by the project.

07 91 23 BACKER ROD

Closed cell polyethylene foam or as recommended by the sealant manufacturer, with the diameter at least 25 percent greater than the joint width.

07 92 13 ELASTOMERIC JOINT SEALANT

Materials

Polyurethane, polysulfide, or silicone, ASTM C920, Type S or M, Grade NS, Class 25 or 50.

Execution

Sealant depth equal to the width of the joint up to $\frac{1}{2}$ in. (13 mm), with a minimum depth of $\frac{1}{4}$ in. (6 mm).

Sealant depth $\frac{1}{2}$ in. (13 mm) for joint widths from $\frac{1}{2}$ in. to 1 in. (13 mm to 25 mm).

For sealants with a ± 25 percent movement capability, the joint width should be four times the expected movement of the joint.

Proper priming and backer rods are required.

2-32 EXTERIOR STONE ON FRAMING SYSTEM

Description

Figure 2-32 is similar to Fig. 2-31 in that the stone is supported by a steel framework, but instead of assembling prefabricated units in the shop or on site, the framework is installed on the building first and then individual pieces of stone are attached to the framework. This procedure makes the system more applicable for low-rise buildings since the stone must be applied from the outside.

Limitations of Use

- This system is generally not applicable for high-rise buildings.

Figure 2-32 Exterior stone on framing system 04 42 26

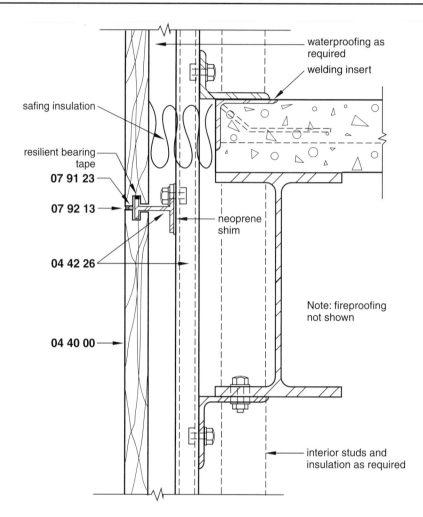

waterproofing as required

welding insert

safing insulation

resilient bearing tape
07 91 23

07 92 13

neoprene shim

04 42 26

Note: fireproofing not shown

04 40 00

interior studs and insulation as required

- This system requires stone with a minimum thickness of $1\frac{1}{4}$ in. (32 mm), although a minimum thickness of $1\frac{1}{2}$ in. (38 mm) or more may be required, depending on the specific type of anchoring method used.
- The stone veneer cannot support any load other than its own weight, the wind load, and the vertical dead load of any veneer immediately above it.
- The deflection of horizontal supports cannot exceed 1/600 of the span under full load of the veneer.
- Connections and panel joints must accommodate relative movement between stories caused by wind and seismic forces as required by the applicable building code.

Detailing Considerations

- The number and spacing of stone anchors are generally determined by the strength of the stone and the imposed wind loads on the panel.
- The requirements for waterproofing, flashing, and weeps behind the stone must be reviewed and incorporated into the design.
- Safing insulation is required to fill space between floor structure and stone veneer.

- The stone veneer and its attachments must be designed to resist a horizontal force equal to twice the weight of the stone. See Table 2-6 for stone weights.
- Horizontal supports, attachments, and other structural framing for the stone must be of noncombustible, corrosion-resistant materials.
- Provisions must be made for adjustable erection connections to provide for building tolerances.
- Provisions must be made for accommodating thermal movement, deformation, differential movement, and structural frame movement. Some of these problems can be minimized by attaching the steel truss frame at columns or other compressive members only to carry gravity loads.

Coordination Required

- The expected construction tolerances of the structural system being used must be determined to design an appropriate connection system.
- Insulation may need to be placed on the inside of the steel frame system.
- Window systems must be designed to work with the framing system selected.

Likely Failure Points

- Buckling of the veneer if provisions are not made for vertical movement such as frame shortening or structural movement
- Cracking or breaking off of the stone veneer caused by inadequate provisions for lateral movement of the building
- Buckling or cracking of the veneer due to undersized joints or installation of sealant during cold weather
- Water leakage caused by improperly designed or installed waterproofing and weeps
- Spalling of the stone caused by freeze/thaw cycles of moisture trapped in the stone by water repellents

Materials

04 40 00 STONE

Granite (ASTM C615), marble (ASTM C503), or limestone (ASTM C568).

Minimum $1\frac{1}{4}$ in. (32 mm) thick; $1\frac{1}{2}$ in. (38 mm) minimum thickness recommended.

Exterior corners should have a quirk miter.

Provide drips where required.

Provide sloped surfaces on the top of exposed horizontal pieces of stone.

04 42 26 GRID-SYSTEM-SUPPORTED STONE CLADDING

Steel channel sections, tubular sections, or Z-members as required by the span and imposed loads.

Alternately, the stone panel may be supported by clip angles along the bottom edge of the stone.

Dissimilar metals must be protected from galvanic action by shims of neoprene or other appropriate materials.

07 91 23 BACKER ROD

Closed cell polyethylene foam or as recommended by the sealant manufacturer, with the diameter at least 25 percent greater than the joint width.

07 92 13 ELASTOMERIC JOINT SEALANT

Materials

Polyurethane, polysulfide, or silicone, ASTM C920, Type S or M, Grade NS, Class 25 or 50.

Execution

Sealant depth equal to the width of the joint up to $\frac{1}{2}$ in. (13 mm), with a minimum depth of $\frac{1}{4}$ in. (6 mm).

Sealant depth $\frac{1}{2}$ in. (13 mm) for joint widths from $\frac{1}{2}$ in. to 1 in. (13 mm to 25 mm).

For sealants with a ±25 percent movement capability, the joint width should be four times the expected movement of the joint.

Proper priming and backer rods are required.

CHAPTER 3

METAL DETAILS

3-1 STRUCTURAL STEEL COLUMN ERECTION TOLERANCES

Description

Figure 3-1 illustrates some of the erection tolerances permitted by the American Institute of Steel Construction (AISC) for the plumbness of columns and attached spandrel beams. Along with the mill tolerances and plan tolerances shown in Section 3-3, this diagram permits realistic detailing of the attachment of other materials, such as exterior cladding, to a steel frame. However, AISC 303 states that the accumulated mill and fabrication tolerances cannot cause erection tolerances to be exceeded.

Figure 3-1 shows the permissible envelope within which the working points of columns can fall. When misalignment of beams is caused by an acceptable variation in column alignment, the beams are considered acceptable as well. Figure 3-2 illustrates the permissible variations of a beam attached to a column, which is within the allowable tolerance envelope shown in Fig. 3-1.

In general, with the tolerances shown in Fig. 3-1, if connections that allow for a 3 in. (76 mm) adjustment are provided, the exterior of a building (the building line in the detail) can be maintained in a true vertical plane up to the 20th story. If no further adjustment is provided in buildings of over 20 stories, the exterior can be maintained within $1/16$ in. (1.6 mm) per story.

Limitations of Use

- Additional tolerances exist for steel fabrication and erection. Refer to AISC 303, *Code of Standard Practice for Steel Bridges and Buildings*, for a complete description.
- Figure 3-1 does not account for differential column shortening between interior and exterior columns during construction or for the effects of temperature changes. However, once the building is complete, these variations are usually not significant for detailing purposes as long as sufficient clearance and adjustment have been provided based on the tolerances shown in this detail and in Section 3-3.
- Figure 3-1 does not indicate mill tolerances for camber or sweep.

Figure 3-1 Structural steel column erection tolerances 05 05 03

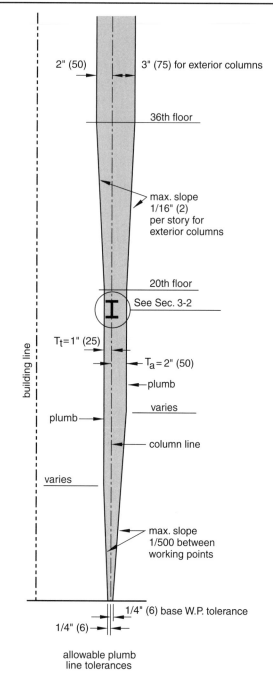

2" (50)

3" (75) for exterior columns

36th floor

max. slope
1/16" (2)
per story for
exterior columns

20th floor

See Sec. 3-2

T_t=1" (25)

T_a= 2" (50)

plumb

varies

building line

plumb

column line

varies

max. slope
1/500 between
working points

1/4" (6) base W.P. tolerance

1/4" (6)

allowable plumb
line tolerances

Detailing Considerations

- The following definitions apply to steel erection tolerances:
  The working point of a column is defined as the actual center of the column at either end of the column as shipped. Therefore, when two column pieces are spliced together, there are two working points adjacent to each other.
- The working point of a beam is the actual centerline of the top flange at either end.

- The mill tolerances shown in Section 3-3 should be added to the erection tolerances shown in this detail if overall dimensions are critical. Complete mill tolerances are given in ASTM A6.
- For members with both ends finished for contact bearing, a variation of $1/32$ in. (0.8 mm) is permitted.
- At the bottom of the column there is a tolerance of $1/4$ in. (6 mm) from the center of any anchor bolt group to the established column line through the group. The center-to-center distance between any two bolts within an anchor bolt group cannot vary by more than $1/8$ in. (3 mm).
- The tolerances for columns adjacent to elevator shafts are slightly more restrictive than those for other columns. These columns cannot vary more than 1 in. (25 mm) from the established column line in the first 20 stories. Above the 20th floor, the displacement can be increased $1/32$ in. (0.8 mm) for each additional story to a maximum of 2 in. (51 mm).
- In addition to providing for required steel tolerances, adequate clearances must be provided for tolerances of attached materials (such as precast concrete) and for the clearances required for working and connecting the various construction materials together.
- In general, a column is considered plumb if the deviation of the working line of the column from a true plumb line does not exceed 1:500.

Coordination Required

- The tolerance for setting anchor bolt groups and embedded items is separate from the steel erection tolerances and must be taken into account when the total tolerance at any given point in the steel frame is determined. However, anchor bolt groups are usually set to a tolerance of $\pm 1/4$ in. (6 mm).
- Adjustments in the height of prefabricated cladding panels must be provided for due to the accumulated shortening of steel columns under load, which will make the steel frame slightly shorter than the unstressed facade.

3-2   STEEL COLUMN/BEAM CONNECTION TOLERANCES

Description

As stated in Section 3-4, horizontal alignment of beams is considered acceptable when the ends are connected to columns that fall within acceptable tolerances. This section describes acceptable variations in both horizontal and vertical placement of beams and tolerances of individual columns between floors.

Figure 3-2(a) illustrates how the horizontal position of an individual beam work point must fall within the allowable column tolerances shown in Fig. 3-1. In addition, the allowable vertical tolerance is determined by measuring from the upper column splice line to the theoretical beam work point. This distance cannot be greater than $3/16$ in. (5 mm) or less than $5/16$ in. (8 mm).

Figure 3-2 Steel column/beam connection tolerances 05 05 03.1

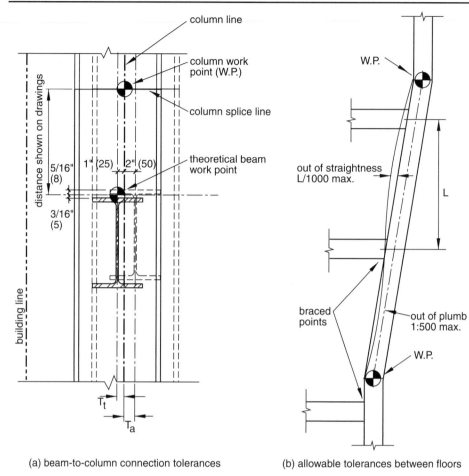

(a) beam-to-column connection tolerances
(b) allowable tolerances between floors

As shown in Fig. 3-2(b), the variation in straightness for a straight compression member must be equal to or less than 1/1000 of the axial length between points that are to be laterally supported. This is the fabrication tolerance given in AISC 303. For curved members, the variation from the theoretical curve must be equal to or less than the variation in sweep that is required for an equivalent straight member of the same length as specified in ASTM A6/A6M.

3-3 STRUCTURAL STEEL COLUMN PLAN TOLERANCES

Description

Figure 3-3 illustrates some of the allowable variations in cross-sectional size and straightness of standard rolled W and HP shapes, commonly used for columns. A *W shape* is a doubly symmetric wide-flange shape used as a beam or column whose inside flange surfaces are substantially parallel. An *HP shape* is a wide-flange shape generally used as a bearing pile whose flanges and webs are of the same nominal thickness and whose depth and width are essentially the same. The tolerances shown are those that most affect architectural detailing and coordination with other materials.

Figure 3-3 Structural steel column plan tolerances 05 05 04

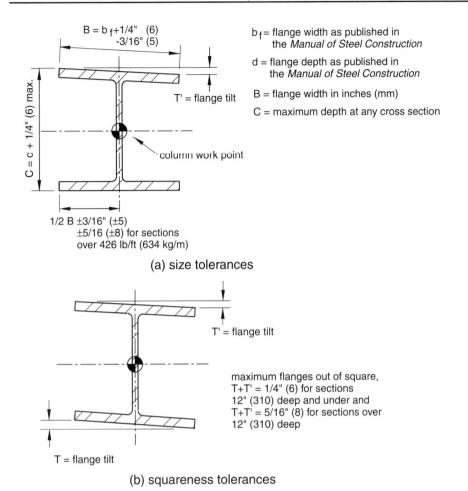

(a) size tolerances

(b) squareness tolerances

Limitations of Use

- Additional tolerances exist for steel fabrication and erection. Refer to AISC 303, *Code of Standard Practice for Steel Buildings and Bridges,* for a complete description.
- These diagrams do not take into account variations in position caused by temperature changes of the exposed steel frame since it is usually the responsibility of the erector and contractor to locate working points in such a way as to compensate for temperature effects.
- These diagrams do not indicate mill tolerances for camber or sweep.

Detailing Considerations

- The dimensional values for *d* and *bf* are those of the actual depth and width of steel members as published in the *Manual of Steel Construction*.
- The working point of a column is defined as the actual center of the column at either end of the column as shipped. Therefore, when two column pieces are spliced together, there are two working points adjacent to each other.

- Refer to Fig. 3-4(b) for accumulated tolerances considering mill tolerances, erection tolerances as shown in Section 3-1, and possible out-of-straightness for individual column sections. The maximum out-of-straightness tolerance is $h/1000$, where h is the distance between braced points

Coordination Required

- Required thicknesses for fireproofing must be added to the tolerances shown in these details.
- In addition to providing for required steel tolerances, adequate clearances must be provided for tolerances of attached materials (such as precast concrete) and for the clearances required for working and connecting the various construction materials together.

3-4 STRUCTURAL STEEL COLUMN LOCATION TOLERANCES

Description

In addition to individual column tolerances for plumb, a row of columns must fall within specified limits. This determines the alignment of the total length of a building and the alignment of individual beams between columns. Figure 3-4(a) shows the tolerances for this alignment between several columns, and Fig. 3-4(b) shows the effect of the accumulated tolerances of mill tolerances, fabrications tolerances, and erection tolerances.

Detailing Considerations

The working points at the tops of exterior columns in a single-tier building or the working points of exterior columns at any splice level for multitier buildings must fall within a horizontal envelope parallel to the building line. This is shown diagrammatically in Fig. 3-4(a). For each column, the working points must also fall within the envelope shown in Fig. 3-1. This horizontal envelope is $1^1/_2$ in. (38 mm) wide for buildings up to 300 ft (91 m) long and is increased $1/_2$ in. (13 mm) for each 100 ft (30 m) but cannot exceed 3 in. (75 mm).

The horizontal location of this $1^1/_2$ in. (38 mm) envelope does not necessarily have to fall directly above or below the adjacent envelope, but it must be within the allowable 1:500 tolerance in plumbness for columns as shown in Fig. 3-2. If the alignment of the columns is within acceptable limits, then any single-piece beam connected to them is considered to be in acceptable alignment.

For cantilevered members, alignment is checked by extending a straight line from the working point at the member's supported end and comparing it with the working line of the cantilevered member. If the misalignment is equal to or less than 1/500 of the distance from the supported end to the free end, then the member is considered aligned, level, or plumb, depending on the direction of the cantilever.

Accumulated Tolerances

Figure 3-4(b) shows the minimum clearance envelope based on steel erection tolerances used with enclosures or attachments that must be held to a precise plan location. This clearance

Figure 3-4 Structural steel column location tolerances 05 05 04.1

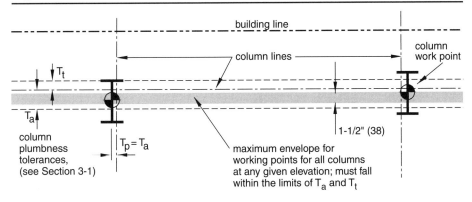

T_a = Tolerance away from building line

T_t = Tolerance toward building line

T_p = Tolerance parallel to building line (see Fig. 3-4(b) below)

(a) tolerances for columns with continuous intermediate beams

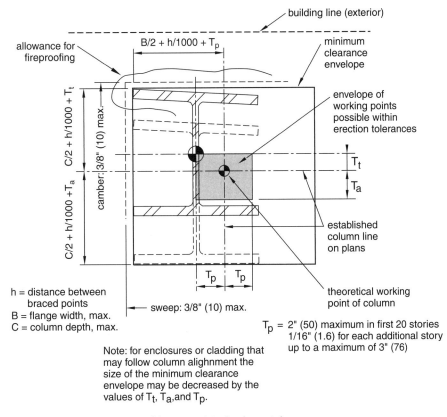

h = distance between
    braced points
B = flange width, max.
C = column depth, max.

sweep: 3/8" (10) max.

T_p = 2" (50) maximum in first 20 stories
1/16" (1.6) for each additional story
up to a maximum of 3" (76)

Note: for enclosures or cladding that
may follow column alighnment the
size of the minimum clearance
envelope may be decreased by the
values of T_t, T_a, and T_p.

(b) accumulated column tolerances

envelope includes the variations in maximum beam depth and width, C and B; the maximum variation in slope between braced points, h; and the allowable erection tolerances toward, away from, and parallel to the building line, T_t, T_a, and T_p (see Section 3-1). The clearance envelope is measured from the theoretical working point of the column, which is the actual center of the steel column at the end of the shipping piece. Current AISC standards state that the accumulation of mill tolerances and fabrication tolerances shall not cause the erection tolerances to be exceeded.

However, when the alignment of lintels, spandrels, wall supports, and similar members is used to connect other building construction elements to the structural steel frame, there should be sufficient provisions for adjustment to allow for the accumulation of mill and fabrication tolerances as well as erection tolerances. Figure 3-4(b) also shows the additional tolerances for camber and sweep of the steel framing.

Because the various tolerances vary with the beam size and height of the building, a tolerance envelope can be calculated for each story, but in most cases the worst condition is determined for detailing purposes. For example, in a 20-story building, the column can vary up to 1 in. (25 mm) toward the building line or 2 in. (50 mm) away from the building line due to erection tolerances. If the column straightness varies by $h/1000$, the envelope could be as much as $1\frac{1}{8}$ in. (29 mm) outward or as much as $2\frac{1}{8}$ in. (54 mm) inward (assuming a 12 ft or 3660 mm distance between braced points). At the midpoint of the column between splice points, camber or sweep could add as much as $\frac{3}{8}$ in. (10 mm) to the basic erection tolerance envelope. Refer to ASTM A6/A 6M for sweep and camber tolerances.

Even though the envelope of working point tolerance for an individual column can be up to 3 in. (76 mm) for a 20-story building, AISC standards require that all exterior columns along one side of a building at each splice line be limited to a $1\frac{1}{2}$ in. (38 mm) wide band, as shown in Fig. 3-4(a). The adjacent envelope above or below each band must be within the 1:500 slope restriction illustrated in Fig. 3-2.

In general, if connections between the steel frame and exterior cladding provide for a total adjustment of 3 in. (76 mm) in a 20-story building, the exterior building line can be maintained in a true vertical plane. Above this, the facade can be erected to within $\frac{1}{16}$ in. (1.6 mm) of plumb per story with a maximum total deviation of 1 in. (25 mm) from a true vertical plane. If dimensional or erection tolerances of the cladding material are substantial, these should be added to the steel tolerances.

3-5 STRUCTURAL STEEL SUPPORT FOR MASONRY

Description

For masonry-clad, steel-framed buildings, various types of support systems are required when the height of the masonry bearing directly on the foundation exceeds the height limitation dictated by the local building code, usually 25 ft (7.62 m). Figure 3-5 shows one method of supporting masonry from a steel beam that allows for both vertical and horizontal adjustment to compensate for erection tolerances of the steel frame. See Fig. 2-12 for masonry supported on a lintel spanning between brick.

Limitations of Use

- This detail indicates the masonry support system only. Refer to the details on masonry construction for requirements of masonry reinforcement, flashing, and materials use. See Section 2-11 for requirements of brick supported on a shelf angle.
- The size of the angles, methods of connection, and spacing of connectors must be verified with a structural engineer based on the loads imposed on the supports.

Figure 3-5 Structural steel support for masonry 05 12 23.1

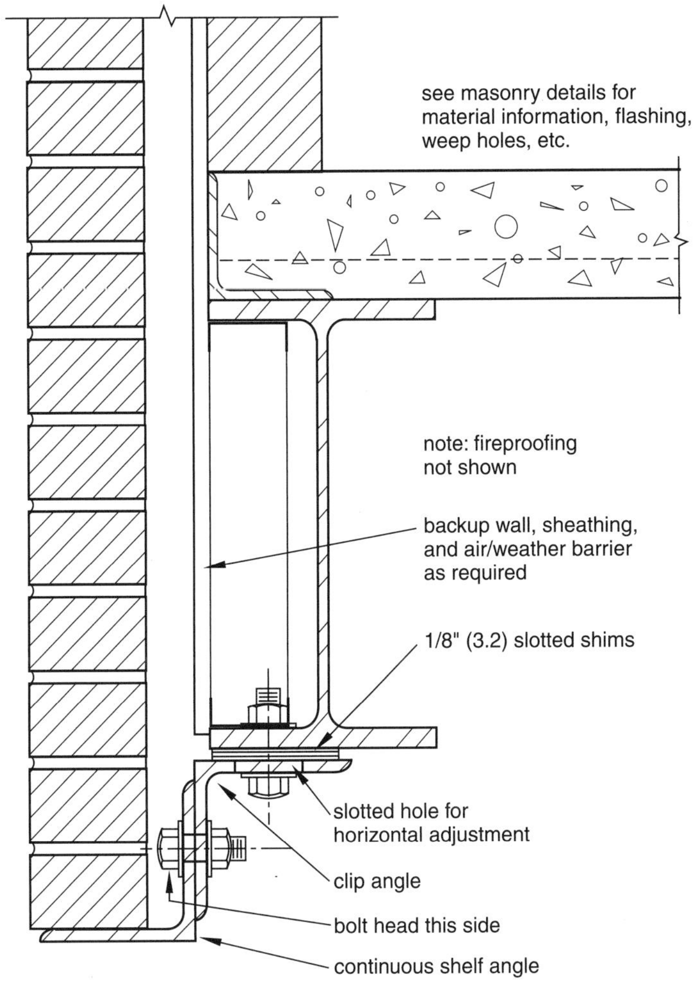

see masonry details for
material information, flashing,
weep holes, etc.

note: fireproofing
not shown

backup wall, sheathing,
and air/weather barrier
as required

1/8" (3.2) slotted shims

slotted hole for
horizontal adjustment

clip angle

bolt head this side

continuous shelf angle

Detailing Considerations

- A clip angle may also be bolted to the web of the beam to make the bottom edge of the masonry flush with the bottom flange of the beam.
- Vertical adjustment may be made by shims, as shown in this detail, or by slotted holes.
- For buildings of less than 20 stories, the total horizontal adjustment required to maintain the face of the masonry in a true vertical plane is about 3 in. (75 mm). Two inches (50 mm) of adjustment toward the building line and 1 in. (25 mm) of adjustment away from the building line should be provided, although this is not always possible. Refer to Section 3-2.

Coordination Required

- Coordinate elevations of the steel frame working points with masonry coursing.
- Refer to Sections 3-1, 3-2, and 3-3 for allowable tolerances of the steel frame.
- Refer to Section 2-11 for masonry detailing requirements.

Likely Failure Points

- Failure of the angles or excessive deflection of the masonry caused by excessive eccentricity when the maximum horizontal adjustment is made toward the building line
- Torsion caused by inadequate bearing of the clip angles to the steel beam with undersized shims

3-6 STRUCTURAL STEEL SUPPORT FOR PRECAST CONCRETE

Description

Figure 3-6 illustrates one of the several methods used to attach precast concrete to a structural steel frame. Because most precast concrete panels are attached to the outside of the structural frame, most multistory attachments are eccentric bearing, as shown in this detail.

Figure 3-6 Structural steel support for precast concrete 05 12 23.3

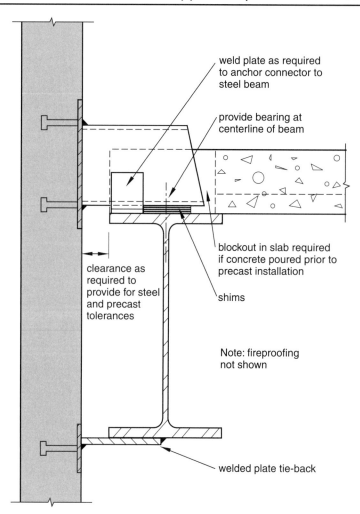

weld plate as required to anchor connector to steel beam

provide bearing at centerline of beam

blockout in slab required if concrete poured prior to precast installation

shims

clearance as required to provide for steel and precast tolerances

Note: fireproofing not shown

welded plate tie-back

Limitations of Use

- The location and type of tie-back connection in Fig. 3-6 are shown for illustrative purposes. The exact location, type, and configuration should be verified with a structural engineer and the precast supplier.
- Seismic shear plates are not shown in this detail.
- With the type of rigid tie-back shown in this detail, the possible volume change of the precast panel and the deflection of the steel frame must be considered. Other types of tie-back details are available that allow vertical movement while transferring lateral forces.

Detailing Considerations

- The connector should be designed for the maximum moment on the panel anchor when the maximum horizontal adjustment is made.
- A leveling bolt, as shown in Fig. 3-7, may be used in lieu of shims.
- Adjustments must be provided for the vertical dimensions of precast panels relative to the structural frame to account for the accumulated shortening of the steel columns.
- Bearing connections should be made at two points per panel at only one level of the structure. Additional connections to the structural frame should be made for lateral support only. Refer to Fig. 1-19.
- If shim plates are used for leveling, an additional weld plate should be used to transfer significant loads.
- In tall buildings, it is usually impractical to provide enough adjustment to allow for the steel erection tolerances allowed by standard practice. Generally, the precast panels will follow the steel frame in tall buildings.

Coordination Required

- Refer to Section 1-17 for types of precast joints.
- Refer to Section 1-13 for allowable tolerances of precast concrete panels.

3-7   STEEL/PRECAST WITH INSULATION

Description

Figure 3-7 is similar to Fig. 3-6 but shows the application of insulation and a backup wall. It also illustrates the use of a leveling bolt instead of shims to adjust the elevation of the precast panel. If possible, the insulation should be applied to the inside of the precast wall to create a continuous layer of insulation with no thermal breaks.

Limitations of Use

- No tie-backs are shown in this detail. They may be attached to the bottom of the steel beam, as shown in Fig. 3-6, or attached to the floor structure of the floor below if the precast panel is one or more stories high.
- All sizes of members must be verified by a structural engineer.

Figure 3-7 Steel/precast with insulation 05 12 23.3

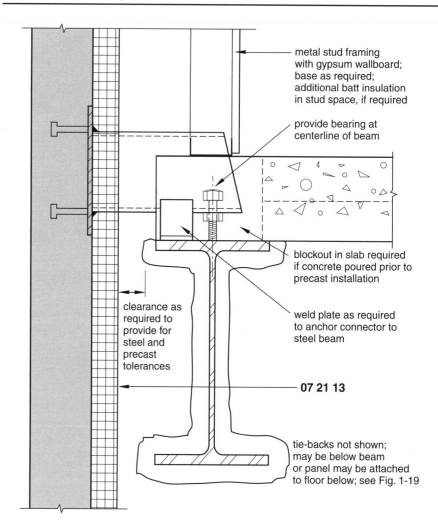

metal stud framing
with gypsum wallboard;
base as required;
additional batt insulation
in stud space, if required

provide bearing at
centerline of beam

blockout in slab required
if concrete poured prior to
precast installation

weld plate as required
to anchor connector to
steel beam

07 21 13

clearance as
required to
provide for
steel and
precast
tolerances

tie-backs not shown;
may be below beam
or panel may be attached
to floor below; see Fig. 1-19

Detailing Considerations

- Additional batt insulation can be installed within stud spaces to provide additional insulation in cold climates.
- The joints between the precast wall and windows, doors, and other openings should be sealed to provide a continuous air barrier because the concrete itself serves as an air barrier.
- The exact position of the interior finish wall will vary, depending on HVAC requirements and the type of bearing connection used.
- See Fig. 1-10 for details of window framing and interior finish.

Coordination Required

- In climate zones 5, 6, and 7, install a vapor retarder on the warm side of the insulation.
- Refer to Section 1-17 for types of precast joints.
- Refer to Section 1-13 for allowable tolerances of precast concrete panels.

Materials

07 21 13 BUILDING BOARD INSULATION

Materials

Expanded or extruded polystyrene, ASTM C578.

Extruded polystyrene may be used in climate zones 1 through 7 (see Fig. 5-5.2) because its lower permeance is better for colder climates.

Expanded polystyrene may be used in climate zones 1 through 5.

Thickness as required for the desired R-value.

Execution

Install in accordance with manufacturers' instructions.

Apply with adhesive, stick pins, or mechanical fasteners.

Boards must be tightly butted, with cracks over $1/16$ in. (1.6 mm) filled with slivers of insulation.

3-8 STRUCTURAL STEEL SUPPORT FOR CURTAIN WALLS

Description

There are several methods for attaching aluminum curtain walls to multistory structural frames; Fig. 3–8 shows one of the most common. It illustrates the use of a grid, or stick, system where the vertical supporting mullions are attached to the building structure first and then the horizontal mullions, spandrel panels, glazing panels, and finishing pieces are attached to the vertical mullions.

Limitations of Use

- This detail does not show the specifics of the curtain wall itself. These vary with individual manufacturers and the specific requirements of the project. Refer to Section 6-11 for more information.
- Anchors and connections must be designed by a structural engineer and approved by the curtain wall manufacturer to transfer all loads imposed on the curtain wall to the structural frame.

Detailing Considerations

- The detail should provide for adjustability in three directions.
- Locate the connection above the floor level for easy accessibility.
- Clearances must be provided for working space access.
- Anchors should be attached to the steel framework by welding in preference to bolted connections.
- Provisions must be made for expansion and contraction of the curtain wall due to temperature changes as well as other differential movements between the curtain wall and the structural frame.

Figure 3-8 Structural steel support for curtain walls 05 12 23.5

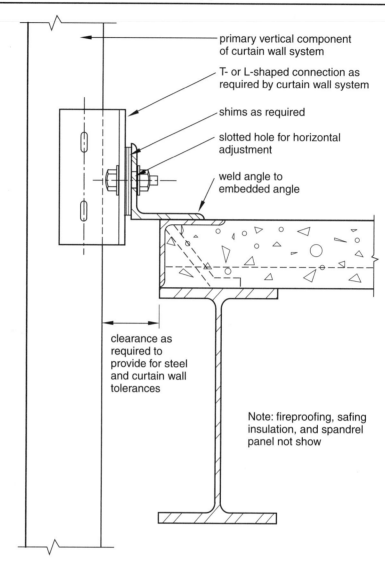

primary vertical component
of curtain wall system

T- or L-shaped connection as
required by curtain wall system

shims as required

slotted hole for horizontal
adjustment

weld angle to
embedded angle

clearance as
required to
provide for steel
and curtain wall
tolerances

Note: fireproofing, safing
insulation, and spandrel
panel not show

Coordination Required

- Refer to Sections 6–11 and 6–12 for additional curtain wall detailing requirements.
- Connection should allow for installation of safing insulation between the edge of the slab and the spandrel panel.

Likely Failure Points

- Anchor failure caused by excessive shimming or excessively long bolted connections
- Anchor failure caused by substituting anchors not originally designed in order to make up for mislocated embedded items in a concrete structure or misaligned anchors attached to a steel structure

Figure 3-9 Open web steel joists 05 21 19

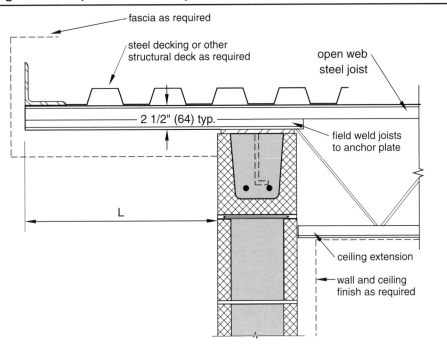

fascia as required

steel decking or other
structural deck as required

open web
steel joist

2 1/2" (64) typ.

field weld joists
to anchor plate

L

ceiling extension

wall and ceiling
finish as required

3-9 OPEN WEB STEEL JOISTS

Description

Open web steel joists provide an efficient way to span medium to long distances. They are lightweight and easy to erect, and the open webbing allows ductwork and other building services to be run through the joists. In addition, the top chord can be sloped to provide roof drainage if required. Open web steel joists can be supported by steel beams, masonry walls (as shown in Fig. 3-9), concrete walls, or heavier open web joist girders.

There are three standard series of open web joists—the K-series, the LH-series, and the DLH-series—with properties as summarized in Table 3-1.

In addition to standard joists, composite joists are available. A composite open web steel joist provides a shear stud connection between the joist's top chord and its overlying concrete slab, allowing the joist and concrete to act together as an integral unit.

Table 3-1	Open Web Steel Joists Series		
Series	Name	Span limits, ft (mm)	Depths in series, in., (mm)
K	Standard	8–60 (2438–18268)	8–30 (203–762)
LH	Long Span	25–80 (7620–24384)	18–48 (457–1219)
DLH	Deep Long Span	89–120 (27127–36576)	52–72 (1321–1829)
Source: Steel Joist Institute.			

Limitations of Use

- All sizing, spacing, and specifications for steel joists must be verified with a structural engineer.

Detailing Considerations

- Floor joists are usually spaced 2 ft (610 mm) on center and roof joists 4 ft (1220 mm) on center, although any spacing can be used to satisfy the structural requirements of the project.
- Positive drainage for roofs should be provided by sloping the joist or by specifying a sloping top chord.
- Extended ends can be provided with the K-series joists, as shown in Fig. 3-9. Each manufacturer supplies a slightly different type of extension, so allowable loads and the length of the extended end will vary. However, the allowable uniform load per linear foot of extended end and the unsupported length, L, may range from 350 lb (1557 N) for a 2 ft-6 in. (762 mm) length to 168 lbf (747 N) for a 5 ft-6 in. (1676 mm) length, depending on the type of end used.
- If longer cantilevered ends are required, the truss may be extended at its full depth.
- Ceiling extensions, as shown in the detail, are also available for supporting a ceiling directly.
- K-series joists must bear a minimum of $2^1/_2$ in. (64 mm) on steel beams and steel bearing plates anchored to masonry or concrete, but it is recommended that the joist bear a minimum of 4 in. (102 mm) over masonry or concrete. LH- and DLH-series joists must bear a minimum of 4 in. (102 mm) on steel beams and steel bearing plates anchored to masonry or concrete, but it is recommended that these joists bear a minimum of 6 in. (152 mm) over masonry or concrete.

3-10   STAIR LAYOUT

Description

Figure 3-10 shows critical working points for designing a simple return stair in such a way that the center railing returns without an awkward jog. Figures 3-11, 3-12, and 3-13 show more detailed views of the base, landing, and upper level. Figures 3-10 through 3-13 can be used to design a stair of any material or with any construction method.

Limitations of Use

- This detail does not indicate the structural requirements of the stair or the specific construction requirements.
- Refer to the *International Building Code* or the local applicable code for details of stairway construction.

Detailing Considerations

- In order to provide for a smooth transition of the handrail at the landing, the upper flight must lead the lower flight by one tread.

Figure 3-10 Stair layout 05 51 00.1

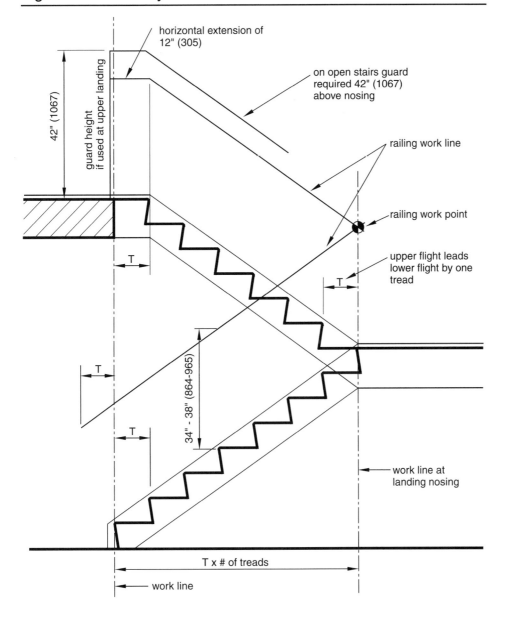

- The railing work line represents the top of the railing.
- For multiple floor stair layouts, the upper flight in this detail should be increased by two risers. Then the stairway can be stacked as many times as required, and the return flight will always lead the lower flight by one tread.

Coordination Required

- The stairway openings should be based on the lower flight of stairs.
- The size, shape, and design of the handrail may affect the exact location of the switch-back. If the railing work point does not fall on the vertical work line, the railing will not be exactly parallel with the nosing work line or the other components of the stairway.

3-11 STAIR LAYOUT AT BASE

Description

Figure 3-11 shows a more detailed view of the overall stair layout shown in Fig. 3-10. The vertical work line is established at the nosing of the first riser. The railing work point and the lower stringer work point should also fall on this vertical work line if all the components of the stair are to be parallel.

Limitations of Use

- This detail only illustrates the geometry of laying out any type of stair. Refer to Section 3-14 for construction details of one type of steel stair.
- Sizes of treads and risers are based on code requirements for commercial stairs. Residential stairs have different minimum and maximum dimensions.

Detailing Considerations

- The railing height must be between 34 in. and 38 in. (864 mm to 965 mm) above the nosing to be in compliance with the requirements of the *International Building Code*.

Figure 3-11 Stair layout at base 05 51 00.2

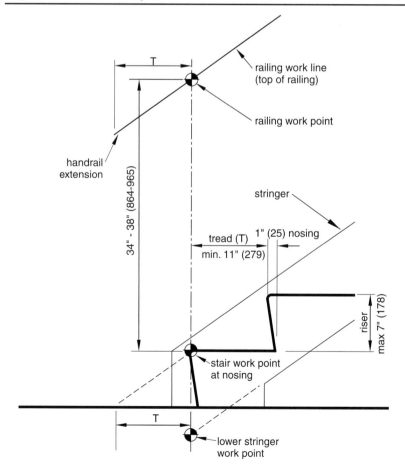

- The stair members such as the nosing line, stringer line, and handrail will be parallel if their work points fall on the vertical work lines.
- In order to comply with barrier-free standards, the minimum tread dimension is 11 in. (279 mm) and the maximum riser dimension is 7 in. (178 mm). However, shorter treads and higher risers are permitted in residential construction.
- Barrier-free standards require that the undersides of nosings not be abrupt. They must be sloped, as shown in this detail, or have sloped transitions (no more than 60 degrees) from the vertical riser to the protruding nosing.
- Building codes and barrier-free standards require that the handrail at the bottom of a stairway extend at least the width of one tread. The end of the handrail must return to the railing post or the wall.
- The relationship between the riser height and the tread width is important for a comfortable, safe stairway. Generally, the required riser height is determined by dividing the floor-to-floor height by an even number such that the riser does not exceed 7 in. (178 mm). Then the tread is determined by one of several formulas. One formula that can be used is $2R + T = 25$, where R is the riser height in in. (mm) and T is the tread depth in in. (mm).

3-12 STAIR LAYOUT AT LANDING

Description

Figure 3-12 shows a more detailed view of the overall stair layout shown in Fig. 3-10. The vertical work line is established at the nosing of the top riser, just as with the base detail. The railing work point and the lower and upper stringer work points should also fall on this vertical work line if all the components of the stair are to be parallel. One of the critical elements of this detail is the one-tread lead of the first riser of the upper flight. If this is done, the railing can make a smooth switchback without an awkward rise at the turn.

Detailing Considerations

- In order to comply with building code and accessibility standards, the handrail at a switchback must be continuous.
- The stair members such as the nosing line, stringer line, and handrail will be parallel if their work points fall on the vertical work lines.
- The exact elevation of the upper and lower stringer work points will vary, depending on the type of stringer used and the exact construction details of the stringer.
- For L-shaped stairways, the first riser of the upper flight should also begin one tread distance from the nosing of the last riser of the lower flight in order to make a smooth transition of the handrail.

Coordination Required

- For barrier-free requirements refer to Section 3-11.

Figure 3-12 Stair layout at landing 05 51 00.3

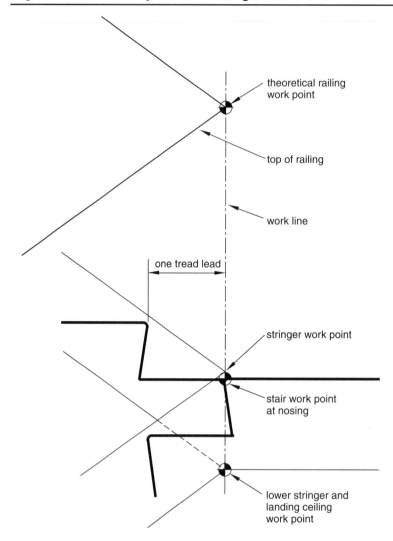

3-13 STAIR LAYOUT AT TOP LANDING

Description

Figure 3-13 shows a more detailed view of the overall stair layout shown in Fig. 3-10. The vertical work line is established at the nosing of the last riser. The railing work point and the lower stringer work point should also fall on this vertical work line if all the components of the stair are to be parallel.

Detailing Considerations

- In this detail, the edge of the landing structure is shown schematically to fall on the work line of the bottom nosing. However, the edge of the landing may fall

Figure 3-13 Stair layout at top landing 05 51 00.4

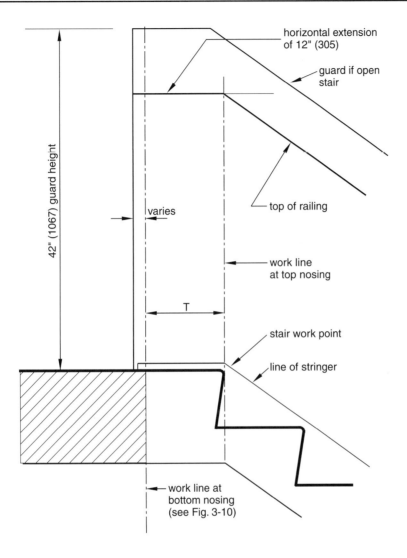

along the last riser of the flight, which makes it easier to detail the structure of the landing.

- Building code and barrier-free standards require that the handrail at the top of a stairway extend at least 12 in. (305 mm) beyond the top riser and that it be parallel to the floor. The end of the handrail must return to the railing post or the wall.
- Handrails must be between $1\frac{1}{4}$ in. and $1\frac{1}{2}$ in. (32 mm and 38 mm) across, with the inside edge at least $1\frac{1}{2}$ in. (38 mm) from the wall or other obstruction.
- The stair members such as the nosing line, stringer line, and handrail will be parallel if their work points fall on the vertical work lines.

Coordination Required

- For barrier-free requirements refer to Section 3-11.

3-14   METAL STAIRS

Description

Metal stairs constructed of preformed steel risers and treads are one of the most common types of stairway construction. See Fig. 3-14. In most cases, the tread is filled in with $1\frac{1}{2}$ in. (38 mm) to 2 in. (51 mm) of concrete. If other finish materials are required, they are applied over this basic construction. Utility stairs and some exit stairs are constructed with a deformed metal plate as the tread.

Limitations of Use

- Railings and balusters are not shown in this detail.
- The underside of the stair is not finished in this detail. However, it may be finished with gypsum wallboard on steel framing, plaster on lath, or other types of decorative surfaces if permitted by the applicable building code.

Detailing Considerations

- Stringers are typically constructed of channel sections, with the toe of the channel facing away from the stair.

Figure 3-14 Metal stairs 05 51 13

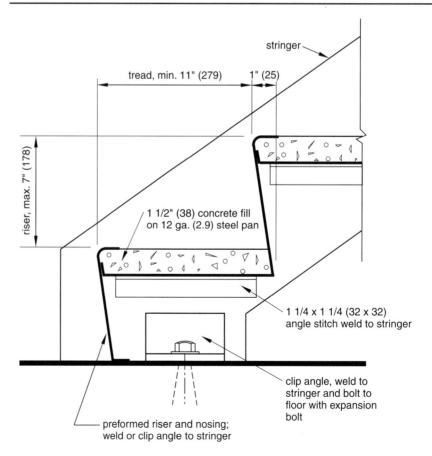

- Nonslip nosings can be substituted for nosings integral with the riser.
- In order to conform to barrier-free design standards, the radius of the nosing cannot exceed $\frac{1}{2}$ in. (13 mm).
- Barrier-free standards require that the underside of nosings not be abrupt. They must be sloped, as shown in this detail, or have sloped transitions (no more than 60 degrees) from the vertical riser to the protruding nosing.
- Balusters must be spaced with a maximum clear dimension of 4 in. (102 mm).

Coordination Required

- Refer to Section 3-10 for barrier-free requirements.
- Verify requirements for noncombustible finishes in exit stairways and other locations.

3-15 ORNAMENTAL METAL/GLASS GUARD

Description

There are many ways to detail guards and corresponding stairway handrails. Figure 3-15 shows the use of a tempered glass baluster capped with an ornamental metal rail. The glass is held

Figure 3-15 Ornamental metal/glass guard 05 52 13

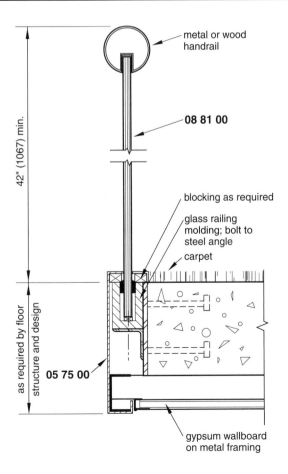

metal or wood handrail

08 81 00

42" (1067) min.

as required by floor structure and design

blocking as required

glass railing molding; bolt to steel angle

carpet

05 75 00

gypsum wallboard on metal framing

in place with a metal shoe that is secured to the structure with bolts. These types of railing systems are made by several manufacturers, but they each use similar construction details.

Detailing Considerations

- Most building codes require a minimum guard height of 42 in. (1,067 mm).
- The metal shoe holding the glass may be mounted on top of the floor, attached to the edge of the floor structure, or fastened to a separate structural support, as shown in Fig. 3-15.
- The support system must be designed to withstand a lateral force as designated by the applicable building code. In most cases, the railing must be capable of supporting a lateral load of 50 plf (0.73 kN/m) along the top rail or a concentrated lateral load of 200 lb (0.89 kN) applied in any direction.
- If open guardrails are used, the clear opening between railings must be such that a 4 in. (102 mm) sphere cannot pass through or as required by the applicable building code.
- Wood handrails are available in addition to ornamental metal rails.
- This detail may be adapted to serve as a stairway guard if a handrail is attached to the glass at a height between 34 in. and 38 in. (864 mm to 965 mm) above the nosing, with the size of the handrail meeting the requirements of building and accessibility codes.

Coordination Required

- For some openings, a draftstop below the floor line may be required.

Materials

05 75 00 ORNAMENTAL METAL FASCIA

Common ornamental metals include the following:

18, 20, or 22 gage (0.0500 in., 0.0375 in., or 0.0312 in. [1.270 mm, 0.953 mm, or 0.792 mm]) type 304 or 430 stainless steel with #3, #4, #6, #7, or #8 finish.

Copper alloys 110 (copper), 220 (commercial bronze), 230, 280 (Muntz metal), or 385 (architectural bronze) with a buffed specular or fine satin directional textured finish.

08 81 00 GLASS BALUSTER

$1/2$ in. or $3/4$ in. (13 mm or 19 mm) tempered or laminated glass.

Provide $1/4$ in. (6 mm) of space between adjacent panels.

Verify the maximum lengths of glass panels with the manufacturer.

The railing must span at least three panels of glass.

3-16   EXPANSION JOINT AT FLOOR AND WALL

Description

Expansion joints of the types shown in Fig. 3-16 are used to provide for major building movements and for dividing sections of very large buildings into independent structural

Figure 3-16 Expansion joint at floor and wall 05 54 00.1

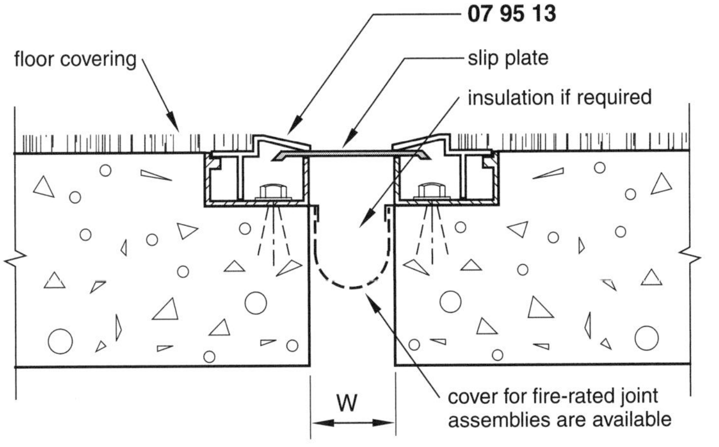

07 95 13

floor covering

slip plate

insulation if required

W

cover for fire-rated joint assemblies are available

(a) floor joint

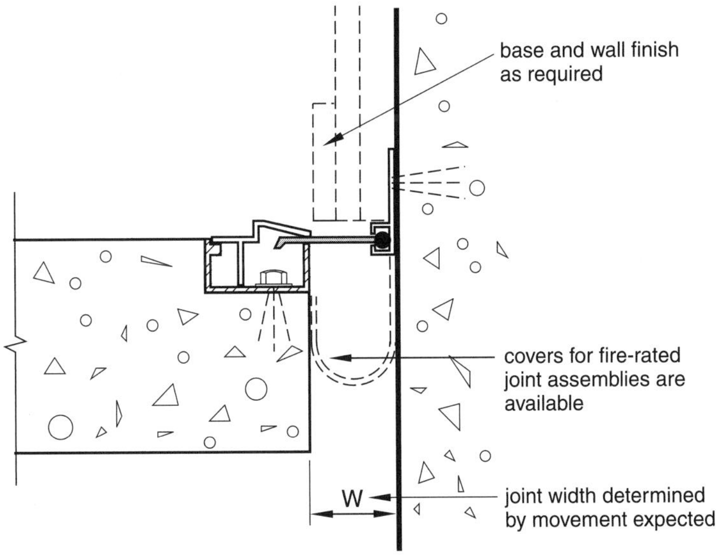

base and wall finish as required

covers for fire-rated joint assemblies are available

W

joint width determined by movement expected

(b) wall joint

units. Figure 3-16(a) shows a diagrammatic representation of a floor-to-floor expansion joint; however, many manufacturers offer a variety of products to satisfy specific requirements. Figure 3-16(b) illustrates a common type of floor-to-wall expansion joint.

Limitations of Use

- Figure 3-16(a) shows a unit capable of horizontal movement only. However, expansion joints are available for both horizontal and vertical movement.
- This detail is not applicable to seismic joints. Special assemblies are available for seismic use, but they require a specific engineering study to determine what type and amount of movement must be accommodated.
- Similar ceiling and wall assemblies are not shown but are also required to provide a complete through-building joint.

Detailing Considerations

- Surface-mounted joint assemblies are also available.
- Recessed types, as shown in Fig. 3-16, permit blockouts to be made during the concrete pour with the joint assemblies installed later. Other types are available that can be cast directly into the concrete.
- Covers that fit below the joint are available for fire-rated assemblies.
- For wet areas, integral gutters may be placed below the joint cover.
- For other types of concrete joints, refer to Figs. 1-5, 1-6, and 1-7.
- In high-traffic areas, use abrasive or nonslip finishes.

Coordination Required

- Select joint assemblies compatible with the finish material to be used.
- Verify expected joint movement with a structural engineer.

Likely Failure Points

- Crushing of the cover when the joint width is undersized for the actual building movement
- Damage to the structure or finish materials due to noncontinuous joints through the entire building

Materials

07 95 13 EXPANSION JOINT COVER ASSEMBLIES

Assemblies are available to accommodate joint widths, W, from 1 in. to 8 in. (25 mm to 200 mm).

Expansion joints are available in a variety of finishes. Typical finishes include anodized aluminum, stainless steel, and bronze.

Assemblies are available for tile and carpet for flush installation with concrete or other materials.

CHAPTER 4

WOOD DETAILS

4-1 PLATFORM FRAMING AT FOUNDATION

Description

Platform framing, as shown in Fig. 4-1, is a standard method of wood construction for residential and small commercial structures. It allows the floor construction to provide a surface for laying out the wall framing, which is then tilted into place. Platform framing may be constructed over a basement or a crawl space, and the framing may be set on a sill plate over a full-width foundation wall or a stepped foundation, as shown in Fig. 4-2.

Limitations of Use

- This detail does not show finish flooring.
- This detail does not include special framing for seismic loads.
- This detail does not show dampproofing or drainage material outside of the foundation wall. Local conditions must be studied to develop requirements for foundation moisture control. See Section 5-1 for more information.

Detailing Considerations

- Two inch × 6 in. (38 mm × 140 mm) studs may be used in lieu of 2 in. × 4 in. (38 mm × 89 mm) studs in cold climates to allow greater depth for thicker insulation.
- Concrete foundation walls must be a minimum of 6 in. (152 mm) wide for one-story buildings and 8 in. (203 mm) wide for two-story buildings or as specified by the local building code.
- Joists closer than 18 in. (457 mm) or wood girders closer than 12 in. (305 mm) to exposed ground in crawl spaces must be treated wood or wood with natural resistance to decay.
- Bridging should be installed between end supports if the span exceeds 8 ft (2440 mm). Maximum spacing of bridging is 8 ft 0 in. (2440 mm) on center.
- If the floor is above a crawl space, insulation may be placed between the joists.

Figure 4-1 Platform framing at foundation 06 11 00.1

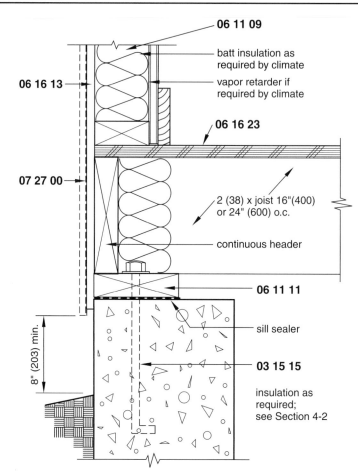

- 06 11 09
- batt insulation as required by climate
- vapor retarder if required by climate
- 06 16 13
- 06 16 23
- 07 27 00
- 2 (38) x joist 16"(400) or 24" (600) o.c.
- continuous header
- 06 11 11
- sill sealer
- 8" (203) min.
- 03 15 15
- insulation as required; see Section 4-2

Coordination Required

- Refer to Section 2-8 for brick veneer construction.
- If a center girder bearing is used, its detail should be coordinated with the foundation wall framing to equalize the amount of shrinkage at both ends of the joist bearing.
- Termite protection is required in some locations.
- Foundation insulation is required in cold climates. See Section 5-4.
- Crawl spaces must be ventilated with openings having a net area of at least 1 in.^{2} (645 mm^2) for each 150 ft^2 (13.9 m^2) of under-floor area or as required by the local code.
- A vapor barrier may be required on the warm side of the insulation in cold climates. This may be a separate sheet of polyethylene film or it may be integral with the insulation. In hot, humid climates, air-conditioned buildings may require that the vapor barrier be placed on the outside of the insulation.
- Verify required draft stops in all concealed openings between floors and between floors and the roof and other areas near stairs, soffits, ducts, and similar openings.
- Conditioned basements must be provided with insulation and vapor retarders as required by the climate and local codes.

Materials

03 15 15 ANCHOR BOLT

Minimum $\frac{1}{2}$ in. (13 mm) diameter bolts embedded at least 7 in. (178 mm) in concrete.

Maximum spacing of 6 ft 0 in. (1829 mm) with a minimum of two bolts per sill piece, with one bolt located within 12 in. (305 mm) of either end of each piece.

06 11 09 WOOD STUD

Minimum 2 in. × 4 in. (38 mm × 89 mm) nominal size.

Spacing 16 in. (406 mm) or 24 in. (610 mm) on center.

06 11 11 SILL PLATE

Minimum 2 in. × 4 in. (38 mm × 89 mm) nominal size.

Treated wood or foundation redwood.

Place sill plate over sill sealer.

06 16 13 INSULATING SHEATHING

Minimum $\frac{1}{2}$ in. (13 mm) thickness. Thicker insulation may be used as required by the climate.

Standard plywood or particleboard sheathing may be substituted with building paper over.

If insulating sheathing is used, provide plywood at corners or use other suitable lateral bracing. See Sections 4-4, 4-5, and 4-6 for more information on lateral bracing.

If insulating or asphalt-impregnated sheathing is used, an air infiltration barrier may be applied over the sheathing.

06 16 23 FLOOR SHEATHING

Plywood or particleboard with an underlayment and a finish floor over or a combination subfloor-underlayment.

Plywood: APA-rated sheathing. Various span ratings are available, but normally a 32/16 span-rated plywood $\frac{1}{2}$ in. (13 mm) thick may be used over joists spaced 16 in. (406 mm) on center.

Particleboard: $\frac{1}{2}$ in. (13 mm) 2-M-W grade may be used over joists spaced 16 in. (406) on center. Three-quarter inch (19 mm) particleboard is used over joists 24 in. (610 mm) on center.

07 27 00 AIR BARRIER

Nonwoven, spun-bonded olefin sheet membrane, liquid-applied membrane, or self-adhering membrane, ASTM E1677.

Vapor-permeable or vapor-impermeable as required by local climatic conditions.

Install according to manufacturer's instructions.

Refer to Section 5-5 for more information.

Figure 4-2 Platform framing at stepped foundation 06 11 00.2

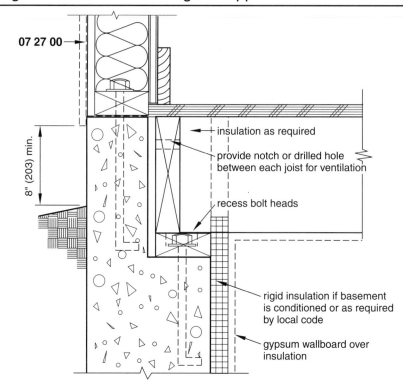

8" (203) min.

07 27 00

insulation as required

provide notch or drilled hole
between each joist for ventilation

recess bolt heads

rigid insulation if basement
is conditioned or as required
by local code

gypsum wallboard over
insulation

4-2   PLATFORM FRAMING AT STEPPED FOUNDATION

Description

Figure 4–2 illustrates a method to keep the finish floor level of the building close to the grade level. Although this detail shows grade at the foundation, a concrete porch or patio may be placed against the stepped foundation to provide a same-level entry from exterior to interior. The detail may be modified to align the top of the foundation with the top of the floor sheathing.

Limitations of Use

- This detail does not show finish flooring.
- This detail does not include special framing for seismic loads.
- This detail does not show dampproofing or drainage material outside of the foundation wall. Local conditions must be studied to develop requirements for foundation moisture control. See Section 5–1 for more information.

Detailing Considerations

- The space behind the rim joists should be ventilated by notching the rim joists or drilling holes between each joist.
- Insulation should be installed between each joist.

- If required, hold down clamps or straps may be used, as shown in Fig. 4-4.
- Conditioned basements need insulation and vapor retarders as required by the climate. Rigid insulation may be placed on the inside of the wall and extended into the joist space or stopped at the ceiling finish with batt insulation used between joists.

Coordination Required

- In unconditioned basements or crawl spaces, the floor must be insulated.
- In unconditioned basements or crawl spaces, all heating pipes and air ducts should be insulated and all penetrations and gaps into the first floor must be sealed.

Materials

See Section 4-1 for material requirements.

4-3 PLATFORM FRAMING AT ROOF

Description

Figure 4-3 is a continuation of Fig. 4-1 and illustrates a typical framing condition at the ceiling and roofline. The eaves may extend the desired distance from the face of the building.

Figure 4-3 Platform framing at roof 06 11 00.3

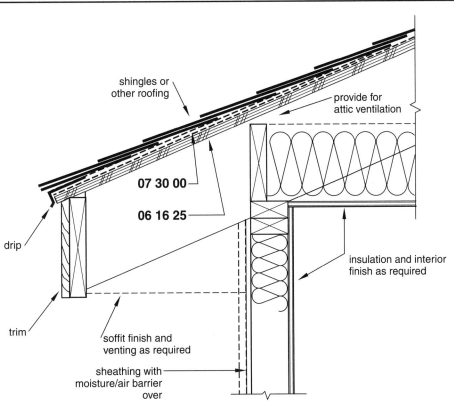

Limitations of Use

- This detail does not include special framing for seismic loads.
- In cold climates, a cold roof may be detailed that provides air circulation below the roof sheathing and roofing separate from the insulated attic.

Detailing Considerations

- The minimum slope of the roof depends on the type of roofing material used.
- For various roof finishes refer to Sections 5-9, 5-10, and 5-11.
- Prefabricated roof trusses may be used in lieu of standard joist and rafter framing.

Coordination Required

- The attic should be ventilated, either with edge venting, as shown in this detail, with gable vents, or with both.
- A vapor barrier may be required on the warm side of the insulation in cold climates. This may be a separate sheet of polyethylene film or it may be integral with the insulation. In hot, humid climates, air-conditioned buildings may require the vapor barrier to be placed on the outside of the insulation.
- Verify required draft stops in all concealed openings between floors and between floors and the roof and other areas near stairs, soffits, ducts, and similar openings. Large attic spaces may need to be subdivided into smaller areas as required by the local code.

Materials

06 16 25 ROOF SHEATHING

Plywood: APA-rated sheathing. Various span rating are available, but normally a 24/0 span rated plywood 3/8 in. (10 mm) thick may be used over rafters spaced 16 in. (406 mm) or 24 in. (610 mm) on center. The 16 in. center spacing will carry a heavier load. If required, thicker panels may be used. Verify loading conditions and rafter spacing based on the span rating and panel thickness.

Particleboard: 3/8 in. (10 mm) 2-M-W grade may be used over rafters spaced 16 in. (406 mm) on center if blocking or edge clips are used. One-half inch (13 mm) particleboard is used over joists 24 in. (610 mm) on center or 16 in. (406 mm) on center if blocking or edge clips are not used.

Bonded with exterior glue.

07 30 30 UNDERLAYMENT

Fifteen pound nonperforated asphalt-saturated felt, ASTM D 4869, or cold-applied, self-adhering membrane, ASTM D 1970.

Apply asphalt-saturated felt horizontally, lapping edges a minimum of 2 in. (50 mm) and ends 4 in. (100 mm).

Apply self-adhering membrane according to the manufacturer's directions.

Figure 4-4 Multistory framing at foundation 06 11 00.4

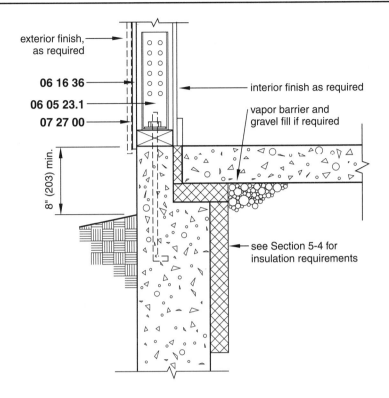

exterior finish,
as required

06 16 36

06 05 23.1

07 27 00

8" (203) min.

interior finish as required

vapor barrier and
gravel fill if required

see Section 5-4 for
insulation requirements

4-4   MULTISTORY FRAMING AT FOUNDATION

Description

When wood-framed Type V construction is used for multistory construction, shear, uplift, and overturning forces are greater than those for simple one-story frame buildings and the corresponding detailing can be more complex. Building codes require that a defined, continuous load path be created that is capable of transferring the loads to the foundation. The exact methods of structuring wood frame buildings vary with the loads imposed and the materials and products used to resist them. Figure 4-4, as well as Figs. 4-5 and 4-6, illustrate one method for detailing multistory wood framed buildings to resist uplift and overturning forces.

Limitations of Use

- Although the detailing for seismic restraint is similar to that shown in Fig. 4-4, a structural engineer should be consulted for exact requirements based on the seismic zone and the occupancy type of the building.
- This detail does not illustrate other methods of resisting shear loads.

Detailing Considerations

- Various products are available to transfer loads. Verify with the manufacturer the exact products, sizes, and installation methods required to resist the loads imposed on the structure. One common alternative is a steel strap anchored to the foundation, extending over the sheathing, and fastened to the studs. Consult individual manufacturers for available products.

- Anchor bolts should be ⅝ in. (16 mm) in diameter.
- In lieu of the individual hold-down fastener shown, a continuous rod may be used that extends from the foundation to the top plate of the upper story. When these products are used, a shrinkage compensation device is included to compensate for accumulated wood shrinkage, which can otherwise cause gaps to form between the hold-down and the structure.
- Provide a vapor retarder on the warm side of the insulation, if required by the climate and the building usage. See Section 5-5 for more information.

Coordination Required

- Sheathing type and fastener spacing must be specified to resist shear forces.
- Verify the type and size of fasteners used with the manufacturer.
- Certain types of pressure-treated wood used for the sill plate may not be compatible with some connector finishes. Verify requirements with the manufacturer.

Likely Failure Points

- Failure of individual shear panels and studs or overall structural failure when continuous tie-down systems are not connected to each story

Materials

06 05 23.1 HOLD-DOWN

Connector of the type, size, and finish as recommended by the manufacturer to resist the loads imposed.

Finish galvanized, ASTM A153, or stainless steel type 304 or 316.

Install according to the manufacturer's recommendations.

06 16 36 WOOD PANEL PRODUCT SHEATHING

APA-rated plywood sheathing, ½ in. (13 mm), exterior grade or as required by structural requirements and load analysis or oriented strand board APA-rated sheathing.

Installations requirements determined by the local code.

Install with the long dimension parallel to the studs.

Nails spaced 6 in. (152 mm) on center and 3 in. (76 mm) on center at edges for structural sheathing.

07 27 00 AIR BARRIER

Nonwoven, spun-bonded olefin sheet membrane, liquid-applied membrane, or self-adhering membrane, ASTM E1677.

Vapor-permeable or vapor-impermeable as required by local climatic conditions.

Install according to the manufacturer's instructions.

Refer to Section 5-5 for more information.

4-5 MULTISTORY FRAMING AT FLOOR LINE

Description

Figure 4-5 is a continuation of Fig. 4-4, showing a common way to provide a floor-to-floor hold-down system in multistory wood frame construction. As mentioned in Section 4-4, straps located on the outside of the sheathing may also be used that tie studs from one floor to the floor above. Alternately, a continuous tie-down rod may be run from the foundation to the roofline. Continuous tie-down systems can resist overturning forces of over 40,000 lb (177,929 N).

Limitations of Use

- This method should be used for structures with three stories or less.

Figure 4-5 Multistory framing at floor line 06 11 00.5

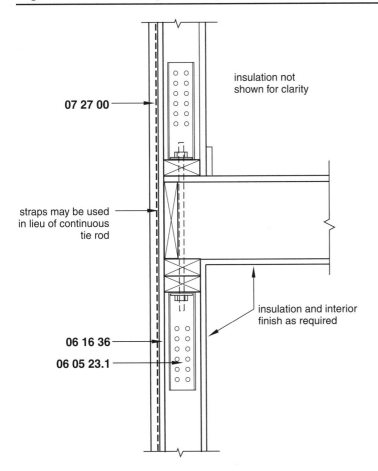

Detailing Considerations

- Straps attached to the upper- and lower-story studs through the sheathing may be used when the overturning force does not exceed 4000 to 5000 lb (17, 793 N to 22,241 N).
- If a continuous tie rod is used, it must be attached to every floor.

Materials

See Section 4-4 for material requirements.

4-6 MULTISTORY FRAMING AT ROOF

Description

Figure 4-6 shows the detailing condition at the roofline for the multistory wood frame construction also shown in Figs. 4-4 and 4-5. Straps or a continuous tie-down rod may also be used, depending on the overturning and uplift forces involved.

Figure 4-6 Multistory framing at roof 06 11 00.6

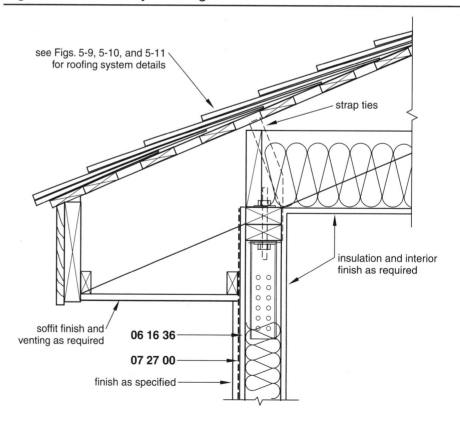

see Figs. 5-9, 5-10, and 5-11 for roofing system details

strap ties

insulation and interior finish as required

soffit finish and venting as required

06 16 36

07 27 00

finish as specified

Detailing Considerations

- When separate connectors are used for stud-to-top-plate and top-plate-to-roof-structure connections, they should be located on the same side of the top plate.

Likely Failure Points

- Reduction in connection capacity if stud-to-top-plate and top-plate-to-roof hardware are located on opposite sides of the top plate

Materials

See Section 4-4 for material requirements.

4-7 STRUCTURAL INSULATED PANEL AT FOUNDATION

Description

Structural insulated panels (SIPs) are high-performance composite building panels consisting of a core of rigid foam insulation, typically expanded polystyrene, sandwiched between two structural skins of oriented strand board (OSB). They are custom-designed for each job and built in a factory to exacting specifications. SIPs are used for walls, floors, and roofs in residential and commercial buildings. SIPs speed construction and offer high R-values without thermal bridging. Once set in place and anchored, the OSB surfaces are ready for interior and exterior finishing. They are available in nominal thicknesses of 4 in. and 6 in. (102 mm and 152 mm) for walls and 8 in., 10 in., and 12 in. (203 mm, 254 mm, and 305 mm) for floors and roofs. The actual thickness of the insulation is generally $3^1/_2$ in. (89 mm) or $5^1/_2$ in. (140 mm) to match standard widths of wood framing.

The detail shown in Fig. 4-7 illustrates one method of joining an SIP to a foundation. Wall panels may also be placed on SIP floor panels supported by sill plates or the SIP wall panel may be supported on a subfloor placed on standard floor joists, as with conventional platform framing. However, by detailing as shown in Fig. 4-7, the full insulation properties of the panel are utilized by carrying it close to the foundation. Additional batt or rigid insulation can be used to complete the thermal envelope.

Limitations of Use

- SIP construction varies slightly with each manufacturer. Verify the manufacturer's standard details and review shop drawings as required.
- Interior surfaces must be protected with a thermal barrier, such as gypsum wallboard, with a minimum thickness of $1/_2$ in. (13 mm).

Detailing Considerations

- Verify the manufacturer's limitations on the maximum size for panels. Typical sizes range from 4 ft by 8 ft (1220 mm by 2440 mm) to 8 ft by 24 ft (2440 by 7315 mm).

Figure 4-7 Structural insulated panel at foundation 06 12 00.1

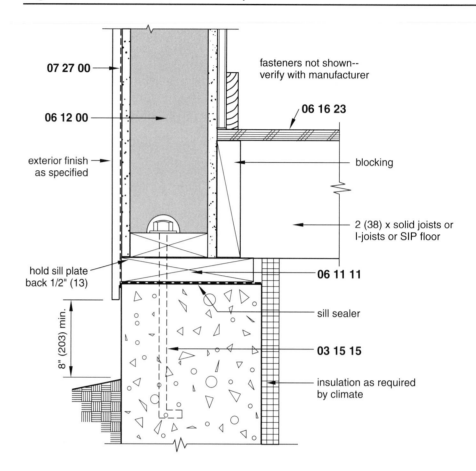

- The manufacturer's standard fasteners must be used.
- Continuous beads of sealant must be applied at junctions of foam and wood blocking and at other areas as recommended by the manufacturer.
- Although there are no industry standards for manufacturing tolerances, many manufacturers work with a tolerance from ± 1/8 in. (3 mm) to ± 1/4 in. (6 mm) for size, placement, and vertical and horizontal alignment of erected panels.
- Panels are typically precored for installation of electrical services. Verify this with the manufacturer.

Coordination Required

- Verify other construction details with the manufacturer.
- A suitable air/moisture barrier must be installed on the outer surface of the panels.
- Install a vapor retarder on the warm side of the insulation if required by the climate and the building use. See Section 5-5 for more information.
- All exterior finishes and roofing must comply with applicable codes.
- Verify that the panels may be used as shear walls in the seismic design category. Generally, they are acceptable in categories A, B, or C.

Materials

03 15 15 ANCHOR BOLT

Minimum 1/2 in. (13 mm) diameter bolts embedded at least 7 in. (178 mm) in concrete or as determined by the structural engineer or manufacturer.

Maximum spacing of 6 ft 0 in. (1829 mm) with a minimum of two bolts per sill piece, with one bolt located within 12 in. (305 mm) of either end of each piece.

06 11 11 SILL PLATE

Minimum 2 in. (38 mm) nominal thickness. Width as required for the SIP and joist bearing.

Treated wood or foundation redwood.

Place the sill plate over the sill sealer.

Sill plate for attachment of panels should be held back 1/2 in. (13 mm) for full bearing of the outside skin of the SIP.

06 12 00 STRUCTURAL INSULATED PANEL

Manufacturer's standard insulation panel, thickness as required for structure and insulation values. It should be treated for insect resistance.

Panels should be in compliance with ICC ES AC04, *Acceptance Criteria for Sandwich Panels.*

Polystyrene insulation, ASTM C578.

OSB, APA rated, conforming to structural I, with exposure 1 rating; DOC PS-2 span rating of 24/16 or greater.

Install in accordance with the manufacturer's instructions.

06 16 23 FLOOR SHEATHING

Plywood or particleboard with an underlayment and a finish floor over or a combination subfloor-underlayment.

Plywood: APA-rated sheathing. Various span ratings are available, but normally a 32/16 span-rated plywood 1/2 in. (13 mm) thick may be used over joists spaced 16 in. (406 mm) on center.

Particleboard: 1/2 in. (13 mm) 2-M-W grade may be used over joists spaced 16 in. (406) on center. Three-quarter inch (19 mm) particleboard is used over joists 24 in. (610 mm) on center.

07 27 00 AIR BARRIER

Nonwoven, spun-bonded olefin sheet membrane, liquid-applied membrane, or self-adhering membrane, ASTM E1677.

Vapor-permeable or vapor-impermeable as required by local climatic conditions.

Install according to the manufacturer's instructions.

Refer to Section 5-5 for more information.

Figure 4-8 Structural insulated panel at roof 06 12 00.2

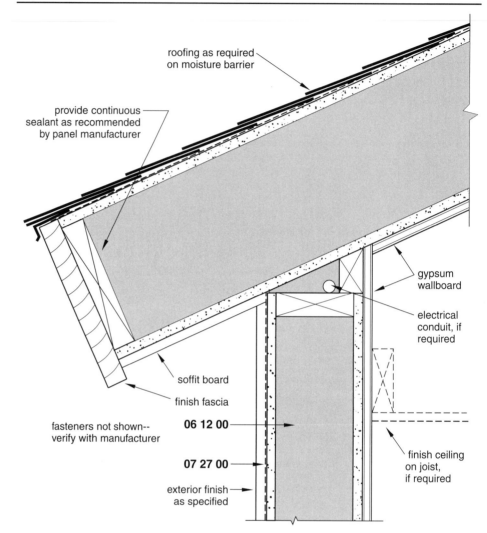

roofing as required
on moisture barrier

provide continuous
sealant as recommended
by panel manufacturer

gypsum
wallboard

electrical
conduit, if
required

soffit board

finish fascia

fasteners not shown--
verify with manufacturer

06 12 00

07 27 00

finish ceiling
on joist,
if required

exterior finish
as specified

4-8 STRUCTURAL INSULATED PANEL AT ROOF

Description

Figure 4-8 is a continuation of Fig. 4-7 showing one possible framing method at the roof. In addition to the construction shown in Fig. 4-8, the SIP roof panel may stop at the outside face of the wall panel, and the eaves and soffit may be constructed with conventional stick framing. The eave may also be constructed as an extension of the roof panel with a horizontal soffit framed conventionally.

Limitations of Use

- SIP construction varies slightly with each manufacturer. Verify the manufacturer's standard details and review shop drawings as required.

- An ice shield membrane is not shown in this detail. Verify if it is required by the climate and the building use.

Detailing Considerations

- Electrical service may be run in the triangular space below the roof, as shown in Fig. 4-8.
- Horizontal ceilings may be constructed by joining standard joist framing to ledgers attached to the wall panel. Verify exact details with the manufacturer.
- The fascia may be perpendicular to the slope of the roof or vertical.
- See Section 4-7 for other detailing considerations.

Coordination Required

- The type of eave configuration may determine how the wall/roof connection is detailed.

Materials

See Section 4-8 for material requirements.

4-9   GLULAM BEAM AT FOUNDATION WALL

Description

Figure 4-9 shows a common connection of a glulam beam to a concrete or masonry bearing wall. For light loading conditions, the beam may rest directly on the wall without anchoring if it is restrained by joists and floor sheathing. Other conditions will require restraint against horizontal loads and uplift as well as rotation.

Limitations of Use

- The anchorage shown is schematic only. The number and size of connectors depend on the loads carrier and must be calculated for each condition.
- Sizes and stress ratings for individual applications must be determined based on the spans and loads carried.

Detailing Considerations

- If a bearing plate is not used, the beam should rest on a moisture-resistant barrier.
- The connector should be located near the bottom of the beam to minimize the effect of shrinkage between the bottom of the beam and the fastener.
- Connectors or bolts should not be located near the center of the ends of large beams.
- For deep beams, lateral support may be required to prevent rotation. However, the restraint should not be fastened to the beam in order to allow for shrinkage.

Figure 4-9 Glulam beam at foundation wall 06 18 13.1

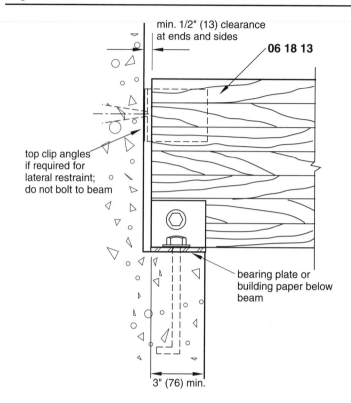

min. 1/2" (13) clearance
at ends and sides

06 18 13

top clip angles
if required for
lateral restraint;
do not bolt to beam

bearing plate or
building paper below
beam

3" (76) min.

Coordination Required

- Verify that the applicable building code permits the use of heavy timber construction.
- Special protection from insects and decay may be required in some locations.

Likely Failure Points

- Splitting of the beam caused by concentrated tension or shear stresses from connectors located near the center of the beam
- Splitting of the beam caused by notching

Materials

06 18 13 GLUED LAMINATED BEAM

ANSI/AITC A190.1 and AITC 117.

Available in standard common widths of $3^{1}/_{8}$ in., $5^{1}/_{8}$ in., $6^{3}/_{4}$ in., $8^{3}/_{4}$ in., $10^{3}/_{4}$ in., and $12^{1}/_{4}$ in. (79 mm, 130 mm, 171 mm, 222 mm, 273 mm, and 311 mm) according to AITC 113. Other sizes may be available.

Rectangular beams are available in depths that are multiples of $1^{1}/_{2}$ in. (38 mm) or $3/_{4}$ in. (19 mm).

Available in three appearance grades: industrial, architectural, and premium.

Figure 4-10 Glulam beam at column 06 18 13.2

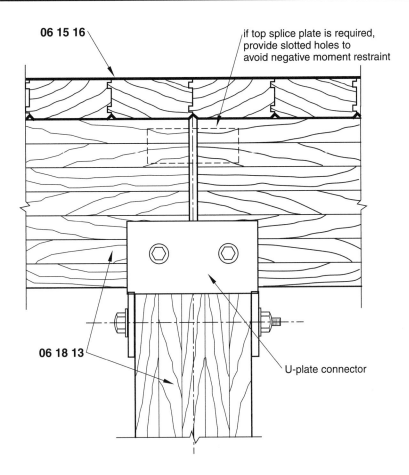

06 15 16

if top splice plate is required,
provide slotted holes to
avoid negative moment restraint

06 18 13

U-plate connector

4-10 GLULAM BEAM AT COLUMN

Description

Figure 4-10 shows one method of connecting beam ends to a solid or glued laminated timber column using a manufactured U-plate connector. A similar detail can be used for connecting a glulam beam to a steel column.

Limitations of Use

- The anchorage shown is schematic only. The number and size of connectors depend on the loads carrier and must be calculated for each condition.

Detailing Considerations

- A T-plate may be used in place of the fabricated connection shown in this detail.
- If the column extends through the floor line, beams may rest on steel seats attached to the column.
- Standard sheathing may be used in lieu of the decking shown in this detail.

Coordination Required

- Verify that the applicable building code permits the use of heavy timber construction.
- Special protection from insects and decay may be required in some locations.

Likely Failure Points

- Splitting of the beam caused by concentrated tension or shear stresses from connectors located near the center of the beam
- Splitting caused by rigid attachment of a splice plate near the top of the beam

Materials

06 15 16 ROOF DECKING

AITC 112.

Solid or laminated decking, nominal 2 × 6 in., 3 × 6 in., or 4 × 6 in. (38 mm × 140 mm, 64 mm × 140 mm, or 89 mm × 140 mm).

Other thicknesses and widths are available.

06 18 13 GLUED LAMINATED BEAM AND COLUMN

ANSI/AITC A190.1 and AITC 117.

Available in standard common widths of $3\frac{1}{8}$ in., $5\frac{1}{8}$ in., $6\frac{3}{4}$ in., $8\frac{3}{4}$ in., $10\frac{3}{4}$ in., and $12\frac{1}{4}$ in. (79 mm, 130 mm, 171 mm, 222 mm, 273 mm, and 311 mm) according to AITC 113. Other sizes may be available.

Rectangular beams are available in depths that are multiples of $1\frac{1}{2}$ in. (38 mm) or $\frac{3}{4}$ in. (19 mm).

Available in three appearance grades: industrial, architectural, and premium.

4-11 GLULAM PURLINS AT BEAM

Description

Figure 4-11 shows the preferred method of connecting a purlin to a beam with a saddle connection. For light loads, clip angles or face hangers may be used if the bolts in the main carrying beam are placed in the upper half of the member.

Limitations of Use

- The anchorage shown is schematic only. The number and size of connectors depend on the loads carried and must be calculated for each condition.

Detailing Considerations

- Connectors in the purlin should be located as close as possible to the bottom of the member and in any case no farther away than 5 in. (127 mm).

Figure 4-11 Glulam beam at beam 06 18 13.3

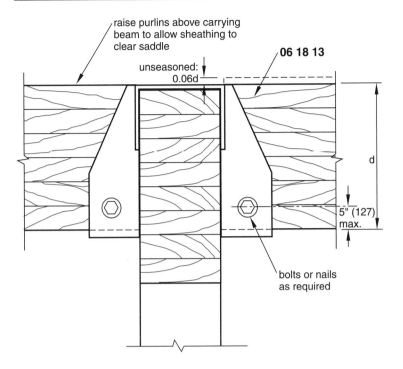

- Purlins may need to be raised to allow sheathing or decking to clear the saddle.
- Concealed purlin hangers may be used where appearance is a factor.
- Joist hangers may be used for carrying light loads and standard joist construction.
- When the purlins are made of seasoned material, design the top of the purlin to be located at 0.01 times its depth.
- When the purlins are made of unseasoned material with a moisture content at or above the fiber saturation point when installed, allow for 6 percent shrinkage. Design the top of the purlin to be located at 0.06 times its depth.

Coordination Required

- Verify that the applicable building code permits the use of heavy timber construction.
- Special protection from insects and decay may be required in some locations.

Likely Failure Points

- Splitting of the purlin caused by concentrated tension or shear stresses from connectors located near the center of the purlin
- Splitting of the beam caused by notching
- Splitting of the members caused by shrinkage when long rows of bolts are used parallel to the grain in angle connectors

Materials

06 18 13 GLUED LAMINATED PURLIN

ANSI/AITC A190.1 and AITC 117.

Available in standard common widths of 3$^{1}/_{8}$ in., 5$^{1}/_{8}$ in., 6$^{3}/_{4}$ in., 8$^{3}/_{4}$ in., 10$^{3}/_{4}$ in., and 12$^{1}/_{4}$ in. (79 mm, 130 mm, 171 mm, 222 mm, 273 mm, and 311 mm) according to AITC 113. Other sizes may be available.

Rectangular purlins are available in depths that are multiples of 1$^{1}/_{2}$ in. (38 mm) or $^{3}/_{4}$ in. (19 mm).

Available in three appearance grades: industrial, architectural, and premium.

4-12   GLULAM ROOF BEAM

Description

Glulam beams with heavy timber decking may be used for pitched roofs, as shown in Fig. 4-12. Standard roof sheathing may also be used. However, because the glulam beams are usually left exposed, insulation must be placed above the decking or sheathing.

Figure 4-12 Glulam roof beam 06 18 13.4

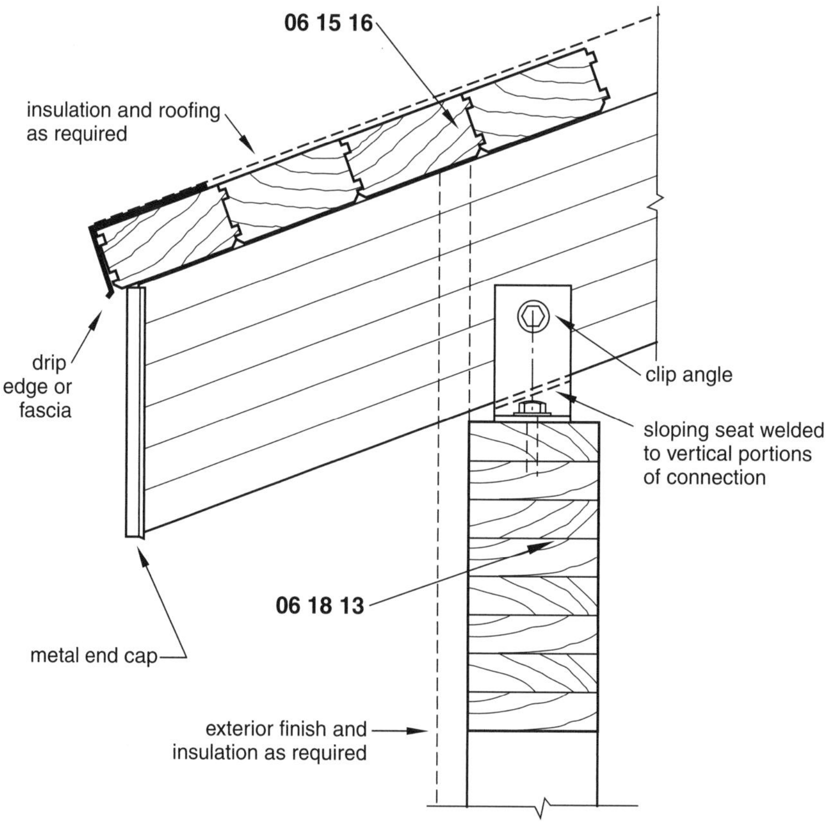

Limitations of Use

- The anchorage shown is schematic only. The number and size of connectors depend on the loads carried and must be calculated for each condition.
- This detail does not show tie rods or other horizontal bracing that may be required to resist the outward thrust of open roof structures.

Detailing Considerations

- Additional insulation may be required in cold climates. A nail base insulation can be applied over roofing felt for direct application of shingles or other roofing materials.
- The ends of glulam beams must be protected from the weather with metal caps or other appropriate means. If metal caps are used, provide a minimum $1/2$ in. (13 mm) clear air space between the metal and the end of the beam.
- In most cases the sloping roof beam should not be notched, which can cause splitting of the beam. However, minor notching may be considered subject to engineering review.

Coordination Required

- A vapor barrier may be required above the decking and below any applied insulation, depending on the local climate and interior building conditions. See Section 5-5.
- If insulation is placed above the decking, solid wood blocking nominally 6 in. (152 mm) wide and as thick as the insulation should be placed at the bottom of the roof slope.
- Verify that the applicable building code permits the use of heavy timber construction.

Materials

06 15 16 ROOF DECKING

AITC 112.

Solid or laminated decking, nominal 2 × 6 in., 3 × 6 in., or 4 × 6 in. (38 mm × 140 mm, 64 mm × 140 mm, or 89 mm × 140 mm).

Other thicknesses and widths are available.

Install decking with the tongues facing toward the peak of the roof.

06 18 13 GLUED LAMINATED BEAM

ANSI/AITC A190.1 and AITC 117.

Available in standard common widths of $3^1/8$ in., $5^1/8$ in., $6^3/4$ in., $8^3/4$ in., $10^3/4$ in., and $12^1/4$ in. (79 mm, 130 mm, 171 mm, 222 mm, 273 mm, and 311 mm) according to AITC 113. Other sizes may be available.

Rectangular beams are available in depths that are multiples of $1^1/2$ in. (38 mm) or $3/4$ in. (19 mm).

Available in three appearance grades: industrial, architectural, and premium.

Figure 4-13 Glulam column at base 06 18 16

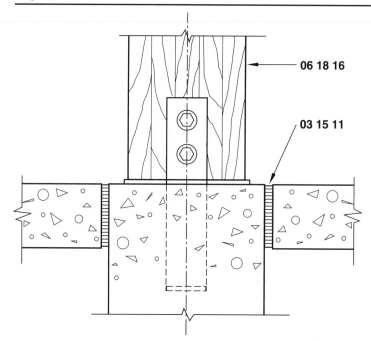

06 18 16

03 15 11

4-13   GLULAM COLUMN AT BASE

Description

Columns must be secured to foundation walls and piers. Figure 4-13 illustrates one common method of attaching a column to a steel anchor embedded in concrete.

Limitations of Use

- The anchorage shown is schematic only. The number and size of connectors depend on the loads carrier and must be calculated for each condition.
- Figure 4-13 does not indicate finish floor materials.

Detailing Considerations

- If a bearing plate is not used, the column should rest on a moisture-resistant barrier.
- If untreated columns are subject to moisture splash or standing water, the column bearing elevation should be raised a minimum of 1 in. (25 mm) above the floor, although 3 in. (76 mm) is preferred.
- Provide barriers or some type of protection if the columns are subject to damage from moving vehicles.
- Clip angles may be used in place of the anchoring device shown in this detail.

Coordination Required

- Separate interior column foundations from slabs-on-grade, as shown in Fig. 4-3.
- Verify that the applicable building code permits the use of heavy timber construction.
- Special protection from insects and decay may be required in some locations.

Likely Failure Points

- Swelling or decay of the column caused by locating the column base below the floor line or by inadequate protection from moisture on the floor

Materials

03 15 11 EXPANSION JOINT FILLER

Compressible joint fillers may be bituminous-impregnated fiberboard or glass fiber or one of several other types of joint fillers. The filler may be used with or without a sealant, depending on the situation.

06 18 13 GLUED LAMINATED COLUMN

ANSI/AITC A190.1 and AITC 117.

Available in standard common widths of $3^1/_8$ in., $5^1/_8$ in., $6^3/_4$ in., $8^3/_4$ in., $10^3/_4$ in., and $12^1/_4$ in. (79 mm, 130 mm, 171 mm, 222 mm, 273 mm, and 311 mm) according to AITC 113. Other sizes may be available.

Rectangular columns are available in depths that are multiples of $1^1/_2$ in. (38 mm) or $3/_4$ in. (19 mm).

Available in three appearance grades: industrial, architectural, and premium.

4-14 BASE CABINET

Description

Figure 4-14 illustrates the typical construction components of a custom millwork cabinet. Such cabinets are manufactured in a mill shop to the size and specification requirements of the designer. Construction details and specifications of millwork have been standardized by the Architectural Woodwork Institute (AWI) and are described in *Architectural Woodwork Quality Standards Illustrated*. Three grades of millwork are established: premium, custom, and economy. Each grade has its own requirements for items such as materials and grades, joint construction, tolerances, finishes, and others. This detail represents a common configuration with a single-drawer unit, doors, and a backsplash, although almost any design is possible with dimensions adjusted to fit the requirements of the project. The drawing represents a finish of plastic laminate on particleboard, but wood veneer and lumber construction may also be used.

Figure 4-14 Base cabinet 06 41 00.1

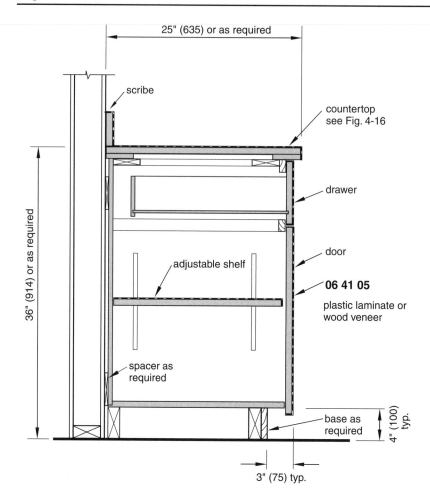

Limitations of Use

- Figure 4-14 does not include stock manufactured casework.
- Pulls, drawer slides, and hinges are not shown in this detail. They must be selected based on the requirements of each job.

Detailing Considerations

- Figure 4-14 illustrates flush overlay construction. Other types of construction include reveal overlay, reveal overlay with inset doors, and flush construction with or without a face frame.
- Various types of countertops are available. Refer to Fig. 4-16.
- The species, cut, and grade of veneer must be specified as well as the AWI grade.
- The cabinet base should allow for adjustment on uneven floors.
- When adjustable shelves are shown, the mill shop has the option of providing either multiple holes with plastic or metal pins or metal or plastic shelf standards.

Table 4-1 Materials and Thicknesses for Cabinet Components

Component	Material	Minimum thickness, in. (mm)
Body members—ends, divisions, bottoms and tops	Panel product	$3/4$ (19)
Rails, face frames, bases	Lumber or panel product	$3/4$ (19)
Backs	Panel product	$1/4$ (6.4)
Doors, max. 30 in. w × 60 in. h (762 mm × 2032 mm)[a]	Medium-density particleboard or medium-density fiberboard core	$3/4$ (19)
Drawer sides, backs and subfronts	Lumber or panel product	$1/2$ (12.7)
Drawer bottoms	Panel product	$1/4$ (6.4)
Drawer fronts	Lumber or panel product	$3/4$ (19)
Wood shelves (min. thicknesses given for spans listed)[b]	Lumber	$3/4$ (19) up to 36 (914) 1-$1/16$ (27) up to 48 (1219)
Shelves (min. thicknesses given for spans listed)	Veneer core plywood	$3/4$ (19) up to 36 (914) 1-$1/16$ (27) up to 48 (1219)
Shelves (min. thicknesses given for spans listed)	Medium-density particleboard or fiberboard	$3/4$ (19) up to 32 (813) 1 (25.4) up to 42 (1067)

[a]Limits are for doors with like materials and thicknesses on both faces. Larger doors require special design, engineering, and fabrication. Verify the thickness and design with the woodwork manufacturer.
[b]Maximum load for the sizes given is 50 psf (244 kg/m^2). Consult the woodwork manufacturer for required thicknesses and materials to minimize deflection for spans and loads required.
Source: based on Architectural Woodwork Institute standards.

- This detail shows the drawer front fabricated with the sides and bottom. However, the mill shop has the option of fabricating a drawer shell and then applying a separate exposed front fastened with screws from inside the drawer.
- Full extension drawer slides must be specified if required.

Materials

06 41 05 CABINET FRAMING, DOORS, AND DRAWERS

Hardwood veneer, plastic laminate, or a combination of materials.

Refer to AWI *Quality Standards* for details of materials for individual parts of a cabinet based on the grade.

Unless otherwise specified, AWI has established standards for thicknesses of various cabinet components, as shown in Table 4-1.

4-15 UPPER CABINET

Description

Figure 4-15 is similar to Fig. 4-14 and shows the construction of a custom wall-mounted millwork cabinet. These cabinets are typically used above base cabinets or as stand-alone storage units. As with base cabinets, details and specifications of millwork have been standardized by AWI. Refer to the AWI *Quality Standards* for more specific information on millwork requirements.

Figure 4-15 Upper cabinet 06 41 00.2

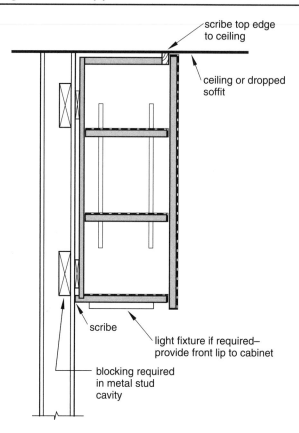

Limitations of Use

- This detail does not include stock manufactured casework.
- Pulls, drawer slides, and hinges are not shown in this detail. They must be selected based on the requirements of each job.

Detailing Considerations

- The top of the cabinet may be detailed against the ceiling or the cabinet may be placed below a dropped soffit. The space between the top of the cabinet and the ceiling may also be left open.
- The bottom edge of the doors may extend below the cabinet bottom, as shown in Fig. 4-15, to allow for a finger pull in lieu of door pull hardware.
- Scribe pieces should be provided where the cabinet touches a wall to allow for out-of-plumb or out-of-line partitions.
- This detail illustrates flush overlay construction. Other types of construction include reveal overlay, reveal overlay with inset doors, and flush construction with or without a face frame.
- The species, cut, and grade of veneer must be specified as well as the AWI grade.
- When adjustable shelves are shown, the mill shop has the option of providing either multiple holes with plastic or metal pins or metal or plastic shelf standards.

Coordination Required

- Solid wood blocking should be shown on the drawings and specified to provide a firm backing for attachment of the cabinet.
- If undercabinet lighting is indicated, provide a front lip to conceal the fixture and locate the exact height of the electrical conduit that connects to the fixture so that it can be stubbed out accurately by the electrician prior to wall finishing.

Materials

Refer to Section 4-14 for material requirements.

4-16   COUNTERTOPS

Description

Countertops may be constructed in several different configurations and surfaced with a variety of materials. Figure 4-16 shows three common types of countertops faced with both plastic laminate and wood veneer. Figure 4-16(a) shows a simple top with a square front edge and a straight backsplash. Figure 4-16(b) profiles a common type used for kitchen and bath counters with a rounded inside corner for easy cleaning and a lipped edge to prevent water runoff. Figure 4-16(c) illustrates a wood veneer top with a matching hardwood edge for more decorative applications.

In addition to these finishes, countertops may be constructed of solid lumber and edge glued or laminated, as with butcher block tops, although these types are not as common as laminate or wood veneer. Countertops may also be finished with ceramic tile, artificial stone, metal, and other materials as appropriate for the application.

Detailing Considerations

- Hardwood edges on wood veneer tops may be molded to a desired profile in addition to being cut square.
- Edges on premium grade plastic laminate have the laminate applied to the edge before the top laminate is applied.
- Edges on premium grade veneer tops are glued under pressure. Edges on custom grade tops can be pressure glued or glued and nailed, while edges on economy grade tops can be pressure glued, glued and nailed, or simply nailed.
- If countertops are installed without a base cabinet, they can be supported at the wall line with a wood cleat or a metal angle. Additional wood or metal support may be required along the front edge if there are no intermediate supports.
- Extra material should be provided along the backsplash for a scribe fit when the countertop is installed. In lieu of a scribe piece, a reveal at the wall will conceal any minor variations of the wall, as shown in Fig. 4-16(c).

Figure 4-16 Countertops 06 41 00.3

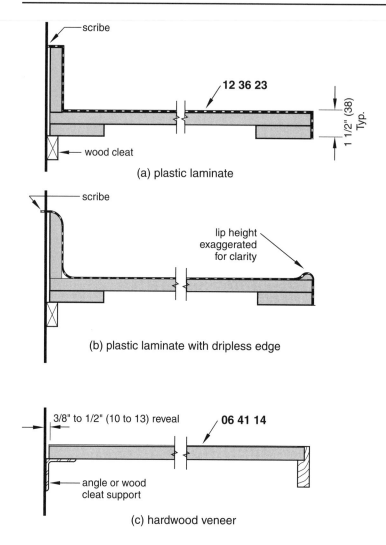

Materials

12 36 23 PLASTIC LAMINATE

Grade I for premium, custom, and economy grades.

Maximum 12 ft (3658 mm) length without joints if available in the color and pattern selected.

Applied to a minimum 3/4 in. (19 mm) thick panel product.

06 41 14 WOOD VENEER

Grade I for premium and custom grades.

Grade II for economy grade.

Maximum 10 ft (3048 mm) length without joints.

Applied to a minimum 3/4 in. (19 mm) thick panel product.

Figure 4-17 Shelving 06 41 00.4

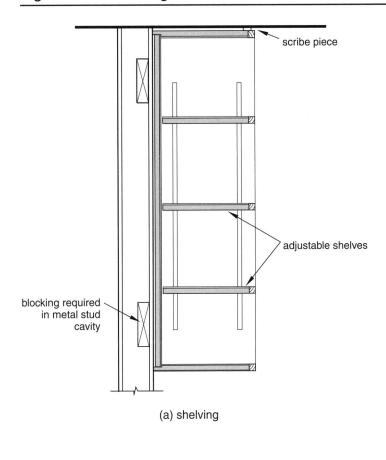

scribe piece

adjustable shelves

blocking required
in metal stud
cavity

(a) shelving

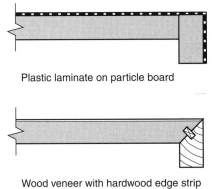

Plastic laminate on particle board

Wood veneer with hardwood edge strip

(b) alternate shelving edge treatments

4-17   SHELVING

Description

Shelving may be mounted on adjustable metal standards, attached to floor-mounted cases, or built into enclosed wall-hung cabinets, as shown in Fig. 4-17(a). In addition, the shelving may be open or enclosed with cabinet doors.

Table 4-2 Maximum Allowable Total Load in Pounds (kg) for Shelf Deflection of $^1/_8$ in. (3 mm) for Shelves of Different Materials, Widths, and Spans

Shelf length, in. (mm)		30 (760)			36 (914)			42 (1067)		
Shelf width, in. (mm)	Shelf thickness, in.	8(203)	10(254)	12(305)	8(203)	10(254)	12(305)	8(203)	10(254)	12(305)
Component	(mm)	lb(kg)	lb(kg)	lb(kg)	lb(kg)	lb(kg)	lb(kg)	lb(kg)	lb(kg)	lb(kg)
Medium-density particleboard faced with 0.05 in. plastic laminate	$^3/_4$(19) $1^1/_2$(38)	58(26) 388(176)	73(33) 485(220)	87(39) 583(264)	34(15) 225(102)	42(19) 281(127)	51(23) 337(153)	21(9) 142(64)	27(12) 177(80)	32(14) 212(96)
High-density particleboard faced with 0.05 in. plastic laminate	$^3/_4$(19)	146(66)	182(83)	218(99)	84(38)	105(48)	126(57)	53(24)	66(30)	80(36)
Birch-faced plywood with $^3/_4$ in. × $^3/_4$ in. softwood edge strip	$^3/_4$(19)	180(81)	225(102)	270(122)	104(47)	130(59)	156(71)	66(30)	82(37)	98(44)
Birch-faced plywood with $^3/_4$ in. × $1^1/_2$ in. softwood dropped edge	$^3/_4$(19)	366(166)	412(187)	458(207)	212(96)	238(108)	265(120)	133(60)	150(68)	167(76)
Douglas fir, coast	$^3/_4$(19)	195(88)	244(111)	293(133)	113(51)	141(64)	169(77)	71(32)	89(40)	107(48)
White oak	$^3/_4$(19)	178(81)	223(101)	267(121)	103(47)	129(59)	155(70)	65(29)	81(37)	97(44)
Red oak, black cherry	$^3/_4$(19)	149(68)	186(84)	224(102)	86(39)	108(49)	129(59)	54(24)	68(31)	81(37)

Note: For calculating total loads, books weigh about 65 pcf (1041 kg/m^3) and paper weighs about 58 pcf (929 kg/m^3).

Limitations of Use

- This detail does not include closet and utility shelving.

Detailing Considerations

- Because one of the most common problems with shelving is excessive deflection under load or outright collapse, the span and thickness of each shelf should be selected for minimum deflection. Shelves are simply thin, wide beams and obey the laws of statics, so any material of any size can be calculated using the standard beam deflection formula. Table 4-2 summarizes these calculations for common shelving materials, configurations, and thicknesses and gives the maximum total load for shelves of various widths and spans so that a $^1/_8$ in. (3 mm) deflection is not exceeded. Deflections other than $^1/_8$ in. (mm) or for other widths and spans can be calculated by direct proportion.
- Scribe pieces should be provided where the cabinet touches a wall to allow for out-of-plumb or out-of-line partitions.
- The species, cut, and grade of veneer must be specified as well as the AWI grade. If plastic laminate is specified, the manufacturer, color, and pattern must be specified.
- When adjustable shelves are shown, the woodwork manufacturer has the option of providing either multiple holes with plastic or metal pins or metal or plastic shelf standards.
- Stop dados with dowels, screws, or concealed interlocking fastening devices are used to attach shelves with side pieces in premium grade and custom grade only. Economy grade shelving uses through dados.

- Edge strips may be hardwood of the same thickness as the shelf, as shown on this drawing. Alternate edge treatments are shown in Fig. 4-17(b).

Coordination Required

- If shelving is mounted on steel stud walls, solid wood blocking should be shown on the drawings so that it can be installed prior to wall finishing.

Likely Failure Points

- Sagging or collapse caused by inadequate anchoring of the cabinet to the wall
- Excessive deflection of the shelving under loads due to inadequate thickness of the shelf or excessive span of the shelf for the imposed load.

Materials

Refer to Section 4-14 for material requirements.

4-18   FLUSH WOOD PANELING

Figure 4-18 shows typical methods of hanging shop-fabricated flush paneling. Because paneling is made in the woodwork manufacturer's shop, the preparation of the substrate and the method of installation are critical to a quality job. The use of cleats, as shown in these details, allows for shimming and installation with a minimum of exposed fasteners. Cleats or Z-clips are attached to the wall, and a corresponding cleat or clip is attached to the back of the wood paneling. The panel is then lifted into place.

Limitations of Use

- There are only premium and custom AWI grades of flush wood paneling.

Detailing Considerations

- Either wood cleats or metal Z-clips, as shown in Fig. 4-18(d), may be used to hang paneling. As shown in Fig. 4-18(a), some space must be allowed at the ceiling line to lift the panels over the cleats or clips, as shown in the detail. Wood cleats are normally made from nominal 1 in. (25 mm) thick material.
- The panel may extend to the floor or various types of base details may be used.
- Similar installation methods are used for plastic laminate clad panels.
- The type of vertical joints must be detailed, either flush joints or articulated joints.
- The species, cut, and matching between adjacent veneers in a panel must be specified. The type of matching within a panel must also be specified, either running match, balance match, or center match. Finally, the matching of panels within an area must be specified, either premanufactured sets, sequence matched panels of uniform size, or blueprint matched panels.

Figure 4-18 Flush wood paneling 06 42 16

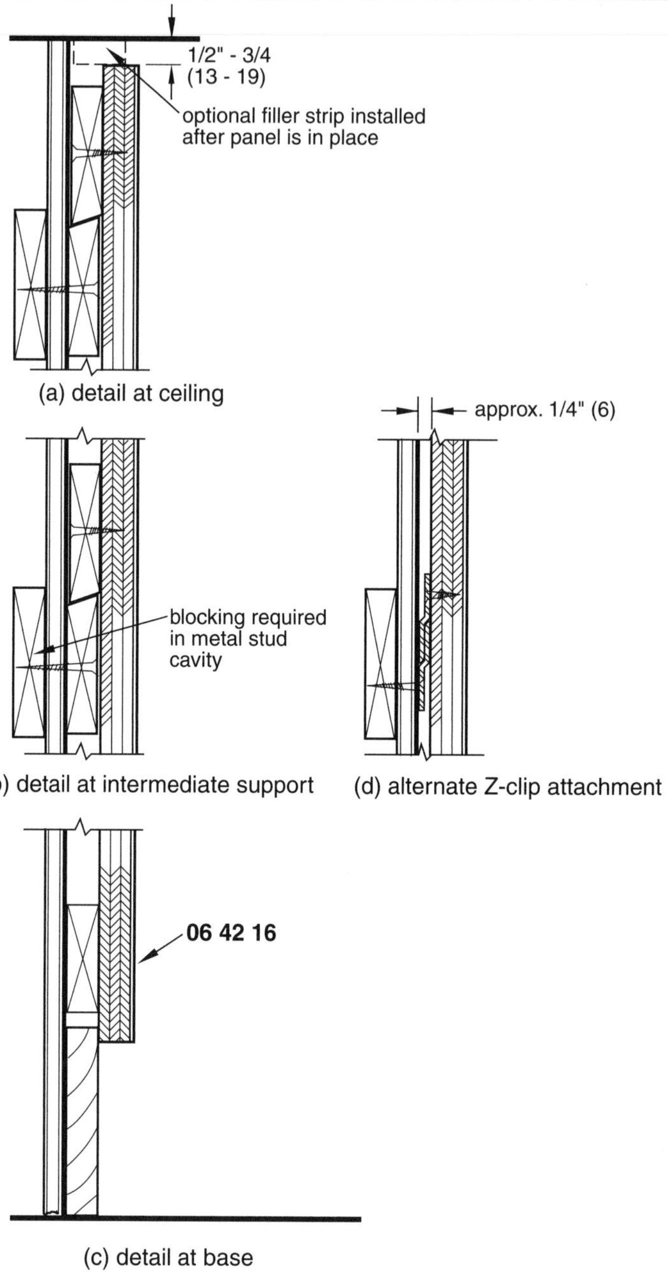

1/2" - 3/4
(13 - 19)

optional filler strip installed
after panel is in place

(a) detail at ceiling

approx. 1/4" (6)

blocking required
in metal stud
cavity

(b) detail at intermediate support

(d) alternate Z-clip attachment

06 42 16

(c) detail at base

Coordination Required

- Wood blocking must be shown on the drawings for installation by other trades.
- Fire-retardant ratings must be determined and specified if required.

Materials

06 42 16 VENEER PANELS

Veneer is mounted on 3/4 in. (19 mm) particleboard or veneer core for premium grade and on 7/16 in. (11 mm) for custom grade. Grade I veneer is used for both premium and custom grades.

Veneers are balance matched within each panel for premium grade. There are no specific requirements for custom grade.

Within an area (room), panels are either sequence matched with panels of uniform size or blueprint matched, depending on which is specified for premium grade. Premanufactured panel sets are used for custom grade.

CHAPTER 5

THERMAL AND MOISTURE PROTECTION DETAILS

5-1 FOUNDATION WATERPROOFING

Description

Figure 5-1 illustrates a typical below-grade concrete wall with sheet membrane waterproofing. Waterproofing is intended to provide protection against penetration of water under hydrostatic pressure. Dampproofing is often used to provide protection against water vapor not under hydrostatic pressure for residential and small commercial foundations. However, many experts maintain that dampproofing provides little protection and recommend waterproofing instead.

Waterproofing membranes may consist of elastomeric sheet materials such as EPDM, neoprene, and butyl rubber, hot- or cold-applied bituminous materials, and liquid-applied elastomeric materials. Cold-applied and elastomeric sheet materials are generally easier to apply, but the specific type of membrane used should be selected based on the requirements of the project. This detail shows the use of an elastomeric or bituminous sheet-applied material.

Limitations of Use

- This detail is not intended to be used for tunnels, for water storage facilities, or under harsh environmental conditions.
- This detail is for below-grade vertical surfaces only.
- This system is not applicable for foundations poured against sheeting or shoring. For these situations, other systems must be used.
- The exact detailing of the waterproofing membrane around the foundation may vary, depending on the severity of the waterproofing problem. Waterproofing may not be required under the floor slab.

Detailing Considerations

- Include drainage systems such as geotextiles and foundation drains.
- Although the finish grade may be soil or permeable landscaping, it is preferable to use impermeable materials such as concrete, pavers, or similar materials to provide positive drainage away from the building.

Figure 5-1 Foundation waterproofing 07 13 00

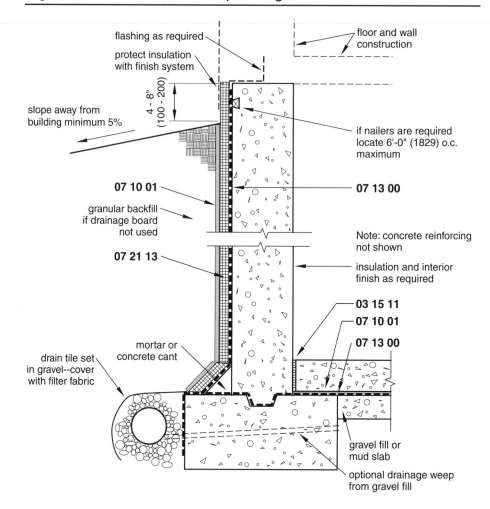

- Minimize the number of penetrations through the waterproofing membrane.
- The membrane should be carried above the grade line and tied into the building flashing and the waterproofing system.
- Tests can be performed that estimate the amount of head that can be expected, and a waterproofing membrane can be selected which is capable of resisting the pressure.
- Some bituminous systems require treated wood nailers to be installed flush with the surface of the concrete.
- Although not recommended, if the membrane is terminated slightly below grade level, cover nail heads with two plies of glass fabric or as recommended by the manufacturer.
- If the surface to be waterproofed is very irregular, a spray-on or liquid-applied membrane may be more appropriate than a sheet material because these types of materials can more easily conform to irregular surfaces.
- Insulation is optional in many cases. Because ground temperature is relatively constant below a certain depth, insulation may only be needed in the upper portion of the wall. The *International Building Code* requires below-grade wall insulation only for climate zones 7 and 8 (see Fig. 5-5.2) unless the basement slab is heated. Verify insulation requirements with local codes. Insulation may be desired for the full height of the wall to help prevent condensation in finished basements.

Coordination Required

- Waterproofing should not be installed until the concrete has completely cured—from 7 to 20 days.
- The entire area subject to hydrostatic pressure must be completely enclosed, including walls, slabs, foundations, and penetrations.
- The surface of the concrete wall must be smooth and free of fins, humps, honeycomb, and other defects that would interfere with the adhesion of the waterproofing membrane to the concrete. Tie holes should be filled with mortar. Form coatings, curing compounds, and release agents can affect the adherence of the waterproof membrane and should be removed prior to application.
- Cants should be made of mortar or concrete. Wood or fiber cants should not be used.
- The protection board, insulation, and drainage system should be placed immediately after the membrane is applied.
- The backfill density should be specified to be between 85 and 88 percent of the Modified Proctor Density to avoid settlement while not causing stress on the walls and preventing proper drainage.
- Building expansion joints require special detailing. The membrane should only span construction joints.
- Verify compatibility of the materials used to seal the membrane with the protection board and insulation.
- Verify compatibility of the soil composition with the waterproofing materials.

Likely Failure Points

- Leaking due to poor installation of the waterproof membrane (The application of waterproofing must be inspected carefully during construction. For complex jobs, the use of an independent inspection company may be advisable.)
- Leaks caused by gaps or joints, which exceed the maximum size that the membrane can span
- Puncture of or damage to the membrane caused by careless backfilling or overcompaction
- Leaks caused by improperly detailed or installed flashing where the waterproofing membrane terminates
- Delamination of directly adhered systems caused by water release from uncured concrete

Materials

03 15 11 EXPANSION JOINT FILLER

Compressible joint fillers may be bituminous-impregnated fiberboard or glass fiber or one of several other types of joint fillers. In some situations, the joint filler may be used alone without a sealant; however, a sealant is generally preferred.

07 10 01 DRAINAGE BOARD SYSTEM/PROTECTION BOARD

In installations where high hydrostatic pressure is present, a drainage board should be used both to protect the membrane and to reduce pressure.

Manufacturer's standard drainage mat with filter fabric.

A $\frac{1}{2}$ in. (6 mm) polystyrene protection board if used directly over waterproofing.

Some manufacturers provide products that combine the waterproofing membrane with a drainage layer. If no insulation is required, these products are a good choice.

Some manufacturers provide grooved insulation boards that combine insulation with the drainage layer, so no separate protection board is required.

07 13 00 ELASTOMERIC OR BITUMINOUS SHEET MEMBRANE WATERPROOFING

Materials

The membrane should have a perm rating less than 1 (57 ng/ • s • m^2 • Pa).

The membrane should be capable of at least 300 percent elongation and capable of spanning $\frac{1}{8}$ in. (3 mm) gaps.

If sheets are exposed above grade, the material must be resistant to weathering.

Execution

Follow the manufacturer's directions for application and use of accessory materials.

Install when temperatures are expected to exceed 40°F (4.4°C).

The top edge of the membrane may be terminated over the top of a wall, but if it is stopped on the vertical surface, it should be under counterflashing or in a reglet.

Reinforce corners, joints, intersections, and penetrations through the wall with materials as recommended by the manufacturer.

07 21 13 RIGID INSULATION

Extruded polystyrene for water resistance and compressive strength, ASTM C578. Thickness as required for thermal insulation.

Refer to Section 5-5 for more information on insulation.

5-2   COLD, LIQUID-APPLIED MEMBRANE DECK WATERPROOFING

Description

Figure 5-2 illustrates one of several methods of waterproofing plaza decks. This is an open-joint drainage system in which the wearing surface is raised on pedestals with gaps between each unit. Water runs off and is directed to drains below the walking surface. With a pedestal system, the wearing surface can be installed horizontally above a sloped drainage surface by the use of shims or proprietary pedestal systems. This detail shows rigid board insulation applied above the membrane, but in many systems the insulation may be omitted and placed inside the structure.

A typical alternative to this method is the closed-joint system, where the wearing surface is a monolithic surface, such as another concrete slab, which is designed to remove most of the runoff at the surface level. See Figure 5-2.1.

Figure 5-2 Cold, liquid-applied membrane deck waterproofing 07 14 00.1

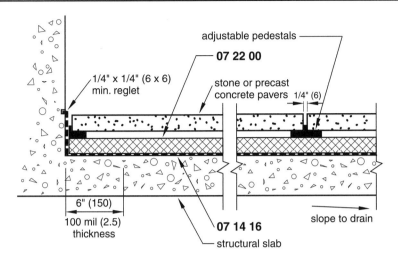

adjustable pedestals
07 22 00

1/4" x 1/4" (6 x 6) min. reglet

stone or precast concrete pavers 1/4" (6)

6" (150)

100 mil (2.5) thickness

07 14 16

structural slab

slope to drain

Limitations of Use

- This detail is not for surfaces subject to vehicular traffic.
- This detail shows the termination at a wall where no differential movement between the slab and the wall is expected.
- Insulation must be selected that will not crush under the concentrated loads of the pedestal system.

Detailing Considerations

- The structural substrate should be cast-in-place concrete, not precast concrete.
- In cold climates, consider the possibility of freezing anywhere within the drainage system above the membrane.
- The recommended location for the insulation is above the membrane.

Figure 5-2.1 Closed joint deck waterproofing 07 14 00.2

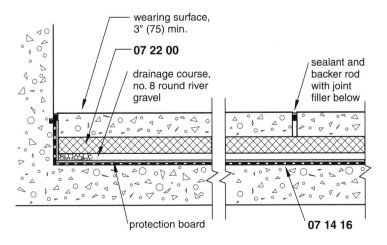

wearing surface, 3" (75) min.

07 22 00

drainage course, no. 8 round river gravel

sealant and backer rod with joint filler below

protection board

07 14 16

- Verify the compatibility of the insulation with the membrane. A protection board between the two may be required.
- The structural slab must limit deflection and movement.
- A hot-applied waterproofing membrane may also be used. Verify the manufacturer's requirements.

Coordination Required

- A minimum slope of $1/8$ in./ft (10 mm/m) is required, but $1/4$ in./ft (20 mm/m) is preferred. The slope should be formed with the structural slab. The deck should be drained away from walls and expansion joints.
- Waterproofing should not be installed until the concrete has completely cured and aged. Concrete should be cured for 7 days and aged for 21 days prior to application of waterproofing.
- A floated or troweled finish is required on the structural slab.
- Form coatings, curing compounds, and release agents can affect the adherence of the waterproof membrane. Verify with the manufacturer that these materials are compatible with the waterproofing. If not, they must be removed.
- Insulation must be selected that supports the dead and live loads transmitted through the pedestals. A concrete protection slab may be required over the insulation to provide adequate bearing for the pedestal system.
- Expansion joints require special detailing.
- Drains should be located at points of maximum deflection.

Likely Failure Points

- Leaks and damage to the membrane caused by trapped water in the structural slab
- Damage caused to the membrane or insulation from freezing water
- Breaking of the membrane caused by excessive movement of the structural slab

Materials

07 14 16 COLD, LIQUID-APPLIED ELASTOMERIC WATERPROOFING

Materials

ASTM C836.

Applied to achieve a 60 mil (1.5 mm) dry film thickness.

Execution

Follow the manufacturer's directions for the application and use of accessory materials.

Install during warm weather if possible.

The membrane may be terminated flush on the wall, but the use of a small reglet, as shown in Fig. 5-2, is preferred.

If the membrane is terminated on a masonry wall, counterflashing is required.

Apply at a thickness of 100 mil (2.54 mm) 6 in. (152 mm) horizontally from the corner and up the full height of the return to the termination point.

07 22 00 BUILDING BOARD INSULATION

Extruded polystyrene, ASTM C578.

Thickness as required for the insulation value.

Compressive strength adequate to support concentrated pedestal loads.

5-3   VEGETATED PROTECTED MEMBRANE ROOFING

Description

A vegetated protected membrane roof, also called a *green roof, vegetated roof cover*, or *eco-roof*, is a system of components designed to allow the growth of vegetation above a waterproofed roof structure. The advantages of a green roof include reduced storm runoff, energy conservation, a reduced heat island effect, carbon dioxide absorption, protection of the roofing, acoustical insulation, and aesthetic appeal. A project can receive Leadership in Energy and Environmental Design (LEED[TM]) credits for having a green roof if it covers at least 50 percent of the total roof area.

There are two types of green roofs: extensive and intensive. *Extensive green roofs* use soil or a planting medium less than 6 in. (150 mm) deep supporting the growth of sedums, meadow grasses, herbs, perennials, or other plants suitable for the local climate. See Figure 5-3. *Intensive green roofs* use soil or a planting medium more than 6 in. (150 mm) deep to support the growth of smaller plants as well as shrubs and trees. Extensive roofs may use a continuous layer of growth medium or the plants may be placed in modular plastic containers. Generally, the modular systems weigh less, are more flexible, and can be easily removed to make roof repairs.

Figure 5-3 Vegetated Protected Membrane Roofing   07 55 63

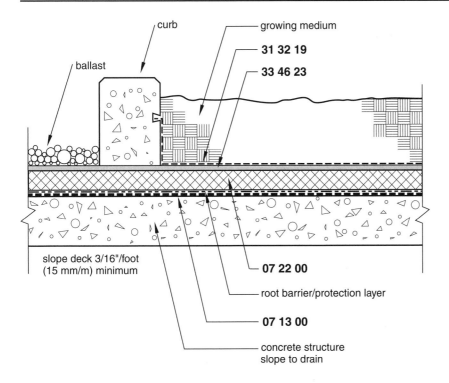

Extensive green roofs are typically designed for their energy conservation advantages, while intensive roofs are also designed to create a park-like setting for public access.

When detailing a green roof, the plant types must be selected first based on aesthetic requirements, climate, available sunlight, wind loading, planting methods, and whether the roof will be extensive or intensive. The plant types and the type of roof structure available will suggest the specific type of system that should be used.

Limitations of Use

- The detail shown here is one of the most common, but it is only one of many that can be used successfully. Other details utilize insulation placed directly on a metal deck with the waterproofing membrane over the insulation. Verify the exact placement of the component parts with the supplier of the plants and based on the type of insulation used.
- The roof structure must be designed to support the wet weight of the assembly. The weight of an extensive roof system may range from 12 to 35 lb/ft^2 (59 to 171 kg/m^2), while that of an intensive system may range from 50 to 300 lb/ft^2 (245 to 1470 kg/m^2).
- A green roof should not cover the entire surface area of the building. Space must be provided around major roof penetrations, the parapet, mechanical equipment, and other areas requiring regular maintenance.

Detailing Considerations

- Roof penetrations should be grouped whenever possible during the initial planning of the roof and located in nonplanted areas.
- The roof should be sloped to drain a minimum of 1.5 percent.
- Verify the minimum waterproofing thicknesses with the manufacturer, depending on the type of green roof and the warranty period required.
- If the roof is installed in an area with high winds, appropriate ballasts should be included in the detail.

Coordination Required

- Verify appropriate vegetation with a qualified horticulturist or another expert based on the type of roof, climate, microclimate, wind load, availability of sunlight, and whether the planting will have irrigation. A drip irrigation system is usually recommended instead of a spray system.
- Waterproofing should not be installed until the concrete has completely cured—from 14 to 28 days. Curing compounds must be compatible with the waterproofing membrane or must be completely removed.
- Verify the required ballast weight and planting medium weight required to secure insulation to prevent flotation of insulation.
- Some types of waterproofing membranes, such as TPO (thermoplastic polyolefin) EPDM, and PVC, can also serve as root barriers. Verify your selection with the manufacturer.

Likely Failure Points

- Leaking due to poor installation of the waterproof membrane (The application of waterproofing must be inspected carefully during construction. For critical jobs, the use of an independent inspection company may be advisable. A flood test or electric field vector mapping [EFVM] should be conducted prior to completion of the installation to check for leaks.)
- Failure of insulation, the drainage layer, or filter products due to incompatible maintenance products including fertilizers, pesticides, and herbicides

Materials

07 13 00 SHEET MEMBRANE WATERPROOFING

Materials

Polyvinyl chloride (PVC), ASTM D4434, or

thermoplastic polyolefin (TPO), ASTM D6878, or

ethylene propylene diene monomer (EPDM), ASTM D4637.

The membrane should have a perm rating below 1 (57 ng/$m^2 \bullet$ s $\bullet$ Pa).

The membrane should be capable of at least 300 percent elongation and capable of spanning $1/8$ in. (3 mm) gaps.

Hot liquid-applied rubberized asphalt or self-adhering bituminous sheets may also be considered, but thermoplastic sheets are generally preferred.

Execution

Follow the manufacturer's directions for application and use of accessory materials.

Install when temperatures are expected to exceed 40°F (4.4°C).

The top edge of the membrane may be terminated over the top of a wall, but if it is stopped on the vertical surface, it should be under counterflashing or in a reglet.

Reinforce corners, joints, intersections, and penetrations through the wall with materials as recommended by the manufacturer.

07 22 00 DECK INSULATION

Extruded polystyrene (XPS), ASTM C578.

Thickness as required for the insulation value.

Compressive strength adequate to support concentrated pedestal loads. XPS insulation is available in strengths of up to 100 psi (690 kPa).

When more than one layer of insulation is required, verify the manufacturer's requirements. Generally, the layer directly on the root barrier must be at least 2 in. (50 mm) thick and be the thicker of the two layers or at least equal to the top layer. Stagger the joints between layers.

31 32 19 GEOSYNTHETIC SOIL STABILIZATION AND LAYER SEPARATION

Manufacturer's standard layer separation. It may be integral with the drainage layer material.

This layer may also serve as a water retention layer.

33 46 23 DRAINAGE LAYER

Manufacturers' preformed drainage sheet, 3/8 in. to 1/2 in. (10 mm to 13 mm), which may include types with entangled filaments, thermoformed dimpled cups, or geonets.

Always locate the drainage layer above the insulation to provide for vapor diffusion.

5-4 SLAB-ON-GRADE FOUNDATION INSULATION

Description

Perimeter foundation insulation is required in many climates to reduce the heat loss from a slab-on-grade through the foundation wall near the grade line (see Fig. 5-4). The insulation must extend below the top of the slab the distance shown in Table 5-1, depending on the climate zone as shown in Figure 5-5.2, or to the top of the footing, whichever is less. The required R–values also vary, depending on the climate zone as shown in Table 5-1.

Detailing Considerations

- Coordinate the position of the exterior wall and the concrete configuration to conceal the insulation next to the slab.
- Insulation may be placed either on the outside or the inside of the wall. The inside location is preferred to prevent damage during backfilling and subsequent construction.
- The insulation below the slab may be omitted.
- Perimeter insulation may be installed vertically from the top of the slab to the bottom of the slab and then horizontally under the floor slab for the total distance shown in Table 5-1.

Figure 5-4 Slab-on-grade foundation insulation 07 21 13

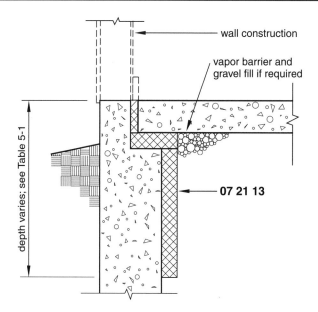

wall construction

vapor barrier and gravel fill if required

depth varies; see Table 5-1

07 21 13

Table 5-1   Insulation Requirements for Slabs-on-Grade

Climate zone (see Fig. 5-5.2)	Depth, in. (mm)	Min. R-value
1	12 (305)	7.5
2	12 (305)	7.5
3	12 (305)	7.5
4, except marine	12 (305)	7.5
5 and marine 4	24 (610)	7.5
6	36 (914)	10
7	36 (914)	10
8	48 (1219)	10

Note. Based on requirements of the *International Building Code.* Verify with local regulations.

Materials

07 21 13 BOARD INSULATION

XPS, ASTM C578.

Nominal R-7.5 or R-10 as required by the climatic zone and local codes. This is generally a nominal 1½ in. (38 mm) or 2 in. (50 mm) thickness.

5-5   WEATHER BARRIER CONCEPTS

Description

The exterior enclosure of a building must provide weather protection against liquid water (and snow), water vapor, air infiltration, and temperature differentials. The ways in which these elements enter the building vary, as do the methods for preventing or minimizing their effects. See Fig. 5-5.1.

The types of construction details developed to provide protection from weather and climate depend on many factors:

- The climatic zone in which the building is located
- The microclimate surrounding the building
- Environmental conditions required inside the building
- The type of structure and exposed cladding being used
- Anticipated building movement
- Other detailing considerations of cost, desired appearance, security, acoustics, fire resistance, durability, and similar parameters

Moisture generated inside a building can also be problematic if there is no way to exhaust it at the source or provide for its diffusion to the exterior.

Climate Zones

The amount of insulation and the type and position of air and water barriers in the exterior enclosure depend largely on the climatic zone in which the project is located. In the United States, climates range from hot and humid to cold and dry. There are eight zones in the United States, including four subzones of moist, dry, marine, and warm–humid. See Figure 5-5.2

Figure 5-5.1 Weather barrier concepts

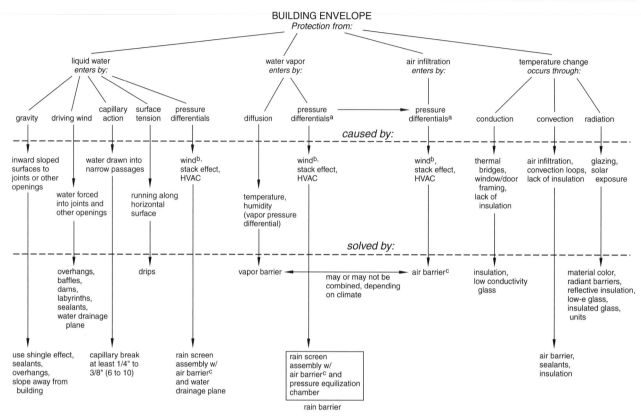

a water vapor enters primarily through air infiltration
b wind has the greatest effect on pressure differentials
c air barriers may be vapor permeable or vapor impermeable

and Table 5-2. An appendix of ASHRAE 90.1 provides a county-by-county listing of the climate zones in the United States as well as the climate zones of other countries.

Water Barriers

Water barriers are the first line of defense against water penetration into a building. They include the exterior surfaces of walls, waterproof membranes within walls, roofing, below-grade waterproofing, drips, and flashing. These surfaces move as much water as possible out of and away from the building or to drainage lines. Historically, building walls employed the barrier concept, through which the exterior walls, joint sealants, and other components prevented water and water vapor from penetrating by providing a continuous barrier exposed to the weather. However, leaks, wind-driven rain, and other forces and construction defects often let water penetrate.

Contemporary cladding systems typically employ the rain screen system, in which the exposed surface provides protection from the elements and is used in conjunction with an air space behind it and a watertight membrane and/or air barrier inside the air space. The air space is vented to the outside, so the pressure is equal on both sides of the rain screen. This minimizes the movement of water due to pressure differentials caused by wind or other forces. Any moisture that does penetrate the rain screen is prevented from entering the backup wall by a vapor barrier and flashing, and is drained down the air space and out of weep holes.

Figure 5-5.2 Climate zones

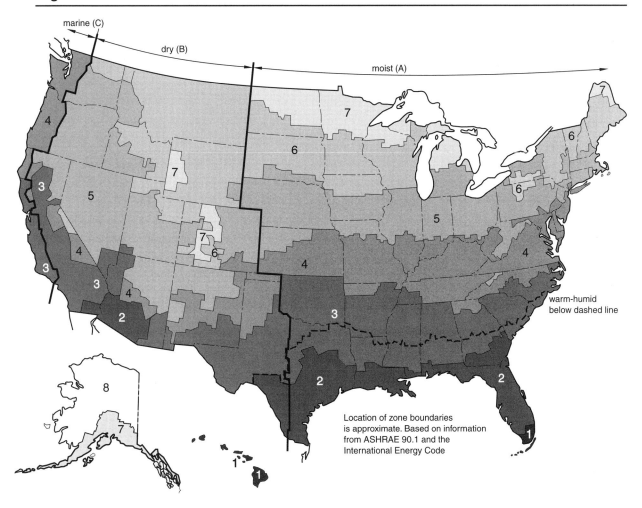

Other openings in the rain screen allow excess water vapor to evaporate. The types of rain screen systems are discussed in more detail in the section on detailing considerations.

Water Vapor Retarders

Water can also enter a building through the migration of water vapor, either by diffusion through materials or by air movement, or by both. Air movement and air barriers are discussed in the next section.

Table 5-2 Climate Zone Descriptions	
Zone number	**Description**
1A, 2A, and 3A south of the warm-humid line	Warm, humid
2B	Warm, dry
3A north of the humid line, 4A	Mixed, humid
3B, 3C, 4B	Mixed, dry
4C	Cool, marine
5A, 6A	Cold, humid
5B, 6B	Cold, dry
7	Very cold
8	Subarctic

Table 5-3 Perm Rating Terminology

Perm rating	Term
less than 0.1	Vapor impermeable
0.1 to 1	Semi-impermeable
1 to 10	Semipermeable
10 or over	Permeable

Note: Anything less than 1 perm is considered to be a vapor retarder (less accurately called a vapor barrier*).*

Vapor diffusion is the slow movement of water molecules through vapor-permeable materials caused by differences in vapor pressure. Differences in vapor pressure are caused by differences in temperature and relative humidity. Generally, there is a tendency for warm, moist air to migrate to areas of cooler, dryer air. In buildings, this can cause problems when warm, moist air reaches its dew point and condenses. If this happens within a wall, the water can degrade insulation and other building materials, promote rust, and support mold growth.

To prevent vapor migration, vapor retarders are used. These may be plastic sheeting (polyethylene), aluminum foil, self-adhering sheet membranes, or fluid-applied membranes. Vapor retarders may also function as air barriers if it is appropriate to place them in the same position within the wall as discussed in the section on air barriers.

Different materials have different permeance ratings. *Permeance* is the property of a material that prevents water vapor from diffusing through it. It is measured in grains of moisture per hour per square foot per inch of mercury difference in vapor pressure, and the unit is the *perm*. In inch-pound units, 1 perm equals 1 $g/h \cdot ft^2 \cdot in.$ Hg. In SI units, permeance is given in nanograms of water per second per square meter per Pascal of vapor pressure, or $ng/s \cdot m^2 \cdot Pa$. One perm in SI units equals a flow rate of 57 $ng/s \cdot m^2 \cdot Pa$.

Table 5-3 gives perm ratings and their corresponding terminology.

The ideal position of vapor retarders within a wall assembly is climate specific and must be considered in conjunction with the location of the air barrier. Generally, vapor retarders are placed on the warm side of insulation in most climatic regions.

In cold regions (generally, climate zones 6, 7, and 8), for example, vapor retarders prevent warm, moist interior air from migrating toward the cooler outdoors and condensing inside the insulation cavity or elsewhere inside the wall. They should be placed on the warm side of the insulation. In these regions, a vapor-*permeable* air barrier should be also placed outside of the insulation to prevent air infiltration while allowing any accumulated moisture to dry out. In most cases, the air barrier is placed outside of the sheathing for support, protection, and ease of construction.

In hot, humid climates (generally, climate zones 1, 2, 3A below the warm-humid line, and 3C) in air-conditioned buildings, the vapor retarder should be placed on the outside of the insulation to prevent the moist, warm air *outside* the building from migrating to the cooler, dehumidified interior spaces. In these climatic regions, the vapor retarder should also serve as the air barrier; that is, the air barrier should be vapor *impermeable*.

In mixed climatic regions (generally, climate zones 4 and 5 and some parts of 3A, 3B, 3C, and 4B), a vapor-*permeable* air barrier should be placed outside of the insulation with no vapor retarder. This allows any vapor or condensation to pass through the wall in either direction.

The *International Building Code* does not require the use of vapor retarders in climate zones 1, 2, or 3 for commercial buildings or in climate zones 1, 2, 3, and 4 for residential construction as prescribed in the *International Residential Code*. When vapor retarders are required, they must have a permeance rating of 1 perm (57 $ng/s \cdot m^2 \cdot Pa$) or less.

The suggestions for mixed climates given above are general guidelines only. The local climate, interior environmental conditions, and specific building materials being used should be reviewed by the designer to determine the preferred use of air and vapor barriers and their placement. For detailed analysis, computer programs are available that can analyze heat and vapor transmission through a proposed wall design throughout the year for a specific climatic region and for specific interior environmental conditions. Two of these are the MOIST program, developed by the National Institute of Standards and Technology, and WUFI/ORNL/IBP, developed jointly by Oak Ridge National Laboratory and the Fraunhofer Institute for Building Physics. Analysis can also be done manually using the dew point method, in which a specific condition and building materials are selected and a temperature gradient line is developed from outside to inside based on the R-values (temperature resistance) of the individual materials.

Air Barriers

Air leakage into buildings can cause a number of problems including excessive moisture, heat loss, poor indoor air quality, and increased heating and cooling costs. The U.S. Department of Energy estimates that up to 40 percent of the energy used to heat and cool a building is due to uncontrolled air leakage.

Although vapor transmission, discussed in the previous section, can be caused by diffusion through materials, vapor transmission by air movement is a larger problem than by diffusion through materials. It is estimated that water vapor carried by air infiltration is 10 to 200 times greater than that carried by diffusion through materials. Air movement is caused by pressure differentials, which are, in turn, caused by wind, the stack effect, or the mechanical system of the building. The stack effect (or chimney effect) is caused by differences in pressure at the top and bottom of a building due to temperature differentials. The effect is most pronounced in high-rise buildings. In a cold climate, air will be warmer in the upper part of the building and cooler at the bottom, causing infiltration of air near the ground and exfiltration at the top.

The solution to the problem of air leakage is to provide a continuous barrier around the conditioned spaces in the building. This is done by using air barrier materials, components, and assemblies to provide a complete air barrier system on vertical and horizontal surfaces exposed to the exterior. Air barrier materials are the primary elements used to provide an air barrier system and include either vapor-permeable or vapor-impermeable barriers. Vapor-impermeable barriers provide both an air barrier and a vapor retarder in the same material. Vapor-permeable barriers include relatively thin sheets of spun-bonded polyolefin, various types of sheathing, vapor-permeable self-adhered membranes, and vapor-permeable fluid-applied products. If the air barrier is vapor permeable it should have a permeance rating of 5 to 10 perms (285 ng/s $\cdot$ m^2 $\cdot$ Pa to 570 ng/s $\cdot$ m^2 $\cdot$ Pa) or greater.

The maximum permeance of an air-barrier material should be 0.004 cfm/ft^2 at 1.57 lbf/ft^2 (0.02 L/s/m^2 at 75 Pa) when tested according to ASTM E2178. Note that 1.57 lbf/ft^2 is 0.3 in. w.g. (water gage) at 68°F (20°C). This value is approximately the permeance of a sheet of $1/2$ in. (13 mm) unpainted gypsum wallboard.

ASHRAE Standard 90.1, *Energy-efficient Design of New Buildings Except Low-rise Residential Buildings,* requires that one of three options be used for many commercial buildings:

1. Individual air barrier material cannot exceed 0.004 cfm/ft^2 at 0.30 in. water (0.02 L/s/m^2 at 75 Pa).
2. Air barrier assemblies cannot exceed 0.04 cfm/ft^2 at 0.30 in. water (0.2 L/s/m^2 at 75 Pa) when tested according to ASTM E1677.

3. Whole building air barriers cannot exceed 0.4 cfm/ft^2 at 0.30 in. water (2.0 L/s/m^2 at 75 Pa) when tested according to ASTM E779.

For individual projects, the requirements of the local building code regarding air and vapor barriers must be determined.

In order for an air barrier system to function properly, the following conditions must be met:

- The air barrier, assemblies, and whole building must meet the minimum permeance ratings listed above or those prescribed by the local building code.
- The air barrier must be continuous around the conditioned spaces including walls, roof, foundation walls, and slabs-on-grade.
- All joints between materials, components, and assemblies must be sealed.
- The air barrier must be securely and tightly joined at other building materials such as windows, doors, roof air barrier components, and foundations.
- All penetrations for pipes, ducts, and similar elements must be sealed.
- The barrier must be securely attached to the structure to prevent billowing, tearing, or breaking away from attachments and other building components. It must resist the loads on it caused by wind, the stack effect, and HVAC systems, both as positive and negative air pressure.
- The air barrier at movement joints must be capable of moving with the joint without breaking or tearing.
- The air barrier must be durable and last the life of the building or be able to be maintained.
- If both a vapor retarder and an air barrier are used and they are separate membranes, the air barrier should be 10 to 20 times more permeable to water vapor diffusion than the vapor retarder to prevent moisture from being trapped between the two layers.

The location of an air barrier within the wall or roof assembly is not important. However, for ease of construction and durability, the air barrier generally should be located behind the exterior cladding and outside of the sheathing. This makes it easier to install, seal, join to other building components, and have it properly supported. If the same material performs the functions of both an air barrier and a vapor retarder, it is usually placed on the outside of the structure and sheathing and behind the cladding. If the air barrier and vapor retarder are made of different materials, their locations within the building envelope depend on the climatic region, the interior environmental conditions, and the specific construction of the envelope.

Common air barriers include spun-bonded polyolefin (house wrap), polyethylene, elastomeric coatings, liquid-applied spray-on or trowel-on materials, self-adhesive membranes, sheathing sealed with tape, silicon-based materials, or some combination of these materials.

Insulation

Combined with properly installed air barriers, thermal insulation provides one of the most important barriers in the building envelope, increasing comfort and saving energy. Selection of the best insulation is problematic because of the many factors that must be considered. Selection criteria include the R-value, long-term thermal performance, required form or installation method for the application, permeability, sustainability issues (described in the next section), ease of application, moisture resistance, fire safety, cost, and how the insulation works with other building materials. In addition, there are many proprietary insulating products and installation methods that should be investigated when deciding on which to specify and detail. They may have different R-values or present unique advantages that the generic form of the insulation does not possess.

The following list of common insulation materials includes brief descriptions of how they are manufactured, common forms, and highlights of environmental considerations.

FIBERGLASS

Fiberglass insulation is produced by melting sand and recycled glass and spinning the product into thin fibers, which are held together with a binder. Fiberglass is most commonly formed into batts, either with or without a paper facing. It is also used as a loose fill for blow-in applications, such as in attics. In batt form, the insulation is placed between studs, floor and roof joists, and other cavities.

Fiberglass commonly contains about 30 percent recycled glass, while up to 90 percent recycled content is possible. There has been some concern that the fibers may be carcinogenic, but no long-term damage has been demonstrated. A small amount of formaldehyde is used in the binder, which has raised some concern. One manufacturer makes a formaldehyde-free product in response to this concern.

CELLULOSE

Cellulose insulation is made from 80 percent to 100 percent recycled paper combined with a fire-retardant additive. For loose-fill applications, a binder is added to prevent settling. It is used for loose-fill attic insulation as well as dry blown-in and wet-spray applications.

The high recycled content of cellulose insulation and its low embodied energy are the main environmental benefits. There have been some concerns about the dust generated during installation and the possible toxicity of some types of fire-retardant treatments. However, with proper installation methods and detailing to ensure that the insulation is isolated from interior spaces and ventilation systems, dust and fibers are not a problem. A low-dust cellulose is available and some manufacturers offer products that use only all-borate fire retardants, which are considered nontoxic.

COTTON

Cotton insulation is made from preconsumer recycled cotton denim scrap material with a small amount of polyester for binding and stability. It is made in loose fill and batt form. Low-toxicity borates are added as a fire retardant.

Cotton insulation has a very high recycled content and requires a minimum amount of energy to manufacture.

MINERAL WOOL

Mineral wool is a generic term for two types of product: rock wool and slag wool. Rock wool is manufactured by melting basalt or other rocks in a high-temperature furnace and then spinning the molten material into long fibers. Binding agents and other materials are added through various manufacturing processes to give the desired properties. Slag wool is manufactured from iron ore blast furnace slag using production methods similar to those of rock wool. Slag wool accounts for about 80 percent of the mineral wool industry. It is formed into batts, blankets, or loose fill material and is used for applications similar to those of fiberglass.

The Environmental Protection Agency (EPA) recommends that rock wool insulation contain at least 50 percent recovered material. However, most manufacturers use 50 percent to 95 percent recycled material, with 75 percent postindustrial content being about average.

PERLITE

Perlite insulation is an expanded form of naturally occurring siliceous volcanic rock. It is manufactured in densities ranging from 2 lb/ft^3 (32 kg/m^3) to 15 lb/ft^3 (240 kg/m^3) and in different forms including loose fill insulation, board insulation, aggregate in lightweight concrete, and as a component in acoustical ceiling tiles. Its most common use for insulation is as loose fill in hollow concrete unit masonry walls and between walls. It is also used as insulation under floating concrete floors.

Perlite is manufactured from a naturally occurring mineral with no recycled content in its loose fill form, but the EPA recommends that perlite composite board contain at least 23 percent postconsumer recovered paper.

EXPANDED POLYSTYRENE BOARD (EPS)

EPS is manufactured by reacting ethylene from natural gas or crude oil with benzene and, through additional chemical processes, forming it into polystyrene beads. The polystyrene beads are then expanded about 40 times with steam and a blowing agent, typically pentane; they are then injected into a mold and further expanded into their final form. Pentane is a non-ozone-depleting chemical. EPS is manufactured in various densities for different applications. Because the material can absorb water, a vapor retarder may be necessary.

EPS is manufactured from petrochemicals and has the highest embodied energy per insulating unit when compared with polyisocyanurate, fiberglass, cellulose, and mineral wool. However, it is manufactured without ozone-depleting chemicals and continues to be a flexible insulation product with a high R-value. It can also use recycled material, although few manufacturing companies are currently doing this.

EXTRUDED POLYSTYRENE BOARD (XPS)

The basic material for XPS is made the same way as EPS, but different blowing agents and forming processes are used to manufacture a closed cell, smooth skin product that is highly resistant to moisture and pressure. XPS has a higher compressive strength than EPS and is more resistant to moisture, making it ideal for roof insulation. XPS is commonly formed into rigid boards for foundation, wall, and roof insulation.

Although XPS has a high insulating value and is strong and highly moisture resistant, one of the main environmental disadvantages, besides requiring petroleum products to manufacture, is that the blowing agent contains ozone-depleting chemicals and can outgass styrene monomer. Some European manufacturers have switched to other blowing agents and the currently used hydrochloro-fluorocarbon (HCFC)-based blowing agent, HCFC-14b, is scheduled to be phased out by 2010. Although polystyrene can be recycled, only one manufacturer currently recycles it.

POLYISOCYANURATE BOARD

Polyisocyanurate insulation is manufactured by combining liquid isocyanate and polyol with catalysts and additives. A blowing agent expands the material into a closed cell structure, which is laminated between engineered facing materials. Polyisocyanurate can also be blown in place.

Polyisocyanurate is used in rigid boards for above-grade applications in roof and wall assemblies. Because it can readily absorb moisture, it is not suitable for below-grade uses unless it is used on the inside of foundation walls.

Like polystyrene, polyisocyanurate requires petroleum products in its manufacture, but it uses a hydrocarbon-based blowing agent that has no ozone depletion potential and no global warming potential. Polyisocyanurate also uses recycled materials including polyethylene terephthalate (PET) from beverage bottles. The EPA recommends that polyisocyanurate rigid foam insulation contain at least 9 percent recovered material.

SPRAY POLYURETHANE

Spray polyurethane insulation is a foam plastic that is applied in the liquid state and rapidly expands about 30 to 50 times its original volume as it quickly cures to a solid form. The proportions of the component materials can be adjusted to vary its densities, amount of expansion, and water-resistant properties. As it foams, the material expands to fill all spaces and acts as an effective air barrier. Polyurethane insulation is also made in rigid foam boards, which can be laminated with a variety of facings.

Spray polyurethane is available in either closed cell or open cell form. The closed cell foam has a higher density and a higher R-value, but some manufacturers still use an ozone-depleting blowing agent. Open cell foams have a lower R-value and lower density but use water and carbon dioxide as the blowing agent, making them environmentally more desirable.

Low-density foam is used to insulate open wall cavities, but because of the amount of expansion, it must be cut off flush with wall studs before finish materials are applied. High-density foams used for roof insulation can effectively cover gaps and the roof structure to prevent thermal bridging while providing a base with high compressive strength for the roofing material.

While petrochemicals are required to manufacture polyurethane insulation and some offgassing occurs, these insulation products are relatively sustainable when considering their high insulating and air sealing properties. The EPA recommends that polyurethane foam-in-place insulation contain at least 5 percent recovered material.

ICYNENE

Icynene is a brand name for a water-based, HCFC-free, low-density, open cell polyurethane insulation. When sprayed into open wall or ceiling cavities, it expands about 100 times and cures to a soft foam. It easily adheres to other building materials and maintains its R-value over time. A different formulation is available that can be used in closed cavities for retrofitting. This formulation does not expand as much and expands only in the area of least resistance to prevent damage to walls and structure while still filling the cavity.

SPRAY-ON CELLULOSE

Spray-on cellulose insulation is made as described above for the loose-fill type. When the wet-spray method is used, the spray device mixes the cellulose with a water-activated acrylic binder. When the wet-spray form is used in walls, a vapor-permeable exterior sheathing should be used.

The EPA recommends that spray-on cellulose insulation contain at least 75 percent postconsumer recovered paper.

SPRAY CEMENTITIOUS INSULATION

Cementitious insulation is a cement-based foam that uses an expanding agent and compressed air to foam the material in place. This type of insulation is inorganic, fire-resistant, lightweight, moisture-resistant, and pest-resistant. Air-Krete™ is one type that is made from magnesium oxide derived from sea water. The cured product has an R-value of 3.9 (27). Cementitious insulation is commonly used to insulate stud cavities.

Although considered environmentally safe, the material has two disadvantage: it is easily damaged by water and it is highly friable.

REFLECTIVE INSULATION

Reflective insulation is made from thin aluminum sheets combined with paper, plastic, or other materials to reduce heat transfer through radiation. Reflective insulation products are typically combined with other materials, such as plastic bubbles or foam, to form small, enclosed air spaces, which also reduces heat transfer by convection. Spray-applied interior radiation control coatings are also available for use on interior surfaces. They are typically lower in cost than foil-type barriers, especially for retrofit applications. In all cases, to be effective, the reflective material must be adjacent to an air space.

Reflective insulation products are typically used in attic spaces to reduce the solar heat gain. Reflective insulation is also used in walls and above unheated crawl spaces.

SUSTAINABILITY ISSUES

As with other building materials, sustainability of insulation involves consideration of its raw material acquisition, manufacture, use in place, and disposal or recycling potential. However, its primary purpose, that of slowing the transfer of heat, is the most important environmental consideration because the long-term energy savings from insulation generally outweigh the disadvantages any particular insulation may have.

From the standpoint of sustainability no insulation material is perfect; there are advantages and disadvantages to each. When other selection factors are considered, such as the required R-value, physical form, cost, water resistance, installation method, combustibility, vapor permeance, and others, the best insulation for the application may not be the most environmentally perfect. However, insulation technology is constantly changing, and many of the environmentally detrimental aspects of insulation are being overcome with new materials and manufacturing techniques. For example, the manufacture of XPS has evolved from the use of highly ozone-depleting chlorofluorocarbons (CFCs) for blowing agents to various types of HCFCs, which are less hazardous but still undesirable. Some manufacturers are now switching to hydrofluorocarbons (HFCs) in anticipation of a planned phase-out of HCFCs by 2010.

Detailing Considerations

There are two basic approaches for creating a weather-resistant exterior wall. One uses a barrier system and the other uses the rain screen principle. The rain screen wall is generally the preferable type. If it is detailed and executed properly, water penetration is virtually eliminated, even with minor imperfections in construction and as the building ages. In contrast, a barrier system wall must be built perfectly and maintained with no leaks over the life of the building to function well.

In a barrier wall system, the exterior cladding serves as the exterior finish, protects the building from the elements, and serves to prevent water, snow, and condensation from entering the building. A solid multiwythe masonry wall or an exterior insulation and finish system applied directly to the structural wall are examples of barrier wall systems. In both cases, if there are small cracks or other defects in any part of the wall, gravity-driven or wind-driven water can seep into the structure or the interior of the building.

In a rain screen wall, the exterior cladding is separated from the waterproof and airtight barriers with an air space cavity. The exterior cladding serves as the finish and protects the remainder of the wall from the gross effects of the weather. Any moisture that penetrates the cladding is prevented from entering the building by a drainage plane of water-resistant material and is directed back to the exterior with flashing, weep holes, or other openings at the bottom of the cavity. Insulation is located inside the drainage plane. The moisture barrier may be either air permeable or impermeable, depending on the climate, interior environmental conditions, and other factors as described in the previous sections on vapor and air barriers.

There are two basic types of rain screen walls. One is a drained and back-ventilated system; the other, the true rain screen, is pressure-equalized. In the former, the exterior cladding does not prevent water from penetrating due to pressure differentials between the exterior of the building and the air cavity. In the latter, the air cavity is vented enough to equalize the pressure on both sides of the exterior cladding to reduce the amount of wind-driven water into the cavity and onto the drainage plane. In a pressure-equalized rain screen, a continuous air barrier is required. In addition to an air barrier, a pressure-equalized design subdivides the air cavity into separate compartments so that air does not flow from high-pressure areas to low-pressure areas as the wind pressure varies across the building.

Figure 5-5.3 illustrates two basic configurations of the elements that make up a well-designed exterior cladding system using the rain screen principle. The concepts described in this section apply to all of the other building envelope details in this book.

Figure 5-5.3(a) illustrates an exterior wall with the insulation in the stud cavity. Figure 5-5.3(b) shows the installation applied to the outboard side of the structural wall. If the structural wall is formed with wood or metal studs, the stud cavity may also be insulated.

Placing the water-resistant drainage plane on the outside of the sheathing, as shown in Figure 5-5.3(a), with an insulated stud cavity makes construction easy and is one of the most common methods used for residential construction. However, the drainage plane/air barrier is subject to damage during construction, and the location of the insulation will create thermal bridges at the studs. If a vapor barrier is used on the warm side of the insulation, the drainage plane/air barrier must be vapor permeable.

With the drainage plane placed on the warm side of the insulation, as shown in Figure 5-5.3(b), it is protected from temperature extremes and construction damage. In addition, the insulation is continuous and prevents thermal bridging at studs or other construction elements. Because the insulation is exposed to moisture in the air space, it must be made of a water-resistant material such as XPS or closed cell spray polyurethane.

Additional detailing considerations include the following:

- The air barrier must be fully supported and continuous to be effective.
- Connections between the structural wall and the cladding should not allow water to travel across the air space. Built-in drips or clips on the connections should be specified.
- Eliminate air movement and ventilation on the conditioned side of the insulation.
- Only one vapor retarder should be used to allow the wall structure to dry through vapor diffusion, either to the outside or the inside.

Figure 5-5.3 Rain screen weather barrier concepts

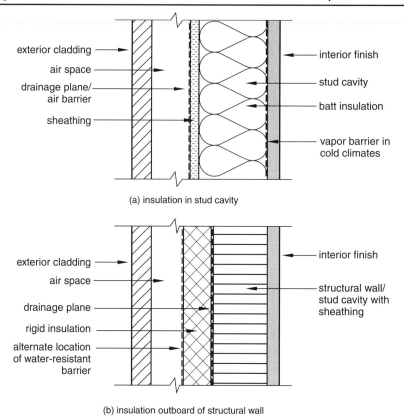

exterior cladding

air space

drainage plane/ air barrier

sheathing

interior finish

stud cavity

batt insulation

vapor barrier in cold climates

(a) insulation in stud cavity

exterior cladding

air space

drainage plane

rigid insulation

alternate location of water-resistant barrier

interior finish

structural wall/ stud cavity with sheathing

(b) insulation outboard of structural wall

- Carefully consider the use of vinyl wallcovering on the inside face of exterior walls in hot, humid climates. If a vapor barrier is not placed on the warm side of the insulation, water vapor may condense behind the wallcovering and cause mold growth. Vapor-permeable paint or other permeable finish materials should be considered.
- In cold and mixed climate regions where vapor transmission from the interior to the exterior is usually a problem, vapor can also travel from outside to inside when the cladding is absorptive (such as masonry) and the wall is heated through solar radiation.
- Eliminate or minimize thermal shortcuts through thermal insulation. High-conductivity materials such as metal window framing or metal studs can significantly reduce the effectiveness of insulation.
- If a radiant barrier is used, it must have an air space on the warm side to be effective.

5-6   EXTERIOR INSULATION AND FINISH SYSTEM AT BASE

Description

An exterior insulation and finish system (EIFS) consists of a synthetic plaster-like finish applied over a rigid insulation board, which is attached to building sheathing. Although portland cement stucco is included in these types of finish systems, the coating generally consists of various types of polymers, usually acrylics, or a mixture of cement and polymers. EIFS finishes provide

Figure 5-6 Exterior insulation and finish system at base

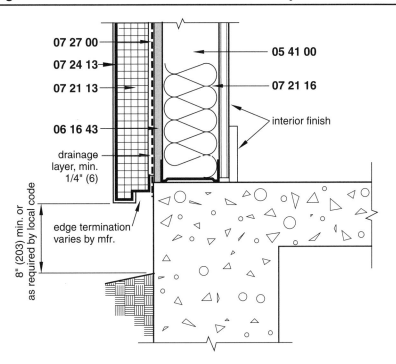

excellent energy savings by placing the insulation outside of the building structure, thereby preventing thermal bridging that can result from systems with insulation in the stud cavities.

The exact formulation of an EIFS varies with each manufacturer, but there are two basic classifications: polymer based (Class PB) and polymer modified (Class PM). A variation of the polymer-based system is the high-impact PB system, which is like the PB system but includes a heavy-duty mesh and an additional layer of base coat.

PB systems use EPS or polyisocyanurate board insulation with the base coat applied directly to the insulation with an embedded fiberglass mesh. The base coat is about $1/16$ in. (1.6 mm) thick and has a high percentage of polymeric binder that gives the system a great deal of flexibility. The finish coat, like that of the PM system, consists of acrylic polymer, sand, pigments, and other additives. The majority of EIFS installations in the United States are PB systems.

PM systems use extruded polystyrene, which is mechanically fastened to the building sheathing and structure along with the reinforcing mesh. The base coats of PM systems are thicker, from $3/16$ in. to $3/8$ in. (5 mm to 10 mm), and include a higher percentage of portland cement than PB systems. As a result, control joints are needed in PM systems to limit cracking. They should be located 10 ft to 12 ft (3048 mm to 3658 mm) apart, with no section exceeding 150 ft^2 (14 m^2).

EIFS finishes can be applied as a barrier system or a drainage system. A barrier system requires that the finish, sealant, and other aspects of the system be constructed and maintained perfectly to prevent water infiltration. As this is generally not possible, EIFS finishes are typically installed as a rain screen or drainage wall where any moisture that does penetrate the finish is drained and directed to the outside with flashing or other details.

Figures 5-6, 5-7, and 5-8 illustrate a PB system. These systems are more flexible than PM systems and do not require expansion joints; also, they are generally less expensive than PM systems. However, PM systems are more resistant to impact than standard PB systems, and the extruded polystyrene has a slightly higher thermal resistance than expanded polystyrene and is more resistant to water penetration.

EIFS systems are proprietary. Each manufacturer supplies a complete system and has specific recommendations for insulation, sealants, and other components that are not part of the system. Variations in detailing should be verified with the manufacturer.

Limitations of Use

- This detail does not include retrofit applications of EIFS systems.
- Local building codes may limit the type or thickness of the insulation.
- EIFS should not be applied below grade, and a minimum distance of 8 in. (203 mm) should be maintained above finished grade or other finished surfaces.

Detailing Considerations

- The structural substrate may be concrete, masonry, or wood or metal studs. On clean masonry surfaces, PB systems may be directly adhered to the masonry.
- Decorative reveals may be constructed by routing joints in the insulation or using different thicknesses of insulation.
- Provide a weather barrier on the outside of the sheathing. This should serve as both an air barrier and a vapor retarder as required by the climate. See Section 5-5.
- A vapor barrier may be required between the interior finish and the batt insulation. Refer to Section 5-5.
- Expansion joints should be sized to accommodate the expected building movement but should not be less than $3/4$ in. (19 mm). Expansion joints are generally required in the following locations:
  - Where there are expansion joints in the substrate or the substrate material changes
  - Where the EIFS abuts dissimilar materials
  - At points of anticipated building movement
  - At changes in building height
  - At floor lines in multilevel wood frame construction (typical shrinkage may range from $1/2$ in. to $3/4$ in. (13 mm to 19 mm) per story near the rim joist)
- Because a high-impact PB system costs more than a standard PB system, its use should be limited to locations where it is needed.
- The size of exposed aggregates is limited in PB systems because of the thin base coat. Larger aggregates require the use of a PM system.
- Provide flashing with drips over windows, doors, soffits, and other horizontal openings to direct water away from the finished surface.
- Avoid locating finishes where they may be subject to continuous water contact such as near grade level, at sidewalls, or in areas of rain splash.
- The finish coat should not be carried into joints where sealant will be applied. The sealant should adhere directly to the base coat.
- Verify that the EIFS coating is vapor permeable to avoid a double vapor retarder situation.

Coordination Required

- Building structure and substrate movement must be limited to avoid cracking.
- The substrate must be even to within $1/4$ in. in 4 ft (6 mm in 1220 mm).

Likely Failure Points

- Improper flashing above openings, at window sills, and at other penetrations in the system
- Delamination of standard exterior gypsum sheathing caused by exposure to moisture (Fiberglass mat–faced gypsum board is recommended instead.)
- Softening of the polymeric finish caused by prolonged contact with water
- No back wrapping of the edges of the EIFS at penetrations or terminations
- Color variations in adjacent panels in the same plane applied on different days due to differing curing conditions or different mixes
- Sealant breaks caused by delamination of the finish coat from the base coat if the finish coat is carried into joints as a base for the sealant
- Cracking at the corners of openings because insulation boards were not notched in an L shape to fit around the corners
- Cracking at the corners of openings because diagonal reinforcing mesh was not installed at the corners
- Lack of adequate slope on sills and other upward-facing surfaces (Minimum slope should be 6:12.)
- Inadequate base and finish coats in reveals and changes in thicknesses of insulation

Materials

05 41 00 METAL STUD

Materials

Zinc-coated, ASTM A653/A653M, Grade G-90.

ASTM C955.

Sized for maximum deflection, under full wind load, of L/240.

Execution

ASTM C1007.

Studs at openings designed to transfer loads of a tributary area within deflection criteria.

06 16 43 SHEATHING

Materials

Fiberglass mat–faced gypsum board (ASTM C1177) or gypsum fiber panels (ASTM C1278).

$1/2$ in. (13 mm) minimum fiberglass mat–faced gypsum board is recommended.

Execution

ASTM C1280.

Seal joints with self-adhering tape as approved by the sheathing manufacturer.

07 21 16 BUILDING INSULATION

Rigid insulation or batt insulation placed between furring or metal studs on the inside wall.

In mild climates, this additional insulation may not be required.

07 21 13 BUILDING BOARD INSULATION

Materials

EPS, 1 pcf (16 kg/m^3) density, minimum $3/4$ in. (19 mm) thick, maximum 4 in. (100 mm) thick, ASTM E2430.

Polyisocyanurate foam boards may also be used.

Mineral wool or fiberglass boards are available with some proprietary systems if a non-combustible system is required, but these must be adhered and mechanically fastened.

Some systems use insulation board grooved on the back side to act as a drainage space against the sheathing and as a weather barrier. Other systems use vertical beads of adhesive to provide a drainage space.

Execution

Install in accordance with manufacturers' instructions.

At least 30 percent of the area of the board must be adhered using the manufacturer's recommended adhesive.

Some building codes may require full adhesion if insulation is applied over paper-faced gypsum sheathing.

Boards must be tightly butted, with cracks over $1/16$ in. (1.6 mm) filled with slivers of insulation.

Stagger boards at corners and make an L-shaped notch for boards around the corners of windows and other openings.

07 24 13 POLYMER-BASED EXTERIOR FINISH

Materials

Base coat consisting of polymers and portland cement, depending on the manufacturer's formulation.

Base coat applied to a thickness of about $1/16$ in. (1.6 mm) with a fiberglass mesh embedded as the base coat is applied.

Impact resistance may be increased by using a heavier mesh and increasing the thickness to approximately $1/2$ in. (13 mm).

A finish coat of acrylic polymer, sand, pigment, and other additives as required by the installation and as recommended by the manufacturer.

Execution

Install in strict accordance with manufacturers' instructions and ASTM C1397, ASTM C1516, or ASTM C1535, as applicable.

The mesh and base coat are used to backwrap the insulation as well as return the finish at door and window openings.

Place extra reinforcing mesh diagonally on the outside corners of door and window openings.

The finish coat must be applied when the surface is in the shade.

07 27 00 AIR BARRIER

Nonwoven, spun-bonded olefin sheet membrane, liquid-applied membrane, or self-adhering membrane, ASTM E1677.

Vapor-permeable or vapor-impermeable as required by local climatic conditions.

Install according to the manufacturer's instructions.

Refer to Section 5-5 for more information.

5-7 EXTERIOR INSULATION AND FINISH SYSTEM AT PARAPET

Description

Figure 5-7 is a continuation of Fig. 5-6 and illustrates one method of terminating an EIFS at a parapet. Although the top of the parapet may be trimmed with the same finish as

Figure 5-7 Exterior insulation and finish system at parapet

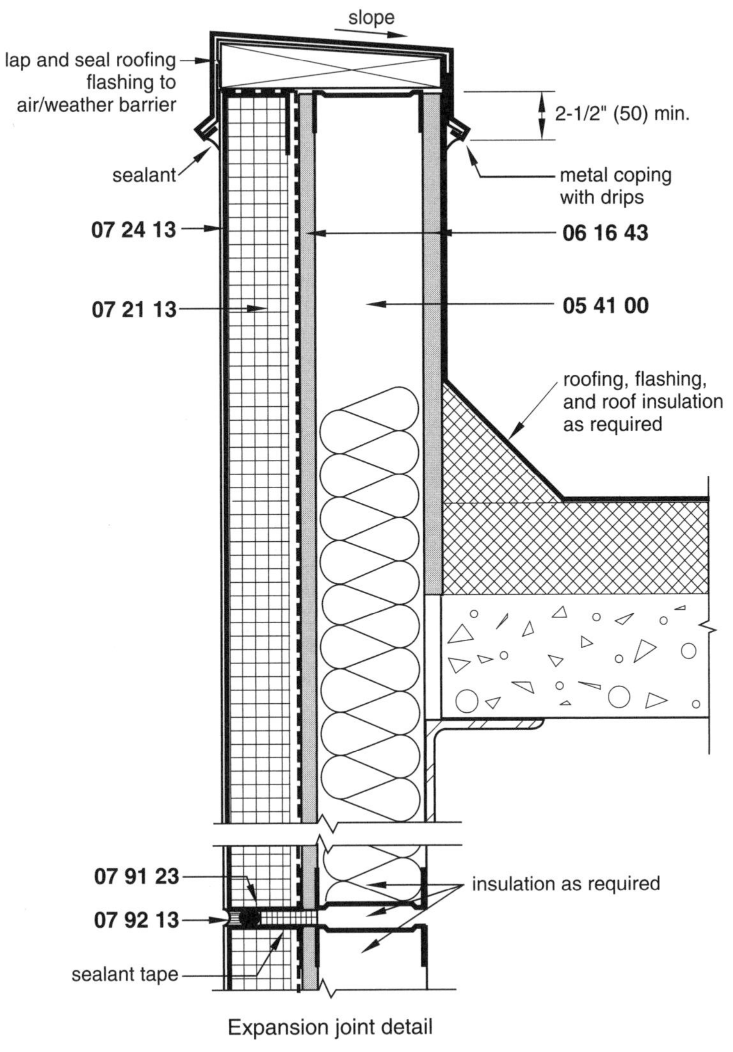

the walls, a metal coping offers better protection from leakage and water damage to the finish.

Limitations of Use

- This detail does not include retrofit applications of EIFS.
- This detail does not show the use of EIFS on the roof side of the parapet.

Detailing Considerations

- The parapet should be high enough to prevent water from blowing over the top and soaking the upper portions of the wall.
- Although the back of the parapet may be finished with the EIFS, the lowest edge should be kept far enough above the roofline to prevent standing water or rain splash from continual wetting of the surface of the EIFS.
- See Section 5-6 for other detailing considerations.

Coordination Required

- Joints should be located where building or substrate movement is expected.
- The metal stud wall should be sized to prevent excessive deflection from wind loads.
- See Section 5-6 for other areas requiring coordination and for likely failure points.

Materials

See Fig. 5-6 for additional material requirements.

07 91 23 BACKER ROD

Closed cell polyethylene foam, with the diameter at least 25 percent greater than the joint width.

As recommended by the sealant manufacturer.

07 92 13 SEALANT

Materials

ASTM C1382, ASTM C1481.

ASTM C920, Type M or S, Grade NS, minimum Class 25, compatible with the finish system type and as recommended by the EIFS manufacturer and the sealant manufacturer.

Execution

ASTM C1193.

Apply sealant to the base coat, not the finish coat, of a PB system.

Sealant depth equal to the width of the joint up to $1/2$ in. (13 mm), with a minimum depth of $1/4$ in. (6 mm).

Sealant depth $1/2$ in. (13 mm) for joint widths from $1/2$ in. (13 mm) to 1 in. (25 mm).

See Section 5-38 for more information on design joints.

5-8 EXTERIOR INSULATION AND FINISH SYSTEM OPENINGS

Description

Figure 5-8 is a continuation of Figs. 5-6 and 5-7 and illustrates one method of detailing commercial window openings in an EIFS. Windows and other openings must be detailed to provide flashing around the opening, to allow water to weep out of the drainage plane, and to provide continuity of the water and air barrier.

Limitations of Use

- This detail shows one method of detailing an aluminum window frame. Details for wood windows and other types of openings may vary, depending on the manufacturers' recommendations.
- Flashing and sealant details for pipes and other small penetrations may differ slightly from those shown here. Verify recommendations with the manufacturer.

Detailing Considerations

- Flashing at the head and sill must include integral end dams.
- Flashing on the interior side and end dams should be upturned a minimum distance equal to the expected water head pressure based on test results or as recommended by the window manufacturer.

Figure 5-8 Exterior insulation and finish system at opening

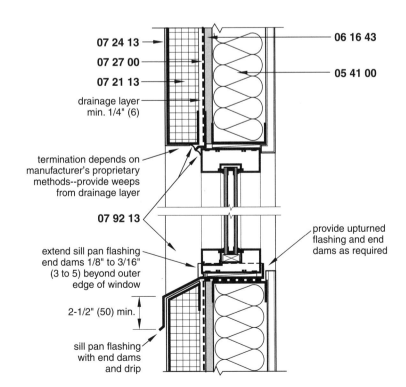

- Subsill membrane flashing below the metal sill flashing should overlap the exterior drainage plane membrane.
- Sealant is required at all flashing extensions beyond the outside plane of the finish surface of the EIFS.
- Sill flashing may be detailed to be concealed. Refer to the *EIMA Guide to Exterior Insulation & Finish System Construction*.
- See Sections 5-6 and 5-7 for other detailing considerations.

Coordination Required

- Verify that opening details provide continuity of the air and moisture barrier.
- Make sure that there is an overlapping transition from the jamb flashing to the end dams of the sub-sill metal flashing.
- See Section 5-6 and 5-7 for other areas requiring coordination and for likely failure points.

Materials

See Figs. 5-6 and 5-7 for additional material requirements.

07 92 13 SEALANT

Materials

ASTM C1382, ASTM C1481.

ASTM C920, Type M or S, Grade NS, minimum Class 25, compatible with the finish system type and as recommended by the EIFS manufacturer and the sealant manufacturer.

Execution

ASTM C1193.

Apply sealant to the base coat, not the finish coat, of a PB system.

Sealant depth equal to the width of the joint up to $1/2$ in. (13 mm), with a minimum depth of $1/4$ in. (6 mm).

Sealant depth $1/2$ in. (13 mm) for joint widths from $1/2$ in. (13 mm) to 1 in. (25 mm).

See Section 5-38 for more information on design joints.

5-9 ASPHALT/GLASS FIBER SHINGLES AT EAVES

Description

Asphalt and glass fiber roofing shingles are two of the most common types of roofing materials for residential and small commercial buildings. Figure 5-9 shows the commonly accepted method of applying these shingles over new construction.

Although this detail represents the traditional method of providing attic ventilation above the ceiling insulation, an alternate detail continues the wall air barrier up to a plane above the rafters. Battens can then be applied to support the roof sheathing and to provide ventilation between the air barrier and the sheathing. This approach vents the roof system, reduces air

Figure 5-9 Asphalt/fiberglass shingles at eaves 07 31 13

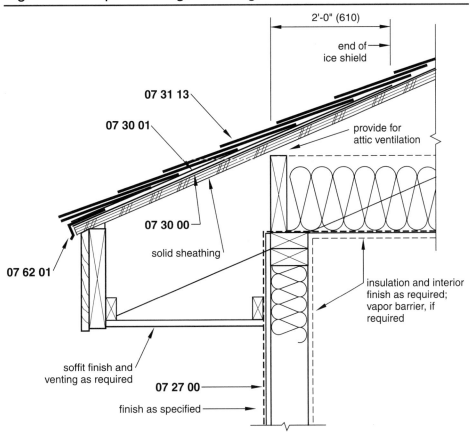

2'-0" (610)

end of → ice shield

07 31 13

07 30 01

provide for attic ventilation

07 30 00

solid sheathing

07 62 01

insulation and interior finish as required; vapor barrier, if required

soffit finish and venting as required

07 27 00

finish as specified

leakage into the attic space, and still allows moisture to escape through the vapor-permeable air barrier. This detailing approach can be used with asphalt shingles as well as with wood shingles and tile roofing.

Detailing Considerations

- Generally, asphalt or glass fiber shingles (and those without tabs and lock-down shingles) should only be applied over roof decks with a minimum slope of 4 in 12. Self-sealing shingles may be applied to roof decks with a minimum slope of 3 in 12 if two layers of asphalt-saturated felt are applied as an underlayment.
- In severe climates or where the January mean temperature is 30°F (−1°C) or less, an ice shield should be applied from the eaves to a point 24 in. (610 mm) inside the outside face of the exterior wall or as required by the local code. This ice shield may be a peel-and-stick proprietary elastomeric or modified bituminous product or two plies of 15 lb felt set in hot mastic.

Coordination Required

- Shingles with the appropriate fire rating must be selected.
- Provide adequate ventilation in the attic space above the insulation.

Materials

07 27 00 AIR BARRIER

Nonwoven, spun-bonded olefin sheet membrane, liquid-applied membrane, or self-adhering membrane, ASTM E1677.

Vapor-permeable or vapor-impermeable as required by local climatic conditions.

Install according to the manufacturer's instructions.

Refer to Section 5-5 for more information.

07 30 01 ICE SHIELD

Self-adhering polymer-modified bituminous sheet material, ASTM D1970.

Install according to the manufacturer's instructions.

07 30 30 UNDERLAYMENT

15 lb nonperforated asphalt-saturated felt, ASTM D4869, or cold-applied, self-adhering membrane, ASTM D1970.

Apply asphalt-saturated felt horizontally, lapping edges a minimum of 2 in. (50 mm) and ends 4 in. (100 mm).

Apply the self-adhering membrane according to the manufacturer's directions.

07 31 13 SHINGLES

Asphalt or glass fiber–reinforced roofing shingles in the desired style and color.

Use 11 or 12 gage (3.175 mm or 2.779 mm) hot-dip galvanized roofing nails with deformed shanks.

Nails should extend through the sheathing or at least ³/₄ in. (19 mm) into the wood decking.

Apply nails in locations as recommended by the manufacturer.

Apply a starter course along the eaves prior to installing the first course of shingles.

Apply successive courses with exposure and fasteners as required by the type of shingle used and as recommended by the manufacturer.

Provide flashing at valleys, ridges, vertical surfaces, chimneys, and other areas as required. Use step flashing where the rake of the roof intersects vertical surfaces.

07 62 01 DRIP EDGE

Minimum 28 gage (0.396 mm) galvanized steel or another noncorrosive type of edging.

The drip edge should not extend more than 3 in. (75 mm) from the roof edge.

Apply the drip edge over the ice shield and under the underlayment.

Apply to eaves and rakes of the roof with nails spaced 8 to 10 in. (203 to 254 mm) apart.

5-10 WOOD SHINGLES AT EAVES

Description

Wood shingles are manufactured wood roofing products with uniform thicknesses and lengths. Wood shakes are products split from logs and shaped by the manufacturer into one of several types of roofing products. Figure 5-10 illustrates a common method of installing wood shingles, although the application of shakes is similar. The alternate approach of continuing the air barrier above the rafters, as discussed in Section 5-9, may also be used.

Limitations of Use

- This detail is not for the application of wood shingles over existing roofing.
- This detail is for the application of wood shingles only. Wood shakes require slightly different installation procedures.
- Solid sheathing should be used where wind-driven snow is prevalent.

Figure 5-10 Wood shingles at eaves 07 31 29

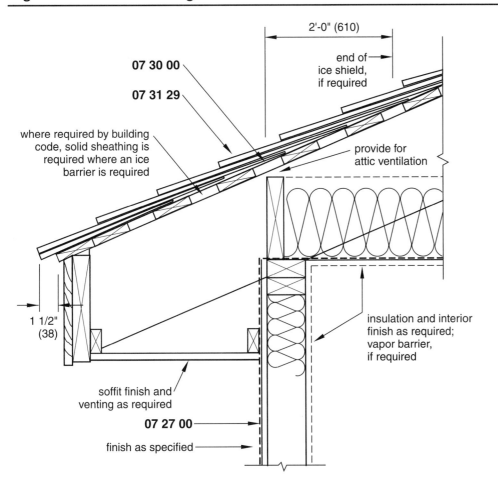

Detailing Considerations

- Generally, the minimum roof slope for shingles and shakes is 4 in 12. Special details and installation procedures are required for slopes less than 4 in 12 but are usually not recommended.
- Wood shingles and shakes may be installed over solid or spaced sheathing. Spaced sheathing allows the shingles to breathe. Spaced sheathing for shingles consists of 1 in. × 4 in. (25 mm × 100 mm) nominal boards spaced on centers equal to the weather exposure of the shingles.
- Breather-type building paper must be applied over solid or spaced sheathing.
- When required by the local code or when ice formation along the eaves is likely, an ice barrier applied over sheathing should be used. See Section 5-9.

Coordination Required

- Local codes may require fire-treated wood shingles or shakes.
- Provide adequate ventilation in the attic space above the insulation.

Materials

07 27 00 Air barrier

Nonwoven, spun-bonded olefin sheet membrane, liquid-applied membrane, or self-adhering membrane, ASTM E1677.

Vapor-permeable or vapor-impermeable as required by local climatic conditions.

Install according to the manufacturer's instructions.

Refer to Section 5-5 for more information.

07 30 30 Underlayment

Asphalt-saturated felt, ASTM D226, Type I.

Apply asphalt-saturated felt horizontally, lapping edges a minimum of 2 in. (50 mm) and ends 4 in. (100 mm).

07 31 29 Wood shingles

Install with the maximum exposure as required by the grade and length of shingle being used or as recommended by the manufacturer. Roofs with slopes from 3 in 12 to 4 in 12 require smaller exposures.

Apply a starter course at the eaves.

Space shingles $1/4$ in. (6 mm) to $3/8$ in. (6 mm to 10 mm) apart.

Overhand shingles 1 in. (25 mm) at gable ends.

Use hot-dipped galvanized or aluminum nails of the sizes required by the type and size of shingle being used.

Provide flashing at valleys, ridges, vertical surfaces, chimneys, and other areas as required. Use step flashing where the rake of the roof intersects vertical surfaces.

5-11   ROOFING TILES AT EAVES

Description

Figure 5-11 shows a common method of installing clay roofing tile. Although clay tile is available in many flat or rolled shapes, the installation of both varieties is very similar. Clay tile requires careful installation and attention to flashing and closure pieces to achieve a watertight roof. The alternate approach of continuing the air barrier above the rafters, as discussed in Section 5-9, may also be used.

Detailing Considerations

- In general, the minimum required roof slope is 4 in 12. Flat shingle tile should only be installed on roofs with a minimum slope of 5 in 12. Roll or flat tiles may be installed on roofs with slopes of $2\frac{1}{2}$ in 12 to 4 in 12 if two layers of 30 lb felt are set in hot asphalt or as required by the local building code.
- In severe climates or where the January mean temperature is 30°F (−1°C) or less, an ice shield should be applied from the eaves to a point 24 in. (610 mm) inside the outside face of the exterior wall. This ice shield may be a proprietary elastomeric or modified bituminous product or two plies of 15 lb felt set in hot asphalt or mastic.
- The first course of tile must be installed over an eaves closure strip.

Figure 5-11 Roofing tiles at eaves 07 32 00

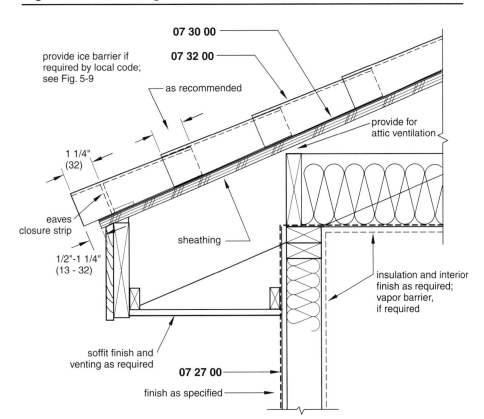

Coordination Required

- Plywood or particleboard sheathing should be spaced a minimum of $1/16$ in. (1.6 mm) apart.
- If gutters are used, flashing should be placed under the roofing felt extending 4 in. to 8 in. (102 mm to 203 mm) from the eaves.
- In high-wind areas, hurricane clips or other fastening devices may be required.

Materials

07 30 00 UNDERLAYMENT

30 lb nonperforated, asphalt-saturated felt, ASTM D226, Type II; or asphalt-saturated and coated base sheet, ASTM D2626, Type I; or asphalt roll roofing, ASTM D6380, Class M.

Apply horizontally, lapping edges a minimum of 2 in. (51 mm) and ends 4 in. (102 mm).

07 32 00 ROOFING TILE

Roll or flat tiles as selected for the project requirements.

Nails should be 11 gage (3.175 mm) noncorrosive type and should penetrate the sheathing.

Nails should be applied according to the recommendations of the manufacturer but not so tightly as to lift the loose end.

Flat tile roofs require an under-eaves course.

Use ridge tiles, gable end tiles, and other special shapes as required.

Provide flashing at valleys, ridges, vertical surfaces, chimneys, and other areas as required. Use continuous base flashing and counterflashing where the rake of the roof intersects vertical surfaces.

5-12 PREFORMED METAL WALL PANEL AT BASE

Description

Figures 5-12 and Fig. 5-13 show a typical application of a factory-assembled, laminated exterior metal wall panel. These types of panels are non-load-bearing and are fabricated by laminating a layer of metal on either side of an insulating core. The panel is designed to span between supports of a structural framework and provide the finished exterior cladding of the wall assembly. The exterior finish may be aluminum, stainless steel, porcelain enamel, or another proprietary finish. In most cases, glazing or framing for glazing is not an integral part of the panel system and must be detailed separately.

Because metal panel systems are proprietary, the exact method of detailing will vary with the manufacturer and the particular requirements of the project. This section outlines some of the general considerations of most systems.

Figure 5-12 Preformed metal wall panel at base 07 42 13.1

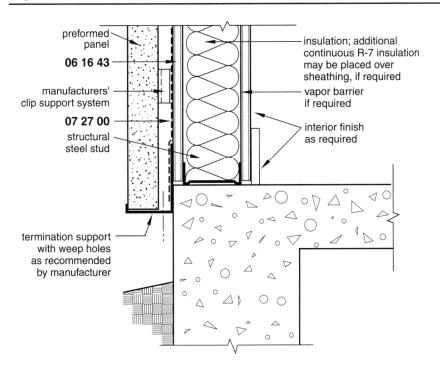

preformed panel
06 16 43

manufacturers' clip support system
07 27 00
structural steel stud

termination support with weep holes as recommended by manufacturer

insulation; additional continuous R-7 insulation may be placed over sheathing, if required

vapor barrier if required

interior finish as required

Detailing Considerations

- This type of exterior wall system employs the rain screen principle, so the exposed joints and sealants provide the primary weather barrier, with the air/moisture barrier behind them providing secondary water protection.
- The insulating core may be very thin and only thick enough to provide rigidity to the panel or it may be thicker and provide significant insulating properties to the entire wall assembly. If the rain screen principle is used, extra insulation in the wall panel itself is not needed, as the insulation is provided between the studs and/or as a continuous layer over the sheathing.
- Although these types of wall panels are typically installed flush, with thin joints, they may also be set within an exposed grid framework or batten system.
- The edges of the panels must be detailed to allow for movement resulting from temperature changes, building movement, wind deflection, and other causes.
- Connection details must allow for tolerances of the supporting framework.
- Generally, the greatest economy results from minimizing the number of shapes and sizes of panels.

Coordination Required

- Joints must be sized to allow for the anticipated movement of the panels and the supporting framework.
- Window and door frames should be attached to the supporting framework, not the exterior panel.

- Provide drips at soffits, window heads, and other horizontal surfaces to prevent leakage into horizontal joints and staining of adjacent surfaces.
- Further insulation may be required in addition to that provided in the stud cavity.
- Provide vertical expansion joints where building expansion joints occur.
- Detail connections of panels to the supporting framework to avoid galvanic action.

Materials

06 16 43 SHEATHING

Materials

Fiberglass mat–faced gypsum board (ASTM C1177) or gypsum fiber panels (ASTM C1278).

One-half inch (13 mm) minimum fiberglass mat–faced gypsum board is recommended.

Execution

ASTM C1280.

Seal joints with self-adhering tape as approved by the sheathing manufacturer.

07 27 00 AIR BARRIER

Nonwoven, spun-bonded olefin sheet membrane, liquid-applied membrane, or self-adhering membrane, ASTM E1677.

Vapor-permeable or vapor-impermeable as required by local climatic conditions.

Install according to the manufacturer's instructions.

Refer to Section 5-5 for more information.

5-13 PREFORMED METAL WALL PANEL AT PARAPET

Description

Figure 5-13 is a continuation of Fig. 5-12 and illustrates one way of terminating a preformed wall panel at the parapet. Although Fig. 5-13 shows structural steel studs as the supporting framework, the substrate can also be concrete or masonry. Because wall panel systems are proprietary, follow the specific recommendations of the panel manufacturer.

Detailing Considerations

- If recommended by the manufacturer, preformed coping pieces that match the wall system may be used instead of separate metal copings.
- Masonry backup for the parapet may be used instead of metal studs.
- The edges of the panels must be detailed to allow for movement resulting from temperature changes, building movement, wind deflection, and other causes.
- Connection details must allow for tolerances of the supporting framework.
- See Section 5-12 for other detailing considerations.

Figure 5-13 Preformed metal wall panel at parapet 07 42 13.2

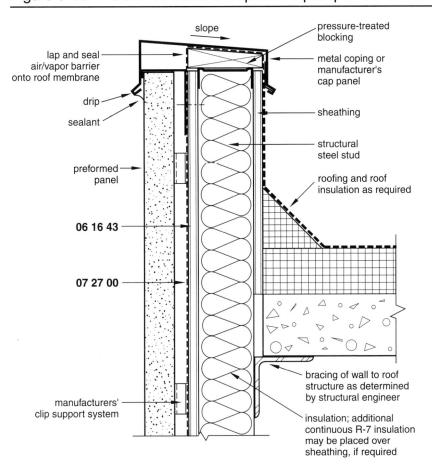

slope

pressure-treated blocking

lap and seal air/vapor barrier onto roof membrane

metal coping or manufacturer's cap panel

drip

sealant

sheathing

structural steel stud

preformed panel

roofing and roof insulation as required

06 16 43

07 27 00

bracing of wall to roof structure as determined by structural engineer

manufacturers' clip support system

insulation; additional continuous R-7 insulation may be placed over sheathing, if required

Coordination Required

- Connection details must allow for differential movement of the panel and its supporting framework caused by wind loading and differences in thermal expansion of the two materials. This is especially important because both faces of the parapet are exposed to the weather.
- Provide drips at soffits, window heads, and other horizontal surfaces to prevent leakage into horizontal joints and staining of adjacent surfaces.
- Further insulation may be required in addition to that provided in the stud cavity.
- See Section 5-12 for other coordination and material requirements.

5-14   ROOFING SYSTEMS ON STEEL DECK

Description

Figure 5-14 illustrates some of the general considerations in developing roofing systems for low-slope steel structural decks. Low-slope roofs are considered those with slopes less than 3 in 12. In most cases, low-slope roofs must have a slope of at least 1/4 in./ft (20 mm/m).

Figure 5-14 Roofing Systems on Steel Deck 07 22 00.1

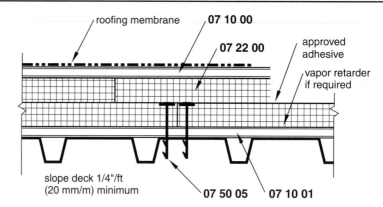

Building codes give requirements for fire resistance, wind resistance, physical properties, and impact resistance of roof assemblies as well as for accessories such as flashing. In addition, an owner's insurance carrier may require that a roof meet further testing standards.

Required fire ratings of roofs are based on Underwriters Laboratories (UL) classes or Factory Mutual Global (FMG) class ratings. The *International Building Code* requires that roof assemblies meet certain testing standards, depending on the construction type and, in some instances, the fire zone. Roofs are classified into three categories—A (severe exposure), B (moderate exposure), and C (light exposure)—as defined by ASTM E108, *Test Methods for Fire Tests of Roof Coverings* or UL 790, *Tests for Fire Resistance of Roof Covering Materials.* These tests are identical.

For wind resistance, the *International Building Code* requires nonballasted roof assemblies to be tested in accordance with FM 4450, FM 4470, UL 580, or UL 1897. Ballasted roofs must be designed in accordance with ANSI/SPRI RP-4, *Wind Design Guide for Ballasted Single-ply Roofing Systems.*

FMG standards generally apply only to buildings that are insured by companies that use the Factory Mutual system. For fire resistance, FMG has two classes, Class 1 and Class 2. Class 1 is the highest rating and has the lowest insurance rates by FMG-affiliated insurance companies. Class 2 roofs require a higher insurance premium. For wind resistance, there are several Factory Mutual Research Corporation (FMRC) ratings—for example, 1-60 and 1-90. The numbers 60 and 90 refer to negative force, in pounds per square foot, that a roof assembly can withstand.

In all cases, the local building code requirements and the owner's insurance requirements should be determined prior to detailing and specifying roof coverings.

Limitations of Use

- This detail does not include nailable decks, concrete decks, or applying insulation over existing roofs.
- Protected membrane roofing is not included. See Section 5-36.

Detailing Considerations

- The decking should have a minimum slope for drainage of 1/4 in./ft (20 mm/m); however, 1/2 in./ft (40 mm/m) is preferred. If the structural deck is flat, the slope may be achieved with tapered insulation.

- The specific type of insulation used depends on the thermal resistance needed, compatibility with the roofing membrane used, the insulation's ability to span the decking flutes, cost, moisture resistance, and impact resistance. Polyisocyanurate is commonly used for roof insulation because of its high R-value, moisture resistance, impact resistance, and compatibility with a wide variety of roofing membrane types. Refer to Sections 5-16, 5-21, 5-26, and 5-31 for more information on insulation for specific types of roofs.
- A double layer of insulation is the preferred application method, with the first layer mechanically attached to the steel deck and the second layer applied to the first with a material appropriate for the type of insulation used. The joints between layers should be offset to reduce air leaks. In climates where a high R-value is not required, the cover board may be considered the second layer of insulation.
- A cover board, often called an *overlayment* or *recover board,* should be used above the insulation and below the membrane. A cover board protects the insulation from damage during and after construction, supports the roofing membrane, provides added thermal and sound insulation, and protects the insulation from fire. In addition, high temperatures, hot asphalt, and solvent-based adhesives will disintegrate expanded polystyrene and extruded polystyrene. Alternately, insulation with an integral cover board may be used.
- In some cases, an underlayment must be used above the steel deck and below the insulation. This underlayment provides structural support for the insulation and may be required as a thermal barrier. The *International Building Code* provides an exception to the thermal barrier requirement if the insulation is part of a Class A, B, or C roof covering, provided that the roof assembly passes the FM 4450 or UL 1256 test.
- Deck flutes, the long dimension of insulation boards, and felts should run parallel to each other and be perpendicular to the roof slope.
- When a vapor retarder is used, venting of the insulation may be required to allow trapped moisture to escape. This may be accomplished with the use of roof relief vents or edge venting.

Coordination Required

- The insulation or cover board must be compatible with the roofing membrane used.
- The insulation selected must meet the roof class fire rating requirements of the applicable building code.
- The insulation must be able to span the flutes of the steel decking used. If an underlayment is used, verify the thickness required based on the flute spacing.
- For slopes over $1/2$ in./ft (40 mm/m) or as recommended by the manufacturer, roofing felts should be back nailed, that is, nailed to blocking securely attached to the structural deck with the same thickness as the insulation. Verify the required spacing of the blocking with the roofing manufacturer.
- Verify expected deflection of the structural deck so that the slope is not defeated.
- Verify the need for a vapor retarder. It should be installed where it will be warmer than the winter design dew-point temperature. The vapor retarder is generally located between the two layers of insulation to prevent puncturing and to satisfy fire rating requirements. Alternately, if an underlayment is used, the vapor retarder may be located above the underlayment, below the insulation.
- If a separate vapor retarder is used, it should be connected to the wall air and vapor retarders.

Likely Failure Points

- Blistering or delamination of the roofing membrane or insulation failure caused by vapor migration through the insulation
- Loss of some insulating capacity caused by *thermal drift* (Thermal drift is the change in R-value of an insulation as it ages. For example, polyurethane may lose some insulation value as low-conductivity gas escapes and is replaced with air.)
- Incompatibility of the insulation with the roofing membrane, especially bituminous roofs

Materials

07 10 00 COVER BOARD

Glass mat gypsum board, ASTM C1177.

Alternate materials may include wood fiber board, asphaltic board, plywood, and oriented strand board (OSB), among others.

07 10 01 UNDERLAYMENT

Glass mat gypsum board, ASTM C1177.

Thickness as required to span deck fluting and as required for the thermal barrier: 1/4 in., 1/2 in., or 5/8 in. (6 mm, 13 mm, or 16 mm).

07 22 00 ROOF DECK INSULATION

Materials

The following types of rigid insulation are commonly used over steel decking for the types of roofs described in the following details:

Polyisocyanurate foam board, ASTM C591 and ASTM C1289.
Extruded polystyrene, ASTM C578.
Expanded polystyrene, ASTM C578.
Perlite, ASTM C728.

Composite boards are also available that combine insulation and a covering of OSB, plywood, or other material.

Apply in thicknesses as required for the needed thermal resistance.

Verify compatibility with the roofing membrane used.

Execution

Apply insulation in a double layer with a thin layer attached to the steel deck and a thicker layer with higher thermal resistance applied over that layer.

The edges of the insulation should be supported on the deck flanges.

Edges and end joints of double-layer applications should be vertically staggered.

07 50 05 MECHANICAL FASTENERS

Threaded self-tapping screw with a 3 in. (76 mm) diameter disc, spring steel barbed clip, hardened steel serrated nail with a 1 in. (25 mm) diameter head, or another fastener as recommended by the insulation and roofing manufacturer.

Attach the first layer of insulation with the number of fasteners and in the pattern recommended by the insulation manufacturer.

Adhesives are also available from some manufacturers that can be used to apply insulation to a steel deck.

5-15 ROOFING SYSTEMS ON CONCRETE DECK

Description

Figure 5-15 illustrates some of the general considerations in developing roofing systems for low-slope concrete structural decks. Low-slope roofs are considered those with slopes less than 3 in 12. In most cases, low-slope roofs must have a slope of at least $1/4$ in./ft (20 mm/m). Refer to Sections 5-16, 5-21, 5-26, and 5-31 for more information on details for specific types of roofs.

Refer to Section 5-14 for information on code requirements for low-slope roofs.

Limitations of Use

- This detail does not include nailable decks, steel decks, or applying insulation over existing roofs.
- Protected membrane roofing is not included. See Section 5-36.

Detailing Considerations

- The decking should have a minimum slope for drainage of $1/4$ in./ft (20 mm/m); however, $1/2$ in./ft (40 mm/m) is preferred. If the structural deck is flat, the slope may be achieved with tapered insulation.
- A cover board should be used above the insulation and below the membrane for the same reasons given in Section 5-14.

Figure 5-15 Roofing systems on concrete deck

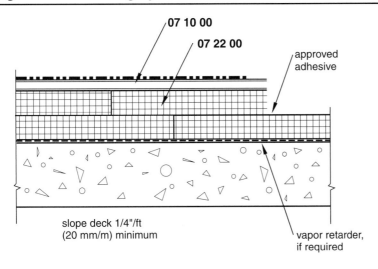

07 10 00
07 22 00
approved adhesive
slope deck 1/4"/ft (20 mm/m) minimum
vapor retarder, if required

- A vapor retarder over the concrete is generally recommended to prevent the migration of moisture into the remainder of the roof system. However, because the roofing membrane also acts as a vapor retarder, carefully consider the need to add a second vapor retarder that could trap moisture in the insulation.
- If a separate vapor retarder is used, connect it to the wall air and vapor retarders.

Coordination Required

- Detail all penetrations through the roof to be airtight and vapor tight.
- Verify the expected deflection of the structural deck so that the slope is not defeated.

Likely Failure Points

- Possible failure points are the same as those for steel deck low-slope roofs

Materials

07 10 00 COVER BOARD

Glass mat gypsum board, ASTM C1177.

Alternate materials may include wood fiber board, asphaltic board, plywood, and OSB, among others.

07 22 00 ROOF DECK INSULATION

Materials

The following types of rigid insulation are commonly used over concrete decking for the types of roofs described in the following details:

Polyisocyanurate foam board, ASTM C591 and C1289.
Extruded polystyrene, ASTM C578.
Expanded polystyrene, ASTM C578.
Perlite, ASTM C728.

Composite boards are also available that combine insulation and a covering of OSB, plywood, or other material.

Apply in thicknesses as required for the needed thermal resistance.

Verify compatibility with the roofing membrane used.

Execution

Apply insulation in a double layer with a thin layer attached to the concrete deck and a thicker layer with higher thermal resistance applied over that layer.

Edges and end joints of double-layer applications should be vertically staggered.

Figure 5-16 Built-up roof at supported deck 07 51 00.1

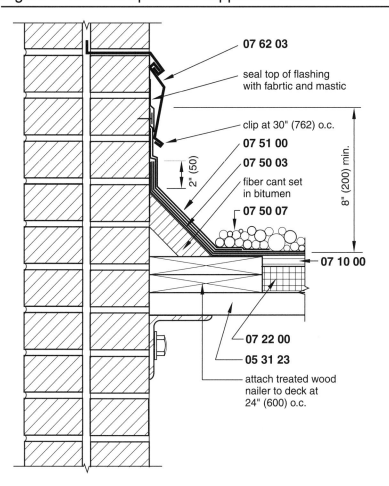

07 62 03

seal top of flashing
with fabrtic and mastic

clip at 30" (762) o.c.
07 51 00
07 50 03
fiber cant set
in bitumen
07 50 07

2" (50)

8" (200) min.

07 10 00

07 22 00
05 31 23
attach treated wood
nailer to deck at
24" (600) o.c.

5-16 BUILT-UP ROOF AT SUPPORTED DECK

Description

Figures 5-16 to 5-20 describe built-up roofing using asphalt–impregnated glass fiber felts applied to rigid insulation over steel decking. Organic fiber and nonwoven synthetic fiber felts are also used. The details are similar for other types of built-up roofs as well. Although Figures 5-16 to 5-20 show generally accepted roofing practice, the exact method of detailing will depend on the specific requirements of the project, local trade practices, decking material, and the exact type of roofing membrane used. In addition, specific recommendations of the roofing manufacturer and the building code, as well as insurance requirements, may require modifications to the details shown here.

Figures 5-16 and 5-17 illustrate the roofing adjacent to a solid masonry wall; however, a similar detail would work with parapets constructed of concrete, steel studs, or other structural materials. This detail does not show wall insulation, air barriers, or interior finish materials. Refer to Figs. 2-6, 2-18, 5-7, 5-13, 5-31, and 6-12 for parapet details showing roofing and wall construction.

Limitations of Use

- Use this detail only where the deck is supported by the wall and no differential movement between the two elements is expected.
- This detail shows a common method of applying this type of roofing and terminating it at the parapet, but the specific manufacturer's instructions should be followed.
- This detail is for roof slopes from 1/4 in./ft (20 mm/m) to 1/2 in./ft (40 mm/m). If the slope is greater, wood nailers for backnailing may be required, as described in Section 5-14.

Detailing Considerations

- A cant strip must be installed between the roof and all vertical surfaces.
- Install crickets as required to ensure drainage on all parts of the roof.
- For wind design, follow the recommendations of ANSI/SPRI WD-1, ANSI/SPRI RP-4, and the requirements of the local authority having jurisdiction. In high-wind areas, a ballasted system may not be appropriate and a smooth roof surfacing may be needed. Other types of surfacing include roofing granules; cut-backs of solvent, asphalt, fillers, and fibers; or fibrated emulsions. Alternately, another type of roofing system may be required.
- Provide walkways to mechanical equipment and other roof-mounted facilities that require frequent access. These may be constructed of 2 × 4 in. (38 mm × 89 mm) redwood or other approved materials. Do not penetrate the roofing membrane with fasteners.
- If a masonry wall is not used, flashing may extend from a coping or from a reglet similar to that in Figs. 1-21, 2-18, 2-24, 2-27, and 5-31.
- In some instances, a vented base sheet or a venting system may be needed to relieve vapor pressure buildup below the roofing membrane. This is especially true if insulating roof decks of lightweight concrete, perlite, or vermiculite are used.

Coordination Required

- Roof slopes should have a minimum slope of 1/4 in./ft (20 mm/m); however, 1/2 in./ft (40 mm/m) is recommended. Deflection and camber of structural members should be taken into account when determining roof slope.
- Drains should be located on the interior to prevent freezing. They should also be located away from columns and at points of maximum deflection. See Fig. 5-39 for a typical drain detail.
- Verify the limitations on the use of gravel ballast in high-wind areas.
- Verify the need for a vapor retarder between the two layers of insulation.
- Field quality control is very important to proper installation. The designer should make frequent site visits or employ a qualified roofing consultant.

Likely Failure Points

- Deterioration of the roofing or structural collapse due to ponding of water if sufficient slope for drainage is not provided
- Uplift of the insulation caused by insufficient fastening of the base layer of insulation

- Blistering or delamination of the roofing membrane or insulation failure caused by vapor migration through the insulation
- Blistering of the roofing caused by direct application of the membrane to polyisocyanurate, polyurethane, and felt-skinned foam-type insulation
- Splitting of the roofing or base flashing caused by direct mechanical attachment of the metal flashing to the roof
- Cracking (alligatoring) of the membrane if a suitable top surfacing is not used (Generally, a ballasted covering is considered the most durable of the surfacing types available.)
- Tearing or splitting of the membrane caused by differential movement between the wall and the roof
- Overspacing of the rolls of felt during installation

Materials

05 31 23 METAL DECK

Minimum 22 gage, 0.0312 in. (0.792 mm) with maximum spans as recommended by FMG, UL, and the requirements of the local building code. Depth and configuration as required by the structural requirements of the roof.

Maximum deck deflection should be limited to the following values:

Span, ft	Deflection, in.	Span, mm	Deflection, mm
4	0.20	1220	5.1
5	0.25	1525	6.4
6	0.30	1830	7.6

07 10 00 COVER BOARD

Glass mat gypsum board, ASTM C1177.

Alternate materials may include paper-faced gypsum board, wood fiber board, asphaltic board, plywood, and OSB, among others.

Verify that the surface of the cover board used is recommended for the application temperature of the roofing asphalt.

07 22 00 ROOF DECK INSULATION

Materials

See Section 5-14 for additional information.

Polyisocyanurate, extruded polystyrene, and expanded polystyrene require a cover board, as described in Section 5-14.

Glass fiber, cellular glass, perlite, or wood fiberboard may be used without an additional layer of protection prior to applying the roofing felts.

Thickness as required by the thermal resistance needed.

Insulation must have sufficient strength to span the flutes of the metal decking.

Verify that the surface of the insulation used is recommended for the application temperature of the roofing asphalt.

Execution

See Section 5-14 for additional information.

Follow the roofing manufacturer's instructions for the type and installation of insulation used as a substrate for the roofing.

Apply insulation in two layers, with the first layer mechanically attached to the steel decking.

07 51 00 BITUMINOUS ROOFING

Materials

Asphalt: ASTM D312, Type II, III, or IV as required.

Asphalt primer: ASTM D41.

No. 40 asphalt-saturated base sheet: ASTM D2626 or asphalt-coated glass fiber base sheet, ASTM D4601.

No. 15 asphalt-saturated organic felts: ASTM D226, Type I.

Asphalt-impregnated glass fiber mat: ASTM D2178, Type III or IV.

A vented base sheet is substituted for the No. 40 base sheet if required.

Execution

Follow the manufacturer's instructions and the recommendations of ASTM E936.

If the parapet is masonry, prime it prior to application of roofing.

Apply No. 40 base sheet in full mopping of asphalt.

Apply three plies of No. 15 felts in asphalt, lapping as recommended by the manufacturer so that felts do not touch other felts.

Apply aggregate ballast at a rate of 400 lb per roof square (19.5 kg/m^2) or as required by local conditions.

At parapets and curbs, apply one ply of asphalt-saturated glass fiber mat extending 2 in. (50 mm) beyond the toe of the curb on the roof and 2 in. (50 mm) above the top of the roofing felts. Modified bituminous flashing may also be used.

Apply reinforced base flashing extending 4 in. (100 mm) beyond the toe of the curb on the roof and 8 in. to 14 in. (200 mm to 360 mm) above the roof surface. Set base flashing in steep asphalt or asphalt roof cement. Nail the top of the base flashing 8 in. (203 mm) on center.

07 50 03 ROOFING ASPHALT

ASTM D312, Type II for roof slopes up to ^{1}/$_2$ in./ft (40 mm/m).

ASTM D312, Type III or IV for slopes up to 3 in./ft (240 mm/m).

07 50 07 BALLAST

ASTM D1863, ^{3}/$_8$ in. (10 mm) nominal diameter gravel, slag, or other approved material.

Apply a flood coat of hot bitumen as soon as possible after the application of the membrane.

Apply at a rate of 4 psf to 5 psf (20 kg/m^2 to 24 kg/m^2) or as required by the local building code.

07 62 03 COUNTERFLASHING

Materials

Minimum 18 gage, 0.055 in. (1.270 mm) noncorrosive metal.

Execution

Secure counterflashing to parapet with 2 in. (50 mm) wide clips 30 in. (750 mm) on center.

Do not solder the counterflashing.

Provide expansion joints in all metal flashing.

5-17   BUILT-UP ROOF AT NONSUPPORTED DECK

Description

Similar to Fig. 5-16, the construction shown in Fig. 5-17 is used where differential movement between the roof and the wall structure is expected. It should be used in conjunction with

Figure 5-17 Built-up roof at non-supported deck 07 52 00.2

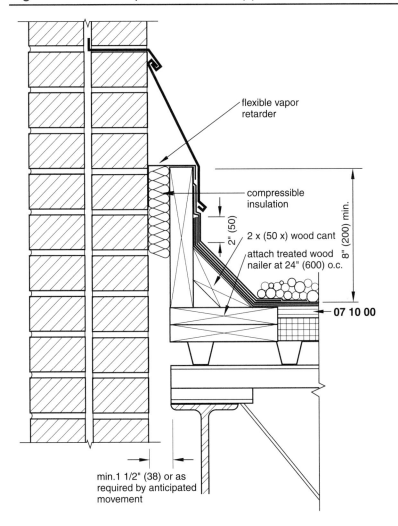

expansion joints, as shown in Fig. 5-18, to minimize the stress on the roofing membrane caused by movement of the substrate.

This detail does not show wall insulation, air barriers, or interior finish materials. Refer to Figs. 2-6, 2-18, 5-7, 5-13, 5-31, and 6-12 for parapet details showing roofing and wall construction.

Limitations of Use

- This detail shows a common method of applying this type of roofing and terminating it at the parapet, but the manufacturer's instructions should be followed.
- This detail is for roof slopes from 1/4 in./ft to 1/2 in./ft (20 mm/m to 40 mm/m).

Detailing Considerations

- The decking and the vertical wood member should not be attached to the wall.
- Preformed, flexible joint covers may be used in lieu of sheet metal counterflashing.
- Use a wood cant strip nailed at 16 in. (406 mm) on center to the nailing strip and wood curb.
- The roof slope should provide for drainage away from the wall.
- If a closure angle is required below the deck level, it should provide for a slip joint.

Coordination Required

See Fig. 5-18 for additional expansion joint requirements.

Likely Failure Points

Splitting of the roofing or base flashing caused by direct mechanical attachment of the metal flashing to the roof

Materials

See Section 5-16 for material requirements.

5-18 BUILT-UP ROOFING AT EXPANSION JOINT

Description

Expansion joints are required to prevent the roofing membrane from being split or otherwise damaged due to building movement. The joint shown in Fig. 5-18 uses a preformed joint cover; however, a sheet metal joint can be constructed, as shown in Fig. 5-23.

Detailing Considerations

- The expected movement of the joint should be calculated and should provide for both expansion and contraction.

Figure 5-18 Built-up roof at expansion joint 07 51 00.3

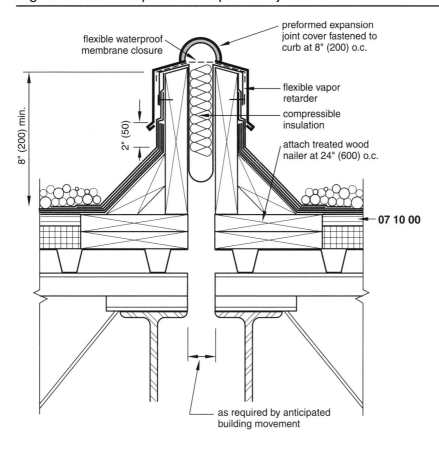

flexible waterproof membrane closure

preformed expansion joint cover fastened to curb at 8" (200) o.c.

flexible vapor retarder

compressible insulation

attach treated wood nailer at 24" (600) o.c.

8" (200) min.

2" (50)

07 10 00

as required by anticipated building movement

- Expansion joints must extend the full width of the roof.
- The roof slope should provide for drainage away from the expansion joint.
- The wood cant strip should be nailed to both the vertical curb piece and the horizontal nailer.

Coordination Required

- Expansion joints should be placed at the same places as the building's structural expansion joints as well as at the following locations:

  At the junctions of the wings of L-, T-, and U-shaped buildings.
  Where the type of decking changes.
  Where the framing or steel decking changes direction.
  At the connections of new construction to existing construction.
  At the junctions where interior heating conditions change.

- Refer to Fig. 5-17 for expansion joints between walls and the roof.
- On very large buildings, area dividers may be required. They should be located at 150 to 200 ft (46 m to 61 m) intervals between roof expansion joints.

Likely Failure Points

- Splitting of the roofing or base flashing caused by direct mechanical attachment of the metal flashing to the roof

Materials

See Section 5-16 for material requirements.

5-19 BUILT-UP ROOF AT EQUIPMENT SUPPORT

Description

Figure 5-19 shows one way to support rooftop mechanical equipment, piping, signs, and similar fixtures. The roofing and flashing requirements are similar to those described in Section 5-16. As an alternative to the reglet and flashing shown, base flashing can be carried over the curb, fastened at 6 in. (152 mm) on center, and covered with a sheet metal cap.

Detailing Considerations

- Do not use pitch pans for equipment supports. Where structural members or supports for heavy equipment must penetrate the decking and roofing membrane, separate the structural member from the roof with curbs similar to those in Fig. 5-20 and provide a metal umbrella securely attached and sealed to the structural member and then connected to the counterflashing.
- Provide drainage crickets around equipment supports as required to prevent the accumulation of water at these points.
- If the roof extends under equipment, provide adequate clearance between the roof and the mechanical unit to allow for equipment maintenance and roof repairs or reroofing.

Figure 5-19 Built-up roof at equipment support 07 51 00.4

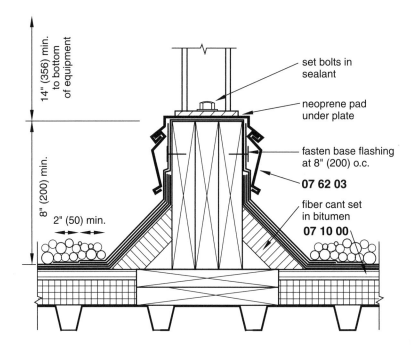

Coordination Required

Provide sufficient space between nearby stacks and other roof penetrations so that the roofing can be installed properly. Generally, maintain a minimum of 12 in. (300 mm) between equipment supports and stacks.

Likely Failure Points

- Splitting of the roof or delamination of the membrane or insulation from the decking caused by dragging or rolling heavy mechanical units across the roof
- Splitting of the roofing or base flashing caused by direct mechanical attachment of the metal flashing to the roof

Materials

See Section 5-16 for material requirements.

5-20   BUILT-UP ROOF AT STACK FLASHING

Description

Figure 5-20 illustrates a roof penetration for any type of stack or pipe, but this is required for high-temperature stacks where a clearance must be maintained between the stack and the roofing curb. This type of stack penetration allows the opening to be built and the roofing to

Figure 5-20 Built-up roof at stack flashing 07 51 00.5

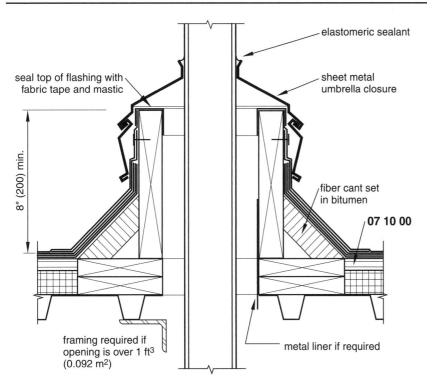

elastomeric sealant

seal top of flashing with fabric tape and mastic

sheet metal umbrella closure

8" (200) min.

fiber cant set in bitumen

07 10 00

framing required if opening is over 1 ft³ (0.092 m²)

metal liner if required

be installed before the stack is placed. A similar detail can be used for roof hatches, skylights, and other penetrations. For other pipe penetrations, a simple storm collar applied over a flashing collar may be used, similar to the one in Fig. 5-30.

Detailing Considerations

- The metal umbrella shown should be welded or securely banded to the pipe.
- In lieu of this detail for short pipe penetrations, sheet lead (minimum of 2.5 psf [12.2 kg/m^2]) may be wrapped around the top of the pipe and flashed under two layers of felt, with the edges sealed with mastic. See Fig. 5-25 for a similar application.
- Compressible insulation may be installed between the roof curb and piping. Verify the requirements for fireproof insulation when heated pipes penetrate the membrane.

Coordination Required

- All openings for plumbing pipes, roof drains, and other penetrations must be formed prior to installing the roof.
- Provide sufficient space between nearby stacks and other roof penetrations so that the roofing can be installed properly. Generally, maintain a minimum of 12 in. (300 mm) between stacks and between stacks and curbs or parapets.

Likely Failure Points

- Splitting of the roofing or base flashing caused by direct mechanical attachment of the metal flashing to the roof
- Water leakage due to sealant failure around the metal umbrella

Materials

See Section 5-16 for material requirements.

5-21 MODIFIED BITUMEN ROOF AT SUPPORTED DECK

Description

Modified bitumens are composed of asphalt, reinforcing fabrics, and polymers used to modify the asphalt to improve the elastic and plastic properties of the membrane. There are two main types of commonly used modified bitumen roofing, atactic polypropylene (APP) and styrene butadiene styrene (SBS). Both use their respective types of polymer blended with asphalt and fillers, and both types are composed of a base sheet and a cap sheet. Cap sheets are available with a smooth surface or covered with mineral granules or a factory-applied surface of metal foil.

Although there are several types of manufactured modified bitumens and methods of application, the details are similar. Depending on the material used, modified bitumens may be torch applied, self-adhered, or mechanically fastened.

Figure 5-21 Modified bitumen roof at supported deck 07 52 00.1

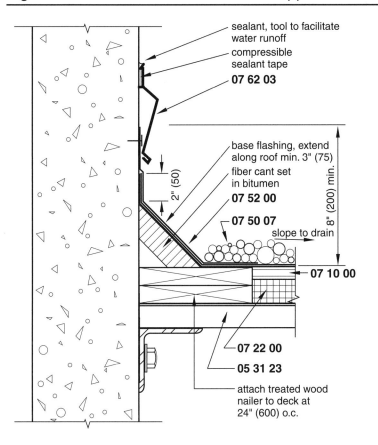

Figures 5-21 to 5-25 show common applications of a loose-laid modified bitumen membrane system using a base sheet. Because modified bitumen systems vary greatly, the manufacturer's recommendations should be followed and details modified according to the manufacturer's requirements.

Limitations of Use

- This detail is only for roofs with a maximum slope of 1 in./ft (80 mm/m).
- Use this detail only where the deck is supported by the wall and no differential movement between the two constructions is expected.

Detailing Considerations

- A cover board is required to protect expanded and extruded polystyrene insulation from the application of some roofing materials and from heat buildup under a black membrane.
- A cant strip must be installed between the roof and all vertical surfaces.
- For wind design, follow the recommendations of ANSI/SPRI WD-1, ANSI/SPRI RP-4, and the requirements of the local authority having jurisdiction. In high-wind areas, a ballasted system may not be appropriate and a covering other than gravel ballast may be required.

- Install crickets as required to ensure drainage on all parts of the roof.
- Provide walkways to mechanical equipment and other roof-mounted facilities that require frequent access.
- If a masonry wall is not used, flashing may extend from a coping or from a reglet similar to Figs. 1-21, 2-18, 2-24, 2-27, and 5-31.
- In some instances, a vented base sheet or a venting system may be needed to relieve vapor pressure buildup below the roofing membrane.

Coordination Required

- Roof slopes should have a minimum slope of 1/4 in./ft (20 mm/m); however, 1/2 in./ft (40 mm/m) is recommended. Deflection and camber of structural members should be taken into account when determining the roof slope.
- Drains should be located on the interior to prevent freezing. They should also be located away from columns at points of maximum deflection. See Fig. 5-39 for a typical drain detail.
- Verify the limitations on the use of gravel ballast in high-wind areas.

Likely Failure Points

- Leaks caused by inadequate connection of the overlapping seams of the membrane
- Leaks due to improper application of adhesives in cold-applied systems
- Deterioration of the roofing or structural collapse due to ponding of water if sufficient slope for drainage is not provided
- Uplift of the insulation due to insufficient fastening of the base layer of insulation
- Blistering or delamination of the roofing membrane or insulation failure caused by vapor migration through the insulation
- Splitting of the roofing or base flashing caused by direct mechanical attachment of the metal flashing to the roof
- Tearing or splitting of the membrane caused by differential movement between the wall and the roof

Materials

05 31 23 METAL DECK

Minimum 22 gage, 0.0312 in. (0.792 mm) with maximum spans as recommended by FMG, UL, and the requirements of the local building code. Depth and configuration as required by the structural requirements of the roof.

Maximum deck deflection should be limited to the following values:

Span, ft	Deflection, in.	Span, mm	Deflection, mm
4	0.20	1220	5.1
5	0.25	1525	6.4
6	0.30	1830	7.6

07 10 00 COVER BOARD

Glass mat gypsum board, ASTM C1177.

Alternate materials may include wood fiber board, asphaltic board, plywood, and OSB, among others.

Verify that the surface of the cover board used is recommended for the application temperature of the roofing asphalt.

07 22 00 ROOF DECK INSULATION

Materials

See Section 5-14 for additional information.

Select the insulation based on the specific modified bitumen and the application method to be used.

Polyisocyanurate, extruded polystyrene, and expanded polystyrene require a cover board, as described in Section 5-14.

Glass fiber, cellular glass, perlite, or wood fiberboard may be used without an additional layer of protection prior to applying the roofing felts.

Thickness as required by thermal resistance needed.

Insulation must have sufficient strength to span the flutes of the metal decking.

Execution

See Section 5-14 for additional information.

Follow the roofing manufacturer's instructions for the type and installation of insulation used as a substrate for the roofing.

Apply insulation in two layers, with the first layer mechanically attached to the steel decking.

07 52 00 MODIFIED BITUMINOUS ROOFING

Materials

Roofing asphalt, ASTM D312, Type III or IV, or ASTM D6152 for SBS.

SBS modified bitumen sheet:

   ASTM D6162, D6163, D6164, and D6298.

APP modified bitumen sheet:

   ASTM D6222, D6223, and D6509.

Base flashing and primers as required by the specific manufacturer's product being used.

Execution

Application Guidelines for Modified Bitumen Roofing Systems, published by the Single-Ply Roofing Industry.

Follow the manufacturer's instructions for the type of membrane and the application method being used.

Prime masonry prior to applying roofing and base flashing.

Lap base sheet a minimum of 2 in. (50 mm) at the edges and 4 in. (100 mm) at the ends.

07 50 07 BALLAST

ASTM D1863, 3/8 in. (10 mm) nominal diameter gravel, slag, or other approved material.

Apply in flood coat of hot bitumen as soon as possible after the application of the membrane.

Apply in amounts required by the building height and local wind conditions to prevent uplift of the membrane.

Precast concrete pavers may be used if the membrane is protected from the abrasive surface of the pavers.

07 62 03 COUNTERFLASHING

Materials

Minimum 18 gage, 0.0500 in. (1.270 mm) noncorrosive metal.

Elastomeric sealant across the top of the surface-applied flashing strip.

In lieu of the counterflashing shown in this detail, a flashing reglet may be used in concrete parapets or coping may be used over the top of the parapet.

Execution

Secure the counterflashing to the parapet with 2 in. (50 mm) wide clips 30 in. (750 mm) on center.

Do not solder the counterflashing.

Provide expansion joints in all metal flashing.

5-22   MODIFIED BITUMEN ROOF AT NONSUPPORTED DECK

Description

Similar to Fig. 5-21, the construction shown in Fig. 5-22 is used where differential movement between the roof and wall structure is expected. It should be used in conjunction with expansion joints, as shown in Fig. 5-23, to minimize the stress on the roofing membrane caused by movement of the substrate.

Detailing Considerations

- The decking and the vertical wood member should not be attached to the wall.
- Preformed, flexible joint covers may be used in lieu of sheet metal counterflashing.
- Use a wood cant strip nailed at 16 in. (406 mm) on center to the nailing strip and wood curb.
- The roof slope should provide for drainage away from the expansion joint.
- If a closure angle is required below the deck level, it should provide for a slip joint.

Coordination Required

See Section 5-23 for additional expansion joint requirements.

Figure 5-22 Modified bitumen roof at nonsupported deck 07 52 00.2

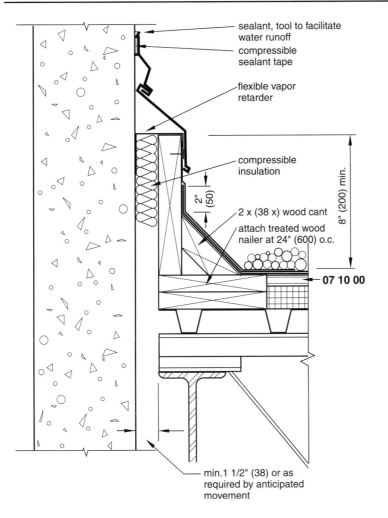

sealant, tool to facilitate water runoff

compressible sealant tape

flexible vapor retarder

compressible insulation

2" (50)

2 x (38 x) wood cant

attach treated wood nailer at 24" (600) o.c.

8" (200) min.

07 10 00

min.1 1/2" (38) or as required by anticipated movement

Likely Failure Points

Splitting of the roofing or base flashing caused by direct mechanical attachment of the metal flashing to the roof

Materials

See Section 5-21 for material requirements.

5-23 MODIFIED BITUMEN ROOF AT EXPANSION JOINT

Description

Expansion joints are required to prevent the roofing membrane from being split or otherwise damaged due to building movement. The joint shown in Fig. 5-23 uses a sheet metal joint cover; however, a preformed joint cover, similar to that shown in Fig. 5-18, can be used.

Figure 5-23 Modified bitumen roof at expansion joint 07 52 00.3

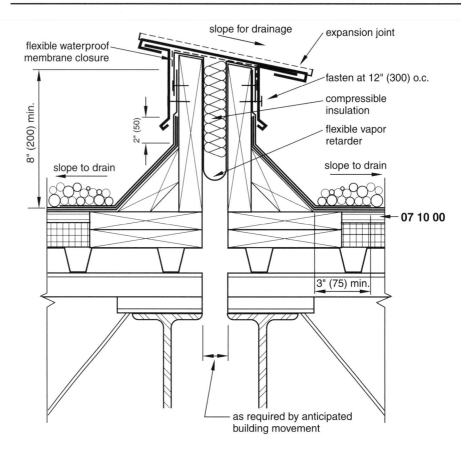

flexible waterproof membrane closure

slope for drainage

expansion joint

fasten at 12" (300) o.c.

compressible insulation

flexible vapor retarder

2" (50)

8" (200) min.

slope to drain

slope to drain

07 10 00

3" (75) min.

as required by anticipated building movement

Detailing Considerations

- The top flashing cap should not be attached to both sides of the flashing underneath to allow for movement in both directions.
- The expected movement of the joint should be calculated and should provide for both expansion and contraction.
- Expansion joints must extend the full width of the roof.
- The roof slope should provide for drainage away from the expansion joint.
- The wood cant strip should be nailed to both the vertical curb piece and the horizontal nailer.

Coordination Required

- Expansion joints should be placed at the same places as the building's structural expansion joints as well as at the following locations:
  - At the junctions of the wings of L-, T-, and U-shaped buildings.
  - Where the type of decking changes.
  - Where the framing or steel decking changes direction.
  - At the connections of new construction to existing construction.
  - At the junctions where interior heating conditions change.

- Refer to Fig. 5-22 for expansion joints between walls and roof.
- On very large buildings, area dividers may be required. They should be located at 150 to 200 ft (46 m to 61 m) intervals between roof expansion joints.

Likely Failure Points

- Leaks caused by lack of adequate slip joints at the ends of the metal cap flashing
- Splitting of the roofing or base flashing caused by direct mechanical attachment of all components of the metal flashing system to the roof

Materials

See Section 5-21 for material requirements.

5-24 MODIFIED BITUMEN ROOF AT EQUIPMENT SUPPORT

Description

Figure 5-24 shows one way to support rooftop mechanical equipment, piping, signs, and similar fixtures. The roofing and flashing requirements are similar to those described in Section 5-21. If structural members or supports for heavy equipment must penetrate the decking and roofing membrane, separate the member from the roof, flash, and provide a metal umbrella securely attached and sealed to the structural member.

Figure 5-24 Modified bitumen roof at equipment support 07 52 00.4

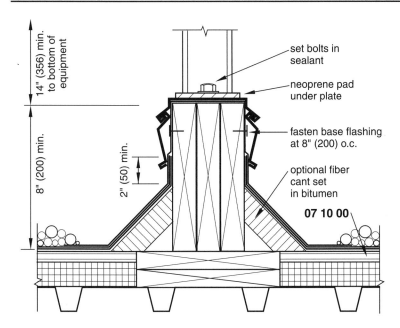

Detailing Considerations

- Follow the manufacturer's recommendations for specific detailing requirements.
- Do not use pitch pans for equipment supports.
- Provide drainage crickets around equipment supports as required to prevent the accumulation of water at these points.
- If the roof extends under equipment, provide adequate clearance between the roof and the mechanical unit to allow for equipment maintenance and roof repairs or reroofing.

Coordination Required

- Provide sufficient space between nearby stacks and other roof penetrations so that the roofing can be installed properly. Generally, maintain a minimum of 12 in. (305 mm) between equipment supports and stacks.

Likely Failure Points

- Splitting of the roof or delamination of the membrane or insulation from the decking caused by dragging or rolling heavy mechanical units across the roof
- Splitting of the roofing or base flashing caused by direct mechanical attachment of the metal flashing to the roof

Materials

See Section 5-21 for material requirements.

5-25   MODIFIED BITUMEN ROOF AT PLUMBING VENT

Description

Figure 5-25 shows a common detail used for plumbing vents and similar types of piping that must penetrate the roof. For roof hatches, skylights, and similar openings, use a curb system similar to that shown in Figs. 5-23 or 5-24.

Limitations of Use

This detail is generally appropriate only for plumbing pipes. If hot stacks must penetrate the roof, use a detail similar to Fig. 5-20 to separate hot stacks from the structure.

Detailing Considerations

The pipe should extend above the roof far enough to meet local building code requirements and good plumbing practice and to avoid obstruction by snow.

Coordination Required

- All plumbing pipes, roof drains, and other penetrations must be in place prior to installing the roof.

Figure 5-25 Modified bitumen roof at plumbing vent 07 52 00.5

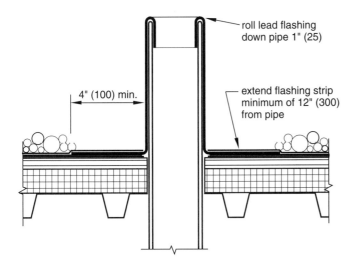

roll lead flashing
down pipe 1" (25)

4" (100) min.

extend flashing strip
minimum of 12" (300)
from pipe

- Provide sufficient space between nearby stacks and other roof penetrations so that the roofing can be installed properly. Generally, maintain a minimum of 12 in. (305 mm) between stacks and between stacks and curbs or parapets.

Materials

- Use sheet lead of 2.5 psf (12.2 kg/m^2) minimum.
- Set the lead flange in mastic and prime before applying the modified bitumen flashing strip.
- See Section 5-21 for other material requirements.

5-26 EPDM ROOF AT SUPPORTED DECK

Description

Ethylene propylene diene monomer (EPDM) single-ply roofing is a thermoset elastomeric material formed by mixing EPDM polymer with oils, carbon black, and other materials. Seams are bonded with bonding adhesive or specially formulated tape. EPDM is one of the most widely used single-ply membrane roofing materials used in the United States. Sheets are available in thicknesses of 45 mils, 60 mils, and 70 mils (1.14 mm, 1.52 mm, and 1.94 mm) and widths of 10 ft, 20 ft, and 45 or 50 ft (3 m, 6 m, and 14 or 15 m). EPDM roofing offers the advantages of easy application, excellent weather resistance, good resistance to movement, good low-temperature flexibility, high resistance to heat aging, and economy when large roofs with few penetrations are covered.

Membranes are available nonreinforced or reinforced. Typically, EPDM membranes are nonreinforced, but reinforced membranes are recommended for mechanically attached installations and where increased resistance to puncturing and tearing is desired in a fully adhered or ballasted application. EPDM is typically black in color, but white sheets are available when reflectivity is needed.

Figure 5-26 EPDM roof at supported deck 07 53 23.1

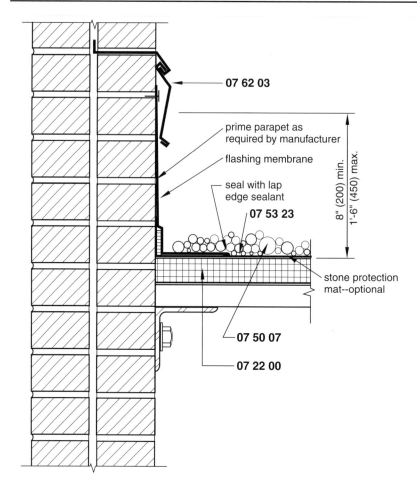

07 62 03

prime parapet as
required by manufacturer

flashing membrane

seal with lap
edge sealant

07 53 23

8" (200) min.
1'-6" (450) max.

stone protection
mat--optional

07 50 07

07 22 00

EPDM membranes may be fully adhered, mechanically attached, partially attached, or loose laid. Figure 5-26 shows the use of a loose-laid system with overlaid ballast to secure the membrane against uplift caused by wind.

Figures 5-26 and 5-27 illustrate the roofing adjacent to a solid masonry wall; however, a similar detail would work with parapets constructed of concrete, steel studs, or other structural materials. This detail does not show wall insulation, air barriers, or interior finish materials. Refer to Figs. 2-6, 2-18, 5-7, 5-13, 5-31, and 6-12 for parapet details showing roofing and wall construction.

Figures 5-26 to 5-30 show common applications of an EPDM system with ballast. Because EPDM systems vary slightly, the manufacturer's recommendations should be followed and details modified according to the manufacturer's requirements.

Limitations of Use

- This detail is only for roofs with a maximum slope of 2 in./ft (160 mm/m).
- Use this detail only where the deck is supported by the wall and no differential movement between the two constructions is expected. See Fig. 5-27 for conditions where movement must be accommodated.
- This detail shows a common method of applying this type of roofing and terminating it at the parapet, but the manufacturer's instructions should be followed.

Detailing Considerations

- For high masonry walls with masonry, stone, or concrete copings, use counterflashing, as shown in Fig. 5-26, and a separate through-wall flashing under the coping.
- Provide walkways to mechanical equipment and other roof-mounted facilities that require frequent access.
- For wind design, follow the recommendations of ANSI/SPRI WD-1, ANSI/SPRI RP-4, and the requirements of the local authority having jurisdiction. In high-wind areas, a ballasted system may not be appropriate and a fully adhered or mechanically fastened system may be required.
- Consider specifying a protection mat above the membrane when using a ballasted system. Because leaks are difficult to find on a ballasted system and because sharp stones or other debris may be present in the ballast, this is good insurance against damage.
- Because EPDM is not highly resistant to certain types of solvents, animal oils, and vegetable oils, the roof should be protected with an epichlorohydrin (ECH) membrane where kitchen exhausts may be located or where the roof may be susceptible to exposure to hydrocarbons, solvents, grease, or oils.

Coordination Required

- Roofs should have a minimum slope of $1/4$ in./ft (20 mm/m); however, $1/2$ in./ft (40 mm/m) is recommended. Deflection and camber of structural members should be taken into account when determining the roof slope.
- Drains should be located on the interior to prevent freezing. They should also be located away from columns at points of maximum deflection. See Fig. 5-39 for a typical drain detail.
- Verify compliance of the roofing system specified with UL requirements.

Likely Failure Points

- Leaks caused by incomplete cementing or taping of the lapped seams
- Deterioration of the roofing or structural collapse due to ponding of water if sufficient slope for drainage is not provided
- Uplift of the insulation caused by insufficient fastening of the base layer of insulation

Materials

07 22 00 ROOF DECK INSULATION

Materials

See Section 5-14 for additional information.

Polyisocyanurate, extruded polystyrene, expanded polystyrene, or composite board may be used as recommended by the membrane manufacturer. Expanded and extruded polystyrene require a cover board because solvent-based adhesives can cause the insulation to disintegrate.

Cellular glass insulation and other insulations with rough surfaces should be covered with a separation sheet to protect the membrane from rough surfaces and sharp edges.

Thickness as required by the thermal resistance needed.

Insulation must have sufficient strength to span the flutes of the metal decking.

Execution

See Section 5-14 for additional information.

Follow the roofing manufacturer's instructions for the type and installation of insulation used as a substrate for the roofing.

Apply insulation in two layers, with the first layer mechanically attached to the steel decking.

07 53 23 EPDM SINGLE-PLY MEMBRANE ROOFING

Materials

ASTM D4637.

ASTM D4811.

Adhesive as required by the membrane manufacturer.

Base flashing: cured membrane identical to the roof membrane or uncured elastomeric membrane.

Execution

Extend the roofing membrane up the side of the parapet and secure it to the vertical face with a fastening strip attached at 12 in. (300 mm) on center or as recommended by the roofing manufacturer.

Extend base flashing up a minimum of 8 in. (200 mm) and a maximum of 18 in. (460 mm). Fasten it to the parapet along the top edge at 6 in. 150 mm) on center or as recommended by the manufacturer.

07 50 07 BALLAST

Washed river gravel $1^1/_2$ in. (38 mm) or $2^1/_2$ in. (64 mm) in diameter (depending on wind speed) applied at a rate of 10 psf to 15 psf (49 kg/m^2 to 73 kg/m^2).

Precast concrete pavers may be used if the membrane is protected from the abrasive surface of the paver. The minimum weight of pavers is 18 psf (88 kg/m^2).

07 62 03 COUNTERFLASHING

Materials

Minimum 18 gage 0.0500 in. (1.27 mm) noncorrosive metal.

In lieu of the counterflashing shown in this detail, a flashing reglet may be used in concrete parapets or coping may be used over the top of low parapets and extended over the base flashing, similar to Fig. 5-31.

Execution

Secure counterflashing to the parapet with 2 in. (50 mm) wide clips 30 in. (760 mm) on center if required.

Do not solder the counterflashing.

Provide expansion joints in all metal flashing.

Secure counterflashing to the reglet at 24 in. (600 mm) on center.

Figure 5-27 EPDM roof at nonsupported deck 07 53 23.2

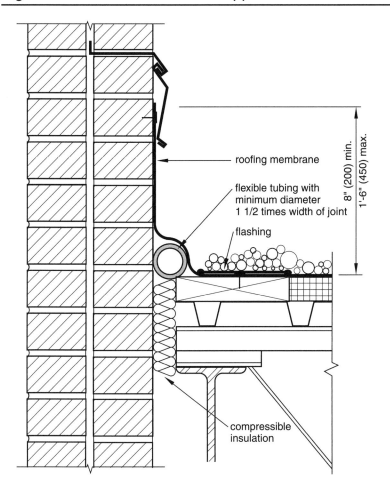

roofing membrane

flexible tubing with
minimum diameter
1 1/2 times width of joint

flashing

8" (200) min.
1'-6" (450) max.

compressible
insulation

5-27   EPDM ROOF AT NONSUPPORTED DECK

Description

Figure 5-27 shows construction where differential movement between the roof and the wall structure is expected. It should be used in conjunction with expansion joints, as shown in Fig. 5-28, to minimize the stress on the roofing membrane caused by movement of the substrate.

This detail and Fig. 5-26 illustrate the roofing adjacent to a solid masonry wall; however, a similar detail would work with parapets constructed of concrete, steel studs, or other structural materials. This detail does not show wall insulation, air barriers, or interior finish materials. Refer to Figs. 2-6, 2-18, 5-7, 5-13, 5-31, and 6-12 for parapet details showing roofing and wall construction.

Detailing Considerations

- The decking and wood nailer should not be attached to the wall.
- A cover board over the insulation may be required or desirable. Refer to Section 5-14.

- The roof slope should provide for drainage away from the expansion joint.
- Slip joints must be provided for the metal reglet flashing and counterflashing.
- If a closure strip is required to support the insulation, it should provide for a slip joint.

Coordination Required

- See Section 5-28 for additional expansion joint requirements.

Likely Failure Points

- Water leakage at the top of the membrane if counterflashing is not used
- Sagging of the membrane at the expansion joint if the flexible tubing is too small

Materials

- Fasten the roofing membrane to the parapet along the top edge at 6 in. (150 mm) on center.
- Fasten the roofing membrane to the wood nailer as required and cover it with flashing. Seal the edges of the flashing with a lap edge sealant.
- See Section 5-26 for other material requirements.

5-28   EPDM ROOF AT EXPANSION JOINT

Description

Although a loose-laid EPDM membrane is less susceptible to damage from substrate movement, expansion joints are still required. Figure 5-28 shows a typical method of designing an expansion joint; however, the recommendations of each manufacturer should be followed.

Limitations of Use

- This type of low-profile expansion joint should not be used over building expansion joints. Instead, use a minimum 8 in. (200 mm) curb with a preformed expansion joint cover similar to that in Fig. 5-18.

Detailing Considerations

- As an alternative to this low-profile expansion joint, a minimum 8 in. (200 mm) curb can be constructed similar to those in Figs. 5-18 and 5-23.
- Taper wood nailers.
- The expected movement of the joint should be calculated and should provide for both expansion and contraction.

Figure 5-28 EPDM roof at expansion joint 07 53 23.3

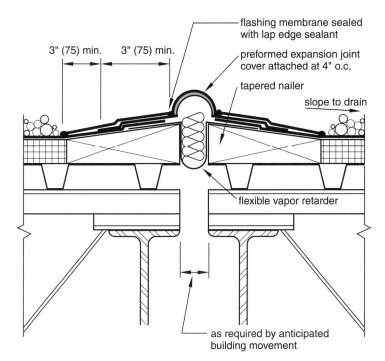

- Expansion joints must extend the full width of the roof.
- The roof slope should provide for drainage away from the expansion joint.

Coordination Required

- Expansion joints should be placed at the following locations:
  - At the junctions of the wings of L-, T-, and U-shaped buildings.
  - Where the type of decking changes.
  - Where the framing or steel decking changes direction.
  - At the connections of new construction to existing construction.
  - At the junctions where interior heating conditions change.
- Refer to Section 5-27 for expansion joints between walls and roof.

Likely Failure Points

- Leaking caused by damage from foot traffic or from being underwater if minor leaks develop

Materials

See Section 5-26 for material requirements.

Figure 5-29 EPDM roof at equipment support 07 53 23.4

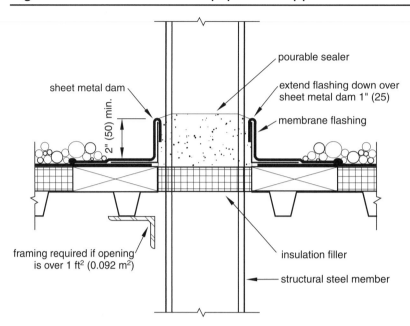

5-29 EPDM ROOF AT EQUIPMENT SUPPORT

Description

Figure 5-29 illustrates a method of flashing around a structural member that penetrates the roof. It allows irregularly shaped supports to be sealed with the use of a pourable sealant. Pipes should be detailed as shown in Fig. 5-30.

Detailing Considerations

- Follow the manufacturer's recommendations for specific detailing requirements.
- The pourable sealant should be sloped away from the support.
- The sheet metal dam should be fastened to the wood nailer at 6 in. (150 mm) on center.
- The membrane flashing should be sealed to the roofing membrane with lap edge sealant or other adhesives as recommended by the manufacturer.
- Provide adequate clearance between the roof and mechanical equipment to allow for equipment maintenance and roof repairs or reroofing.

Coordination Required

- Provide sufficient space between nearby penetrations so that the roofing can be installed properly. Generally, maintain a minimum of 12 in. (300 mm) between equipment supports and other roof penetrations.

Materials

See Section 5-26 for material requirements.

Figure 5-30 EPDM roof at pipe flashing 07 53 23.5

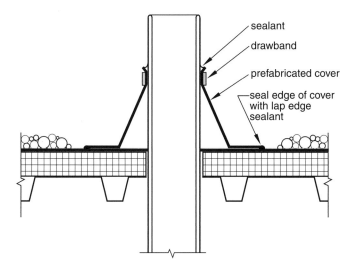

sealant

drawband

prefabricated cover

seal edge of cover
with lap edge
sealant

5-30 EPDM ROOF AT PIPE FLASHING

Description

Figure 5-30 shows one of two methods of flashing around plumbing pipes and similar penetrations. The detail illustrates the use of prefabricated covers, which are available to fit pipes of various diameters. If no prefabricated cover is used, the flashing membrane can be wrapped around the pipe over upturned roofing membrane and sealed to the membrane with lap-edge sealant.

Limitations of Use

- This detail is only appropriate for plumbing pipes. If hot stacks must penetrate the roof, provide a clear opening with curbs similar to that shown in Fig. 5-20 with flashing as shown in Fig. 5-26.

Detailing Considerations

- The pipe should extend above the roof far enough to meet local building code requirements and good plumbing practice and to avoid obstruction by snow.

Coordination Required

- All plumbing pipes, roof drains, and other penetrations must be in place prior to installing the roof.
- Provide sufficient space between nearby stacks and other roof penetrations so that the roofing can be installed properly. Generally, maintain a minimum of 12 in. (300 mm) between stacks and between stacks and curbs or parapets.

Likely Failure Points

▪ Leakage caused by poorly sealed edges.

Materials

See Section 5-26 for other material requirements.

5-31 TPO ROOF AT SUPPORTED DECK

Description

Thermoplastic polyolefin (TPO) single-ply roofing, shown in Fig. 5-31, is a thermoplastic material consisting of polypropylene, ethylene-propylene, or other olefinic materials. Sheets are available in thicknesses of 45 mils, 60 mils, and 80 mils (1.14 mm, 1.52 mm, and 2.03 mm) and in widths of up to 12 ft (3660 mm). TPO membranes are available in white, gray, or black, but white is the most common color used to take advantage of its reflectivity in cool roof applications. Sheets are connected by heat welding and result in seams stronger than taped or glued seams.

Figure 5-31 TPO roof at supported deck 07 54 23.1

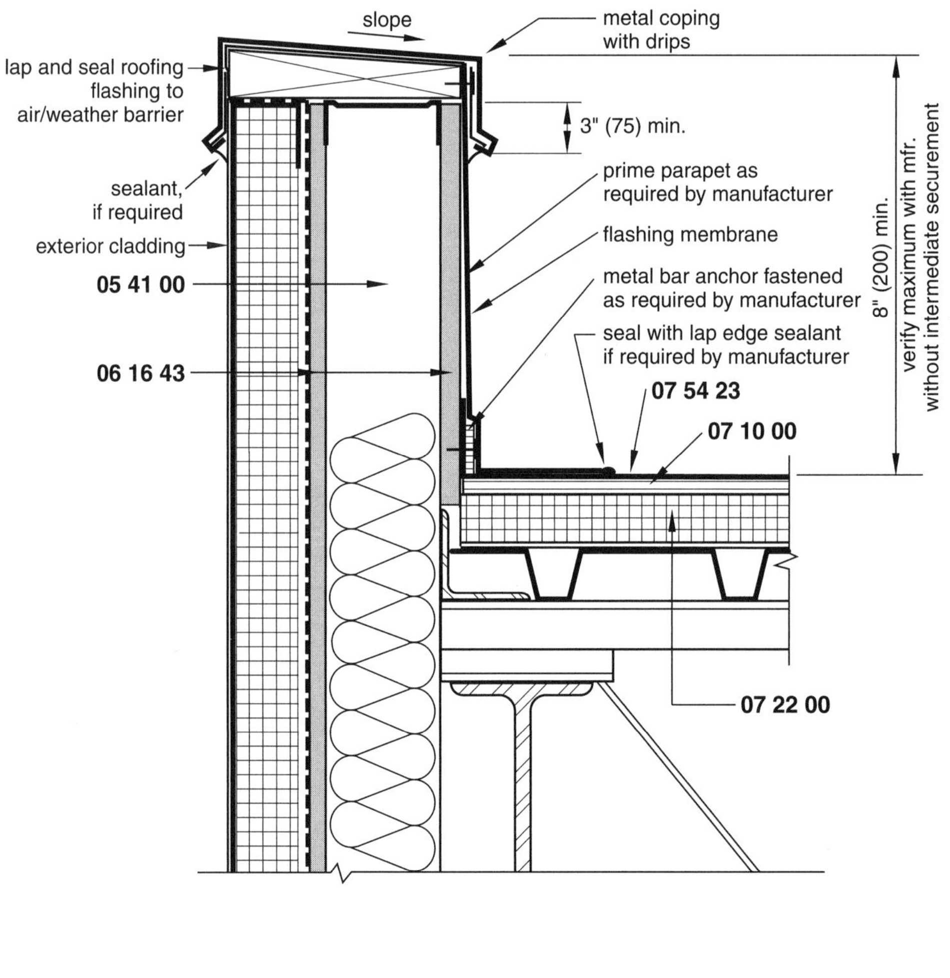

slope

metal coping with drips

lap and seal roofing flashing to air/weather barrier

3" (75) min.

prime parapet as required by manufacturer

sealant, if required

flashing membrane

exterior cladding

05 41 00

metal bar anchor fastened as required by manufacturer

seal with lap edge sealant if required by manufacturer

06 16 43

07 54 23

07 10 00

verify maximum with mfr. without intermediate securement

8" (200) min.

07 22 00

TPO roofing offers many advantages:

- High breaking and tearing strength and puncture resistance.
- Resistance to ultraviolet degradation and premature aging from high temperatures.
- Excellent resistance to ozone, algae, and mold.
- Good flexibility to resist building movement and temperature changes (flexibility is achieved through copolymers rather than plasticizers, as with PVC materials).
- Environmentally safe because the material does not contain chlorine.
- Minimizes volatile organic compound (VOC) release because heat-welded seams are used instead of solvents for connecting sheets.
- High reflectivity for cool roof applications.
- The thermoplastic nature of TPO (as well as PVC roofing) material makes it recyclable during the manufacturing process as well as after use.

TPO roofs may be fully adhered, ballasted, or mechanically attached. Fully adhered systems are highly resistant to wind uplift and may be used in low-slope applications as well as steep-slope roofing or where appearance is important. Traditionally, fully adhered systems relied on the use of a separate adhesive. Newer systems are available that make use of peel-and-stick membranes. Mechanically attached systems are the most common and are installed with fasteners or plates placed along the edge of each sheet. The adjacent sheet covers the fasteners, and the two are heat welded together. If fire resistance is a requirement, fire retardants may be added for fully adhered or mechanically attached applications. Ballasted systems are applied loose laid and covered with river rock 2 in. to 3 in. (50 mm to 75 mm) in diameter applied at a rate of 10 psf to 12 psf (48 kg/m^2 to 59 kg/m^2).

Limitations of Use

- Figure 5-31 shows TPO used with a low parapet. Parapets higher than 24 in. (600 mm), or as stated by the manufacturer, may require intermediate securement on the vertical surface. Verify recommended details with the manufacturer.
- Added fire retardants may be required to meet fire test requirements for unballasted applications.

Detailing Considerations

- A steel structural roof deck is illustrated here. Other deck types are acceptable. Verify minimum requirements for strength, fastener pullout resistance, and other properties with the manufacturer of the roofing system.
- Provide walkways to mechanical equipment and other roof-mounted facilities that require frequent access. These may be an additional layer of membrane or separate pavers or walkways.
- Grease vents may require special treatment to protect against deterioration of the membrane. Exposure to petroleum-based products or other chemicals may required special treatment.
- For wind design, follow the recommendations of ANSI/SPRI WD-1, ANSI/SPRI RP-4, and the requirements of the local authority having jurisdiction. In high-wind areas, a ballasted system may not be appropriate and a fully adhered or mechanically fastened system may be required.

- When the roofing is terminated at the top of a parapet, as shown in Fig. 5-31, the TPO membrane should be carried over the wood cap under the coping and at least 1 in. (50 mm) over the exterior wall or as required by the manufacturer. Other terminations may be used including counterflashing on the parapet, a termination bar, or a reglet.
- Steel decks must be a minimum of 22 gage, 0.0312 in. (0.792 mm).

Coordination Required

- The roof deck and insulation must be capable of resisting anticipated wind uplift loads.
- Vertical sheathing and parapet construction must be capable of resisting positive and negative wind loads.
- The roof should be sloped to drain a minimum of $1/4$ in./ft (20 mm/m).
- Wood nailers must be pressure treated without the use of creosote or asphaltic products.
- Tie the roofing into the air barrier for walls using the manufacturer's approved product.

Materials

05 41 00 METAL STUD

Materials

ASTM C955.

If galvanized: ASTM A653/A653M, Grade G-90.

Sized for maximum deflection, under full wind load, of L/240.

Execution

ASTM C1007.

06 16 43 SHEATHING

Materials

Fiberglass mat–faced gypsum board (ASTM C1177) or gypsum fiber panels (ASTM C1278).

On-half inch (13 mm) minimum fiberglass mat–faced gypsum board is recommended.

Execution

ASTM C1280.

Seal joints with self-adhering tape as approved by the sheathing manufacturer.

07 10 00 COVER BOARD

Glass mat gypsum board, ASTM C1177.

Alternate materials may include wood fiber board, asphaltic board, plywood, and OSB, among others.

Verify that the surface of the cover board used is approved by the TPO manufacturer.

A cover board may not be necessary, depending on the type of insulation used. Composite insulation boards may provide a suitable surface for the TPO.

07 22 00 Roof deck insulation

Materials

See Section 5-14 for additional information.

Polyisocyanurate, extruded polystyrene, expanded polystyrene, or composite board may be used as recommended by the membrane manufacturer. Expanded polystyrene requires a cover board.

Cellular glass insulation and other insulations with rough surfaces should be covered with a separation sheet to protect the membrane from rough surfaces and sharp edges.

Thickness as required by the thermal resistance needed.

Insulation must have sufficient strength to span the flutes of the metal decking.

Execution

See Section 5-14 for additional information.

Follow the roofing manufacturer's instructions for the type and installation of insulation used as a substrate for the roofing.

Apply insulation in two layers, with the first layer mechanically attached to the steel decking.

07 54 2 TPO roofing

Materials

ASTM D6878.

TPO membrane and related products as supplied by the same manufacturer.

Execution

Install according to manufacturers' instructions.

Install according to *Application Guidelines for Self Adhered Thermoplastic and Thermoset Roofing Systems* of the Single-Ply Roofing Industry.

5-32 TPO ROOF AT CURB THRESHOLD

Description

Figure 5-32 shows one way to construct a door-opening threshold leading to the roof area. Exact details may vary due to the differences between the floor level on the interior and the finished roof surface. Ideally, the structural deck on the inside and outside should not be a continuous member, as shown in this detail, so that the interior floor can be level with the threshold while there is a step down to the exterior. In some cases, a wood deck is constructed over the waterproof membrane.

Figure 5-32 TPO roof at curb threshold 07 54 23.2

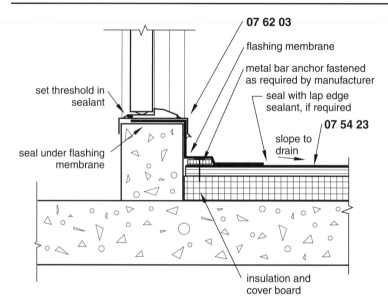

07 62 03

flashing membrane

metal bar anchor fastened as required by manufacturer

seal with lap edge sealant, if required

07 54 23

slope to drain

set threshold in sealant

seal under flashing membrane

insulation and cover board

Limitations of Use

- Individual manufacturers' details may vary.
- This detail does not provide for accessibility.

Detailing Considerations

- Ideally, there should be a minimum of 8 in. (200 mm) from the roof surface to the threshold. If this is not possible, protect the door opening with a roof overhang and use sealant between the flashing and the metal saddle flashing. The threshold should be raised higher than 8 in. (200 mm) in climates with heavy snow accumulation.
- Provide end dams at the edges of the opening.

Coordination Required

- See Section 5-31 for coordination requirements.

Materials

07 54 23 TPO ROOFING

Materials

ASTM D6878.

TPO membrane and related products as supplied by the same manufacturer.

Execution

Install according to manufacturers' instructions.

Install according to *Application Guidelines for Self Adhered Thermoplastic and Thermoset Roofing Systems* of the Single-Ply Roofing Industry.

07 62 03 COUNTERFLASHING

One of the following flashings may be used:

Galvanized steel, ASTM A653/A653M, minimum 26 gage or 0.0187 in. (0.475 mm); it may have a factory-applied coating of polyvinylidene fluoride or another fluorocarbon coating.

Stainless steel, ASTM A167, Type 302 or 304; use Type 316 in corrosive or marine environments, minimum 0.015 in. (0.38 mm), 2D finish.

Copper, ASTM B370, cold rolled hard tempered, minimum 16 oz (455 g/m^2), 0.0216 in. (0.549 mm).

Aluminum, ASTM B 209, minimum 0.0320 in. (0.813 mm), anodized color as required.

5-33 TPO ROOF AT EXPANSION JOINT

Description

The detail shown in Fig. 5–33 is used for major expansion joints in TPO roofing. Some manufacturers allow flat or low-profile joints without the use of curbs, depending on the maximum width of the joint.

Figure 5-33 TPO roof at expansion joint 07 54 23.3

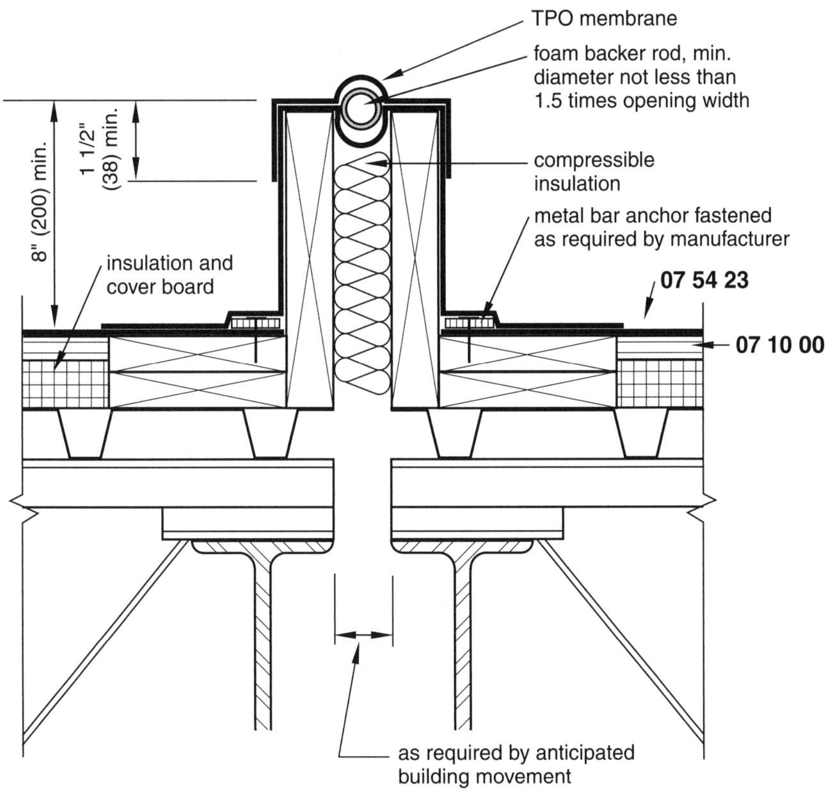

Detailing Considerations

- Verify the expected movement of the joint with the structural engineer.
- The roof slope should provide for drainage away from the expansion joint.
- Expansion joints should extend the full width of the roof.

Coordination Required

- Coordinate the location with that of rooftop-mounted equipment and penetrations with expansion joint locations.
- See Section 5-31 for other coordination requirements.

Materials

07 10 00 COVER BOARD

Glass mat gypsum board, ASTM C1177.

Alternative materials may include wood fiber board, asphaltic board, plywood, and OSB, among others.

07 54 23 TPO ROOFING

Materials

ASTM D6878.

TPO membrane and related products as supplied by the same manufacturer.

Execution

Install according to manufacturers' instructions.

Install according to *Application Guidelines for Self Adhered Thermoplastic and Thermoset Roofing Systems* of the Single-Ply Roofing Industry.

5-34 TPO ROOF AT EQUIPMENT SUPPORT

Description

Figure 5-34 shows one type of equipment support using a point support placed directly on the structural deck rather than a continuous curb. Refer to Figs. 5-24 and 5-29 for other variations of equipment support.

Limitations of Use

- Verify the size and spacing of the steel support members with the structural engineer.

Figure 5-34 TPO roof at equipment support 07 54 23.4

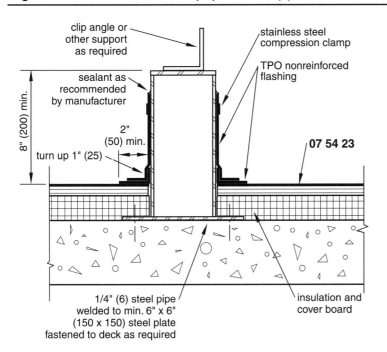

Detailing Considerations

- Various types of support members (clip angles, clamps, beams, bars, etc.) may be welded to the pipe; however, the top of the pipe must extend at least 8 in. (200 mm) above the roof surface or as required by the manufacturer.
- Follow the manufacturer's recommendations for specific detailing requirements.

Coordination Required

- Provide sufficient space between nearby penetrations or curbs so that the roofing can be installed properly. Generally, maintain a minimum of 12 in. (300 mm), or as recommended by the manufacturer, between equipment supports and other roof penetrations or curbs.
- See Section 5-31 for coordination requirements.

Materials

07 54 23 TPO ROOFING

Materials

ASTM D6878.

TPO membrane and related products as supplied by the same manufacturer.

Execution

Install according to manufacturers' instructions.

Install according to *Application Guidelines for Self Adhered Thermoplastic and Thermoset Roofing Systems* of the Single-Ply Roofing Industry.

Figure 5-35 TPO roof at pipe flashing 07 54 23.5

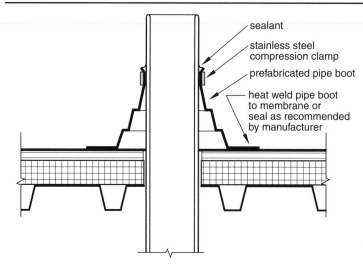

sealant

stainless steel
compression clamp

prefabricated pipe boot

heat weld pipe boot
to membrane or
seal as recommended
by manufacturer

5-35   TPO ROOF AT PIPE FLASHING

Description

Figure 5-35 illustrates a typical pipe penetration through TPO roofing. Most manufacturers provide pipe boots that are compatible with the rest of their products, although details of use may vary slightly.

Limitations of Use

- This detail shows a fully adhered system. A mechanically attached system may require a slightly different detail. Consult individual manufacturers for requirements.
- A separate detail is required for hot pipe penetrations. Verify the maximum pipe temperature allowable for this type of detail with the manufacturer. The TPO flashing is similar to that shown in Fig. 5-34, with the hot pipe inside of an outside pipe. The space between the hot pipe and the outer pipe is covered with a sheet metal hood.

Detailing Considerations

- If the penetration or pipe boot overlaps a field seam, a separate patch may be required over the membrane and under the pipe boot flange.

Coordination Required

- See Section 5-31 for coordination requirements.

Materials

See Section 5-31 for material requirements.

Figure 5-36 Protected membrane roofing 07 55 00

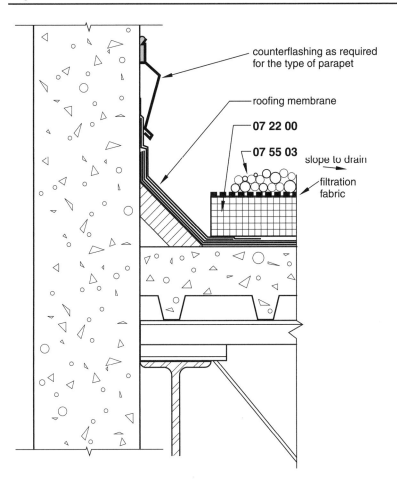

counterflashing as required
for the type of parapet

roofing membrane

07 22 00

07 55 03   slope to drain →

filtration
fabric

5-36   PROTECTED MEMBRANE ROOFING

Description

Unlike standard membrane roofing, a protected membrane roof is designed with the insulation over the waterproof membrane. The membrane may be a built-up roof, a modified bituminous roof, or other single-ply roofing. The purpose of placing the insulation on top is to protect the membrane from physical damage and ultraviolet degradation and to minimize thermal cycling of the membrane, which often causes failures. Figure 5–36 shows a parapet detail using a protected membrane roofing.

Limitations of Use

- This detail is for roof slopes from $1/4$ in./ft (20 mm/m) to $1/2$ in./ft (40 mm/m).

Detailing Considerations

- A firm, smooth decking must be provided for the membrane. This detail shows a concrete deck, but steel decking may also be used if it is covered with a suitable underlayment, such as glass-mat gypsum board.

- Parapet details at nonsupported deck edges, expansion joints, and other roofing details are similar to those shown for standard roofing.
- See Sections 5-16, 5-21, 5-26, and 5-31 for other detailing considerations.

Coordination Required

- See Section 5-16 for coordination requirements.

Materials

07 22 00 ROOF DECK INSULATION

Materials

Extruded polystyrene insulation in the thickness as required for thermal resistance.

Because some water absorption may occur and reduce the R-value slightly, reduce the board's initial R-value by 10 percent.

Execution

The roofing membrane should be cleaned of dirt and debris prior to installation.

Insulation is loose laid, with the long dimension perpendicular to the roof slope.

End joints should be staggered.

The insulation should be covered with a geotextile filtration fabric prior to application of the ballast to keep the ballast from falling into the board joints. Alternately, insulation with a factory-applied mortar surface may be used.

07 55 03 BALLAST

Washed river gravel $3/4$ in. (19 mm) in diameter is applied at a minimum rate of 12 psf (59 kg/m^2) for board 2 in. (50 mm) thick or less. Additional ballast is required for thicker insulation and in high-wind areas. Larger ballast sizes may also be required in high-wind areas. Generally, an extra 5 psf (25 kg/m^2) of ballast should be applied for each additional inch of insulation thickness.

Precast concrete pavers may also be used if they provide adequate weight for the thickness of insulation used.

5-37   GRAVEL STOP

Description

Although parapets are generally recommended for flat roof termination, gravel stops can be used where there is no parapet. Gravel stops, as shown in Fig. 5-37, provide a means of stopping the roofing system and preventing water and gravel from washing over the edge of the roof.

Limitations of Use

- This detail shows the use of an EPDM single-ply roof at a gravel stop termination. Details of other types of roofing may vary slightly.
- This detail is only appropriate where the roof deck is supported by the exterior wall.

Figure 5-37 Gravel stop 07 71 19

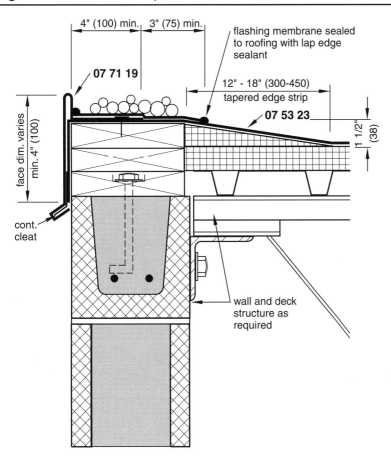

Detailing Considerations

- The roof should be sloped away from the gravel stop to a drain if possible. If scuppers are used, there must be positive drainage to the scupper.
- Provide sufficient expansion joint clearance for the gravel stop.
- The wall and the roof structure must be firmly attached to each other and move as a unit.

Materials

07 53 23 EPDM SINGLE-PLY MEMBRANE ROOFING

See Section 5-26 for material requirements.

07 71 19 GRAVEL STOP

One of the following flashings may be used:

Galvanized steel, ASTM A653/A653M, minimum 26 gage or 0.0187 in. (0.475 mm); it may have a factory-applied coating of polyvinylidene fluoride or another fluorocarbon coating.

Table 5-4 Minimum Thicknesses of Gravel Stops, in. (mm)

Material	Face dimension, in. (mm)							
	4	(102)	5	(127)	6	(152)	7+	(178+)
Galvanized steel	26 ga. 0.0187 in.	0.475	24 ga. 0.0250 in.	0.635	22 ga. 0.0312 in.	0.792	20 ga. 0.0375 in.	0.953
Stainless steel	26 ga. 0.0187 in.	0.475	26 ga. 0.0187 in.	0.475	22 ga. 0.0312 in.	0.792	20 ga. 0.0375 in.	0.953
Copper	16 oz, 0.0216 in.	0.549	16 oz, 0.0216 in.	0.549	20 oz, 0.0337 in.	0.686	20 oz, 0.0337 in.	0.686
Aluminum	0.0253 in.	0.643	0.0320 in.	0.813	0.040 in.	1.024	0.0506 in.	1.290

Stainless steel, ASTM A167, Type 302 or 304; use Type 316 in corrosive or marine environments, minimum 0.015 in. (0.38 mm), 2D finish.

Copper, ASTM B370, cold rolled hard tempered, minimum 16 oz (455 g/m^2), 0.0216 in. (0.549 mm).

Aluminum, ASTM B 209, minimum 0.0320 in. (0.813 mm), anodized color as required.

Minimum thicknesses depend on the face dimension, as shown in Table 5-4.

Execution

Attach to wood nailer at 4 in. (100 mm) on center with ring shank nails or screws.

Set in a bed of roofing cement if used with a built-up roof.

Attach to continuous cleat if the face dimension exceeds 5 in. (127 mm).

For face dimensions of over 5 in. (127 mm) expansion joints should be constructed, with backup plates formed in the same profile as the wall edging. The gravel stop is set in mastic over this, allowing for a 1/4 in. (6 mm) expansion space. A 6 in. (152 mm) cover plate is then set over the joint and nailed in place, with the nails set in the 1/4 in. (6 mm) expansion space. Copper gravel stops may require slightly different detailing.

5-38 VERTICAL AND HORIZONTAL JOINT FILLERS AND SEALANTS

Description

Joint fillers and sealants are two of the primary methods of protecting a building from moisture and air infiltration. They are required in every building and must seal joints of both similar and dissimilar materials in a wide variety of applications. This section describes the basic requirements for detailing and selecting sealants for weathertight joints. See Fig. 5-38.1.

Limitations of Use

- This detail does not include premolded compression seals or expansion joint cover assemblies.
- Joints using the rain screen principle are not included.
- Sealants and calking compounds with low movement capability (5 percent or less) are not included.

Figure 5-38.1 Vertical and horizontal joint fillers and sealants 07 92 00

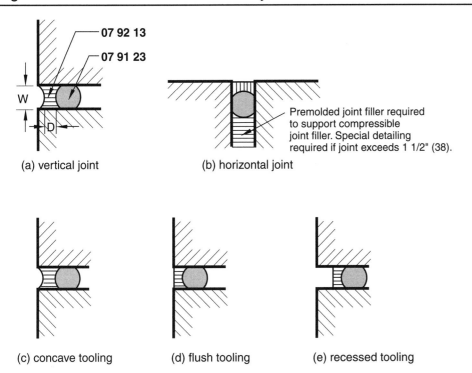

(a) vertical joint

(b) horizontal joint

Premolded joint filler required
to support compressible
joint filler. Special detailing
required if joint exceeds 1 1/2" (38).

(c) concave tooling

(d) flush tooling

(e) recessed tooling

- This section does not include methods of calculating joints that are subject to a combination of movements—for example, simple extension and transverse extension (shear). Refer to ASTM C1472 for a complete discussion of the methods for calculating joint width for these types of conditions.

Determining Joint Width

The width of the joint is determined by the expected movement of the joint, the movement capability of the sealant, construction tolerances, and the temperature at which the sealant is applied. Joint movement may be caused by such factors as thermal expansion and contraction, moisture absorption of the materials being sealed, and the various forms of structural movement. Construction tolerances may include manufacturing, fabrication, and erection tolerances. Detailing a joint either too wide or too narrow for the movement capability of the joint can cause it to fail.

The following procedure gives a method for determining the required width of a butt joint for a liquid-applied sealant as commonly found on the exterior of a building. It does not include provisions for structural movement caused by dead loading, live loading, wind, or seismic events. When designing a joint that may be subject to these types of loads, the structural engineer can be consulted for expected movement dimensions. However, seismic loading is generally not considered in the following procedure because the amount of movement that must be accommodated is too large for a typical sealant joint. Instead, seismic joints are commonly constructed of preformed gasket systems or other specialized products. See Section 2-2 for procedures for sizing vertical brick joints and Section 2-11 for sizing horizontal brick joints.

Joint width can be calculated using the following formula:

$$W = \frac{\Delta L_t + \Delta L_r + \Delta L_i}{S} + T \qquad \text{(eq. 5-1)}$$

where

W = designed sealant joint width, in. (mm)

ΔL_t = dimensional change due to thermal movement, in. (mm)

ΔL_r = dimensional change due to reversible moisture movement, in. (mm)

ΔL_i = dimensional change due to irreversible moisture growth (if any), in. (mm)

S = sealant movement capacity, expressed as a decimal; that is, $\pm 25\%$ is entered as 0.25

T = total construction tolerance including manufacturing, fabrication, and erection tolerances, as applicable

The dimensional change due to thermal movement is calculated according to the following formula:

$$\Delta L_t = (L)\Delta T(e) \qquad \text{(eq. 5-2)}$$

where

L = unrestrained length or sealant joint spacing, in. (mm)

ΔT = maximum temperature difference that the joint will be subjected to, °F (°C)

e = coefficient of thermal linear expansion, in./in./°F (mm/mm/°C)

Coefficients of thermal expansion of common building materials are given in Table 2-5 and can be found in ASTM C1472 and other reference sources. If a particular proprietary material is being used, the manufacturer can be consulted for an exact value.

The maximum temperature difference, ΔT, is based on the winter and summer temperature extremes that the material is likely to encounter according to the simple formula

$$\Delta T = T_s - T_w \qquad \text{(eq. 5-3)}$$

where

T_s = maximum summer temperature

T_w = minimum winter temperature

The minimum winter temperature is the winter heating design dry bulb air temperature as given in the ASHRAE *Fundamentals Handbook*. Design temperatures can also be found in other reference sources.

In the summer, the maximum temperature is a result of both ambient air temperature and increased temperatures due to solar radiation. The solar radiation heat gain is a product of a material's solar absorption coefficient and its heat capacity constant. In winter, increases in temperature due to solar gain are negligible, so only the air temperature is used. The maximum summer temperature, T_s, is obtained by the following formula:

$$T_s = T_A + A_x(H_x) \qquad \text{(eq. 5-4)}$$

where

T_A = hottest summer air temperature (0.4 percent dry bulb air temperature), °F (°C)

A_x = coefficient of solar absorption for the material (dimensionless number)

H_x = heat capacity constant for the material

Table 5-5 Coefficients of Solar Absorption for Common Building Materials

Material	Coefficient (dimensionless)
Aluminum, clear finish	0.60
Aluminum, dull finish	0.40–0.65
Black asphalt or slate	0.85–0.98
Brick, light buff	0.50–0.70
Brick, red	0.65–0.85
Brick, white	0.25–0.50
Concrete	0.65
Copper, tarnished	0.80
Galvanized steel	0.40–0.65
Galvanized steel, white	0.20
Glass, $1/4$ in. (6 mm)	0.15
Glass, $1/4$ in. tinted	0.48–0.53
Glass, $1/4$ in. reflective	0.60–0.83
Mineral board, uncolored	0.75
Paint, dark red, brown, or green	0.65–0.85
Paint, black	0.85–0.98
Paint, white	0.23–0.49
Plaster, white	0.30–0.50
Surface color, black	0.95
Surface color, light gray	0.65
Surface color, white	0.45
Wood, smooth	0.78

Source: ASTM C 1472.

Some coefficients of solar absorption of common building materials are given in Table 5-5, and heat capacity constants are given in Table 5-6.

Lacking precise information on temperature extremes, an ΔT value of 130°F (54°C) can be used, although greater or lesser differences are possible, depending on the local climate.

The change in dimension due to water absorption can come from two processes, reversible moisture growth and irreversible moisture growth. Reversible moisture growth is a material's response to changes in size as it absorbs or rejects water or water vapor. Such materials include porous substances such as wood, concrete, and concrete block. Irreversible moisture growth is caused by a material's permanent change in size with the passage of time. This commonly occurs with face brick. Dimensional changes caused by moisture growth can be calculated with the following formulas:

$$\Delta L_r = \left(\frac{R}{100} \right) L \qquad \text{(eq. 5-5)}$$

$$\Delta L_i = \left(\frac{I}{100} \right) L \qquad \text{(eq. 5-6)}$$

Table 5-6 Heat Capacity Constants

Condition	Constant, IP units (SI units)
Low	100 (56)
Low, with reflection	130 (72)
High	75 (42)
High, with reflection	100 (56)

Source: ASTM C 1472.

Table 5-7 Coefficients of Linear Moisture Growth for Common Building Materials

Materials	Coefficient, percent	
	Reversible (R)	Irreversible (I)
Brick, solid	0.02	+ 0.03
Brick veneer	0.02	+ 0.05
Concrete, standard gravel	0.02 to 0.06	− 0.03 to 0.08
Concrete, lightweight	0.03 to 0.06	− 0.03 to 0.09
CMU, dense	0.02 to 0.04	− 0.02 to 0.045
CMU, lighweight	0.03 to 0.06	− 0.02 to 0.06
Limestone	0.01	—

Note: For values in in./in. or mm/mm, divide the above percentage values by 100.
Source: Compiled from information from the American Concrete Institute and the Brick Industry Association.

where

ΔL_r = dimensional change due to reversible moisture movement, in. (mm)

R = moisture-induced reversible growth, percent

L = length, in. (mm)

ΔL_i = dimensional change due to irreversible moisture growth (if any), in. (mm)

I = moisture-induced irreversible growth, percent

Coefficients of linear moisture growth for some common building materials are given in Table 5-7. For irreversible growth for brick, a value of 0.03 percent is often used.

When the total joint width based on temperature and moisture dimensional changes is calculated, the expected tolerances of materials, fabrication, and installation must be added. Of course, construction tolerances vary with the material. Refer to other details in this book for some industry standard tolerances. Other tolerances can be found in the *Handbook of Construction Tolerances* and from the various trade associations.

Other Detailing Considerations

- If a sealant with a lower movement capability is desired, the joint width can be increased to reduce the percentage of movement.
- The expected movement of any joint can be calculated using the procedure given above; however, the graph in Fig. 5-38.2 is a quick method of estimating the required joint width based on the materials being used and the movement capability of the sealant. The graph assumes a 130°F (54°C) temperature differential and the length of material at 10 ft. (3 m). For shorter or longer material lengths, simply multiply the joint width from Fig. 5-38.1 by the percentage the actual panel is shorter or longer than 10 ft (3 m). For example, the required joint width for a 20 ft (6.1 m) panel would be twice that given by the graph. In addition, the material's construction tolerance and other expected movements *must* be added to the value found in the graph.
- Although the ideal relationship of depth to width may be prescribed by a specific manufacturer, refer to Table 5-8 for suggested dimensions.
- For horizontal joints subject to foot traffic, select a sealant with a hardness not less than 25 or more than 50 when tested in accordance with ASTM C661.
- For very wide joints, consider the use of a steel cover plate or a prefabricated expansion joint assembly.

Figure 5-38.2 Joint width for sealants with various movement capabilities for 10-ft (3 m) panels at ΔT of 130°F (54°C)

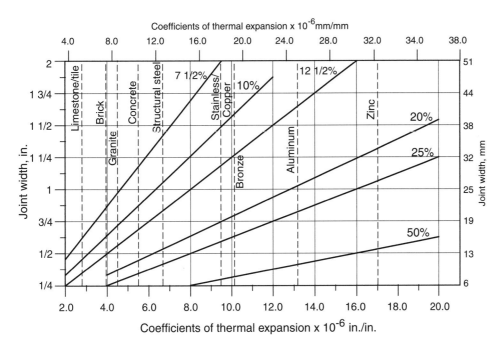

- Compressible elastomeric joint fillers made of neoprene, butyl, or EPDM may be used as a backup as well as a temporary seal before the final sealant is applied.
- If the sealant is likely to adhere to the joint filler, a bond breaker must be used below the sealant. A typical bond breaker is a self-adhesive polyethylene or polytetrafluoroethylene tape.

Coordination Required

- In some instances, a primer may be required. Joints with dissimilar materials that require different primers are often difficult to construct. Follow the manufacturer's recommendations for the type of substrate and the type of sealant used.
- Verify that the substrates do not have coatings that would prevent adhesion.
- Verify that the sealant selected will not cause staining of adjacent surfaces.

Table 5-8   Recommended Depth of Sealants

Joint width, W in in. (mm)	Depth of sealant, D	
	Concrete, masonry, and stone	Metal, glass and other nonporous materials
min. 1/4 in. (6)	1/4 in.	1/4 in. (6)
1/4 in. to 1/2 in. (6 to 13)	Same as width	1/4 in. (6)
1/2 in. to 1 in. (13 to 25)	One-half width	One-half width up to max. of 3/8 in. (10)
1 in. to 2 in. (25 to 51)	Max. 1/2 in. (13)	Max. 3/8 in. (10)

Likely Failure Points

- Tearing of the sealant caused by adherence to three sides of a joint or to both sides and the joint filler
- Bubbling of the sealant caused by puncturing or overcompressing the joint filler during application
- Tearing caused by excessive depth of the sealant
- Lack of adhesion caused by dirty or dew- or frost-covered surfaces
- Omission or misapplication of joint fillers
- Breaking of the sealant if installed during temperature extremes when the joint is at its maximum extension or compression
- Tearing or breaking caused by the use of a low-performance sealant with limited movement capability in a joint with a high percentage of movement
- Lack of adhesion caused by omission of a primer
- Early failure caused by sealant movement during cure (This may happen when sealants requiring atmospheric moisture for curing are used in climates with low relative humidity.)

Applicable Standards

The following are some of the useful standards for design joints and selecting sealants for various applications. In particular, ASTM C1472 gives very detailed procedures for calculating the required width of a sealant joint.

ASTM C661	*Standard Test Method for Indentation Hardness of Elastomeric-Type Sealants by Means of a Durometer*
ASTM C834	*Standard Specification for Latex Sealants*
ASTM C920	*Standard Specification for Elastomeric Joint Sealants*
ASTM C1184	*Standard Specification for Structural Silicone Sealants*
ASTM C1193	*Standard Guide for Use of Joint Sealants*
ASTM C1249	*Standard Guide for Secondary Seal for Sealed Insulating Glass Units for Structural Sealant Glazing Applications*
ASTM C1299	*Standard Guide for Use in Selection of Liquid-Applied Sealants*
ASTM C1401	*Standard Guide for Structural Sealant Glazing*
ASTM C1472	*Standard Guide for Calculating Movement and Other Effects When Establishing Sealant Joint Width*
ASTM C1481	*Standard Guide for Use of Joint Sealants with Exterior Insulation and Finish Systems (EIFS)*
ASTM C1564	*Standard Guide for Use of Silicone Sealants for Protective Glazing Systems*

Materials

07 91 23 JOINT BACKING

Materials

For vertical joints: open cell or closed cell polyethylene foam, sponge rubber rod, or elastomeric tubing. Closed cell foams are generally preferred because they will not absorb moisture. However, open cell foams allow some single-component sealants to cure faster by allowing air and moisture to reach both sides of the sealant.

Table 5-9 Comparative Properties of Sealants

	Butyl	Acrylic, water base	Acrylic, solvent base	Polysulfide, one part	Polysulfide, two part	Polyurethane, one part	Polyurethane, two part	Silicone	Notes
Recommended maximum joint movement, %±	7.5–10	12.5–25	12.5	25	25	25	50	50–100	a
Life expectancy (in years)	5–15	5–10	10–20	10–20	10–20	10–20+	10–20+	20+	
Maximum joint width, in. (mm)	³/₄ (19)	³/₈ (10)	³/₄ (19)	³/₄ (19)	1 (25)	³/₄ (19)	1–2 (25–52)	³/₄ (19)	b
Adhesion to:									
Wood	•	•	•	•	•	•	•		c
Metal	•	•	•	•	•	•	•	•	c
Masonry/Concrete	•	•	•	•	•	•	•	•	c, g
Glass	•	•	•					•	c
Plastic	•	•	•					•	
Curing time (days)	120	5	14	14+	7	7+	3–50	2–14	d, e
Shore A hardness	20–40	30–35	30–50	30–55	25–55	25–55	25–60	15–40	
Self-leveling available	n/a		•	•	•		•	•	
Nonsag available	n/a	•	•	•	•	•	•	•	
Paintable?	No	Yes	Yes	Yes	Yes	Yes	Yes	No	f
Resistance to: (see legend)									
Ultraviolet	1–2	2–3	3–4	2	2–3	3	3	5	
Cut/tear	2	1–2	1	3	3	4–5	4–5	1–2	
Abrasion	2	1–2	1–2	1	1	3	3	1	
Weathering	4–5	3–4	3–4	3	3	3–4	3–4	4–5	
Oil/grease	1–2	2	3	3	3	3	3	2	
Compression	2–3	1–2	1	2	2	4	4	4–5	
Extension	1	1–2	1	1–2	1–2	4–5	4–5	4–5	

Legend: 1 = Poor, 2 = Fair, 3 = Good, 4 = Very good, 5 = Excellent.
Some high-performance silicones have movement capabilities up to 200% extension and 75% compression. Verify with the manufacturer.
Figures given are conservative. Consult manufacturers' literature for specific recommendations.
Primer may be required.
Cure time for low- and medium-modulus silicones to a tack-free condition is about two hours.
Silicone sealants can be applied over a wide temperature range.
Some silicones are field tintable or come in a variety of colors.
Silicones may stain stone and masonry. Verify primer requirements and other limitations with the manufacturer.

Closed cell foams are nonabsorbent to water and gas.

For horizontal joints: closed cell, high-density flexible foams, resin-impregnated fiberboard, or elastomeric tubing.

Execution

Joint fillers should compress at least 25 percent of the joint width.

07 92 13 SEALANT

Materials

ASTM C834, latex sealants.

ASTM C920, single-component or multicomponent compounds.

ASTM C1184, structural silicone sealants.

Refer to Table 5-9 for general guidelines for selecting sealants. Many hybrid sealants are available for specific applications. Verify types with the manufacturer. For example, textured polyurethane sealants are available to appear as grout joints.

Execution

Sealant should be applied at temperatures ranging from 40°F to 100°F (4.4°C to 38°C).

If movement-during-cure problems are anticipated, the risk of failure may be reduced by selecting a sealant with a faster cure time, using open cell joint backing, applying the sealant during cloudy or cool weather, shading the joint during application, or using a procured sealant.

Tool the sealant after application to force the sealant into the joint and to eliminate air pockets. One of the three types of profiles, as shown in Fig. 5.38, may be used, although the concave profile is preferred because it minimizes stress on the bonding surface. The depth of the joint should be designed to allow for reduction in depth caused by concave or recessed tooling.

5-39   ROOF DRAIN

Description

Roof drains must be provided on all roofs to remove water. They should be located whenever possible at the points of maximum structural deflection. In cold climates, they should be located on the interior of the building. Figure 5-39 shows a typical roof drain detail.

Limitations of Use

- This detail shows the use of an EPDM membrane; details for other types of membranes may vary slightly.

Detailing Considerations

- Roof slopes should be a minimum of $1/4$ in./ft (20 mm/m), although $1/2$ in./ft (40 mm/m) is recommended. Roof slopes may be achieved by sloping the structural deck or by using tapered insulation or insulating fill.

Figure 5-39   Roof drain   22 14 26.13

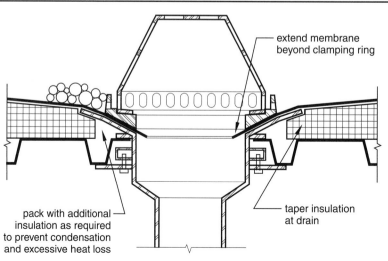

extend membrane
beyond clamping ring

pack with additional
insulation as required
to prevent condensation
and excessive heat loss

taper insulation
at drain

- Recess the drain below the roof surface.
- Provide extra insulation around the drain head, if required, to prevent condensation.
- Design saddles and crickets as required to create positive drainage around obstructions such as penthouses, equipment supports, and large skylights.

Coordination Required

- Through-wall scuppers may be required by the local building code or may be desirable to prevent ponding of water if one or more drains become clogged.
- Drains must be sized to accommodate the heaviest rainfall.
- Roof drains must be in place prior to installing the roofing.
- Compare the camber of structural members and the maximum expected deflection with the proposed drainage pattern to verify that positive drainage will always occur on the completed roof under the heaviest expected loads.

Likely Failure Points

- Leakage caused by standing water due to inadequate drainage
- Structural collapse caused by ponding of water
- Clogging of drains due to inadequate gravel stops or poor inspection and maintenance
- Ice dams formed at the drain caused by excessive heat loss through the tapered insulation

Materials

See Section 5-26 for material requirements.

CHAPTER 6

DOOR AND WINDOW DETAILS

6-1 STEEL DOOR AND FRAME JAMB, MASONRY WALL

Description

Figure 6-1 illustrates a standard installation of a hollow metal, double-rabbeted steel frame in a masonry wall where the frame is butted to the wall. For narrow walls, larger frames can also be detailed to wrap the wall.

Limitations of Use

- This detail is generally not used for main entry doors or where appearance is a primary consideration. However, requirements for fire rating, durability, or security may dictate the use of steel doors and frames.
- Single leaves of exit doors may not be wider than 48 in. (1220 mm).

Detailing Considerations

- Steel frames have a standard 2 in. (51 mm) face dimension with a $5/8$ in. (16 mm) stop. Custom frames can be made with different face dimensions, but the minimum is 1 in. (25 mm). However, a standard 2 in. (51 mm) wide face allows standard door widths to be placed within a modular masonry opening.
- Frames may be single rabbet or double rabbet as required by the job.
- Steel doors are standard $13/8$ in. and $13/4$ in. (34.9 mm and 44.4 mm) thick for Level I doors and $13/4$ in. (44.4 mm) thick for Levels II, III, and IV doors. The standard door height is 7 ft 0 in. (2134 mm), but other heights are available.
- Steel doors may be selected based on the Steel Door Institute's *Recommended Selection and Usage for Standard Steel Doors,* SDI-108.
- Verify tolerances of the masonry and door frame to provide at least a $1/4$ in. (6 mm) wide space for sealant. To accommodate door frame and masonry tolerances while allowing for an acceptable sealant joint, the design clearance between the frame and the masonry should be increased beyond the standard $1/4$ in. (6 mm). However, this may

Figure 6-1 Steel door and jamb frame, masonry wall 08 11 13.1

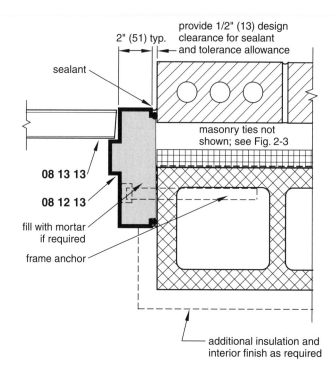

necessitate cutting the block to fit. Alternately, 1½ in. (38 mm) face frames may be used to increase the clearance between the masonry and frame while allowing the use of standard modular masonry openings.

- Steel doors are classified as Grade I, Standard duty, Grade II, Heavy duty, and Grade III, Extra heavy duty. The type selected depends on the endurance level required and the application type. Each grade is further classified into models, depending on whether the door is full flush or seamless and whether it is hollow steel construction or composite construction.
- The clearance between the door and the frame jamb and head is not more than ⅛ in. (3 mm). At the meeting edges of door pairs, the clearance is not more than ¼ in. (6 mm) for standard doors and not more than ⅛ in. (3 mm) for fire-rated doors. Clearance dimensions are subject to a tolerance of ±1/32 in. (0.8 mm).
- Fire-rated louvers are available, if required.

Coordination Required

- Verify that the door size meets exiting and accessibility requirements.
- Verify that the surrounding structure can provide proper anchorage for the door type, size, and weight.
- If a fire-rated assembly is required, the door and frame must be labeled and the hardware must be fire-rated. Fire-rated doors require a mineral fiberboard core.
- Fire-rated opening assemblies must conform to one or more of the following:
  - UL 10B, Standard for Safety for Fire Tests of Door Assemblies.
  - NFPA 252, Fire Tests of Door Assemblies.

- If astragals are required on pairs of doors, they must be factory applied. Door pairs with astragals require door coordinators. Some local building codes may not allow the use of astragals. Some door pairs may be rated without requiring an astragal.
- Refer to Sections 2-3, 2-4, and 2-5 for additional information on brick and masonry.

Likely Failure Points

- Door binding or doors that swing open or closed if the frame is not installed plumb
- Compromise of the fire rating of the assembly if one of the components is not rated or not installed properly

Materials

08 12 13 HOLLOW METAL FRAMES

Materials

ANSI/SDI A250.8, *Recommended Specifications for Standard Steel Doors and Frames.*

Level 1, 18 or 16 gage, 0.042 in. or 0.053 in. (1.0 mm or 1.3 mm).

Level 2, 16 gage, 0.053 in. (1.3 mm).

Level 3, 16 or 14 gage, 0.053 in. or 0.067 in. (1.3 mm or 1.6 mm).

Level 4, 14 or 12 gage, 0.067 in. or 0.093 in. (1.6 mm or 2.4 mm).

Welded or knockdown type.

For interior doors, door stops may extend to the floor or be terminated above the floor at a 90 degree or 45 degree angle. Terminated stops are used to simplify floor cleaning.

Hot-dip galvanized frames should be used in severely corrosive locations. Electrolytic galvanized frames should be used in mildly corrosive locations. Primed steel may be used in other locations.

Execution

Installed according to the recommendations of SDI-122, *Installation & Troubleshooting Guide for Standard Steel Doors & Frames.*

Provide a minimum of three anchors per jamb of the type required for the adjacent construction. Minimum of 18 gage, 0.042 in. (1.0 mm) or $^3/_{16}$ in. (4.76 mm) wire.

Attach the frame to the floor with a minimum 18 gage, 0.042 in. (1.0 mm) floor anchors.

Fill the frames with mortar as the wall is laid up.

Prepared for hardware according to ANSI/BHMA A156.115.

08 13 13 HOLLOW METAL DOORS

Materials

ANSI/SDI A250.8, *Recommended Specifications for Standard Steel Doors and Frames.*

Level I, Standard duty, minimum face thickness of 20 gage or 0.032 in. (0.8 mm).

Level II, Heavy duty, minimum face thickness of 18 gage or 0.042 in. (1.0 mm).

Level III, Extra heavy duty, minimum face thickness of 16 gage or 0.053 in. (1.3 mm).

Level IV, Maximum duty, minimum face thickness of 14 gage or 0.067 in. (1.6 mm).

Full flush or seamless, hollow steel or composite construction as required.

Core material may be honeycomb construction, polyurethane, polystyrene, steel grid, or mineral fiberboard.

Standard door heights are 6 ft 8 in. (2032 mm) and 7 ft 0 in. (2134 mm). Standard door widths are multiples of 2 in. (51 mm) up to 4 ft 0 in. (1219 mm). Custom door sizes are available.

Hot-dip galvanized doors should be used in severely corrosive locations. Electrolytic galvanized doors should be used in mildly corrosive locations. Primed steel may be used in other locations.

Execution

Prepared for hardware according to ANSI/BHMA A156.115.

Install hardware according to ANSI/SDI A250.6, *Recommended Practice for Hardware Reinforcings on Standard Steel Doors and Frames.*

6-2   STEEL DOOR AND HEAD FRAME, MASONRY WALL

Description

Figure 6-2 is a continuation of Fig. 6-1 and illustrates a common method of framing a steel door head. A 4 in. (102 mm) high head frame is often used to allow an assembly with a 7 ft (2134 mm) door to fit within an 8 in. (200 mm) modular masonry opening. However,

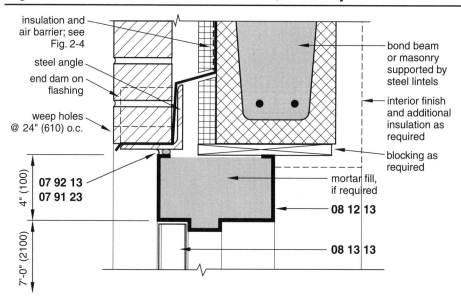

Figure 6-2 Steel door and head frame, masonry wall 08 11 13.2

a 2 in. (51 mm) frame may also be used with custom door heights or nonstandard masonry openings.

Limitations of Use

- This detail is generally not used for main entry doors or where appearance is a primary consideration. However, requirements for fire rating, durability, or security may dictate the use of steel doors and frames.

Detailing Considerations

- Detail the door height and frame face size to work with masonry coursing.
- Frames may be single rabbet or double rabbet as required by the job.
- Fill the head frame with mortar.
- Refer to Section 6-1 for other detailing considerations.

Coordination Required

- Refer to Section 6-1 for the coordination required.

Likely Failure Points

- Binding of the door caused by deflection of the head frame due to inadequate structural support
- Refer to Section 6-1 for additional likely failure points

Materials

07 91 23 BACKER RODS

Closed cell polyethylene foam, with the diameter at least 25 percent greater than the joint width.

07 92 13 ELASTOMERIC JOINT SEALANT

Materials

One-part polysulfide, polyurethane, or silicone, ASTM C920, Type S, Grade NS, Class 25 or 50.

Execution

Sealant depth equal to the width of the joint up to $1/2$ in. (13 mm), with a minimum depth of $1/4$ in. (6 mm).

Sealant depth $1/2$ in. (13 mm) for joint widths from $1/2$ in. to 1 in. (13 mm to 25 mm).

For sealants with a ± 25 percent movement capability, the joint width should be four times the expected movement of the joint.

Proper priming and backer rods are required.

Refer to Section 6-1 for other material requirements.

Figure 6-3 Steel door and jamb frame, gypsum wallboard wall 08 11 13.3

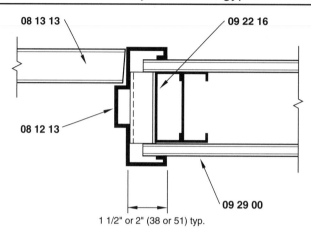

1 1/2" or 2" (38 or 51) typ.

6-3 STEEL DOOR AND FRAME, GYPSUM WALLBOARD WALL

Description

Hollow metal doors and frames, as shown in Fig. 6-3, are often used in gypsum wallboard partitions because of their ease of construction or their durability, or because a higher fire rating can be achieved than is possible with wood doors and frames. Figure 6-3 is similar to that used for plaster partitions except that different types of anchors are used.

Limitations of Use

- This detail is for interior construction only.
- This detail only shows the jamb. However, head detailing is similar except that steel stud runners or other types of head framing are used instead of steel studs.

Detailing Considerations

- Steel frames have a standard 2 in. (51 mm) face dimension with a $5/8$ in. (16 mm) stop. Custom frames can be made with different face dimensions, but the minimum is 1 in. (25 mm).
- Frames may be single rabbet or double rabbet as required by the job. Thin partitions usually require a single-rabbeted frame.
- Fire-rated partitions require the use of 20 gage, 0.032 in. (0.8 mm) studs.
- Steel frames may be used with mineral core flush wood doors for fire ratings of up to $1\frac{1}{2}$ hours.
- Refer to Section 6-1 for other detailing considerations.

Coordination Required

- Doors in walls that extend only to a suspended ceiling may require extra bracing by extending kickers from above the door head to the structure above.

- Verify that the surrounding structure can provide proper anchorage for the door type, size, and weight.
- Refer to Section 6-1 for other coordination items required.

Likely Failure Points

- Shaking or cracking of the wall due to inadequate anchoring of the frame

Materials

08 12 13 HOLLOW METAL FRAMES

Materials

ANSI/SDI A250.8, *Recommended Specifications for Standard Steel Doors and Frames.*

Level 1, 18 or 16 gage, 0.042 in. or 0.053 in. (1.0 mm or 1.3 mm).

Level 2, 16 gage, 0.053 in. (1.3 mm).

Level 3, 16 or 14 gage, 0.053 in. or 0.067 in. (1.3 mm or 1.6 mm).

Level 4, 14 or 12 gage, 0.067 in or 0.093 in. (1.6 mm or 2.4 mm).

Welded or knockdown type.

Door stops may extend to the floor or be terminated above the floor at a 90 degree or 45 degree angle. Terminated stops are used to simplify floor cleaning.

Hot-dip galvanized frames should be used in severely corrosive locations. Electrolytic galvanized frames should be used in mildly corrosive locations. Primed steel may be used in other locations.

Execution

Installed according to the recommendations of SDI-122, *Installation & Troubleshooting Guide for Standard Steel Doors & Frames.*

Provide a minimum of three anchors per jamb of the type required for the adjacent construction. Use a minimum of 18 gage, 0.042 in. (1.0 mm) or $^3/_{16}$ in. (4.76 mm) wire.

Attach the frame to the floor with a minimum 18 gage, 0.042 in. (1.0 mm) floor anchors.

Prepared for hardware according to ANSI/BHMA A156.115.

08 13 13 HOLLOW METAL DOORS

Materials

ANSI/SDI A250.8, *Recommended Specifications for Standard Steel Doors and Frames.*

Level I, Standard duty, minimum face thickness of 20 gage or 0.032 in. (0.8 mm).

Level II, Heavy duty, minimum face thickness of 18 gage or 0.042 in. (1.0 mm).

Level III, Extra heavy duty, minimum face thickness of 16 gage or 0.053 in. (1.3 mm).

Level IV, Maximum duty, minimum face thickness of 14 gage or 0.067 in. (1.6 mm).

Full flush or seamless, hollow steel or composite construction as required.

Core material may be honeycomb construction, polyurethane, polystyrene, steel grid, or mineral fiberboard.

Standard door heights are 6 ft 8 in. (2032 mm) and 7 ft 0 in. (2134 mm). Standard door widths are multiples of 2 in. (51 mm) up to 4 ft 0 in. (1219 mm). Custom door sizes are available.

Hot-dip galvanized doors should be used in severely corrosive locations. Electrolytic galvanized doors should be used in mildly corrosive locations. Primed steel may be used in other locations.

Execution

Prepared for hardware according to ANSI/BHMA A156.115.

Install hardware according to ANSI/SDI A250.6, *Recommended Practice for Hardware Reinforcings on Standard Steel Doors and Frames.*

09 22 16 Nonstructural metal framing

Materials

ASTM C645 and ASTM A653/A653M.

Minimum 25 gage or 0.0175 in. (0.455 mm).

$2\frac{1}{2}$ in., $3\frac{5}{8}$ in., 4 in., or 6 in. (63.5 mm, 92.1 mm, 101.6 mm, or 152.4 mm) as required.

Screws should conform to ASTM C1002.

Execution

Maximum spacing of 24 in. (600 mm) on center.

Installed according to ASTM C754.

Provide a slip joint at the underside of structural slabs or other slabs that may deflect.

09 29 00 Gypsum wallboard

Materials

$\frac{5}{8}$ in. (16 mm), standard or type X if required for fire resistance. ASTM C1396.

Gypsum wallboard tape and joint compound should conform to ASTM C475/C475M.

Screws should conform to ASTM C1002.

Execution

Installed according to ASTM C840, the recommendations of the Gypsum Association, and specific recommendations of the manufacturer.

Wallboard must be applied vertically to $1\frac{5}{8}$ in. (41.3 mm) or $2\frac{1}{2}$ in. (63.5 mm) studs and may be applied horizontally to $3\frac{5}{8}$ in. (92.1 mm) studs.

Stagger joints on opposite sides of the partition.

Applied with 1 in. (25 mm) type S screws 8 in. (203 mm) on center at the edges and 12 in. (305 mm) on center on intermediate studs.

Figure 6-4 Aluminum door frame assembly 08 11 16

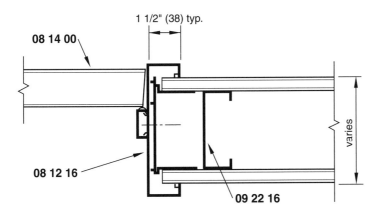

6-4   ALUMINUM DOOR FRAME ASSEMBLY

Description

Aluminum door frames are often used in place of steel frames when a high fire rating is not required, but the other advantages of a metal frame are needed. Aluminum frames are lightweight, strong, durable, easy to fabricate, come in a variety of finishes, and can be used where a 20 minute fire-rated assembly is required. These frames also have a sharper edge to their profile, which many architects prefer over the more rounded edges of steel frames. Although the exact construction of an aluminum frame varies with the manufacturer, Fig. 6-4 shows a typical aluminum jamb anchored to an interior metal stud wall.

Limitations of Use

- Generally, aluminum frames cannot be used on openings requiring a fire rating of more than 20 minutes.

Detailing Considerations

- Frame faces vary in dimension, depending on the manufacturer. A typical size is $1^1/_2$ in. (38 mm).
- Smoke gaskets may be required on some doors. Verify this with the applicable code.
- Most manufacturers offer several types of extrusions for glass sidelight framing, bank railing, and top and bottom tracks as well as door framing.

Coordination Required

- Provide adequate bracing with wall studs or by extending them to the structure above.
- Other metals in contact with the frame should be stainless steel or zinc. Alternatively, contact with dissimilar metals should be prevented with the use of bituminous paint or nonmetallic gaskets.

Materials

08 12 16 ALUMINUM FRAMES

Extruded aluminum complying with ASTM B221, Alloy 6063-T5.

The door stop should have continuous wool pile weatherstripping or silencers.

08 14 00 WOOD DOORS

Materials

Constructed to conform to WDMA I.S. 1A. Other standards as given in Section 1300 or 1400 of the Architectural Woodwork Institute's (AWI) *Quality Standards* for flush doors or stile and rail doors, respectively.

Standard thickness of $1\frac{3}{8}$ in. and $1\frac{3}{4}$ in. (34.9 mm or 44.4 mm) in standard widths from 2 ft 0 in. to 3 ft 0 in. (610 mm to 914 mm). Standard heights of 6 ft 8 in. (2032 mm) and 7 ft 0 in. (2134 mm), although other heights are readily available.

Hollow core or solid core according to the requirements of the project. Several types of solid core construction are available.

Face construction may be paint-grade hardboard, plastic laminate, or wood veneer. Veneer faces are graded according to AWI *Quality Standards* as premium, custom, or economy.

Execution

Door and frame preparation for hardware in accordance with ANSI A156/115W.

Fire-rated doors installed in accordance with NFPA 80.

Doors are hung with $\frac{1}{16}$ in. (1.6 mm) clearance at the hinge jamb, $\frac{1}{8}$ in. (3 mm) clearance at the lock jamb, and a minimum of $\frac{1}{16}$ in. (1.6 mm) and a maximum of $\frac{1}{8}$ in. (3 mm) clearance at the head.

09 22 16 NONSTRUCTURAL METAL FRAMING

Materials

ASTM C645 and ASTM A653/A653M.

Minimum 25 gage or 0.0175 in. (0.455 mm).

$2\frac{1}{2}$ in., $3\frac{5}{8}$ in., 4 in., or 6 in. (63.5 mm, 92.1 mm, 101.6 mm, or 152.4 mm) as required.

Screws should conform to ASTM C1002.

Execution

Maximum spacing of 24 in. (600 mm) on center.

Installed according to ASTM C754.

Provide a slip joint at the underside of structural slabs or other slabs that may deflect.

6-5   WOOD DOOR AND FRAME ASSEMBLY

Description

Wood doors and frames are one of the most common types of door assemblies. The designer has a wide choice of door types, sizes, and finishes, as well as an almost unlimited selection

Figure 6-5 Wood door and frame assembly 08 14 00

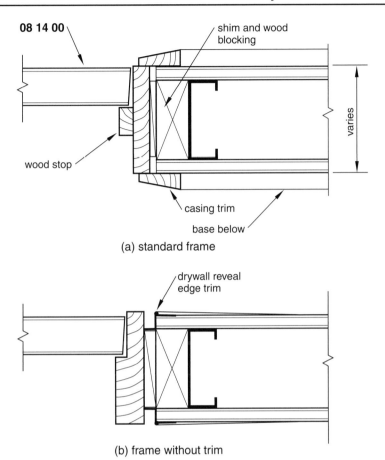

(a) standard frame

(b) frame without trim

of frame configurations and materials. Figure 6-5(a) illustrates the most basic wood door configuration, consisting of a jamb frame, a stop, and casing trim to conceal the joint between the wall and the frame. Other variations on this common configuration include single rabbeted frames with the stop milled integrally with the frame, trimless frames as shown in Fig. 6-5(b), and openings with no frame at all in which the door is mounted on pivots. The detail of the head section is similar to that of the jamb section.

Limitations of Use

- This detail does not include requirements for hardware.
- Wood doors cannot be used in openings requiring a fire rating of greater than $1\frac{1}{2}$ hours.
- Fire-rated doors must meet the requirements of NFPA 252 and carry a label certified by an independent testing agency.
- Pairs of doors with $\frac{3}{4}$ hour, 1 hour, and $1\frac{1}{2}$ hour ratings must have factory-furnished rated astragals.

Detailing Considerations

- At least $\frac{1}{4}$ in. (6 mm) shim space must be provided for setting the frame plumb in the rough opening.

- Adequate clearance must be maintained for the hinge by setting the casing trim back from the face of the jamb or a wide hinge must be used to enable the hinge barrel to clear the trim.
- Casing trim should be thick enough to provide a stopping point for the wall base.
- Wood frames may be used in 20 minute, $1/2$ hour, and $3/4$ hour fire door assemblies if allowed by the applicable building code.
- Smoke gaskets may be required on some doors. Verify this with the applicable building code.

Coordination Required

- Wood blocking is generally required in metal stud walls.
- Hardware, louvers, and lites must be listed or labeled to be used in a labeled door.
- Adequate width of the opening and clearance on either side of the door must be provided for accessibility when required. A minimum clear opening of 32 in. (815 mm) is required between the doorstop and the face of the door when it is open 90 degrees.
- If the door is located in the corner of a room, the hinge jamb should be far enough away from the wall perpendicular to the door to allow for a full 90 degree door opening allowing for clearance for the door handle and door stop.

Likely Failure Points

- Binding of the door due to an out-of-plumb frame
- Loosening of the frame or cracking of the wall finish caused by inadequate stud support or a frame sized too small for the size and weight of the door

Materials

08 14 00 Wood doors

Materials

Constructed to conform to WDMA I.S. 1A. Other standards as given in Section 1300 or 1400 of the AWI *Quality Standards* for flush doors or stile and rail doors, respectively.

Standard thickness of $1 3/8$ in. and $1 3/4$ in. (34.9 mm or 44.4 mm) in standard widths from 2 ft 0 in. to 3 ft 0 in. (610 mm to 914 mm). Standard heights of 6 ft 8 in. (2032 mm) and 7 ft 0 in. (2134 mm), although other heights are readily available.

Hollow core or solid core according to the requirements of the project. Several types of solid core construction are available.

Face construction may be paint-grade hardboard, plastic laminate, or wood veneer. Veneer faces are graded according to AWI *Quality Standards* as premium, custom, or economy.

Execution

Door and frame preparation for hardware in accordance with ANSI A156/115W.

Fire-rated doors installed in accordance with NFPA 80.

Doors are hung with $1/16$ in. (1.6 mm) clearance at the hinge jamb, $1/8$ in. (3 mm) clearance at the lock jamb, and a minimum of $1/16$ in. (1.6 mm) and a maximum of $1/8$ in. (3 mm) clearance at the head.

6-6 ALUMINUM STOREFRONT AT SILL AND HEAD

Description

Storefront systems are used in one-story and low-rise applications where the glass and its framing are supported within an opening rather than being continuously supported across several floors, as with curtain wall construction. Figure 6-6(a) shows a typical installation of a storefront supported by a floor and anchored to framing at the ceiling line.

Figure 6-6 Aluminum storefront at sill and head 08 41 13.1

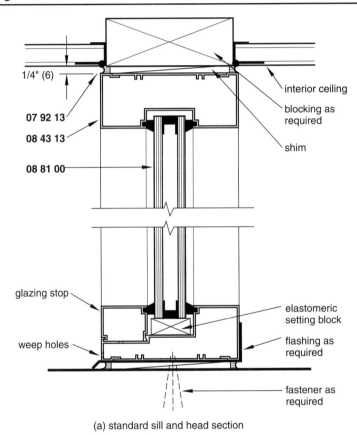

1/4" (6)

07 92 13

08 43 13

08 81 00

interior ceiling

blocking as required

shim

glazing stop

weep holes

elastomeric setting block

flashing as required

fastener as required

(a) standard sill and head section

(b) aluminum storefront slip joint

Figure 6-6(a) shows a flush glazing system where no separate projecting glass stops are used and where the glass is centered in the framing. This is the most typical type of storefront. Systems are also available that position the glass off center. Although this detail shows only glazing, similar framing members are available for doors, transom panels, and opaque panels.

Limitations of Use

- Maximum glass panel sizes are limited by the type and strength of the glass. Verify these limitations with the applicable building code.
- Storefront systems are not appropriate for high-rise construction.

Detailing Considerations

- Storefront systems are available in a variety of standard sizes. One of the most common sizes is $1^3/_4$ in. by $4^1/_2$ in. (44 mm by 114 mm). Other widths available include $1^1/_4$ in. (32 mm), $1^1/_2$ in. (38 mm), and 2 in. (51 mm). Other common depths include 4 in., 5 in., and 6 in. (102 mm, 127 mm, and 152 mm) and square sections for column covers. Refer to specific manufacturers' literature for sizes and profiles available.
- Special profiles are available from some manufacturers, including types with rounded edges, sloped sills, and adjustable mullions for angled corners.
- Either single or insulating glass units may be used.
- In cold climates, sections with thermal breaks should be used.
- Drip flashing is required for overhead sections that are flush with the exterior of the building.
- Long sections of storefront may require expansion joints or slip joints in some mullions.
- Sections may be either inside or outside glazed.

Coordination Required

- Verify if safety glazing is required.
- If the storefront is framed to the underside of a structural member, a slip joint may be required to accommodate deflection, as shown in Fig. 6-6(b).
- Thin sections may require steel stiffeners to support door frames or large glass lites.

Materials

07 92 13 Elastomeric joint sealant

Materials

Solvent release acrylic, one-part polysulfide, polyurethane, or silicone, ASTM C920, Type S, Grade NS, Class 25 or 50.

Execution

Sealant depth equal to the width of the joint up to $1/_2$ in. (13 mm), with a minimum depth of $1/_4$ in. (6 mm).

Sealant depth $1/_2$ in. (13 mm) for joint widths from $1/_2$ in. to 1 in. (13 mm to 25 mm).

For sealants with a ±25 percent movement capability, the joint width should be four times the expected movement of the joint.

Proper priming and backer rods are required.

08 43 13 ALUMINUM-FRAMED STOREFRONTS

Materials

6063-T5 alloy extruded to the size and shape required.

Storefront systems should meet the requirements of ASTM E283, E330, and E331.

Maximum deflection under a wind load of L/175.

Standard anodized finishes include clear, light bronze, medium bronze, dark bronze, and black. Fluorocarbon paints and siliconized polyester finishes are also available.

Execution

Set plumb and level with a $1/4$ in. (6 mm) shim space between the framing and substrate.

08 81 00 GLASS GLAZING

Materials

Flat glass: ASTM C1036.

Heat-treated flat glass: ASTM C1048.

Insulating glass: ASTM E774.

Safety glazing must conform to CPSC 16 CFR 1201.

Execution

Installed according to recommendations of the *Glazing Manual* of the Glass Association of North America.

Set on elastomeric setting blocks located at the quarter points of the glass.

Set in a frame with a dry or wet glazing system as recommended by the manufacturer.

6-7   ALUMINUM STOREFRONT AT MULLION AND JAMB

Description

Figure 6-7 is a continuation of Fig. 6-6 and shows typical detailing at vertical members of a storefront system. As with the head and sill, jambs are typically set within a fixed opening defined by another substrate. Intermediate mullions are provided to support the glass as required by wind loading and the span distances.

Limitations of Use

- Maximum glass panel sizes are limited by the type and strength of the glass. Verify these limitations with the applicable building code.

Detailing Considerations

- Two-piece mullions, which allow for expansion, may be used.
- Adjustable mullions are available from some manufacturers that allow angled corners to be made by rotating the section.
- Refer to Section 6-6 for other detailing considerations.

Figure 6-7 Aluminum storefront at mullion and jamb 08 41 13.2

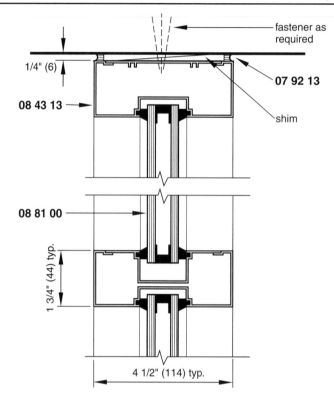

Coordination Required

- Thin sections may require steel stiffeners in vertical members to support door frames or large glass lites.
- Verify the tolerances of the jamb substrate. A design clearance greater than 1/4 in. (6 mm) may be required to accommodate tolerances and provide for a minimum 1/4 in. (6 mm) sealant space.
- Refer to Section 6-6 for other detailing considerations.

Materials

See Section 6-6 for material requirements.

6-8 ALL-GLASS ENTRANCE DOOR

Description

Glass doors are frequently used for both interior and exterior applications. Safety glass doors differ from storefront entrances in that they do not have vertical framing members; the edges of the glass are exposed, as shown in Fig. 6-8. The top and bottom of the glass door may be framed with continuous metal rails (shoes) or simply provided with patch plates that give the means to support the door on top and bottom pivots and a closer. In most cases, door pulls

Figure 6-8 All glass entrance door 08 42 26.1

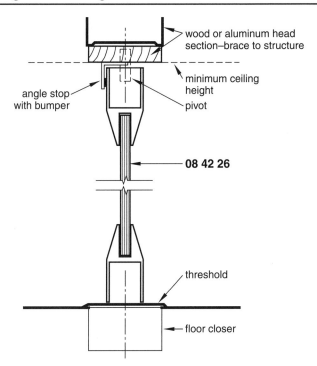

wood or aluminum head
section–brace to structure

minimum ceiling
height

angle stop
with bumper

pivot

08 42 26

threshold

floor closer

are provided and mounted through holes drilled in the glass, although some manufacturers offer special lever handles or locksets that are clamped onto the glass and function much as standard hardware.

Limitations of Use

- Glass doors without frames cannot be used where a fire-rated opening is required.
- Glass doors may not be allowed where smokeproof doors are required. Verify allowable use with the applicable building code.
- Special detailing and structural considerations are required in seismic zones.

Detailing Considerations

- Doors should be a minimum width of 3 ft 0 in. (914 mm).
- Various types of shoe configurations are available. This detail shows a shoe with a tapered edge. Square and rounded edges are also available.
- Head sections may be used in lieu of the wood section shown in this detail.
- Overhead closers may be located in a head section or transom bar if sufficient anchorage is provided.
- Thresholds are optional, but a cover plate is required over the closer.
- Metal shoes are available in finishes of polished or satin stainless steel, polished or satin brass, and anodized aluminum. Other finishes may be available from certain manufacturers.

Coordination Required

- Fixed side lites can be framed with metal shoes with the same profile as an adjacent door.
- Adequate bracing must be provided for the head section, especially near the pivot.
- If a floor pivot is used, verify that there is sufficient clearance within the thickness of the floor structure.

Materials

08 42 00 ALL-GLASS ENTRANCE DOORS

$1/2$ in. (13 mm) or $3/4$ in. tempered glass conforming to ASTM C1048.

Safety glazing must conform to CPSC 16 CFR 1201, Category II.

6-9 ALL-GLASS GLAZING SYSTEM

Description

This type of glazing system, illustrated in Fig. 6-9, consists of glass walls supported only at the top and bottom by framing, with lateral support provided by glass fins mounted perpendicular

Figure 6-9 All-glass glazing system 08 42 26.2

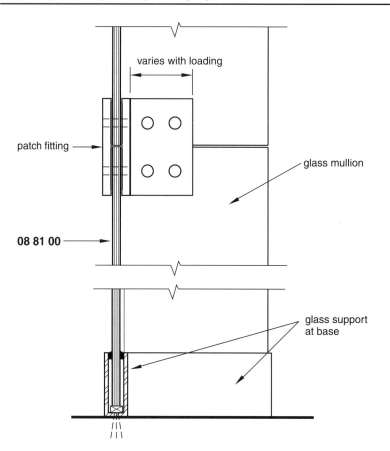

patch fitting

glass mullion

08 81 00

glass support
at base

to the primary glass plane. Individual pieces of glass are connected with special patch fittings, and joints are sealed with silicone sealant. This type of system is capable of spanning vertically up to 30 ft (9144 mm) if all the dead load is carried by the base and up to 75 ft (22.86 m) if the upper sections of glass are suspended from special clamps attached to an adequate structural support. Because the vertical supports are glass and the top and bottom framing members can be recessed into the ceiling and floor, this system provides an almost completely unobstructed view opening. Glass doors can be used with the system by using special patch fittings similar to those described in Section 6-8.

This system is typically used to enclose spaces with high ceilings where a minimum of visible framing is desired, as seen from both the outside and the inside. For typical high-rise applications and for buildings with standard floor-to-floor heights, this system has been largely replaced with structural silicone glazing, as described in Sections 6-14 and 6-15.

Limitations of Use

- Specific details of this type of system for a particular project should be developed with the assistance of the glazing system manufacturer and the glazing contractor.
- This system may not be used where a fire-rated wall is needed or where protected openings are required.

Detailing Considerations

- Deflection, building movement, and thermal movement must be considered when designing the support system.
- If glass is suspended, adequate structural support is required in addition to sufficient space above the ceiling for the clamping mechanism.
- The glass support may be recessed into the floor.

Materials

08 81 00 Glass

Main glass panels 3/8 in. (10 mm), 1/2 in. (13 mm), or 3/4 in. (19 mm) thick tempered glass.

Glass mullions 3/4 in. (19 mm) thick. Depth as required by wind loading.

Insulated glass panels may also be used where thermal control is required. The glass may be clear, tinted, low-emissivity, or reflective. Laminated glass may also be used.

Patch fittings are available in finishes of anodized aluminum, polished and satin stainless steel, polished and satin brass, and chrome. In addition, epoxy powdered coatings may be available.

6-10   ALL-GLASS GLAZING SYSTEM AT MULLION AND JAMB

Description

Figure 6-10 is a continuation of Fig. 6-9 and shows typical conditions at two vertical points in an all-glass glazing system. This type of system is often used to enclose the back wall of racquetball and handball courts as well as building entrances.

Figure 6-10 All-glass glazing system at mullion and jamb 08 42 26.3

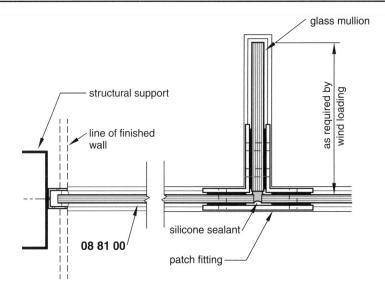

Limitations of Use

- Refer to Section 6-9 for limitations of use.

Detailing Considerations

- The glass at the jambs may be fixed in either surface-mounted or recessed frames.
- The glass system may also be designed with a space frame or a structural steel framework supporting the patch fittings.
- Refer to Section 6-9 for other detailing considerations.

Materials

08 81 00 GLASS

See Section 6-9 for material requirements.

6-11   ALUMINUM CURTAIN WALL AT SPANDREL

Description

A curtain wall is any exterior wall that is non-load-bearing, is supported by the structural framing, and functions primarily to enclose the building. It carries only its own weight and transfers wind loads to the building structure. An aluminum curtain wall is a metal curtain wall comprised primarily of aluminum, glass, and opaque panels supported by a metal framework. Although metal curtain walls can also be constructed of stainless steel or bronze, aluminum is most common because of its light weight, strength, and ability to be extruded into a wide variety of shapes.

Figure 6-11 Aluminum curtain wall at spandrel 08 44 13.1

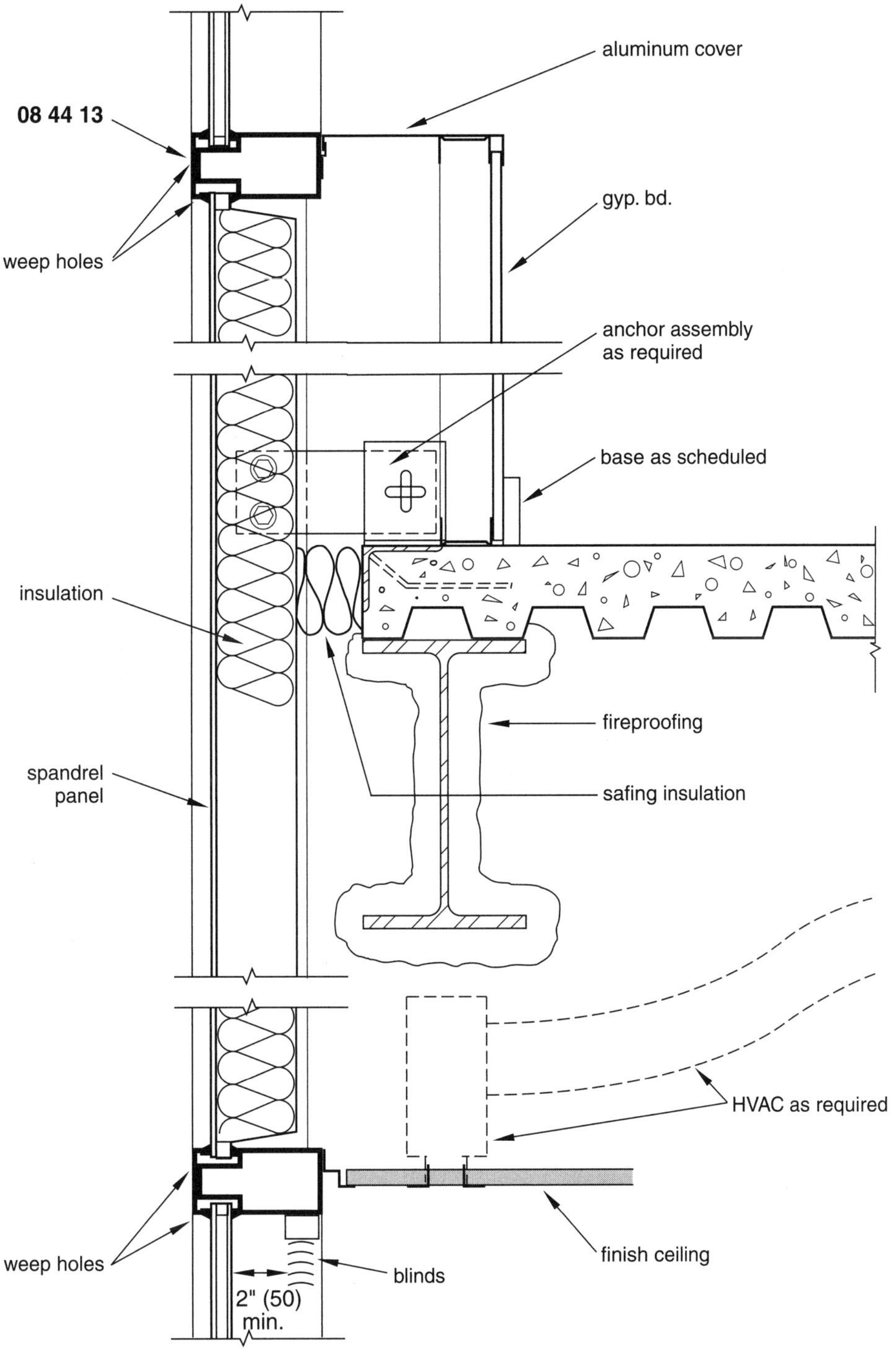

08 44 13

weep holes

insulation

spandrel
panel

weep holes

2" (50)
min.

blinds

aluminum cover

gyp. bd.

anchor assembly
as required

base as scheduled

fireproofing

safing insulation

HVAC as required

finish ceiling

Curtain walls are categorized as standard, custom, or a combination of both. Standard curtain walls use components "out of the catalog" with little, if any, modification. Custom curtain walls are designed specifically for one project. With each type, there are basically two classifications of systems. These are stick systems and unit, or unitized, systems.

Figure 6-11 and Figs. 6-12 and 6-13 illustrate a stick system in which mullions are installed first by attaching them to the building structure. Then the horizontal rails are placed.

This is followed by the installation of the spandrel panels and glazing. Unit systems are premanufactured in the factory, with the glass and spandrel panels already installed, and are attached to the building in one piece. These systems are the most common because much of the work can be completed in the factory under controlled conditions and they can be installed from the inside, without the need for scaffolding or extensive hoist work.

Because there is an almost unlimited number of ways aluminum curtain walls can be designed, this detail only illustrates some of the primary design considerations with which an architect should be familiar. Each manufacturer's product is slightly different, so final details are developed with the assistance of the manufacturer.

Limitations of Use

- This detail only shows a schematic representation of the curtain wall profile. Exact profiles and details vary with each manufacturer or are developed as custom systems. A diagrammatic representation of one type of section is shown in Fig. 6-13.
- Only one method of anchoring the curtain wall to the structural frame is shown.
- The exact configuration of the sill cover will vary, depending on the type of heating system used, the amount of anchoring that must be concealed, the size of the window opening, and the desired finished appearance.

Detailing Considerations

- Most curtain walls are based on the rain screen principle, in which resistance to water penetration is obtained by allowing air pressure to equalize on both sides of the exterior wall covering, while an additional airtight barrier and insulation protect the building's interior from air penetration and thermal transfer. Any moisture that does penetrate the exterior barrier is allowed to drain out through weep holes. Specific details provided by the curtain wall manufacturer should indicate provisions for weep holes, pressure equalization, and a baffle system within the horizontal and vertical members. Mullions and column covers should be blocked off horizontally at locations not exceeding two stories. The detail of mullions should provide for the continuity of the air seal from one piece of glass to the next.
- Tight-fitting joints should have capillary breaks (pressure-reducing pockets) to prevent water from penetrating the system through capillary action.
- Curtain wall movement caused by temperature changes and building movement must be provided for. This varies with the geographical location, but a temperature difference of 180°F (82°C) is a good number to use in calculations. This will produce movement of about 1/4 in. (6 mm) in a 10 ft (3048 mm) section of aluminum. Both horizontal and vertical movement must be accommodated.
- Condensation control must be provided. Potential condensation problems depend on the local climate, the humidity of the indoor air, and the detailing of the wall assembly, but in general, condensation can be controlled by providing a vapor barrier on the warm side of the insulation, by insulating impervious interior surfaces, and by providing drainage for any condensation that may occur within the wall.
- Anchoring should provide for three-way adjustability to account for building frame tolerances and erection tolerances. Anchors should be located on top of the floor slab to facilitate installation and adjustment.

- Curtain walls may be preglazed in the factory if a unit system is used or glazed at the job site.
- In most cases, it is advantageous to design the curtain wall so that it can be installed from inside the building. However, in some cases where construction scheduling or excessive interior obstructions make this difficult, systems can be designed for exterior installation.
- Weep holes must be provided within the framing system to equalize pressure and to allow any moisture that penetrates the system to drain to the outside.
- Weep holes should be provided below each glass unit and between the setting blocks.
- A firestop must be placed between the back of the curtain wall and the structural framing. This may be safing insulation or other approved infill. The firestop must also function as a smoke stop. The firestop should be located below the curtain wall anchoring and allow for differential movement between the structure and the wall. Firestops must extend through column covers and other vertical openings.

Coordination Required

- Curtain wall details for a specific job should be developed with the assistance of the manufacturer. Even standard curtain walls may require specific adaptations.
- Provisions for a window washing track may need to be included in some of the mullions. These tracks are usually located on the column lines.
- Coordinate the location of the weep holes with the setting block locations.
- Tolerances of the building frame must be considered. Refer to Sections 1-2, 1-3, and 1-23 for concrete tolerances and Sections 3-1, 3-2, 3-3, and 3-4 for steel tolerances.
- Provisions for convector covers and shades or blinds may need to be incorporated into the curtain wall design.
- A simple method of abutting interior partitions to vertical mullions must be developed. The spacing of the mullions should be compatible with the expected typical room sizes of the building, the type of ceiling used, and the structural bay spacing.
- If convector covers are used, provisions should be made for sound seals below the covers when interior partitions abut a mullion.

Likely Failure Points

- Leakage of water if a sufficient number or size of weep holes is not provided or if capillary breaks are not provided where tight-fitting joints occur
- Leakage if the air barrier separating the pressure-equalizing air space from the building interior is not maintained
- Cracking or breakage of glass caused by excessive thermal stresses (These may be caused by shading devices, heating or cooling from the HVAC system being too close to the glass, excessive bite on heat-reflecting or heat-absorbing glass, shades or blinds placed too close to the window, or any condition of conditions that causes the temperature of one portion of the glass to be very different from that of another portion.)
- Buckling of the curtain wall or leakage if sufficient provisions are not made for the various types of movement to which the assembly is subjected
- Failure of sealed joints caused by improper priming, inadequate backup material, or improperly sized joints

- Corrosion of aluminum framing if it is in contact with dissimilar metals or if it is used in severe environments

Materials

08 44 13 ALUMINUM CURTAIN WALL

Alloy 6063-T5 or 6063-T6 with Class I anodic coatings (AAMA 611) or high-performance factory-applied fluoropolymer thermoset coatings (AAMA 2604). Maximum deflection of L/175 or $3/4$ in. (19 mm), whichever is less.

Tested for air leakage, structural performance, and water penetration according to ASTM E283, E330, E331, and E547 and AAMA 501.4 as appropriate. Tests for sound transmission and thermal performance may also be desirable.

The type of glass selected will depend on the specific requirements of the project. It may be heat strengthened, tempered, or laminated in single or insulating units. The glass may be clear, reflective, or tinted.

Glass thickness depends on the size of the opening and the wind loading. One-quarter inch (6 mm) glass is commonly used in a variety of situations, with insulating units being 1 in. (25 mm) thick.

Sealants must be the high-performance type capable of ±25 or ±50 percent movement and with a high degree of resistance to ultraviolet light and other weathering. This includes polysulfide, polyurethane, and silicone conforming to ASTM C920. Butt joints should be sized four times the anticipated movement of the joint. Refer to Section 5-38 for information on sealants.

The erection sequence will depend on the type of system selected.

Glazing may be done from the exterior or interior, but interior glazing systems may be preferable for many buildings.

The glazing system should provide for weep holes at the bottom of the glass and the spandrel frame.

6-12 ALUMINUM CURTAIN WALL AT ROOF

Description

Figure 6-12 is a continuation of Fig. 6-11 and shows one way to detail a curtain wall that is designed to continue to the top of the parapet. There are many variations of parapet details, depending on the appearance desired, the type of roof structure, the method of attachment of the curtain wall to the building structure, coping requirements, the required height of the parapet, and the manufacturers' standard curtain wall elements.

Limitations of Use

- Davits or swing staging are not shown for clarity.
- A horizontal mullion is shown at the roofline. Depending on the distance between the coping and the top of the uppermost vision glass, an intermediate mullion may not be required.
- Refer to Section 6-11 for other limitations of use.

Figure 6-12 Aluminum curtain wall at roof 08 44 13.1

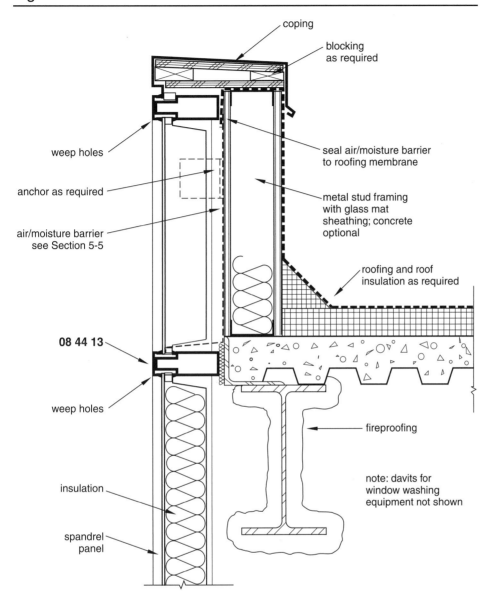

coping

blocking
as required

weep holes

seal air/moisture barrier
to roofing membrane

anchor as required

metal stud framing
with glass mat
sheathing; concrete
optional

air/moisture barrier
see Section 5-5

roofing and roof
insulation as required

08 44 13

weep holes

fireproofing

note: davits for
window washing
equipment not shown

insulation

spandrel
panel

Detailing Considerations

- In cold climates, special consideration must be given to warm air exfiltrating out of the occupied space into the space behind the spandrel panel at the parapet and then condensing. As shown in this detail, an air/vapor retarder may extend from the curtain wall mullion up behind the top spandrel panel and be sealed to the roofing membrane.

- In lieu of metal stud framing with glass mat gypsum wallboard sheathing, a concrete parapet wall may be used. This can simplify construction and provide additional structural support to the curtain wall and the coping assembly.

- If the moisture membrane is terminated at the spandrel panes in the framing, weep holes must be provided to drain condensation and wind-driven rain. The cavity may also be vented.

■ If metal stud framing is used, provide insulation in the stud cavity near the structural roof deck to continue the thermal barrier provided by the roof insulation and spandrel insulation.

Coordination Required

■ The finish of the coping must be coordinated with the curtain wall supplier.
■ If the coping will be subjected to additional loading from maintenance or window washing activities, special detailing or a thicker coping may be required.
■ Refer to Section 6-11 for other coordination requirements.

Likely Failure Points

■ Condensation of water vapor behind the uppermost spandrel panel caused by building air and vapor leaking into the space behind the spandrel
■ Refer to Section 6-11 for other likely failure points

Materials

08 44 13 ALUMINUM CURTAIN WALL

Refer to Section 6-11 for material requirements.

6-13   ALUMINUM CURTAIN WALL AT MULLION

Description

Figure 6-13 shows a schematic representation of one type of curtain wall framing. Because specific configurations vary with each manufacturer and may be custom extruded, only general detailing guidelines are included here. This detail shows the mullion of a stick system in which the structural portion of the mullion is anchored to the building structure, after which the horizontal rails are placed. Then the glass and spandrel panels are secured with pressure plates. Interior and exterior covers are snapped into place to complete the installation.

Limitations of Use

■ Figure 6-13(a) shows a fixed mullion. Split mullions, as shown in Fig. 6-13(b), are required in certain locations to provide for thermal expansion and building movement.
■ The use of pressure plate glazing is shown. Glass may also be installed with glazing stops either from the interior or exterior of the building.
■ This detail shows a standard anchoring system. Refer to Figs. 6-14 and 6-15 for structural silicone glazing systems.

Detailing Considerations

■ The size and shape of the mullion depend on the structural requirements of the job, the amount of bite required on the glass, the manufacturer's standard or custom extrusions, and the desired exterior and interior appearance.

Figure 6-13 Aluminum curtain wall at mullion 08 44 13.2

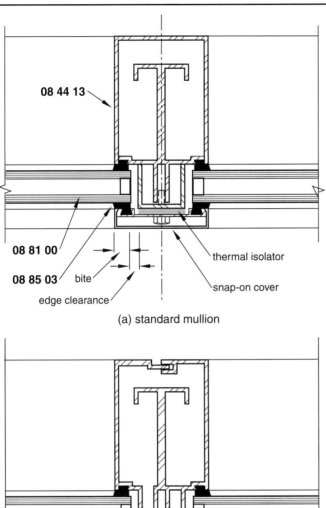

08 44 13

08 81 00

08 85 03 bite

edge clearance

thermal isolator

snap-on cover

(a) standard mullion

(b) split mullion

- The amount of bite of the glass, the edge clearance, and the face clearance must be determined based on the type and thickness of the glass. The bite is the distance the glass is recessed into the framing.
- Thermal breaks, as shown in this detail, must be provided to minimize heat loss and heat gain.

Coordination Required

- A simple method of attaching interior partitions to the mullion must be developed. The connection between partitions and mullions must allow for horizontal movement of the mullion caused by variable wind loading.
- Convector covers should be supplied and installed by the curtain wall installer.

Likely Failure Points

- Glass failure caused by excessive deflection of the mullion
- Failure of insulating glass caused by water immersion due to insufficient weep holes
- Refer to Section 6-11 for other likely failure points

Materials

08 44 13 GLAZED ALUMINUM CURTAIN WALL

Size, shape, thickness, and finish as required by the structural and aesthetic requirements of the project.

Curtain walls may be finished with clear or colored anodized coatings, fluorocarbons, siliconized acrylics and polyesters, plastisols, and porcelain enamel. Organic coatings should conform to AAMA 2603 or AAMA 2605.

Refer to Section 6-11 for additional material requirements.

08 81 00 GLASS GLAZING

Flat glass: ASTM C1036.

Heat-treated flat glass: ASTM C1048.

Insulating glass: ASTM E774.

Safety glazing must conform to CPSC 16 CFR 1201, Category II.

Glass may be heat strengthened, tempered, or laminated in single or insulating units. It may be clear, reflective, tinted or low-emissivity, depending on the specific requirements of the project.

Weep holes should be provided between setting blocks and between setting blocks and the edge of the glass framing.

For insulating glass units, the seal must be compatible with the setting blocks, edge blocks, and other accessories.

Glass should be installed according to the manufacturer's requirements, the recommendations of the *Glazing Manual* of the Glass Association of North America, and the recommendations of the Sealed Insulating Glass Manufacturers Association.

08 85 03 GLAZING TAPE

Glazing systems may be either wet or dry, depending on the requirements of the project.

Dry glazing materials include butyl or polyisobutylene tapes, dense neoprene gaskets, and cellular neoprene. Wet glazing material are high-performance sealants such as silicone.

The specific type of glazing system depends on the type of glass selected.

6-14   FOUR-SIDED STRUCTURAL SILICONE GLAZING AT SPANDREL

Description

Structural silicone glazing is a method of glazing without the use of standard metal framing. Instead, a high-strength silicone sealant is used to bond glass to glass or glass to metal framing.

Figure 6-14 4-sided structural silicone glazing at spandrel 08 44 26.1

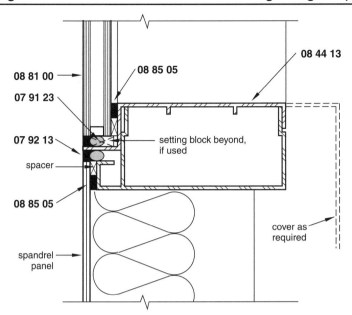

There are three types of silicone glazing systems: the all-glass system, the two-sided or strip-window system, and the four-sided or total-wall system. The all-glass system uses thick glass mullions to give lateral support to large areas of glass connected with metal patch plates. This system is described in Section 6-10. Two-sided systems utilize glass supported in standard metal frames at the sill and head, with the edges butt jointed and sealed with silicone sealant. The four-sided system, as shown in Figs. 6-14 and 6-15, relies on structural silicone to bond the glass to a metal frame on the interior side of the glass.

There are several variations of both the two-sided system and the four-sided system. Two-sided systems may simply have sealant applied in the thin joints of the edge-butted sections or the edges may be adhered to and supported by a metal frame behind the glass. Four-sided systems may be either inside glazed or outside glazed and may be assembled as a semiunitized or unitized system. With a semiunitized system, an aluminum main frame is attached to the building structure similar to a conventional stick system curtain wall. Then glass units attached to a subframe with silicone are mechanically fastened to the main frame. A unitized system, as shown in Fig. 6-14, consists of glass factory-applied to split mullions. These units are then attached to the building structure.

From the exterior, a four-sided system appears as a smooth plane of glass and spandrel panels broken only by thin flush joints. The interior appears similar to that of any aluminum curtain wall system. Although structural silicone may be field applied or factory applied, in-plant application is the preferred method because higher quality control can be maintained and the sealant can be cured under controlled conditions.

Limitations of Use

- Figure 6-14 indicates the aluminum framing diagrammatically. Exact profiles vary with each manufacturer and with the specific structural requirements of the project.
- Figure 6-14 shows the use of insulating glass, but single-glazed units may also be used.
- The sealant cannot be painted. The standard color is black.

Detailing Considerations

- Framing must be detailed to prevent transfer of loads caused by the weight of the glass, building movement, and expansion and contraction of the glass. Adequate expansion joints must be provided.
- Because the exterior lite is exposed, the insulating glass sealant must be capable of withstanding positive and negative wind loading.
- Although field glazing can be done, factory glazing is preferred.

Coordination Required

- The adhesion of the sealant to the glass and the aluminum framing must be tested for each project.
- All of the sealants, setting blocks, spacers, and glazing tapes used must be verified for compatibility. The sealant used to construct the insulating glass unit must be verified as compatible with the silicone sealants used.
- Glass installed under concrete or masonry exposed to the weather should be cleaned frequently to remove possible corrosive materials washed from the concrete or masonry during rainstorms.
- Special provisions for a window washing track may be required for high-rise buildings.
- Refer to Section 6-11 for other coordination requirements.

Likely Failure Points

- Failure of the glass seal or the structural seal caused by incompatibility of materials used
- Delamination of laminated glass caused by incompatible sealants
- Failure of the structural sealant on some types of coated glass

Materials

07 91 23 BACKER ROD

Open or closed cell polyurethane foam, with the diameter at least 25 percent greater than the joint width. Use polyethylene tape for shallow joints where there is insufficient space for a backer rod.

07 92 13 ELASTOMERIC JOINT SEALANT

One-part or two-part silicone glazing sealant for a weather seal only.

ASTM C920, Type S, Grade NS, Class 25 or 50.

Joint size is based on the expected movement of the joint and the expansion of the glass. Joints are normally 1/4 in. (6 mm) to 1/2 in. (13 mm) wide, but they may need to be as large as 3/4 in. (19 mm). The ratio of width to depth should be about 2 to 1.

08 44 13 GLAZED ALUMINUM CURTAIN WALL

Alloy 6063-T5 or 6063-T6 with Class I anodic coatings (AAMA 611) or high-performance factory-applied fluoropolymer thermoset coatings (AAMA 2604). Maximum deflection of L/175 or 3/4 in. (19 mm), whichever is less.

The exact size, shape, and profile will be determined by the structural and aesthetic requirements of the project.

Tested for air leakage, structural performance, and water penetration according to ASTM E283, E330, E331, and E547 and AAMA 501.4 as appropriate. Tests for sound transmission and thermal performance may also be desirable.

The type of glass selected will depend on the specific requirements of the project. It may be heat strengthened, tempered, or laminated in single or insulating units. The glass may be clear, reflective, or tinted.

Glass thickness depends on the size of the opening and the wind loading. One-quarter inch (6 mm) glass is commonly used in a variety of situations, with insulating units being 1 in. (25 mm) thick.

The sealant supplier must confirm that adequate adhesion is possible with the finish selected.

The erection sequence will depend on the type of system selected.

Glazing may be done from the exterior or interior, but interior glazing systems may be preferable for many buildings.

The glazing system should provide for weep holes at the bottom of the glass and the spandrel frame.

08 81 00 GLASS GLAZING

Materials

ASTM C1036 or ASTM C1048. Insulating glass meeting the requirements of ASTM C1249, ASTM E773, and ASTM E2190.

Glass should have a clean-cut edge.

Glass may be annealed, heat-strengthened, tempered, or insulating units. Laminated glass must be selected carefully because of the possible incompatibility of the sealants and the laminating material. The bow and warp conditions of heat-strengthened and tempered glass must be within required tolerances of the sealant manufacturer.

Glass may be clear, reflective, tinted or low-emissivity, depending on the specific requirements of the project. However, some coated glasses may be inappropriate because of poor adhesion of the sealant to the glass coating.

For insulating glass units, the seal must be compatible with the silicone sealant, setting blocks, and other accessories.

Glass thickness is determined by standard tables based on the wind loading and the spacing of the supports.

If setting blocks are used, they should be 0.1 in. (2.5 mm) in length for each square foot (0.09 m^2) of glass area, but in no case less than 4 in. (100 mm). They must be compatible with the silicone and have a Shore A durometer of 85 $\pm$ 5. In some cases, four-sided systems that are shop glazed horizontally and cured properly do not need setting blocks.

Execution

Glass should be installed according to the manufacturer's requirements, the recommendations of the *Glazing Manual* of the Glass Association of North America, and the recommendations of the Sealed Insulating Glass Manufacturers Association.

Setting blocks should be placed at quarter points.

08 85 05 STRUCTURAL SILICONE GLAZING SEALANT

Two-part, high-modulus, neutral cure silicone sealant formulated for structural adhesion of glass. One-part sealants are also available.

ASTM C1401 and C1184.

Sealant width is determined by the wind load and the span of the glass. Verify the required dimension with the sealant manufacturer.

Sealant depth is determined by the total joint design and must be less than the width of the joint, with a minimum dimension of 1/4 in. (6 mm).

Primers may be required for bonding to aluminum and other materials.

Tool sealant beads to ensure adequate contact between the sealant and the substrate.

Cleaning and priming of substrates is critical to a satisfactory job. The manufacturer's instructions must be followed carefully.

6-15   FOUR-SIDED STRUCTURAL SILICONE GLAZING AT MULLION

Description

Figure 6-15 is a continuation of Fig. 6-14 and shows a typical condition at a mullion of a four-sided silicone glazing system. This detail shows a unitized system where the glass lites are factory applied to the framing and attached to the building structure in single pieces. The application of the backing rod and weather seal completes the installation.

Figure 6-15   4-sided structural silicone glazing at mullion   08 44 26.2

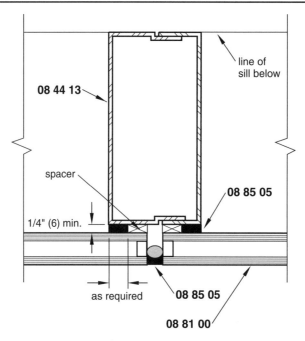

Limitations of Use

- Figure 6-15 detail indicates the aluminum framing diagrammatically. Exact profiles vary with each manufacturer and with the specific structural requirements of the project.
- Refer to Section 6-14 for other limitations of use.

Detailing Considerations

- With a unitized system, special provisions for expansion in the horizontal direction may not be needed because each mullion is a split mullion.
- Refer to Section 6-14 for other detailing considerations.

Coordination Required

- Refer to Section 6-14 for coordination requirements.

Likely Failure Points

- Cracking or breakage of glass caused by excessive thermal stresses (These may be caused by shading devices, heating or cooling from the HVAC system being too close to the glass, excessive bite on heat-reflecting or heat-absorbing glass, shades or blinds placed too close to the window, or any condition that causes the temperature of one portion of the glass to be widely different from that of another portion.)
- Refer to Section 6-14 for other likely failure points.

Materials

Refer to Section 6-14 for material requirements.

6-16 ALUMINUM WINDOW, MASONRY WALL

Description

Aluminum windows are used in a variety of wall types and for residential as well as commercial construction. They are also widely used for replacement windows in renovation work. They are relatively inexpensive and lightweight, and are available in a variety of operating types, sizes, and finishes. Figure 6-16 shows an operable window with thermal breaks set in new masonry construction.

Detailing Considerations

- The exact sizes and profiles of aluminum frames vary with each manufacturer. Refer to individual product catalogues for specific types and installation requirements.
- Various profiles of aluminum sills are available to work with new construction as well as replacement applications.
- Window frames with thermal barriers are available, as shown in this detail.

Figure 6-16 Aluminum window, masonry wall 08 51 13.3

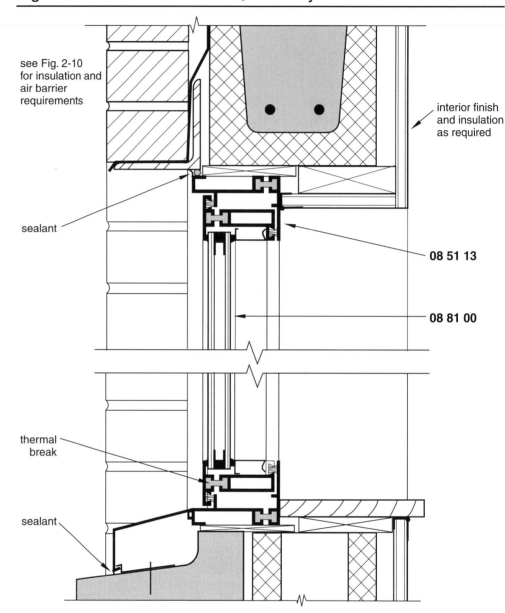

see Fig. 2-10
for insulation and
air barrier
requirements

interior finish
and insulation
as required

sealant

08 51 13

08 81 00

thermal
break

sealant

Coordination Required

- Verify the minimum ventilating area required by the applicable building code.
- Verify the glass types to satisfy applicable energy codes.
- Verify the need for exit window sizes, if required, in residential sleeping rooms.

Materials

08 51 13 ALUMINUM WINDOW

Windows in accordance with ANSI/AAMA 101. Various types and grades are available
with difference performance ratings.

Tested for air leakage, structural performance, and water penetration according to ASTM E283, E330, E331, and E547 and AAMA 501.4, as appropriate. Tests for sound transmission and thermal performance may also be desirable.

Weatherstripping in accordance with AAMA 701.

Window types may be fixed sash, horizontal slider, casement, projected, or single hung.

Standard finishes include clear anodized, bronze anodized in several shades, black anodized, and white and brown PVC coated. Other finishes are available on special order from many manufacturers.

08 81 00 GLASS

Flat glass: ASTM C1036.

Heat-treated flat glass: ASTM C1048.

Insulating glass: ASTM E774.

Low-emissivity glass and reflective glass may also be used.

6-17   STEEL WINDOW, MASONRY WALL

Description

Steel windows offer the advantages of strength, narrow profiles, durability, security, and less thermal expansion than aluminum. They are frequently used for industrial applications and in detention facilities, although their narrow profile makes them appropriate in any situation where a minimum frame appearance is desired. The shape of the window frame shown in Fig. 6-17 is the traditional profile for steel windows, but others are available, both for new installations and for retrofit applications. Consult specific manufacturers' catalogs for available sizes and types.

Detailing Considerations

- Profiles are available for either single or double glazing.
- Windows may be either inside or outside glazed.
- Equal or unequal legs (as shown in this detail) are available, depending on the specific mounting details of the project.
- Weep holes should not be used.
- Rain drips may be required at intermediate horizontal framing.
- Weatherstripping should be specified on all operable units.
- Three-quarter hour fire-rated windows are available if glazed with $1/4$ in. (6 mm) wire glass or other fire-resistant glazing.
- Frames with thermal breaks are available in profiles other than the one shown here.

Coordination Required

- Verify the need for exit window sizes, if required, in residential sleeping rooms.
- Select sizes and mounting details to work with standard masonry coursing.

Figure 6-17 Steel window, masonry wall 08 51 23

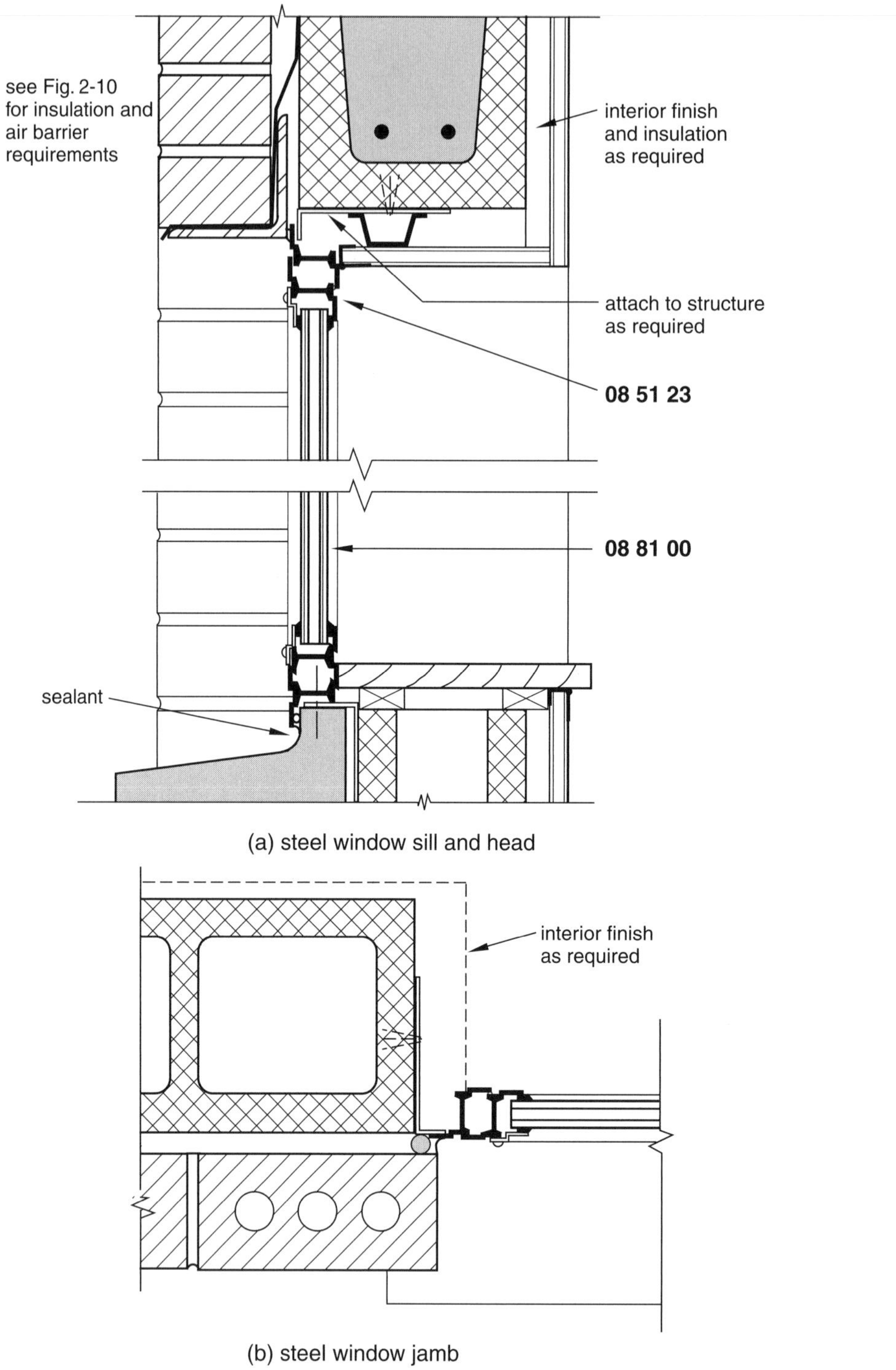

see Fig. 2-10
for insulation and
air barrier
requirements

interior finish
and insulation
as required

attach to structure
as required

08 51 23

08 81 00

sealant

(a) steel window sill and head

interior finish
as required

(b) steel window jamb

Likely Failure Points

- Formation of internal condensation in some climates due to rapid heat transfer through the steel
- Racking of the window if frames are undersized for the size and type of glass used

Materials

08 51 23 STEEL WINDOW

Fabricated from hot rolled new billet steel in accordance with specifications of the Steel Window Institute.

Frames are classified as standard intermediate, heavy intermediate, and heavy custom as defined by the minimum combined weight per linear foot of the outside frame and vent members.

> Standard intermediate: 3.0 plf (4.46 kg/m)
> Heavy intermediate: 3.5 plf (5.21 kg/m)
> Heavy custom: 4.2 plf (6.25 kg/m)

Window types may be fixed sash, horizontal slider, casement, projected, or pivoted.

Windows may be factory painted, supplied with a prime coat, or galvanized.

08 81 00 GLASS

Materials

> Flat glass: ASTM C1036.
>
> Heat-treated flat glass: ASTM C1048.
>
> Insulating glass: ASTM E774.
>
> Safety glazing must conform to CPSC 16 CFR 1201, Category II.

Execution

> Installed according to recommendations of the *Glazing Manual* of the Glass Association of North America.
>
> Set on elastomeric setting blocks located at the quarter points of the glass.
>
> Set in a frame with a dry or wet glazing system as recommended by the manufacturer.

6-18   WOOD WINDOW, MASONRY WALL

Description

Wood windows have traditionally been used in residential construction and some small-scale commercial construction. However, with improved exterior claddings that increase durability and minimize maintenance, wood windows are being used more frequently in many types of commercial applications. Figure 6-18 shows one application of a wood window in a masonry cavity wall. With either aluminum or rigid vinyl exterior claddings, wood windows offer the advantages of durability, high insulating value, minimal condensation problems, low maintenance, and aesthetic appeal. They are available in fixed sash, casement, single-hung, double-hung, sliding, and awning types.

Detailing Considerations

- Provide rough wood framing securely anchored to the masonry opening.
- If additional insulation is required, place it between the brick and the concrete masonry. See Section 2-4.

Figure 6-18 Wood window, masonry wall 08 52 00.3

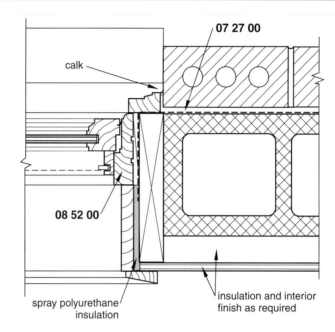

A vapor barrier may be required. Refer to Section 5-5 for more information.

- A vapor barrier may be required. Refer to Section 5-5 for more information.
- Provide a 1/4 in. (6 mm) shim space on either side of the rough opening and a 1/2 in. (13 mm) shim space for leveling the window unit.
- Jamb extensions are available for most manufacturers' windows to account for the extra depth of the masonry wall.
- See Sections 2-4, 2-5, and 2-6 for more information on masonry cavity walls.

Coordination Required

- Wood windows may be glazed with double or triple pane glass units. Tinted, reflective, and low-emissivity glass is available.
- Coordinate modular masonry openings with the available window sizes and rough blocking required. In many cases, the masonry will have to be cut to work with rough opening sizes of standard window units.
- Sleeping rooms may require emergency egress windows. Verify the size and positioning required by the applicable building code.
- Verify that the windows selected meet the performance requirements of the applicable building code for air infiltration.
- Some manufacturers offer glazing that has narrow-slat aluminum blinds set inside the sash for light control.

Materials

07 27 00 AIR BARRIER

Nonwoven, spun-bonded olefin sheet membrane, liquid-applied membrane, or self-adhering membrane, ASTM E1677.

Vapor-permeable or vapor-impermeable as required by local climatic conditions.

Install according to the manufacturer's instructions.

Refer to Section 5-5 for more information.

08 52 00 WOOD WINDOW

Manufactured according to AAMA/WDMA/CSA 101/I.S.2/A440-08.

Exterior finish of primed wood or clad in rigid vinyl or aluminum, depending on the manufacturer's available options.

Interior finish of bare treated wood, primed for paint, prestained, or otherwise prefinished according to the manufacturer's options.

Custom sizes and shapes are available from many manufacturers.

6-19   WOOD WINDOW, WOOD FRAME WALL

Description

This detail shows the standard installation of a premanufactured wood window in a 2 in. by 4 in. (51 mm by 102 mm) stud wall. The rough opening is formed, and the window unit is set on the sill, shimmed into place, and secured to the rough framing. Calking and interior trim complete the installation. Many clad windows are manufactured with an integral fin that is placed on the outside of the sheathing and used to secure the window to the frame. Figure 6-19 shows a typical sill and head detail. Refer to Fig. 6-18 for a jamb detail, which, in a frame wall, is similar to the head.

Detailing Considerations

- Provide a $1/4$ in. (6 mm) shim space on either side of the rough opening and a $1/2$ in. (13 mm) shim space for leveling the window unit.
- A vapor barrier may be required. Refer to Section 5-5 for more information.
- Jamb extensions are available for 2 in. by 6 in. (51 mm by 152 mm) construction and other wall thicknesses.
- Interior trim may be of any shape and configuration required by the interior design.

Coordination Required

- Wood windows may be glazed with double or triple pane glass units. Tinted, reflective, and low-emissivity glass is available.
- Sleeping rooms may require emergency egress windows. Verify the size and positioning required by the applicable building code.
- Verify that the windows selected meet the performance requirements of the applicable building code for air infiltration.

Materials

07 27 00 AIR BARRIER

Nonwoven, spun-bonded olefin sheet membrane, liquid-applied membrane, or self-adhering membrane, ASTM E1677.

Figure 6-19 Wood window, wood frame wall 08 52 00.4

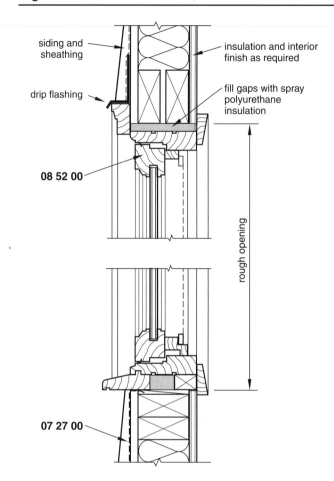

siding and sheathing

drip flashing

08 52 00

insulation and interior finish as required

fill gaps with spray polyurethane insulation

rough opening

07 27 00

Vapor-permeable or vapor-impermeable as required by local climatic conditions.

Install according to the manufacturer's instructions.

Refer to Section 5-5 for more information.

08 52 00 WOOD WINDOW

Manufactured according to AAMA/WDMA/CSA 101/I.S.2/A440-08.

Exterior finish of primed wood or clad in rigid vinyl or aluminum, depending on the manufacturer's available options.

Interior finish of bare treated wood, primed for paint, prestained, or otherwise prefinished according to the manufacturer's options.

Custom sizes and shapes are available from many manufacturers.

6-20   INTERIOR, FRAMED GLAZED OPENING AT JAMB

Description

Figure 6-20 illustrates one method of glazing interior openings in a metal stud partition. Although the diagram shows a glazing frame of wood, steel or aluminum framing may also

Figure 6-20 Interior, framed glazed opening at jamb 08 81 00.1

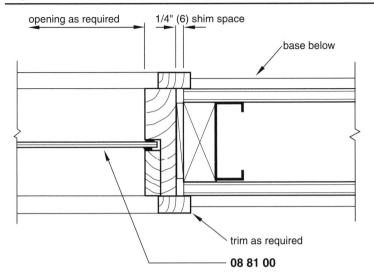

be used. As long as the glass is securely set in a frame, the variety of profiles in wood or metal is limited only by manufacturing and cost constraints.

Limitations of Use

- In most situations, this type of glazed opening cannot be used in a fire-rated wall. Glazing in most fire-rated partitions must be wire glass set in steel frames. Special fire-rated glazing is also available that can be used in 30, 60, and 90 minute rated partitions if it is detailed in accordance with the manufacturer's instructions. See Section 6-24.

Detailing Considerations

- The glazing stop may be set flush with the frame, as shown in this detail, or separately applied glazing stops may be set on top of the jamb frame.
- Interior glazing is often set in wood frames without glazing tape or sealant, but glass in aluminum or steel frames should be set with glazing tape or sealant.
- A minimum 1/4 in. (6 mm) shim space must be provided.
- If a wood frame is set in a metal stud partition, wood blocking should be provided either on the inside or the outside of the metal stud.
- If sound control is a consideration, use laminated glass.

Coordination Required

- Glass used in hazardous locations must be safety glass, which must meet the requirements of CPSC 16 CFR 1201, Category II. Generally, tempered or laminated glass is required. Crash rails may be used in lieu of tempered glass if they are installed according to the applicable building code.
- The maximum allowable glazed area in corridor partitions must be verified with the applicable building code.

Materials

08 81 00 GLASS

ASTM C1036 or ASTM C1048. One-quarter inch (6 mm) tempered glass for large openings.

Thicker glass may be required for very large openings or where additional sound control is desired. Thinner glass can be used in small openings.

Install according to the requirements of the *Glazing Manual* of the Glass Association of North America.

6-21   INTERIOR, FRAMED GLAZED OPENING AT SILL AND HEAD

Description

Figure 6-21 is a continuation of Fig. 6-20 and shows one method of framing the glass at the sill and head. Both conditions may be identical to that of the jamb if the opening does not

Figure 6-21 Interior, framed glazed partition at sill and head   08 81 00.2

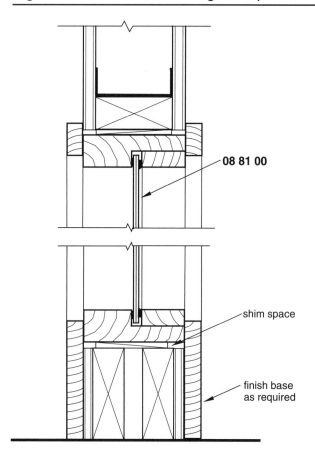

extend to the floor and is treated as a window. If the glass extends to the floor line, the sill must provide for the base used in the room.

Limitations of Use

- Refer to Section 6-20 for limitations of use.

Detailing Considerations

- Adequate shim space must be provided at the sill to account for irregularities in floor level.
- If the level of the sill is less than 18 in. (457 mm) above the floor or the edge of the glass is within 24 in. (610 mm) of a door, safety glazing must be used.

Coordination Required

- The trim should be detailed to be compatible with the type of base used.
- Refer to Section 6-20 for additional coordination requirements.

Materials

08 81 00 GLASS

ASTM C1036 or ASTM C1048. One-quarter inch (6 mm) tempered glass for large openings.

Thicker glass may be required for very large openings or where additional sound control is desired. Thinner glass can be used in small openings.

Install according to the requirements of the *Glazing Manual* of the Glass Association of North America.

6-22 INTERIOR FRAMELESS GLAZED OPENING AT JAMB

Description

In some situations, designers prefer to glaze interior openings without framing so that the glass wall is less conspicuous and has a more contemporary appearance. Figures 6-22 and 6-23 show one glazing method using as little framing as possible. A bead of silicone sealant is shown, but in applications where sound control or draft control is not required, the joint between the wall and the edge of the glass may be left open.

Limitations of Use

- This type of glazed opening cannot be used in a fire-rated wall. Glazing in most fire-rated partitions must be wire glass set in steel frames. Special fire-rated glass is available that can be used in 30, 60, and 90 minute rated partitions if it is detailed in

Figure 6-22 Interior, frameless glazed opening at jamb 08 81 00.3

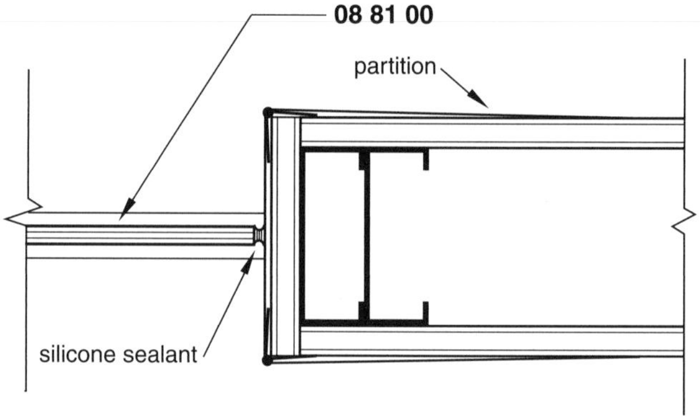

accordance with the manufacturer's instructions. However, one manufacturer provides a fire-rated glazing product that can be used without vertical mullions for a rating of up to 60 minutes.

Detailing Considerations

- The glass thickness should be selected based on the size of the opening and the amount of glass shake that is acceptable.
- Where two pieces of glass abut, the edges are sealed with silicone sealant or the joint is left open.
- Silicone sealant may be either clear or black. Clear sealant often shows bubbles, which can be objectionable.
- Laminated glass should be used where additional sound control is required.
- The glass jamb may be a finished edge of a wall, as shown in this detail, or may be wood or metal framing without a glazing reglet.

Coordination Required

- If frameless glass is used adjacent to a glass door, the thickness of the glass should match the thickness of the door.
- If privacy control is required, provisions must be made for blinds or drapes to cover the opening. Blinds are often concealed in recessed pockets in the ceiling.

Materials

08 81 00 GLASS

ASTM C1036 or ASTM C1048. One-quarter inch (6 mm) tempered glass for large openings.

Thicker glass may be required for very large openings or where additional sound control is desired. Thinner glass can be used in small openings.

Install according to the requirements of the *Glazing Manual* of the Glass Association of North America.

6-23 INTERIOR FRAMELESS GLAZED OPENING AT SILL AND HEAD

Description

Figure 6-23 illustrates one type of detailing at the floor and ceiling of the glass wall shown in Fig. 6-22. The glass is installed by lifting it up at a slight angle into the head frame and then setting it into the sill frame. Although a floor-to-ceiling glass is indicated, the sill may be raised off the floor if required.

Limitations of Use

- Refer to Section 6-23 for limitations of use.

Detailing Considerations

- There are several ways to secure the glass at the ceiling, depending on the particular conditions of the structure and the type of ceiling used. If a small amount of visible framing is not objectionable, a metal channel can be applied directly to the ceiling.

Figure 6-23 Interior, frameless glazed opening at sill and head 08 81 00.4

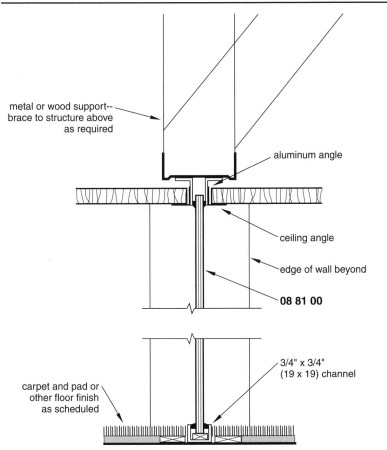

metal or wood support-- brace to structure above as required

aluminum angle

ceiling angle

edge of wall beyond

08 81 00

3/4" x 3/4" (19 x 19) channel

carpet and pad or other floor finish as scheduled

- If fixed channels are used, the top channel must be higher than the bottom channel to allow the glass to be installed by lifting it into the top framing, swinging it plumb, and then letting it down into the bottom framing.
- Using two angles at the head, as shown in this detail, allows one channel to be adjusted and set after the glass is properly placed and makes installation easier than using a fixed-channel section.
- The bottom framing may be recessed in the floor if there is adequate clearance and it does not weaken the floor structure.
- Refer to Section 6-23 for other detailing considerations.

Coordination Required

- Refer to Section 6-23 for the coordination required.

Materials

08 81 00 GLASS

ASTM C1036 or ASTM C1048. One-quarter inch (6 mm) tempered glass for large openings.

Thicker glass may be required for very large openings or where additional sound control is desired. Thinner glass can be used in small openings.

Install according to the requirements of the *Glazing Manual* of the Glass Association of North America.

6-24 INTERIOR FIRE-RESISTANT RATED GLAZING

Description

The *International Building Code* recognizes two types of fire-rated glazing: fire-protection-rated glazing and fire-resistance-rated glazing. *Fire-protection-rated glazing* is wired glass set in steel frames or other types of glazing that meet the requirements of NFPA 252 or NFPA 257. Such glazing must have a 45 minute rating and is limited to use in 1 hour rated fire partitions, fire barriers, or doors. The *International Building Code* sets limits on the size of fire-protection-rated glazed areas in doors and partitions.

Fire-resistant-rated glazing is glass or other glazing material that has been tested as part of a fire-resistance-rated wall assembly according to ASTM E119. Glazing products that qualify include a range of products such as special tempered glass, ceramic glazing, and gel-filled glazing. These products can have fire ratings ranging from 20 minutes to 2 hours, and many of them also meet the impact resistance requirements of CPSC 16 CFR 1201, Category II (which wired glass cannot) and can withstand the hose stream test part of the E119 test procedure. Because of the higher fire ratings possible, this type of glazing can be used in 1 hour and 2 hour rated partitions in sizes much larger than those of traditional wired glass and in larger sizes in doors and windows. Because the *International Building Code* no longer allows wired glass in hazardous locations unless it can meet the requirements of CPSC 16 CFR 1201, Category II, these new products have largely replaced wired glass in many applications.

Figure 6-24 Interior, fire-resistant rated glazing 08 88 60

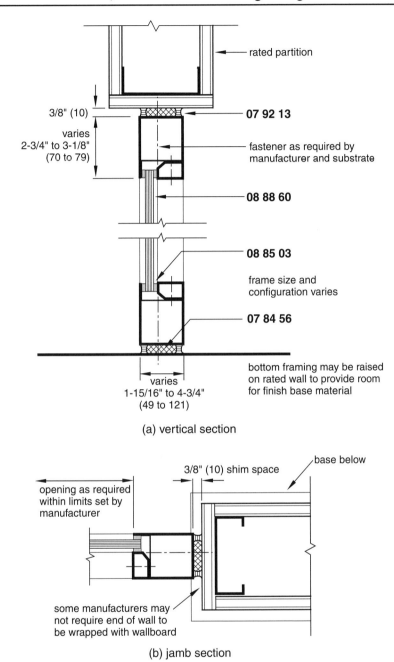

rated partition

3/8" (10)

varies
2-3/4" to 3-1/8"
(70 to 79)

07 92 13

fastener as required by
manufacturer and substrate

08 88 60

08 85 03

frame size and
configuration varies

07 84 56

bottom framing may be raised
on rated wall to provide room
for finish base material

varies
1-15/16" to 4-3/4"
(49 to 121)

(a) vertical section

base below

3/8" (10) shim space

opening as required
within limits set by
manufacturer

some manufacturers may
not require end of wall to
be wrapped with wallboard

(b) jamb section

Figure 6-24 shows a typical use of fire-resistant-rated glazing in an interior partition. Because the glazing products, thicknesses, and framing materials and methods are proprietary to individual manufacturers, Fig. 6-24 illustrates only one possible size and shape of frame and attachment to a fire-rated partition. In general, frames are larger than traditional hollow metal or wood frames and require special attachment methods in order to pass the ASTM E119 test.

Limitations of Use

- Fire-resistant-rated glazing is proprietary and is based on a coordinated system of glazing, framing, attachment methods, and accessory products. Consult with individual manufacturers for required glass thickness, frame materials, and attachment methods based on project requirements of the required fire rating, impact resistance, heat transfer, the hose stream test, and other parameters.

- The maximum overall size of glazing lites between frames is based on whatever was tested and approved by the manufacturer. Verify maximum heights, widths, and areas of specific products and fire-ratings with the individual manufacturers.
- Special fire-resistant-rated glazing is more expensive than traditional wired glass. In many applications, wired glass may be used as a low-cost, readily available product. Wired glass may meet the more stringent requirements of CPSC 16 CFR 1201 if it is laminated to tempered glass or has an acceptable film applied.

Detailing Considerations

- Frames for fire-resistant-rated glazing are typically larger than hollow metal frames or wood frames.
- Some manufacturers offer fire-rated wood frames for glazing with lower ratings, such as a 45 minute rated glazing in a 1 hour rated partition.
- Butt-jointed glazing is available from one manufacturer that eliminates the need for intermediate frames in interior walls.
- Special types of glazing, such as tinted, etched, and bullet-resistant glass, may be incorporated in the system. Verify allowable types with the manufacturer.

Coordination Required

- Different manufacturers require slightly different details of the fire-rated partition in which the framing is placed. It may not be necessary to wrap the end of the partition with gypsum wallboard, as shown in Fig. 6-24.
- Verify the type of door hardware required with the manufacturer based on the product used and the fire rating required.
- Fire doors and windows must be installed in accordance with NFPA 80.
- Verify that the nonrated sealant is compatible with the setting blocks, shims, and fire safing insulation.

Materials

07 84 56 FIRE SAFING INSULATION

As supplied by the manufacturer.

Intumescent sealant or mineral wool.

07 92 13 ELASTOMERIC JOINT SEALANT, NONRATED

One-part polysulfide, polyurethane, or silicone, ASTM C920, Type S, Grade NS, Class 25 or 50. Color as required.

Sealant depth equal to the width of the joint up to $1/2$ in. (13 mm), with a minimum depth of $1/4$ in. (6 mm).

Verify other requirements with the manufacturer of the glazing system.

08 85 03 GLAZING TAPE

For smaller panels, closed cell PVC foam or as required by the manufacturer.

Fire-rated glazing tape is supplied by the manufacturer on large panels or where required by the fire rating.

08 88 60 FIRE-RESISTANT-RATED GLAZING

Of the type, thickness, and composition established by the manufacturer.

ASTM E119, NFPA 80, NFPA 252, NFPA 257, CPSC 16 CFR 1201, Category II, and other test requirements as applicable for the intended use.

Install in accordance with the *Glazing Manual* of the Glass Association of North America and the requirements of the manufacturer.

Set with hardwood or noncombustible (calcium silicate) shim materials as required by the manufacturer.

CHAPTER 7

FINISH DETAILS

7-1 GYPSUM WALLBOARD SHAFT LINING

Description

Figure 7-1(a) illustrates a two-hour rated partition for stairways, elevator shafts, and mechanical shafts when required in Type I and Type II fire-resistive buildings. The configuration of this type of shaft allows construction to take place outside the shaft. Figure 7-1(b) shows a detail of an elevator call button.

Limitations of Use

- This partition is non-load-bearing.
- Openings into two-hour shaft walls must be protected with a self-closing fire assembly with a one-and-a half-hour rating.
- Penetrations through shaft linings of noncombustible conduit and pipe must be sealed. Noncombustible pipe and conduit may also be installed in the wall cavity as long as both wall and floor penetrations are tightly sealed with noncombustible material that does not allow the passage of smoke.

Detailing Considerations

- When both sides of the shaft wall must be finished, a single layer of $1/2$ in. (13 mm) wallboard is applied to either side of the assembly instead of a double layer on one side only.
- A 1 hour rated shaft liner is obtained by using a single layer of $5/8$ in. (16 mm) type X wallboard in lieu of the double layer shown in this detail.
- Sound attenuation insulation can be placed in the wall cavity for greater acoustical control.
- Penetrations in the shaft wall with elevator call buttons and the like may require additional protection, as shown in Fig. 7-1(b).
- Control joints should be installed in unbroken partitions exceeding 30 ft (9144 mm).

Figure 7-1 Gypsum wallboard shaft lining 09 21 16

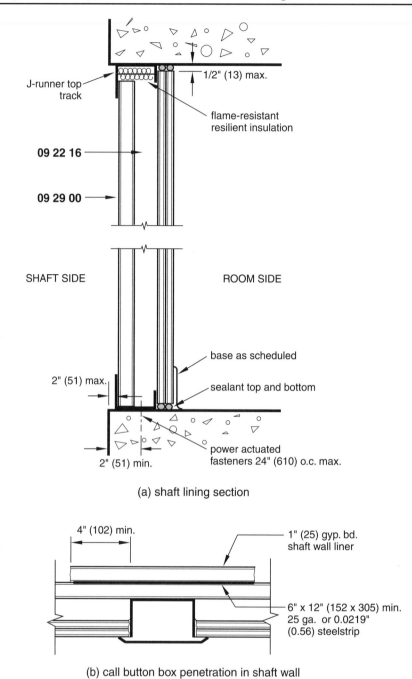

J-runner top track

1/2" (13) max.

flame-resistant resilient insulation

09 22 16

09 29 00

SHAFT SIDE

ROOM SIDE

base as scheduled

2" (51) max.

sealant top and bottom

2" (51) min.

power actuated fasteners 24" (610) o.c. max.

(a) shaft lining section

4" (102) min.

1" (25) gyp. bd. shaft wall liner

6" x 12" (152 x 305) min. 25 ga. or 0.0219" (0.56) steelstrip

(b) call button box penetration in shaft wall

Coordination Required

- For elevator shafts, the expected pressure caused by moving elevator cars should be determined to select the correct gage and depth of studs. Refer to manufacturers' literature for limiting heights of partitions and other structural requirements.
- Deeper studs than those shown in this detail may be required to accommodate elevator control devices.
- Elevator door equipment must be mounted independently of the shaft wall.

- Elevator door assemblies must comply with ANSI A17.1. Wall framing for the shaft wall entrance must meet the specific requirements of the elevator manufacturer.
- If runners or studs are attached to steel structural framing, they should be installed before spray-on fireproofing is applied.

Likely Failure Points

- Cracking of the inside finish surface of the wallboard or attached brittle finish material due to exceeding the maximum wall height or insufficient stiffness of the stud for the pressures encountered in the shaft
- Cracking around openings caused by the insufficient gage of framing members or improper attachment of door frames to partition framing
- Failure of the stud-to-runner attachment under air pressure loading due to the under-sized gage of the runner

Materials

09 22 16 NONSTRUCTURAL METAL FRAMING

Materials

ASTM C645 and ASTM A653/A653M.

Minimum 24 gage or 0.0227 in. (0.58 mm) J-runner track.

Minimum 25 gage or 0.0175 in. (0.455 mm) studs.

$2^1/_2$ in. (63.5 mm) or 4 in. (101.6 mm) deep CH or CT-type studs as required. Various types of proprietary studs are available. The depth used depends on the required wall height, air pressure loading (if applicable), and requirements for elevator controls (if applicable).

Screws should conform to ASTM C1002.

Execution

Maximum spacing of 24 in. (600 mm) on center.

Installed according to ASTM C754.

Provide a slip joint at the underside of structural slabs or other slabs that may deflect.

Follow specific recommendations of the manufacturer for installation of door jambs, openings for ducts, anchoring of elevator entrance frames, and attachment to the structural frame.

09 29 00 GYPSUM WALLBOARD

Materials

$^5/_8$ in. (16 mm), type X. ASTM C1396.

1 in. (25 mm) thick by 24 in. (610 mm) wide shaft wall liner cut 1 in. (25 mm) less than the floor-to-ceiling height.

Two layers of $^1/_2$ in. (13 mm) type X wallboard.

Gypsum wallboard tape and joint compound should conform to ASTM C475/C475M.

Screws should conform to ASTM C1002.

Execution

Installed according to ASTM C840, the recommendations of the Gypsum Association, and specific recommendations of the manufacturer.

Base and face layers applied vertically, with joints staggered.

7-2 GYPSUM WALLBOARD, NONRATED PARTITION

Description

Nonrated partitions with metal framing, as shown in Fig. 7-2(a), may be constructed from the floor to the underside of a suspended ceiling. This type of partition is anchored to the ceiling by screwing the top track into the ceiling suspension system and fastening the bottom runner to the floor with power-actuated fasteners.

One variation of this construction is shown in Fig. 7-2(b), using a gypsum wallboard ceiling and acoustical batt insulation above the ceiling.

Limitations of Use

- This type of partition cannot be used where a fire-rated separation is required.
- This partition is non-load-bearing.
- This type of partition should not be used where a moderate or high degree of acoustical separation between rooms is needed.

Detailing Considerations

- Common stud sizes for this type of partition include $2\frac{1}{2}$ in. (64 mm) and $3\frac{5}{8}$ in. (92 mm). The size selected depends primarily on the height of the partition and the necessary services concealed within the partition such as electrical boxes, conduit, and plumbing pipe.
- Either $\frac{1}{2}$ in. (13 mm) or $\frac{5}{8}$ in. (16 mm) wallboard may be used, but $\frac{5}{8}$ in. (16 mm) is recommended.
- Provide gypsum wallboard trim along exposed edges near the ceiling.
- Where the partition abuts an exterior window mullion, provide a compressible foam gasket between the mullion and the vertical framing member. This will provide a sound and light seal as well as prevent condensation from damaging the partition materials. A perimeter relief joint, as shown in Fig. 7-12, may also be required to accommodate movement of the mullion.
- Control joints should be installed in unbroken partitions exceeding 30 ft (9144 mm).

Coordination Required

- Wood blocking or metal reinforcement should be provided for attachment of wall-hung fixtures that are too heavy to be carried by toggle bolts or hollow-wall anchors.
- Required provisions for pipes and recessed fixtures will determine the depth of studs, along with the height of the studs.

Figure 7-2 Gypsum wallboard, nonrated partition 09 29 03.1

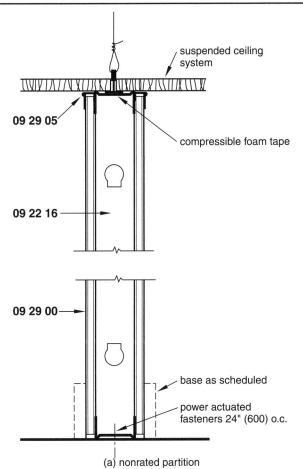

suspended ceiling
system

09 29 05

compressible foam tape

09 22 16

09 29 00

base as scheduled

power actuated
fasteners 24" (600) o.c.

(a) nonrated partition

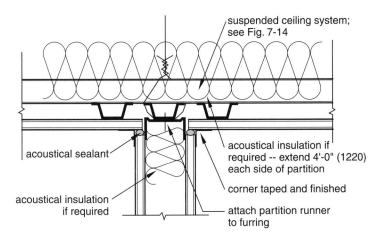

suspended ceiling system;
see Fig. 7-14

acoustical sealant

acoustical insulation if
required -- extend 4'-0" (1220)
each side of partition

corner taped and finished

acoustical insulation
if required

attach partition runner
to furring

(b) sound-isolating partition/ceiling intersection

Likely Failure Points

- Cracking of the partition due to building movement when the partition is tightly joined to the building structure at both ends (This may occur in high-rise buildings subject to drift. Perimeter relief joints located at columns and exterior walls, as shown in Fig. 7-12, may be used to alleviate this problem.)
- Strong side lighting from windows or grazing artificial light may show minor surface irregularities (Avoid these lighting conditions or use a textured surface or a Level 5 finish, as defined in GA 214, published by the Gypsum Association. This includes a thin skim coat of joint compound over the entire wall.)
- Variations in the appearance of a painted surface on smooth walls due to the difference in suction of the gypsum wallboard panel paper and joint compound (When gloss paint is used or the final finish is critical, specify that the entire partition should receive a Level 5 finish.)
- Cracking or other defects in the joints caused by poor alignment of the framing members or improper joint treatment (Installation should be in accordance with the recommendations of the manufacturer and the Gypsum Association.)

Materials

09 22 16 NONSTRUCTURAL METAL FRAMING

Materials

ASTM C645 and ASTM A653/A653M.

Minimum 25 gage or 0.0175 in. (0.455 mm).

2$\frac{1}{2}$ in., 3$\frac{5}{8}$ in., 4 in., or 6 in. (63.5 mm, 92.1 mm, 101.6 mm, or 152.4 mm) as required.

Screws should conform to ASTM C1002.

Execution

Maximum spacing of 24 in. (600 mm) on center.

Installed according to ASTM C754.

Provide a slip joint at the underside of structural slabs or other slabs that may deflect.

09 29 00 GYPSUM WALLBOARD

Materials

$\frac{5}{8}$ in. (16 mm), type X. ASTM C1396.

Gypsum wallboard tape and joint compound should conform to ASTM C475/C475M.

Screws should conform to ASTM C1002.

Execution

Installed according to ASTM C840, the recommendations of the Gypsum Association, and specific recommendations of the manufacturer.

Wallboard must be applied vertically to 1$\frac{5}{8}$ in. (41.3 mm) or 2$\frac{1}{2}$ in. (63.5 mm) studs and may be applied horizontally to 3$\frac{5}{8}$ in. (92.1 mm) studs.

Stagger joints on opposite sides of the partition.

Applied with 1 in. (25 mm) type S screws 8 in. (203 mm) on center at edges and 12 in. (305 mm) on center on intermediate studs.

09 29 05 GYPSUM WALLBOARD TRIM

Corrosion-protected coated steel, aluminum, or plastic.

L, LC, or U trim sized to fit the thickness of wallboard used.

L and LC trim provide for smooth finishing of the edge with joint compound, while U trim shows an exposed metal edge but requires no finishing compound.

Vinyl trim and proprietary trim are also available.

7-3 GYPSUM WALLBOARD, SLIP JOINT AT STRUCTURAL SLAB

Description

Slip joints, as shown in Fig. 7-3, are required where the top of a gypsum wallboard partition abuts construction that may deflect enough to cause the partition to buckle and the wallboard to crack if a tight connection is made. Deflection may be caused by a dead load, live loading, building settlement, concrete creep, expansion and contraction caused by temperature differentials, or other causes.

Limitations of Use

- This partition is non-load-bearing.
- The detail shown in Fig. 7-3 is limited to a total deflection of about 1/2 in. (13 mm). This allowable deflection is based primarily on the amount of compression the fire-rated

Figure 7-3 Gypsum wallboard, slip joint at structural slab 09 29 03.2

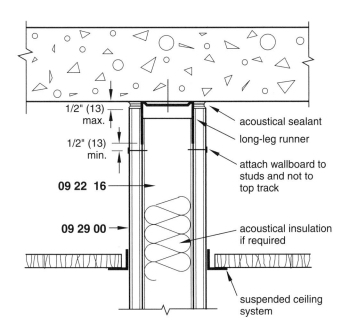

Table 7-1 Maximum Stud Heights[a]

Stud depth, in. (mm)	Structural criteria[b]			
	L/120[c] height, ft-in. (mm)		L/240[d] height, ft-in. (mm)	
	Stud thickness, gage, in. (mm)[e]		Stud thickness, gage, in. (mm)[e]	
	25 gage, 0.0175 (0.455)	20 gage, 0.0329 (0.836)	25 gage, 0.0175 (0.455)	20 gage, 0.0329 (0.836)
1 5/8	**8'-9"[f]**	11'-2"	7'-11"	8'-11"
(41.3)	**(2670)**	(3400)	(2410)	(2720)
2 1/2	**11'-3"**	15'-1"	10'-7"	11'-9"
(63.5)	**(3430)**	(4600)	(3230)	(3580)
3 5/8	**13'-6"**	19'-1"	13'-5"	15'-2"
(92.1)	**(4110)**	(5820)	(4090)	(4620)
4	**14'-3"**	20'-11"	14'-2"	16-7"
(101.6)	**(4340)**	(6380)	(4320)	(5050)
6	**15'-0"**	27'-5"	15'-0"	21'-9"
(152.4)	**(4570)**	(8360)	(4570)	(6630)

[a]The heights in this table are based on various industry sources and represent conservative values. The exact limiting height varies, depending on manufacturers' values and which dated version of ASTM C754 may be required by the local building code. Some manufacturers' values also vary, depending on whether one or two layers of gypsum wallboard are being used and whether stud spacing is 16 in. (406 mm) or 24 in. (610 mm) on center.
[b]The values in this table assume a 5 psf (240 Pa) load, stud spacing of 24 in. (610 mm) on center, and a single layer of gypsum wallboard on either side of the partition. A 5 psf loading is typically the minimum required by most codes.
[c]L/120 refers to the maximum allowable deflection based on the length, L, of the stud. Partition heights are the heights from the bottom runner to the top runner, not the finished ceiling height. L/120 is the maximum deflection limit allowed by most building codes. Some manufacturers recommend a maximum of L/240.
[d]L/240 is the recommended maximum deflection for partitions with brittle finishes, such as veneer plaster. Some manufacturers also recommend this value for all partitions. For partitions with brittle finishes, some manufacturers recommend a maximum deflection value of L/360.
[e]Heights in mm are rounded to the nearest 10 mm from the ft-in. values.
[f]Figures shown in bold type are the most common.

sealant is capable of absorbing. Refer to Section 7-4 for a detail that uses a proprietary product to allow for greater deflection.

- This partition does not qualify as a fire-rated partition unless the requirements given in Section 7-7 are met.
- This type of partition may also be used for acoustical separation if the perimeter is sealed and all penetrations are sealed. A higher Sound Transmission Class (STC) rating may be achieved by adding acoustical insulation and additional layers of wallboard.

Detailing Considerations

- Common stud sizes for this type of partition include 2 1/2 in., 3 5/8 in., and 4 in. (63.5 mm, 92.1 mm, and 101.6 mm). The size selected depends primarily on the height of the partition and the necessary services concealed within the partition, such as electrical boxes, conduit, and plumbing pipe. Refer to Table 7-1 for maximum unsupported partition heights.
- Either 1/2 in. (13 mm) or 5/8 in. (16 mm) wallboard may be used, but 5/8 in. (16 mm) is recommended.
- This detail may be adapted for double-layer construction as long as the finish layer is not attached to the top track.
- Control joints should be installed in unbroken partitions exceeding 30 ft (9144 mm).
- If the partition is to serve as an acoustical separation, the lower edge of the wallboard at the floor line should be sealed.

Coordination Required

- Wood blocking or metal reinforcement should be provided for attachment of wall-hung fixtures that are too heavy to be carried by toggle bolts or hollow-wall anchors.
- Required provisions for pipes and recessed fixtures will determine the depth of studs, along with the height of the studs.

Likely Failure Points

- Cracking of wallboard if it is attached to the top runner or if minimum clearance distances, as shown in the detail, are not maintained
- Cracking of the partition due to building movement when the partition is tightly joined to the building structure at both ends (This may occur in high-rise buildings subject to drift. Perimeter relief joints located at columns and exterior walls, as shown in Fig. 7-12, may be used to alleviate this problem.)
- Other defects as described in Section 7-2

Materials

09 22 16 NONSTRUCTURAL METAL FRAMING

Materials

ASTM C645 and ASTM A653/A653M.

Minimum 25 gage or 0.0175 in. (0.455 mm).

Top track is a long-leg runner.

$2^1/2$ in., $3^5/8$ in., 4 in., or 6 in. (63.5 mm, 92.1 mm, 101.6 mm, or 152.4 mm) as required.

Screws should conform to ASTM C1002.

Execution

Maximum spacing of 24 in. (600 mm) on center.

Installed according to ASTM C754.

Studs should be cut $1/2$ in. (13 mm) shorter than the floor-to-slab dimension.

Attach the top track to the structure with appropriate fasteners at 24 in. (610 mm) on center maximum.

Attach gypsum wallboard to studs near the top track a minimum distance of $1/2$ in. (13 mm) below the bottom edge of the track. Gypsum wallboard should not be attached to the top track.

09 29 00 GYPSUM WALLBOARD

Materials

$1/2$ in. (13 mm) or $5/8$ in. (16 mm) thickness, ASTM C1396.

Gypsum wallboard tape and joint compound should conform to ASTM C475/C475M.

Screws should conform to ASTM C1002.

Execution

Installed according to ASTM C840, the recommendations of the Gypsum Association, and specific recommendations of the manufacturer.

Wallboard must be applied vertically to 1⁵⁄₈ in. (41.3 mm) or 2¹⁄₂ in. (63.5 mm) studs and may be applied horizontally to 3⁵⁄₈ in. (92.1 mm) studs.

Stagger joints on opposite sides of the partition.

7-4 GYPSUM WALLBOARD, PROPRIETARY SLIP JOINT

Description

When deflection above a full-height partition is expected to exceed the amount that can be accommodated with a detail, as shown in Fig. 7-3, various proprietary products can be used. One such product, shown in Fig. 7-4, includes a uniquely shaped runner that allows attachment of separate pieces of gypsum wallboard fastened to the runner such that they can slide over the partition wallboard to maintain a fire rating and allow deflections or extensions up to 3 in. (76 mm), depending on which variation of the product is used. The runner and outside pieces of gypsum wallboard move with the structural floor above, independent of the partition. Deflection of up to 6 in. (152 mm) can also be accommodated.

Figure 7-4 Gypsum wallboard, proprietary slip joint 09 29 03.3

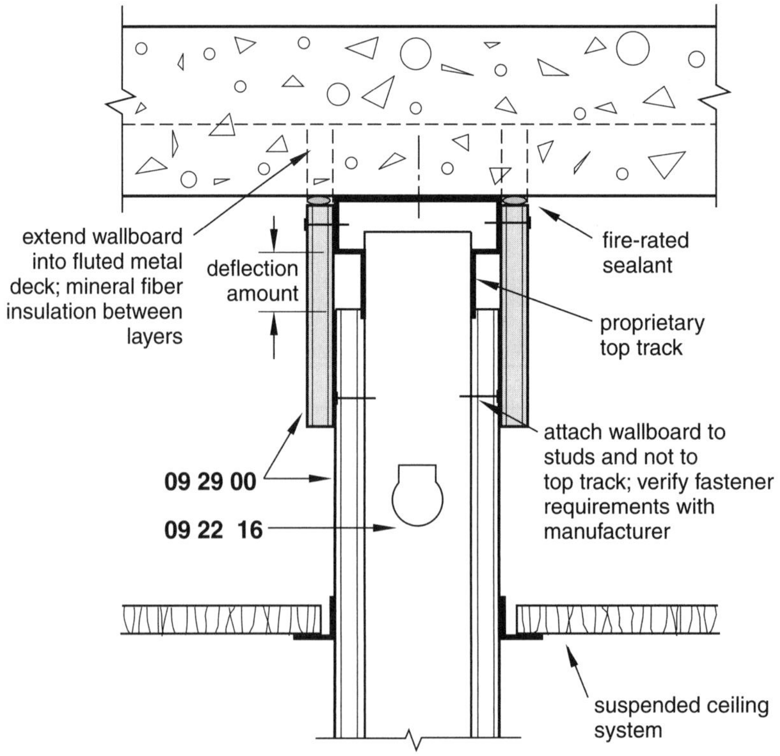

extend wallboard into fluted metal deck; mineral fiber insulation between layers

deflection amount

fire-rated sealant

proprietary top track

attach wallboard to studs and not to top track; verify fastener requirements with manufacturer

09 29 00

09 22 16

suspended ceiling system

Limitations of Use

- Each of the manufacturer's products has been tested and approved by Underwriters Laboratories (UL). However, the manufacturer's instructions for installation must be followed to provide a fire-rated partition. Refer to the product literature for exact details based on fire rating, deflection amount, and floor slab type.
- This product is for horizontal applications only.

Detailing Considerations

- Top tracks and details are available for either one-hour-rated or two-hour-rated partitions. A two-hour-rated detail is similar to Fig. 7-4 except that two layers of wallboard are used on both the partition and the smaller pieces attached to the top track.
- Figure 7-4 shows the partition perpendicular to the direction of the fluted metal decking. There is a slightly different detail for conditions when the partition is parallel to the decking. Verify required details with the manufacturer.
- This detail can be used with floor and roof assemblies.
- The product has been tested for as a fire-resistive joint system and for cycling capabilities in accordance with ASTM E 1966 and UL 2079.

Coordination Required

See Section 7-3 for coordination considerations.

Likely Failure Points

- Cracking of wallboard if the upper sections of wallboard are inadvertently fastened to the partition wallboard and studs
- Refer to Section 7-3 for partition material requirements

7-5 ONE-HOUR GYPSUM WALLBOARD PARTITION, WOOD FRAMING

Description

Figure 7-5 illustrates the simplest type of one-hour-rated wood-framed partition. In addition to providing a one-hour rating, it can be used as an interior bearing wall. Additional acoustical control can be provided as outlined below. Wood-framed partitions are generally limited to residential and small commercial projects, depending on the building type.

Limitations of Use

- The floor/ceiling assembly to which this partition is connected must have at least a one-hour rating.
- Electrical boxes may be used in this type of partition if they occur on one side only in each framing space and if the opening does not exceed 16 in.^{2} (0.01 m^2). The crack

Figure 7-5 One-hour gypsum wallboard partition, wood framing 09 29 03.4

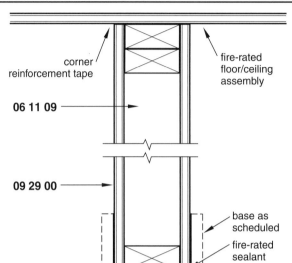

corner reinforcement tape

fire-rated floor/ceiling assembly

06 11 09

09 29 00

base as scheduled

fire-rated sealant

between the electrical box and the wallboard must be filled with joint compound or other approved material.

- This type of partition provides limited acoustical control (STC approximately 34 if the perimeter is sealed). Additional methods may be employed to increase the STC rating while maintaining the fire rating (see Fig. 7-6).
- Glass mesh mortar units should be used as a base for tile in bathrooms and other high-moisture areas.

Detailing Considerations

- Perimeter relief joints should be provided in structures subject to lateral movement.
- Acoustical control may be provided by using one or a combination of the following detailing methods: double layers of wallboard; sealing all penetrations and perimeter cracks with acoustical sealant, including sound attenuation insulation; using a staggered stud system; and using resilient furring channels on one or both sides of the partition.
- Control joints should be installed in unbroken partitions exceeding 30 ft (9144 mm).

Coordination Required

- Wood blocking may be required for attachment of wall-hung fixtures that occur between studs.
- Openings must be rated as required by the local building code.

Likely Failure Points

- Cracking of the partition due to excessive deflection of the structure above
- Other defects as described in Section 7-2

Materials

06 11 09 Wood stud and framing

Minimum 2 in. by 4 in. studs (51 mm × 102 mm), nominal size 16 in. (400 mm) or 24 in. (600 mm) on center.

Framing should be installed to meet minimum requirements of the Federal Housing Administration (FHA) and local building codes.

09 29 00 Gypsum wallboard

Materials

$5/8$ in. (16 mm), type X. ASTM C1396.

Gypsum wallboard tape and joint compound should conform to ASTM C475/C475M.

Screws should conform to ASTM C1002.

Execution

Installed according to ASTM C840, the recommendations of the Gypsum Association, and specific recommendations of the manufacturer.

Wallboard must be applied vertically to $1^5/8$ in. (41.3 mm) or $2^1/2$ in. (63.5 mm) studs and may be applied horizontally to $3^5/8$ in. (92.1 mm) studs.

Stagger joints on opposite sides of the partition.

Applied with 1 in. (25 mm) type S screws 8 in. (203 mm) on center at edges and 12 in. (305 mm) on center on intermediate studs.

7-6 SOUND-RATED ONE-HOUR GYPSUM WALLBOARD PARTITION

Description

Figure 7-6 illustrates one method to provide a sound-rated partition in wood-framed construction for residential and small commercial construction. This detail uses a combination of acoustical insulation within the partition as well as resilient channels.

Limitations of Use

- This detail is limited to building types that allow wood construction for interior partitions.
- The floor/ceiling assembly to which this partition is connected must have at least a one-hour rating.

Detailing Considerations

- A higher STC rating can be achieved by using a double layer of gypsum wallboard. The partition shown in Fig. 7-6 has an STC rating of about 50 to 54.

Figure 7-6 Sound-rated one-hour gypsum wallboard partition 09 29 03.5

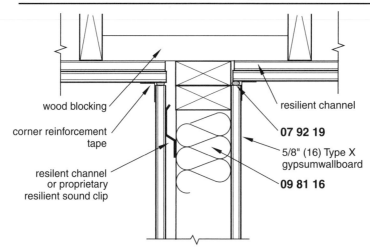

wood blocking

corner reinforcement
tape

resilent channel
or proprietary
resilient sound clip

resilient channel

07 92 19

5/8" (16) Type X
gypsumwallboard

09 81 16

- Proprietary resilient clips may also be used. These utilize a horizontal application of metal furring strips attached to resilient material, which is attached to the studs. Manufacturers claim that a higher STC rating is achieved than with resilient channels.
- Resilient channels must be installed with the open side facing up.

Coordination Required

- Ceiling construction should also use resilient channels.
- See Section 7-5 for other coordination requirements.

Likely Failure Points

- Loss of sound rating due to incorrectly applied resilient channels for proprietary clips

Materials

07 92 19 ACOUSTICAL JOINT SEALANT

ASTM C834.

Nondrying, nonhardening, latex–based.

09 81 16 ACOUSTIC BLANKET INSULATION

Fire-rated fibrous type made from mineral substances such as fiberglass, rock or slag fabricated in rolls, and unfaced conforming.

ASTM C665, Type I.

Refer to Section 7-5 for other material requirements.

7-7 ONE-HOUR GYPSUM WALLBOARD PARTITION, METAL FRAMING

Description

The partition shown in Fig. 7-7 is one of several types of metal-framed partitions that provide a one-hour rating. It must extend from the floor to the structural slab above unless the ceiling assembly alone provides a one-hour rating.

Limitations of Use

- This partition is considered non-load-bearing. However, heavy-gage steel studs may be used to provide a load-bearing partition, subject to engineering review.
- Electrical boxes may be used in this type of partition if they occur on one side only in each framing space and if the opening does not exceed 16 in.^{2} (0.01 m^2). The crack

**Figure 7-7 One-hour gypsum wallboard partition, metal framing
09 29 03.6**

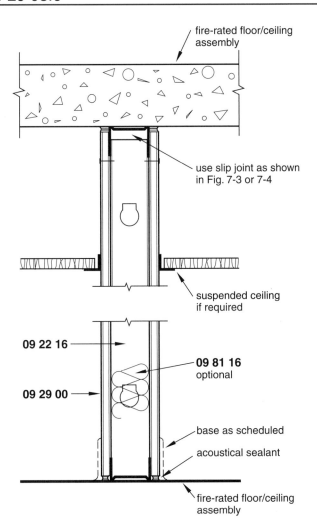

between the electrical box and the wallboard must be filled with joint compound or other approved material.

- This type of partition provides limited acoustical control (STC approximately 42 if the perimeter is sealed). Additional methods may be employed to increase the STC rating while maintaining the fire rating (see the detailing considerations below).
- The floor/ceiling assembly used with this partition must have a one-hour rating.

Detailing Considerations

- Common stud sizes for this type of partition include 2½ in., 3⅝ in., and 4 in. (63.5 mm, 92.1 mm, and 101.6 mm). The size selected depends primarily on the height of the partition and the necessary services concealed within the partition, such as electrical boxes, conduit, and plumbing pipe. Studs of 1⅝ in. (41.3 mm) may be used if the wallboard is applied vertically. Refer to Table 7-1 for maximum unsupported partition heights.
- If the top of the partition abuts a fluted metal deck, any voids between the top track and the surface of the metal deck must be filled and sealed with wallboard and joint compound or with other approved material.
- Perimeter relief joints, as shown in Fig. 7-12, should be provided in structures subject to lateral movement.
- When the partition extends above a suspended ceiling, that portion above the ceiling does not require finish joint treatment to maintain the fire rating.
- Acoustical control may be provided by using one or a combination of the following detailing methods: double layers of wallboard; sealing all penetrations, including sound attenuation insulation; using a staggered stud system; and using resilient furring channels on one or both sides of the partition.
- In wet areas, ceramic tile may be applied over ½ in. (13 mm) glass mesh mortar unit backer board in lieu of regular gypsum wallboard.
- Control joints should be installed in unbroken partitions exceeding 30 ft (9144 mm).

Coordination Required

- All gaps in the partition caused by penetrations (such as from ducts, conduit, and pipe) must be sealed.
- Fire dampers must be provided in ducts where they cross fire-rated partitions.
- Wood blocking or metal reinforcement should be provided for attachment of wall-hung fixtures that are too heavy to be carried by toggle bolts or hollow-wall anchors.
- Required provisions for pipes and recessed fixtures, along with the height of the studs, will determine the depth of studs.

Likely Failure Points

- Cracking of wallboard if slip joints are not provided (See Figs. 7-3 and 7-4.)
- Cracking of the partition due to building movement when the partition is tightly joined to the building structure at both ends (This may occur in high-rise buildings subject to drift. Use perimeter relief joints, as shown in Fig. 7-12, to alleviate this problem.)
- Other defects as described in Section 7-2

Materials

09 22 16 Nonstructural metal framing

Materials

ASTM C645 and ASTM A653/A653M.

Minimum 25 gage or 0.0175 in. (0.455 mm).

$2\frac{1}{2}$ in., $3\frac{5}{8}$ in., 4 in., or 6 in. (63.5 mm, 92.1 mm, 101.6 mm, or 152.4 mm) as required.

Screws should conform to ASTM C1002.

Execution

Maximum spacing of 24 in. (600 mm) on center.

Installed according to ASTM C754.

Provide a slip joint at the underside of structural slabs or other slabs that may deflect.

09 29 00 Gypsum wallboard

Materials

$\frac{5}{8}$ in. (16 mm), type X. ASTM C1396.

Gypsum wallboard tape and joint compound should conform to ASTM C475/C475M.

Screws should conform to ASTM C1002.

Execution

Installed according to ASTM C840, the recommendations of the Gypsum Association, and specific recommendations of the manufacturer.

Wallboard must be applied vertically to $1\frac{5}{8}$ in. (41.3 mm) or $2\frac{1}{2}$ in. (63.5 mm) studs and may be applied horizontally to $3\frac{5}{8}$ in. (92.1 mm) studs.

Stagger joints on opposite sides of the partition.

Applied with 1 in. (25 mm) type S screws 8 in. (203 mm) on center at edges and 12 in. (305 mm) on center on intermediate studs.

09 81 16 Acoustic blanket insulation

See Section 7-6 for material requirements.

7-8 TWO-HOUR GYPSUM WALLBOARD PARTITION, WOOD FRAMING

Description

Figure 7-8 illustrates the simplest type of two-hour-rated, load-bearing, wood-framed partition. This type of partition is generally limited to residential and small commercial projects where combustible materials are permitted.

Figure 7-8 Two-hour gypsum wallboard partition, wood framing
09 29 05.1

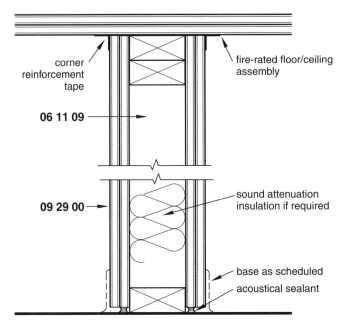

Limitations of Use

- The floor/ceiling assembly above must have at least a two-hour rating.
- Refer to Section 7-5 for other limitations of use.

Detailing Considerations

Refer to Section 7-5 for detailing considerations.

Coordination Required

Refer to Section 7-5 for coordination requirements.

Likely Failure Points

Refer to Section 7-5 for likely failure points.

Materials

06 11 09 WOOD STUD AND FRAMING

See Section 7-5.

09 29 00 GYPSUM WALLBOARD

Materials

ASTM C1396. Base layer ⅝ in. (16 mm), type X or veneer base. Face layer ⅝ in. (16 mm), type X.

Gypsum wallboard tape and joint compound should conform to ASTM C475/C475M.

Screws should conform to ASTM C1002.

Execution

Installed according to ASTM C840, the recommendations of the Gypsum Association, and specific recommendations of the manufacturer.

The base layer is applied at right angles to studs. The face layer is applied at right angles to studs, with joints staggered 24 in. (610 mm) over joints of the base layer.

Stagger joints on opposite sides of the partition.

7-9 TWO-HOUR GYPSUM WALLBOARD PARTITION, METAL FRAMING

Description

The partition shown in Fig. 7-9 is one of several types that provide a two-hour rating. It must extend from the floor to the structural slab above unless the ceiling assembly alone provides a two-hour rating. A double layer of $5/8$ in. (16 mm) wallboard without sound attenuation insulation provides an STC of about 48. This rating can be increased using insulation and resilient furring channels.

Limitations of Use

Refer to Section 7-7 for limitations of use.

Detailing Considerations

- Common stud sizes for this type of partition include $2^{1}/_{2}$ in., $3^{5}/_{8}$ in., and 4 in. (63.5 mm, 92.1 mm, and 101.6 mm). Refer to Table 7-1 for maximum unsupported partition heights.
- Refer to Section 7-7 for other detailing considerations.

Coordination Required

Refer to Section 7-7 for coordination requirements.

Likely Failure Points

Refer to Section 7-7 for likely failure points.

Figure 7-9 Two-hour gypsum wallboard partition, metal framing
09 29 05.2

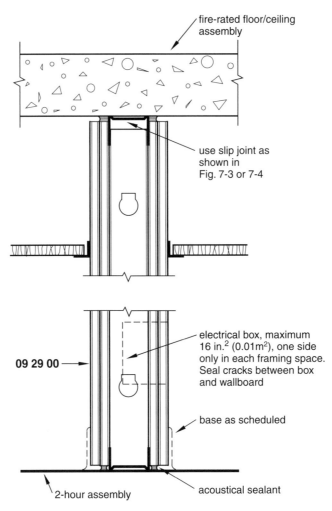

fire-rated floor/ceiling assembly

use slip joint as shown in Fig. 7-3 or 7-4

electrical box, maximum 16 in.^{2} (0.01m^2), one side only in each framing space. Seal cracks between box and wallboard

09 29 00

base as scheduled

2-hour assembly

acoustical sealant

Materials

09 29 00 GYPSUM WALLBOARD

Materials

ASTM C1396. Base layer $^5/_8$ in. (16 mm), type X or veneer base. Face layer $^5/_8$ in. (16 mm), type X.

Gypsum wallboard tape and joint compound should conform to ASTM C475/C475M.

Screws should conform to ASTM C1002.

Execution

Installed according to ASTM C840, the recommendations of the Gypsum Association, and specific recommendations of the manufacturer.

The base layer is applied at right angles to studs. The face layer is applied at right angles to studs, with joints staggered 24 in. (610 mm) over joints of the base layer.

Stagger joints on opposite sides of the partition.

7-10 THREE-HOUR GYPSUM WALLBOARD PARTITION

Description

Three-hour-rated partitions are often required as separation walls between certain mixed occupancies. Figure 7-10 illustrates one type of construction that provides such a rating.

Limitations of Use

- This partition is non-load-bearing.
- The horizontal assemblies to which this partition is attached must continue the three-hour rating if both assemblies form the separation. If only a vertical area separation wall is required, then the three-hour-rated wall must continue from the foundation to above the roof and special details are required to achieve a continuous separation, with the floor and roof assemblies stopping on either side of the partition.
- This type of partition provides good acoustical control if sound attenuation insulation is placed in the cavity (STC of approximately 59).

Figure 7-10 Three-hour gypsum wallboard partition 09 29 07.1

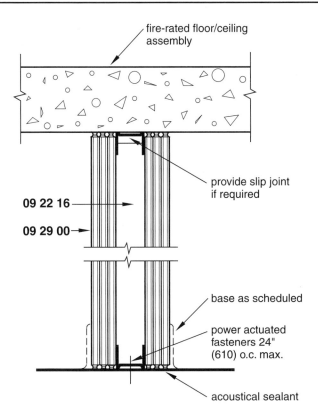

Detailing Considerations

- This partition requires the use of $1^5/_8$ in. (41.3 mm) studs.
- If the top of the partition abuts a fluted metal deck, any voids between the top track and the surface of the metal deck must be filled and sealed with wallboard and joint compound or with other approved material.
- Perimeter relief joints should be provided in structures subject to lateral movement.
- When the partition extends above a suspended ceiling, that portion above the ceiling does not require finish joint treatment to maintain the fire rating.

Coordination Required

- All gaps in the partition caused by penetrations from conduit or pipes must be firestopped with an approved material that will pass the ASTM E 119 test.
- Fire dampers must be provided in ducts where they cross fire-rated partitions.

Likely Failure Points

- Cracking of wallboard if slip joints are not provided (See Figs. 7-3 and 7-4.)
- Cracking of the partition due to building movement when the partition is tightly joined to the building structure at both ends (This may occur in high-rise buildings subject to drift. Perimeter relief joints located at columns and exterior walls, as shown in Fig. 7-12, may be used to alleviate this problem.)
- Refer to Section 7-2 for other likely failure points.

Materials

09 22 16 NONSTRUCTURAL METAL FRAMING

Materials

ASTM C645 and ASTM A653/A653M.

$1^5/_8$ inch, minimum 25 gage or 0.0175 in. (0.455 mm) studs.

Screws should conform to ASTM C1002.

Execution

Maximum spacing of 24 in. (600 mm) on center.

Installed according to ASTM C754.

Provide a slip joint at the underside of structural slabs or other slabs that may deflect.

Follow specific recommendations of the manufacturer for installation of door jambs, openings for ducts, anchoring of elevator entrance frames, and attachment to the structural frame.

09 29 00 GYPSUM WALLBOARD

Materials

ASTM C1396.

Three layers of $1/_2$ in. (13 mm) thick type X wallboard on each side.

Gypsum wallboard tape and joint compound should conform to ASTM C475.

Screws should conform to ASTM C1002.

Execution

Installed according to ASTM C840, the recommendations of the Gypsum Association, and specific recommendations of the manufacturer.

Base layers are applied vertically; the face layer is applied horizontally. For three-hour chase partitions, all layers are applied vertically.

Stagger joints on opposite sides of the partition.

Seal the perimeter.

7-11   THREE-HOUR FIRE-RATED COLUMN COVER

Description

Structural framing members in Type IA buildings must have a three-hour fire rating. Figure 7-11 illustrates steel column protection using gypsum wallboard on a heavy column. In fire tests, a heavy column is a W14 × 228 or heavier. If light columns are used, such as a W10 × 49, an extra layer of wallboard is required to achieve the same protection.

Figure 7-11 Three-hour fire-rated column cover 09 29 07.2

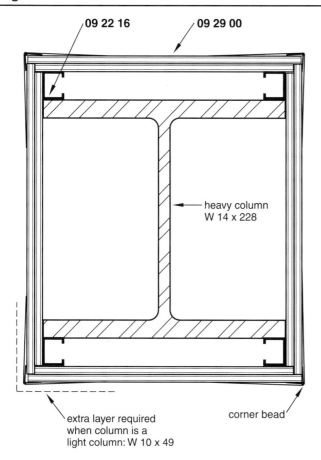

heavy column
W 14 x 228

extra layer required
when column is a
light column: W 10 x 49

corner bead

09 22 16

09 29 00

Limitations of Use

- When significant lateral movement of the structural frame is expected and the wallboard will be exposed, it may be better to use spray-on fireproofing and furr around the column to separate the finish wall from the frame.

Detailing Considerations

- Corners should be finished with corner bead and joint compound.
- Wallboard must continue from the structural slab to the fire-rated construction above.
- A two-hour-rated column cover can be achieved by using a single layer of $1/2$ in. (13 mm) type X wallboard attached to $15/8$ in. (41.3 mm) metal studs at each corner of a heavy column or two layers of $5/8$ in. (16 mm) type X wallboard attached to $15/8$ in. (41.3 mm) metal studs at each corner of a light column.

Likely Failure Points

- Cracking of the wallboard from movement of the structural frame

Materials

09 22 16 NONSTRUCTURAL METAL FRAMING

ASTM C645 and ASTM A653/A653M.

$15/8$ in., 25 gage (0.018 in. [0.46 mm]) studs attached to corners of column.

Screws should conform to ASTM C1002.

09 29 00 GYPSUM WALLBOARD

ASTM C1396.

Two layers of $1/2$ in. (13 mm) type X wallboard if used over a heavy column.

Three layers of $5/8$ in. (16 mm) type X wallboard if used over a light column.

Gypsum wallboard tape and joint compound should conform to ASTM C475/C475M.

Screws should conform to ASTM C1002.

Installed according to ASTM C840, the recommendations of the Gypsum Association, and specific recommendations of the manufacturer.

7-12 PERIMETER RELIEF JOINT

Description

In order to accommodate building movement when gypsum wallboard partitions are attached to exterior walls, columns, and other portions of the building frame, vertical relief joints, as shown in Fig. 7-12, should be detailed to prevent the partitions from buckling or cracking. This type of joint, similar to that shown in Fig. 7-3, allows the structure to move independently of the partition with a slip joint.

Figure 7-12 Perimeter relief joint 09 29 09

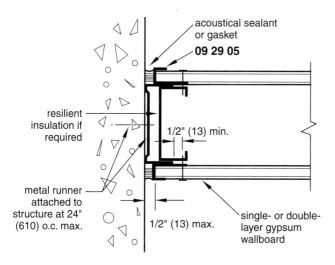

Limitations of Use

- This joint is for non-load-bearing partitions.

Detailing Considerations

- Wallboard should be attached to the stud no closer than ¹/₂ in. (13 mm) from the metal runner.
- Resilient insulation may be placed in the gap between the runner and the stud for improved acoustical control.
- If a furred wall is used perpendicular to the partition, it should not be attached to the partition, nor should the inside corner joint be taped and finished.
- If the partition extends to the structure above the suspended ceiling a slip joint, as shown in Figs. 7-3 or 7-4 should also be used.

Likely Failure Points

- Cracking of the partition if the wallboard is inadvertently attached to the runner

Materials

09 29 05 GYPSUM WALLBOARD TRIM

Corrosion-protected coated steel, aluminum, or plastic.

L, LC, or U trim sized to fit the thickness of wallboard used.

L and LC trims provide for smooth finishing of the edge with joint compound, while U trim shows an exposed metal edge but requires no finishing compound.

Vinyl trim and proprietary trim are also available.

7-13 ONE-HOUR GYPSUM WALLBOARD CEILING, WOOD FRAMING

Description

One-hour floor/ceiling assemblies are often required in residential and small commercial construction. Figure 7-13 shows one of the many ways of achieving a one-hour rating with provisions for acoustical control. If acoustical control is not required, the wallboard may be attached directly to the wood joist and the acoustical insulation omitted.

Detailing Considerations

- The wood flooring may consist of a minimum ½ in. (13 mm) plywood subfloor with either 1 in. (25 mm) nominal tongue-and-groove finish flooring or ⅝ in. (16 mm) plywood or particleboard finish flooring to which carpet, tile, or other finishes are applied.
- Water-resistant wallboard or glass-mat gypsum board should be used in high-moisture areas.

Coordination Required

- The required acoustical rating will determine which system to use.
- Openings must be rated as required by the local building code.

Figure 7-13 One-hour gypsum wallboard ceiling, wood framing
09 29 11.1

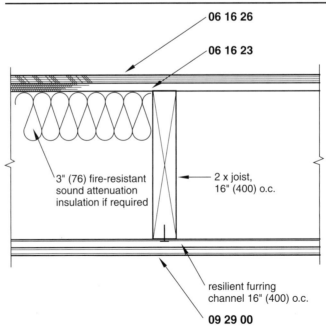

06 16 26

06 16 23

3" (76) fire-resistant sound attenuation insulation if required

2 x joist, 16" (400) o.c.

resilient furring channel 16" (400) o.c.

09 29 00

Materials

06 16 23 SUBFLOORING

Plywood or particleboard with an underlayment and a finish floor over or a combination subfloor-underlayment.

Plywood: APA-rated sheathing. Various span ratings are available, but normally a 32/16 span-rated plywood $\frac{1}{2}$ in. (13 mm) thick may be used over joists spaced 16 in. (406 mm) on center.

Particleboard: $\frac{1}{2}$ in. (13 mm) 2-M-W grade may be used over joists spaced 16 in. (406) on center; $\frac{3}{4}$ in. (19 mm) particleboard is used over joists 24 in. (610 mm) on center.

06 16 26 UNDERLAYMENT

Minimum $\frac{5}{8}$ in. (16 mm) plywood underlayment or $\frac{5}{8}$ in. (16 mm) Type I, Grade M-1 particleboard.

09 29 00 GYPSUM WALLBOARD

Materials

ASTM C1396, type X.

$\frac{1}{2}$ in. (13 mm) or $\frac{5}{8}$ in. (16 mm) thickness.

Gypsum wallboard tape and joint compound should conform to ASTM C475/C475M.

Screws should conform to ASTM C1002.

Water-resistant type for backing in areas subject to moisture or as a backup for tile in wet areas.

Execution

Installed according to ASTM C840.

1 in. (25 mm) type S screws or wallboard nails 6 in. (152 mm) on center if wallboard is attached directly to joists.

7-14   TWO-HOUR SUSPENDED GYPSUM WALLBOARD CEILING

Description

Figure 7-14 illustrates one of the most common designs for a suspended gypsum wallboard ceiling. It conceals the structural system and provides space for ducts, recessed light fixtures, conduit, and piping. If a highly accessible, smooth ceiling is required, an acoustical concealed spline system may be used.

Figure 7-14 Two-hour suspended gypsum wallboard ceiling 09 29 11.2

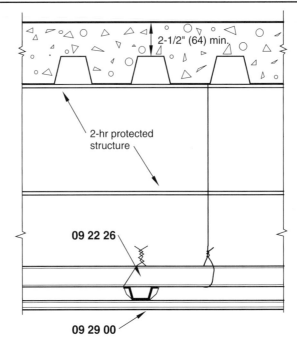

2-1/2" (64) min.

2-hr protected structure

09 22 26

09 29 00

Limitations of Use

- This detail should not be used where a high percentage of access is required.
- The maximum light fixture sizes and the percentage of ceiling area that they occupy may be limited.
- The maximum percentage of duct area per ceiling area may be limited.
- The location of light fixtures, air supply registers, sprinkler heads, and other ceiling penetrations cannot be easily moved.

Detailing Considerations

- Trapeze support systems are required for duct work, heavy piping, and similar elements above the ceiling.
- Codes may require protection over light fixtures.

Coordination Required

- Access doors must be located to provide for servicing of valves, electrical junction boxes, fire dampers, HVAC components, and similar equipment.
- Openings for pipes, electrical outlet boxes, and ducts cannot exceed an aggregate area more than 100 in.^{2} (0.065 m^2) for every 100 ft^2 (9.29 m^2) of ceiling area.
- Electrical outlet boxes must be steel with a maximum area of 16 in.^{2} (0.01 m^2).
- Fire dampers are required on ducts passing through a fire-resistive assembly.
- Access doors must be fire-rated assemblies to match the rating of the ceiling.

Materials

09 22 26 CEILING SUSPENSION SYSTEM

Materials

Minimum No. 8 SWG or 0.1719 in. (4.4 mm) galvanized wire hangers.

1½ in. (38 mm) cold-rolled steel channels.

25 gage or 0.0175 in. (0.455 mm), ⅞ in. (22 mm) deep galvanized hat-shaped furring channels, ASTM C645.

Execution

1½ in. (38 mm) channels spaced 4 ft 0 in. (1220 mm) on center and suspended with wire hangers spaced 4 ft 0 in. (1220 mm) on center.

Furring channels spaced 2 ft 0 in. (610 mm) on center and tied to 1½ in. (38 mm) channels with No. 18 double-stranded galvanized wire or attached with approved clips.

09 29 00 GYPSUM WALLBOARD

Materials

ASTM C1396, type X.

⅝ in. (16 mm) thickness.

Gypsum wallboard tape and joint compound should conform to ASTM C475/C475M.

Screws should conform to ASTM C1002.

Execution

Installed according to ASTM C840.

7-15 CERAMIC TILE FLOOR, THIN-SET ON WOOD FRAMING

Description

Figure 7-15 illustrates the use of tile on a structurally sound wood floor over an underlayment of glass mesh mortar units. It is used where the total weight and thickness of the floor must be kept to a minimum and where low cost is a consideration. The detail is appropriate for residential and light commercial installations. Instead of a glass mesh mortar unit, other types of proprietary products are available to use as an underlayment for thin-set tile applications.

For light residential applications, tile may be set directly on a ⅜ in. (10 mm) plywood underlayment over a ⅝ in. (16 mm) plywood subfloor using an organic adhesive. Tile may also be thin-set on a concrete subfloor.

Limitations of Use

- Although water resistant, this floor is not considered waterproof. A waterproof membrane must be used if greater water resistance is needed.
- This floor system is not appropriate for floors that require resistance to chemicals.
- The deflection of the wood joists and subfloor must be limited to 1/360 of the span.

Figure 7-15 Ceramic tile floor, thin-set on wood framing 09 31 13.1

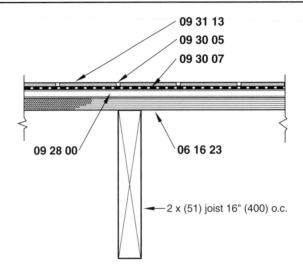

- Only dry-set or latex–portland cement mortar may be used with this detail.
- Maximum spacing of floor joists is 16 in. (400 mm) on center.

Detailing Considerations

- The space between glass mesh mortar units should be 1/8 in. (3 mm) and filled with mortar.
- Joints of glass mesh mortar units must occur over joists.
- Provide expansion joints as required.

Coordination Required

- Maximum variation in the surface of the subfloor must not exceed 1/8 in. in 10 ft (3 mm in 3050 mm).
- Verify the ability of the existing wood floor to support the extra weight of the tile.
- If latex–portland cement mortar is used, it must be allowed to dry out for 14 to 60 days before the tile is exposed to water.

Likely Failure Points

- Cracking of tile if the deflection of the subfloor exceeds the recommendations
- Cracking or loosening of the tile due to an improperly prepared subfloor

Materials

06 16 23 Subflooring

Plywood or particleboard with an underlayment and a finish floor over or a combination subfloor-underlayment.

Plywood: APA-rated sheathing. Various span ratings are available, but normally a 32/16 span-rated plywood $\frac{1}{2}$ in. (13 mm) thick may be used over joists spaced 16 in. (406 mm) on center.

Particleboard: $\frac{1}{2}$ in. (13 mm) 2-M-W grade may be used over joists spaced 16 in. (406) on center; $\frac{3}{4}$ in. (19 mm) particleboard is used over joists 24 in. (610 mm) on center.

The maximum variation in the surface cannot exceed $\frac{1}{8}$ in. in 10 ft (3 mm in 3 m).

The maximum deflection of the structural floor is 1/360 of the span, including dead and live loads

09 28 00 GLASS MESH MORTAR UNIT

Proprietary sheets certified by the manufacturer as suitable for the intended use.

Laminate sheets to plywood with latex–portland cement mortar.

Fasten sheets through plywood into joists with corrosion-resistant fasteners as recommended by the manufacturer.

09 30 05 TILE GROUT

Materials

Ceramic tile grouts, ANSI A118.6.

Latex–portland cement grout is preferred for most installations.

Sand–portland cement may be used for ceramic mosaic tile, quarry tile, and paver tile on floors and walls. It is not used for glazed wall tile on walls or floors.

Dry-set grout may be used except with quarry or paver tile.

Other special types of grout may be required based on the application and tile type. Refer to the Tile Council of North America (TCNA) *Handbook for Ceramic Tile Installation*.

Execution

Install according to ANSI A108.10.

Tiles must be wetted when using commercial portland cement or sand–portland cement grout.

Damp curing is generally required. Refer to the manufacturer's recommendations for requirements.

09 30 07 DRY-SET OR LATEX–PORTLAND CEMENT MORTAR

Dry-set mortar, ANSI A118.1, or latex–portland cement mortar, ANSI A118.4.

Installed according to ANSI A108.5 from $\frac{3}{32}$ in. (2.4 mm) to $\frac{1}{8}$ in. (3 mm) thick.

The substrate must level to within $\frac{1}{4}$ in. in 10 ft (6 mm in 3 m).

09 31 13 THIN-SET CERAMIC TILE

Glazed wall tile, ceramic mosaic tile, quarry tile, or paver tile.

ANSI A137.1 or equivalent European Norms (EN) specifications.

Installed according to ANSI A108.5 and the recommendations of the TCNA *Handbook for Ceramic Tile Installation*.

7-16 CERAMIC TILE WALL, THIN-SET

Description

Figure 7-16 illustrates the use of tile on a structurally sound metal stud wall over a sheathing of glass mesh mortar units. As with Fig. 7-15, this construction is used in wet areas where the weight and wall thickness must be kept to a minimum and where moderate cost is a consideration.

The detail is appropriate for residential and light commercial installations in areas such as kitchens, toilet rooms, and showers, as well as in dry areas. Instead of a glass mesh mortar unit, other types of proprietary products are available to use as an underlayment for thin-set tile applications. Instead of metal studs, wood studs may be used.

Limitations of Use

- Studs must be well braced.
- This construction is for interior use only.
- A 1/2 in. (13 mm) thick glass mesh mortar unit may be required for a one-hour fire rating. This must be verified with the manufacturer and with local building codes.
- Only dry-set or latex–portland cement mortar may be used with this detail.

Detailing Considerations

- Minimum stud width for both wood and metal studs is 3 1/2 in. (13 mm).
- Metal studs must be a minimum of 20 gage or 0.0375 in. (0.952 mm).
- Provide expansion joints as required.
- The space between glass mesh mortar units should be 1/8 in. (3 mm) and filled solid with mortar.

Figure 7-16 Ceramic tile wall, thin set 09 31 13.2

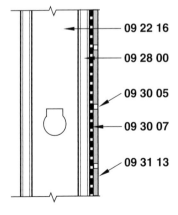

09 22 16

09 28 00

09 30 05

09 30 07

09 31 13

Coordination Required

- Maximum stud spacing is 16 in. (406 mm) on center.
- Wood studs should be dry and straight.
- If latex–portland cement mortar is used, it must be allowed to dry out for 14 to 60 days before the tile is exposed to water.

Likely Failure Points

- Telegraphing of the glass mesh mortar unit joints through the tile if the joints are not finished flush
- Cracking of the grout if the studs are not stiff enough

Materials

09 22 16 METAL STUD AND TRACK

Materials

ASTM C645 and ASTM A653/A653M.

Minimum 20 gage or 0.0375 in. (0.952 mm).

$3^5/_8$ in., 4 in., or 6 in. (92.1 mm, 101.6 mm, or 152.4 mm) as required.

Screws should conform to ASTM C1002.

Execution

Maximum spacing of 24 in. (600 mm) on center.

Installed according to ASTM C754.

Provide a slip joint at the underside of structural slabs or other slabs that may deflect.

09 28 00 GLASS MESH MORTAR UNIT

Proprietary sheets certified by the manufacturer as suitable for the intended use.

Laminate sheets to plywood with latex–portland cement mortar.

Provide a $1/_8$ in. (3 mm) space between the units and fill it solid with dry-set or latex–portland cement mortar.

Provide a 2 in. (51 mm) glass fiber mesh tape embedded in a skim coat of mortar over all joints and corners.

Fasten through plywood into joists with corrosion-resistant fasteners as recommended by the manufacturer.

09 30 05 TILE GROUT

Materials

Ceramic tile grouts, ANSI A118.6.

Latex–portland cement grout is preferred for most installations.

Sand–portland cement may be used for ceramic mosaic tile, quarry tile, and paver tile on floors and walls. It is not used for glazed wall tile on walls or floors.

Dry-set grout may be used except with quarry or paver tile.

Other special types of grout may be required based on the application and tile type. Refer to TCNA *Handbook for Ceramic Tile Installation*.

Execution

Install according to ANSI A108.10.

Tiles must be wetted when using commercial portland cement or sand–portland cement grout.

Damp curing is generally required. Refer to the manufacturer's recommendations for requirements.

09 30 07 Dry-set or latex–portland cement mortar

Dry-set mortar, ANSI A118.1, or latex–portland cement mortar, ANSI A118.4.

Installed according to ANSI A108.5 from $3/32$ in. (2.4 mm) to $1/8$ in. (3 mm) thick.

The substrate must level to within $1/4$ in. in 10 ft (6 mm in 3 m).

09 31 13 Thin-set ceramic tile

Glazed wall tile, ceramic mosaic tile, quarry tile, or paver tile.

ANSI A137.1 or equivalent EN specifications.

Installed according to ANSI A108.5 and the recommendations of the TCNA *Handbook for Ceramic Tile Installation*.

7-17 MOVEMENT JOINT WITH THIN-SET TILE

Description

Movement joints are required over all cold joints and saw-cut control joints, as shown in Fig. 7-17. They are also required where the tile abuts restraining surfaces such as columns, walls, pipes, and curbs; where backing materials change; and where dissimilar floors occur. Movement joints are not required in small interior rooms less than 12 ft (3658 mm) wide or in corridors less than 12 ft (3658 mm) wide.

Figure 7-17 Movement joint with thin-set tile 09 31 13.3

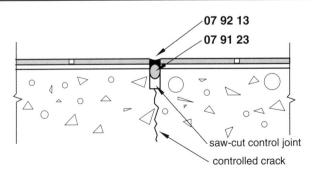

Table 7-2 Recommended Ceramic Tile Expansion Joint Width and Spacing

	Exterior			Interior		
	All tile		Decks Exposed to Sky in Northern Climates	Ceramic Mosaic and Glazed Wall Tile	Quarry and Paver Tile	Exposed to Direct Sunlight or Moisture
Spacing, ft	8	12	12	20–25	20–25	8–12
(m)	(2.59)	(3.66)	(3.66)	(6.10–7.62)	(6.10–7.62)	(2.59–3.66)
width, in.	$^3/_8$	$^1/_2{}^a$	$^3/_4$ (19)	$^1/_8$–$^1/_4{}^b$	$^1/_4{}^c$	$^1/_4$
(mm)	(10)	(13)		(3–6)	(6)	(6)

[a]Increase the width by $^1/_{16}$ in. (2 mm) for each 15°F (8.3°C) tile surface temperature change greater than 100°F (37.8°C) between the summer high and the winter low.
[b]The preferred minimum is $^1/_4$ in. (6 mm), but the joint should never be less than $^1/_8$ in. (3 mm).
[c]Same as grout joint but not less than $^1/_4$ in. (6 mm).

Limitations of Use

- Special application areas such as food processing plants, dairies, factories, swimming pools, shower rooms, and the like may require special sealants and joint design.

Detailing Considerations

- Tile movement joints should be located to coincide with control joints, isolation joints, construction joints, and building expansion joints.
- A movement joint must not be narrower than the structural joint behind it.
- The edges of the tile to which sealant will be applied must be clean and dry. Use a primer as recommended by the sealant manufacturer.
- Movement joints should be spaced and sized according to the recommendations in Table 7-2.
- Refer to Sections 1-5, 1-6, and 1-7 for concrete joints.

Coordination Required

- The location of the structural joints should be based on the location of the tile joints.
- Joints should be installed when the mortar bed and tile are installed rather than sawcutting after installation.

Likely Failure Points

- Tile failure due to improperly sized joints or inadequate spacing
- Sealant failure due to improper selection, joint preparation, or application
- Cracking of the tile or joints when tile movement joints do not align with structural joints

Materials

07 91 23 BACKER ROD

Closed cell polyethylene foam, butyl rubber, or open cell and closed cell polyurethane foam with a rounded top surface.

Sealant must not adhere to the backer rod.

07 92 13 ELASTOMERIC JOINT SEALANT

Materials

Exterior

Vertical joints	Silicone or urethane, ASTM C920, Type S, Grade NS, Class 25.
Horizontal, traffic areas	Two-part polyurethane, ASTM C920, Type M, Grade P, Class 25. Shore A hardness of 35 or greater.

Interior

Vertical joints	Silicone or polyurethane, ASTM C920, Type S, Grade NS, Class 25.
Vertical joints, wet areas	Silicone, ASTM C920, Type S, Grade NS, Class 25, mildew resistant.
Horizontal, traffic areas	Two-part polyurethane, ASTM C920, Type M, Grade P, Class 25. Shore A hardness of 35 or greater.
Horizontal, nontraffic	Silicone, ASTM C920, Type S, Grade NS, Class 25 or one-part polyurethane or polysulfide, ASTM C920, Type S, Grade NS, Class 25.

Execution

Sealant depth equal to the width of the joint up to $1/2$ in. (13 mm), with a minimum depth of $1/4$ in. (6 mm).

Sealant depth $1/2$ in. (13 mm) for joint widths from $1/2$ in. to 1 in. (13 mm to 25 mm).

For sealants with a ± 25 percent movement capability, the joint width should be four times the expected movement of the joint.

Prepare the edges of the tile as recommended by the sealant manufacturer.

Apply primer on the tile edges if recommended by the sealant manufacturer.

7-18   CERAMIC TILE FLOOR, THICK-SET ON MEMBRANE OVER CONCRETE

Description

When deflection of the structural slab is expected, tile should be installed over a full mortar bed, as shown in Fig. 7-18. The tile and reinforced mortar bed are separated from the structural slab with a cleavage membrane to allow the two floor elements to move independently. This system should be used on precast and posttensioned floors and/or when other types of floor movement are expected.

In addition to providing for movement, the full mortar bed allows minor variations in the floor level to be made up with the mortar. The tile can be set on the full mortar bed while it is still plastic or on a cured mortar bed using a bond coat of dry-set or latex–portland cement mortar. If a waterproof floor is required, a waterproof membrane can be used in place of the cleavage membrane.

Figure 7-18 Ceramic tile floor, thick-set on membrane over concrete 09 32 13.1

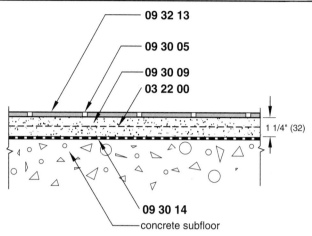

09 32 13
09 30 05
09 30 09
03 22 00

1 1/4" (32)

09 30 14
concrete subfloor

Limitations of Use

- Although this floor provides an excellent floor for heavy and extra-heavy use, it is not appropriate for areas where chemical resistance is required unless epoxy mortar and furan grout are used.
- For floors subjected to continuous wetting, a waterproof membrane must be used, similar to that shown in Fig. 7-19.

Detailing Considerations

- If any floor slope is required, it must be in the subfloor.
- Provide expansion joints as shown in Fig. 7-22.
- Reinforcing mesh must be used.
- The mortar bed should not exceed 2 in. (51 mm).

Coordination Required

- Maximum variation in the surface of the subfloor must not exceed 1/4 in. in 10 ft (6 mm in 3050 mm).
- The concrete slab must be depressed to allow the tile to match the adjacent floor finishes.
- The concrete slab should have a steel trowel finish.
- Interior movement joints in the tile must be located over control joints in the concrete slab, as shown in Fig. 7-17.

Likely Failure Points

- Cracking of the joints if grout is not properly damp cured

Materials

03 22 00 WELDED WIRE FABRIC

2 in. by 2 in. × W0.3 × W0.3 (51 × 51 — MW2 × MW2) or equivalent.

ASTM A82 and A 185.

Stop reinforcing at control joints.

09 30 05 TILE GROUT

Materials

Ceramic tile grouts, ANSI A118.6.

Latex–portland cement grout is preferred for most installations.

Sand–portland cement may be used for ceramic mosaic tile, quarry tile, and paver tile on floors and walls. It is not used for glazed wall tile on walls or floors.

Dry-set grout may be used except with quarry or paver tile.

Other special types of grout may be required based on the application and the tile type. Refer to the TCNA *Handbook for Ceramic Tile Installation.*

Execution

Install according to ANSI A108.10.

Tiles must be wetted when using commercial portland cement or sand–portland cement grout.

Damp curing is generally required. Refer to the manufacturer's recommendations for requirements.

09 30 09 PORTLAND CEMENT MORTAR

Materials

Portland cement, ASTM C-150, Type 1.

Sand, ASTM C-144.

For floors, a mixture of cement and damp sand in a proportion of 1:6.

Bond coat when installed on a cured mortar bed: dry-set mortar, ANSI A118.1 or latex–portland cement mortar, ANSI A118.4.

Execution

Set the tile in the mortar bed while the mortar bed is still plastic, according to ANSI A108.1A, or set the tile on a cured (20 hours at 70°F (21°C) or above) mortar bed with dry-set or latex–portland cement mortar according to ANSI A108.1B.

Nominal $1\frac{1}{4}$ in. (32 mm) thick mortar bed.

09 30 14 ANTIFRACTURE MEMBRANE

Polyethylene film, minimum 4 mil (0.1 mm), ASTM C171 or D 4397, or

High solids, cold liquid-applied membrane, ASTM C836, or

Chlorinated polyethylene sheeting, ASTM D4068, or

PVC membrane, ASTM D4551, or

15 lb (730 g/m^2) asphalt–saturated roofing felt, or

Manufacturer's proprietary product conforming to ANSI A118.12.

09 32 13 MORTAR-BED CERAMIC TILE

Glazed wall tile, ceramic mosaic tile, quarry tile, or paver tile.

ANSI A 137.1 or equivalent EN specifications.

Installed according to ANSI A108.1A or ANSI A108.1B.

7-19 CERAMIC TILE FLOOR, FULL MORTAR BED

Description

Figure 7-19 shows one method of constructing a waterproof shower floor. It is used in conjunction with Fig. 7-21 for commercial showers or where continuous wetting is present. When the use of a full mortar bed on the walls is not required, glass mesh mortar units may be used over metal or wood studs with the wall tile thin-set.

Limitations of Use

- The minimum slope of the membrane to the drain is ¼ in./ft (20 mm/m).
- This detail should not be used for steam rooms.
- If glass mesh mortar units are used in lieu of a full mortar bed on the wall, metal studs must be furred out enough to allow the waterproof membrane to remain flush with the face of the furring so that the glass mesh mortar units can extend straight down. If wood studs are used, they must be notched for the same reason.

Figure 7-19 Ceramic tile floor, full mortar bed 09 32 13.2

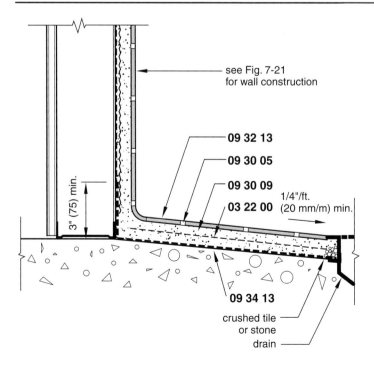

Detailing Considerations

- The slope should be provided by the subfloor or cement mortar fill below the membrane.
- The waterproof membrane must be turned up wall at least 3 in. (76 mm).
- Provide stone or broken tile around drain weep holes to prevent blockage by mortar.

Coordination Required

- The proper slope required with the subfloor must be prepared by other trades. This may require a depressed slab.
- Accessible showers that have no curb at the entry require a minimum of 4 ft 0 in. (1220 mm) from the entry to the drain opening.

Likely Failure Points

- Water leakage due to an improperly sealed or damaged membrane
- Cracking of the joints if the grout is not properly damp cured
- Missing or insufficient slope of the subfloor

Materials

03 22 00 WELDED WIRE FABRIC

2 in. by 2 in. × W0.3 × W0.3 (51 × 51 − MW2 × MW2) or equivalent.

ASTM A82 and A 185.

Stop reinforcing at control joints.

09 30 05 TILE GROUT

Refer to Section 7-18.

09 30 09 PORTLAND CEMENT MORTAR

Materials

Portland cement, ASTM C-150, Type 1.

Sand, ASTM C-144.

For floors, a mixture of cement and damp sand in a proportion of 1:4 with an admixture to make the mortar bed water resistant.

Bond coat when installed on a cured mortar bed: dry-set mortar, ANSI A118.1, or latex–portland cement mortar, ANSI A118.4.

Execution

Set the tile in the mortar bed while the mortar bed is still plastic, according to ANSI A108.1A, or set the tile on a cured (20 hours at 70°F [21°C] or above) mortar bed with dry-set or latex–portland cement mortar, according to ANSI A108.1B.

Nominal 1 in. to 1½ in. (25 mm to 38 mm) thick mortar bed.

09 34 13 WATERPROOFING-MEMBRANE CERAMIC TILING

Single-ply or multicomponent liquid-applied membranes, ANSI A118.10.

Extend edges up the wall a minimum of 4 in. ± 1 in. (100 mm ± 50 mm).

09 32 13 MORTAR-BED CERAMIC TILE

Glazed wall tile, ceramic mosaic tile, quarry tile, or paver tile.

ANSI A137.1 or equivalent EN specifications.

Installed according to ANSI A108.1A or ANSI A108.1B.

7-20 CERAMIC TILE CEILING

Description

Figure 7-20 illustrates one method for suspending a ceramic tile ceiling using a suspended framework of cold-rolled steel channels. Tile may also be applied to glass–mesh mortar units or gypsum wallboard applied directly to the structural ceiling framing.

Limitations of Use

- The suspended ceiling system must be capable of supporting the weight of the tile and mortar.
- This detail should not be used for steam rooms.

Detailing Considerations

- Install lath, mortar bed, and tile in accordance with ANSI A108.1A.
- Movement joints are required if the area exceeds the limits given in Section 7-17 and Table 7-2.
- Spacing of the framing support should not exceed 16 in. (406 mm).

Figure 7-20 Ceramic tile ceiling 09 32 13.3

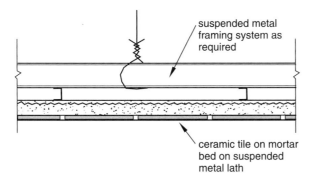

suspended metal framing system as required

ceramic tile on mortar bed on suspended metal lath

Coordination Required

- The backing surface must be flat to within ¼ in. in 10 ft (6 mm in 3 m).
- Verify the maximum weight if loose insulation is placed over the framing.

Likely Failure Points

- Cracking of joints or collapse of the ceiling if framing is undersized

Materials

Refer to Section 7-19 for material requirements.

7-21   CERAMIC TILE WALL, FULL MORTAR BED

Description

Figure 7-21 is one of the most durable wall-tile setting systems. The full mortar bed method incorporates a thick bed of cured mortar as the base for the application of tile using a bond coat of dry-set or latex–portland cement mortar. It is typically used in commercial construction, either in dry or limited water-exposure areas or in wet areas such as gang showers, laundries, and tubs. A full mortar bed application allows minor variations in plumb to be corrected as the mortar bed is applied.

Limitations of Use

- The total thickness of the scratch coat and the cured mortar coat should not exceed 1 in. (25 mm).
- The mortar bed must be thoroughly cured prior to application of the tile.

Figure 7-21 Ceramic tile wall, full mortar bed 09 32 13.4

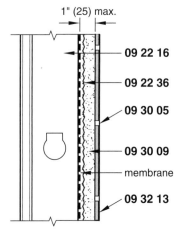

Detailing Considerations

- In wet areas, a single-ply or multicomponent liquid-applied membrane conforming to ANSI A118.10 may be used.
- If required, provide expansion joints similar to those in Fig. 7-22.
- This type of full mortar bed application may also be used over masonry and wood studs.

Coordination Required

- Maximum stud spacing is 16 in. (406 mm) on center.
- The strength of the structure below the wall should be checked to verify that it can support the weight of the wall. A full mortar bed wall with tile may weigh approximately 18 to 20 psf (88 to 98 kg/m^2).

Likely Failure Points

- Cracking of the wall due to deflection of the structure below caused by the additional weight of the wall
- Cracking of the joints if the mortar bed is not properly cured prior to tile application
- Cracking of the joints if the grout is not properly damp cured

Materials

09 22 16 Nonstructural metal framing

Materials

ASTM C645 and ASTM A653/A653M.

Minimum 25 gage or 0.0175 in. (0.455 mm).

2^1/$_2$ in., 3^5/$_8$ in., 4 in., or 6 in. (63.5 mm, 92.1 mm, 101.6 mm, or 152.4 mm) as required.

Screws should conform to ASTM C1002.

Execution

Maximum spacing of 24 in. (600 mm) on center.

Installed according to ASTM C754.

Provide a slip joint at the underside of structural slabs or other slabs that may deflect.

09 22 36 Metal lath

ASTM C847.

Galvanized or painted flat expanded metal lath, minimum 2.5 lb/yd^2 (1.4 kg/m^2).

Rib lath should not be used.

Diamond lath should be used on studs spaced not more than 16 in. (406 mm) on center.

09 30 05 Tile grout

Materials

Ceramic tile grouts, ANSI A118.6.

Latex–portland cement grout is preferred for most installations.

Sand–portland cement may be used for ceramic mosaic tile, quarry tile, and paver tile on floors and walls. It is not used for glazed wall tile on walls or floors.

Dry-set grout may be used except with quarry or paver tile.

Other special types of grout may be required based on the application and the tile type. Refer to the TCNA *Handbook for Ceramic Tile Installation.*

Execution

Install according to ANSI A108.10.

Tiles must be wetted when using commercial portland cement or sand–portland cement grout.

Damp curing is generally required. Refer to the manufacturer's recommendations for requirements.

09 30 09 PORTLAND CEMENT MORTAR

Materials

Portland cement, ASTM C-150, Type 1.

Sand, ASTM C144.

Lime, ASTM C206, Type S or ASTM C207, Type S.

For walls (scratch coat), a mixture of cement, sand, and lime in a proportion of 1:4:$\frac{1}{2}$ if dry sand is used or 1:5:$\frac{1}{2}$ if damp sand is used.

For walls (mortar bed), a mixture of cement, sand, and lime in a proportion of 1:5:$\frac{1}{2}$ to 1:7:1 using damp sand.

Bond coat when installed on a cured mortar bed: dry-set mortar, ANSI A118.1B, or latex–portland cement mortar, ANSI A118.4.

Execution

Set the tile in the mortar bed while the mortar bed is still plastic, according to ANSI A108.1A, or set the tile on a cured (20 hours at 70°F [21°C] or above) mortar bed with dry-set or latex–portland cement mortar, according to ANSI A108.1B.

1 in. (25 mm) maximum thickness of the scratch coat and mortar bed.

09 32 13 MORTAR-BED CERAMIC TILE

Glazed wall tile, ceramic mosaic tile, quarry tile, or paver tile.

ANSI A 137.1 or equivalent EN specifications.

Installed according to ANSI A108.1A or ANSI A108.1B and the recommendations of the TCNA *Handbook for Ceramic Tile Installation.*

7-22   CERAMIC TILE EXPANSION JOINT

Description

Expansion joints, as shown in Fig. 7-22, are required in a full-mortar bed ceramic tile installation where there is a large expanse of tile and where the tile abuts restraining surfaces such as columns, walls, pipes, and curbs. They are also required where backing materials

Figure 7-22 Ceramic tile expansion joint 09 32 13.5

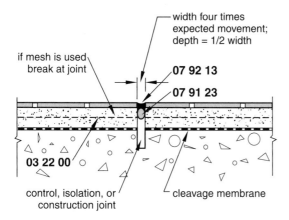

width four times expected movement; depth = 1/2 width

if mesh is used break at joint

07 92 13

07 91 23

03 22 00

control, isolation, or construction joint

cleavage membrane

change and where dissimilar floors occur. Expansion joints are not required in small interior rooms less than 12 ft (3658 mm) wide or in corridors less than 12 ft (3658 mm) wide.

Limitations of Use

- Special application areas such as food processing plants, dairies, factories, swimming pools, and the like may require special sealants and joint design.

Detailing Considerations

- Tile expansion joints should be located to coincide with control joints, isolation joints, construction joints, and building expansion joints.
- An expansion joint must not be narrower than the structural joint behind it.
- Expansion joints should be spaced and sized according to the recommendations in Table 7-2.
- Refer to Sections 1-5, 1-6, and 1-7 for concrete joints.

Coordination Required

- The location of the structural joints should be based on the location of the tile joints.
- Joints should be installed as the mortar bed and tile are installed rather than sawcutting after installation.

Likely Failure Points

- Tile failure due to improperly sized joints or inadequate spacing
- Sealant failure due to improper selection, joint preparation, or application
- Cracking of the tile or joints when tile expansion joints do not align with structural joints

Materials

03 22 00 WELDED WIRE FABRIC

2 in. by 2 in. × W0.3 × W0.3 (51 × 51 − MW2 × MW2) or equivalent.

ASTM A82 and A185.

Stop reinforcing at control joints.

07 91 23 BACKER ROD

Closed cell polyethylene foam, butyl rubber, or open cell and closed cell polyurethane foam with a rounded top surface.

Sealant must not adhere to the backer rod.

07 92 13 ELASTOMERIC JOINT SEALANT

Refer to Section 7-17 for sealant requirements

7-23 ONE-HOUR ACOUSTICAL CEILING ASSEMBLY

Description

Figure 7-23 illustrates a noncombustible or one-hour-rated suspended acoustical ceiling system. Various types of suspension systems are available, but not all of them are fire-rated. Fire

Figure 7-23 One-hour acoustical ceiling assembly 09 50 13.1

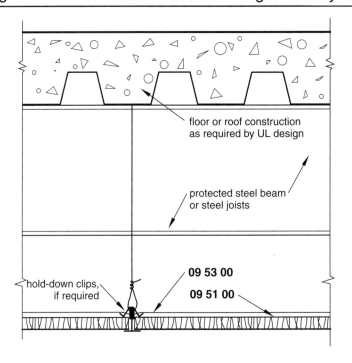

ratings of both suspension systems and ceiling tiles should be verified with manufacturers' literature.

Limitations of Use

- In order for a floor/ceiling or roof/ceiling system to qualify as a fire-rated assembly, the following conditions must be met:
  - The assembly must conform to a UL design.
  - The suspension system must be fire rated.
  - The ceiling tile must be fire rated.
  - The ceiling must be free of overlaid material not specified in the UL design.
- UL designs limit the maximum fixture size and the percentage of ceiling area that fixtures may occupy.
- UL designs limit the maximum duct area per ceiling area.
- When seismic restraint is required, installation should comply with ASTM E580/E580M.

Detailing Considerations

- Trapeze support systems are required for ductwork, heavy piping, and similar elements above the ceiling.
- Codes may require protection of light fixtures, as shown in Fig. 7-24.
- If the weight of the ceiling panels is not sufficient to resist an upward force of 1 lb/ft^2 (48 Pa), wire, hold-down clips, or other approved devices must be used to prevent the vertical displacement of the panels.
- If a rectangular grid is used, its direction should be compatible with the shape of the room in which it is used.
- Required noise reduction coefficient (NRC) ratings should be verified with available fire-rated tiles.

Coordination Required

- Openings for pipes, electrical outlet boxes, and ducts cannot exceed an aggregate area more than 100 in.^{2} (64 500 mm^2) for every 100 ft^2 (9.29 m^2) of ceiling area.
- Individual electrical outlet boxes must be steel with a maximum area of 16 in.^{2} (10 323 mm^2).
- Fire dampers are required on ducts passing through a fire-resistive assembly as required by local codes.
- Access doors must be fire-rated assemblies to match the rating of the ceiling.
- All provisions for penetration of the floor system required by the local building code must be followed.

Likely Failure Points

- Deflection of the suspension system due to inadequately installed hanger rods
- Missing or incorrectly installed hold-down clips

Materials

09 51 00 ACOUSTICAL CEILING

Class I finish (maximum flame spread rating of 25).

Fire rated as listed in the manufacturer's literature.

09 53 00 ACOUSTICAL CEILING SUSPENSION SYSTEM

ASTM C635/C635M.

When the ceiling tile is part of a fire-resistive assembly and its weight is not sufficient to resist an upward force of 1 lb/ft^2 (48 Pa), the panels must be restrained with clips or other approved devices to prevent vertical displacement.

Installed according to ASTM C636/C636M.

7-24   TWO-HOUR ACOUSTICAL CEILING ASSEMBLY

Description

Figure 7-24 shows the typical components of a two-hour suspended acoustical ceiling. However, each ceiling system manufacturer provides many types of two-hour systems, and the manufacturer's literature should be reviewed for particular requirements and designs that are available.

Figure 7-24 Two-hour acoustical ceiling assembly 09 50 13.2

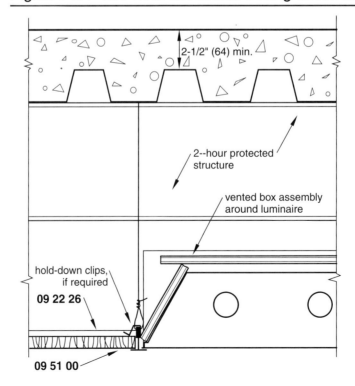

2-1/2" (64) min.

2--hour protected structure

vented box assembly around luminaire

hold-down clips, if required

09 22 26

09 51 00

Limitations of Use

- In order for a floor/ceiling or roof/ceiling system to qualify as a fire-rated assembly, the following conditions must be met:
  - The assembly must conform to a UL design.
  - The suspension system must be fire rated.
  - The ceiling tile must be fire rated.
  - The ceiling must be free of overlaid material not specified in the UL design.
- UL designs limit the maximum fixture sizes and the percentage of ceiling area that they may occupy.
- UL designs limit the maximum duct area per ceiling area.
- When seismic restraint is required, installation should comply with ASTM E 580/E 580M.

Detailing Considerations

- Many codes require that light fixtures in fire-rated floor/ceiling assemblies be protected with semirigid mineral wool boards or tents or with box assemblies constructed of gypsum wallboard. Figure 7-24 shows the use of a vented box around the fixture.
- Trapeze support systems are required for ductwork, heavy piping, and similar elements above the ceiling.
- If the weight of the ceiling panels is not sufficient to resist an upward force of 1 lb/ft^2 (48 Pa), wire, hold-down clips, or other approved devices must be used to prevent the vertical displacement of the panels
- If a rectangular grid is used, its direction should be compatible with the shape of the room in which it is used.
- Required NRC ratings should be verified with available fire-rated tiles.

Coordination Required

- Openings for pipes, electrical outlet boxes, and ducts cannot exceed an aggregate area of more than 100 in.^{2} (64,500 mm^2) for every 100 ft^2 (9.29 m^2) of ceiling area.
- Individual electrical outlet boxes must be steel with a maximum area of 16 in.^{2} (10,323 mm^2).
- Fire dampers are required on ducts passing through a fire-resistive assembly.
- Access doors must be fire-rated assemblies to match the rating of the ceiling.

Likely Failure Points

- Breach of the fire-resistive surface caused by improperly installed light protection
- Deflection of the suspension system due to inadequately installed hanger rods
- Missing or incorrectly installed hold-down clips

Materials

09 51 00 ACOUSTICAL CEILING

Class I finish (maximum flame spread rating of 25).

Fire rated as listed in the manufacturer's literature.

09 53 00 ACOUSTICAL CEILING SUSPENSION SYSTEM

Materials

ASTM C635/C635M.

When the ceiling tile is part of a fire-resistive assembly and its weight is not sufficient to resist an upward force of 1 lb/ft² (48 Pa), the panels must be restrained with clips or other approved devices to prevent vertical displacement.

Execution

Installed according to ASTM C636/C636M.

7-25   STONE FLOORING, THIN-SET

Description

The drawings in Fig. 7-25 represent two methods of applying stone flooring so that a minimum overall thickness is maintained. Figure 7-25(a) illustrates the application of stone to a concrete subfloor using dry-set mortar, and Fig. 7-25(b) shows the application of thin stone slabs to a wood-framed floor using adhesive. Stone applied over concrete slabs may be large, full-thickness pieces or thin tiles. Stone set over wood subfloors is generally limited to thin tiles.

Figure 7-25 Stone flooring, thin-set 09 63 40.1

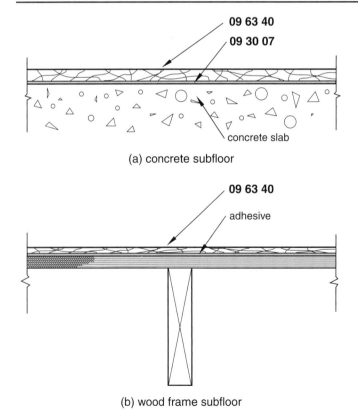

(a) concrete subfloor

(b) wood frame subfloor

Limitations of Use

- Stone should only be set over subfloors that are not subject to deflection or movement.
- Stone on wood subfloors is limited to residential and light commercial construction.

Detailing Considerations

- The thickness of adjacent flooring materials must be considered.
- For wood subfloors, use nonstaining adhesive recommended by the manufacturer of the stone.
- Grout floors with portland cement or another approved grouting material.

Coordination Required

- Wood subfloors should be structurally sound and level to within $1/16$ in. in 3 ft (2 mm in 1 m).
- Concrete subfloors should be level to within $1/4$ in. in 10 ft (20 mm in 1 m).

Likely Failure Points

- Cracking of the grout joints or stone if the subfloor deflects.

Materials

09 30 07 DRY-SET OR LATEX–PORTLAND CEMENT MORTAR

Dry-set mortar, ANSI A118.1, or latex–portland cement mortar, ANSI A118.4.

Installed according to ANSI A108.5 from $3/32$ in. (2.4 mm) to $1/8$ in. (3 mm) thick.

The substrate must level to within $1/4$ in. in 10 ft (20 mm in 1 m).

09 63 40 STONE FLOORING

Granite, marble, slate, or other available stone.

Granite, ASTM C615.

Marble, ASTM C503.

Slate, ASTM C629.

Avoid the use of polished finishes for general flooring areas because they can be slippery, especially when wet.

7-26 STONE FLOORING, FULL MORTAR BED

Description

For commercial construction or when movement or deflection of the structural slab is expected, stone flooring should be installed over a full mortar bed, as shown in Fig. 7-26. The stone and its setting bed are separated from the structural slab with an antifracture membrane to allow the two floors to move independently.

Figure 7-26 Stone flooring, full mortar bed 09 63 40.2

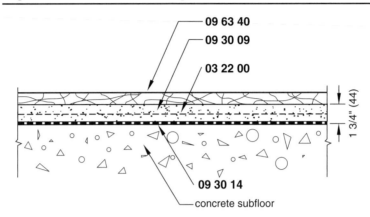

concrete subfloor

Limitations of Use

- This system is more expensive than others and should only be used where required by structural considerations or where a heavy-duty floor is needed.

Detailing Considerations

- Stone may be full-thickness (approximately ³/₄ in. [19 mm]) or thin stone.
- Grout floors with portland cement or another approved material.

Coordination Required

- The concrete slab subfloor may be depressed to allow the stone to match the finish elevation of adjacent materials.
- Verify the structural capability of the subfloor for the extra weight of the flooring and setting bed.

Materials

03 22 00 WELDED WIRE FABRIC

2 in. by 2 in. × W0.3 × W0.3 (51 × 51 − MW2 × MW2) or equivalent.

ASTM A82 and A185.

Stop reinforcing at control joints.

09 30 09 PORTLAND CEMENT MORTAR

Materials

Portland cement, ASTM C-150, Type 1.

Sand, ASTM C-144.

For floors, a mixture of cement and damp sand in a proportion of 1:3.

Bond coat when installed on a cured mortar bed: dry-set mortar, ANSI A118.1, or latex–portland cement mortar, ANSI A118.4.

Execution

Set the tile in the mortar bed while the mortar bed is still plastic, according to ANSI A108.1A, and tamp the stone into place.

09 30 14 ANTIFRACTURE MEMBRANE

Polyethylene film, minimum 4 mil (0.1 mm), ASTM C171 or D4397, or

High solids, cold liquid-applied membrane, ASTM C836, or

Chlorinated polyethylene sheeting, ASTM D4068, or

PVC membrane, ASTM D4551, or

15 lb (730 g/m^2) asphalt-saturated roofing felt, or

Manufacturer's proprietary product conforming to ANSI A118.12.

09 63 40 STONE FLOORING

Granite, marble, slate, or other available stone.

Granite, ASTM C615.

Marble, ASTM C503.

Slate, ASTM C629.

Avoid the use of polished finishes for general flooring areas because they can be slippery, especially when wet.

7-27   WOOD PARQUET FLOORING

Description

Parquet flooring consists of individual pieces of hardwood arranged to form a particular pattern and laminated to a substrate of additional plies of wood. Premanufactured units range from $3/8$ in. to $3/4$ in. (10 mm to 19 mm) thick, are available in various sizes, and are available prefinished or unfinished. Refer to the manufacturer's literature for available types. As shown in Fig. 7-27, parquet flooring is applied to a sound, level subfloor.

Limitations of Use

- Parquet flooring should not be installed over existing or old flooring materials.
- Depending on the manufacturer, these units may only have a Class B fire rating.
- This type of flooring may be used over on-grade concrete slabs, but the slabs must be properly cured, with no moisture present.

Detailing Considerations

- The subfloor must be level to within $1/4$ in. in 10 ft (20 mm in 1 m).
- Provide a minimum of $3/4$ in. (19 mm) expansion space at wall lines.
- The base must be detailed to conceal the floor expansion space.

Figure 7-27 Wood parquet flooring 09 64 23

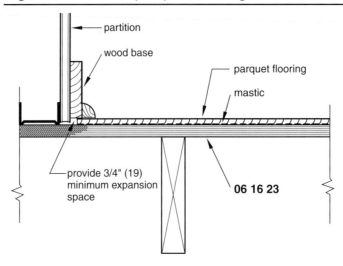

Coordination Required

- The subfloor must be sound and firmly attached to joists.
- Provide air circulation below the structure. Cover crawl spaces with 6 mil (0.15 mm) polyethylene.

Likely Failure Points

- Warping of the finish floor due to the presence of moisture
- Buckling of the floor because of insufficient expansion space
- Uneven floor due to an improperly prepared slab (The slab should be level, as stated above, with no high spots or depressions.)

Materials

06 16 23 SUBFLOORING

Plywood or particleboard with an underlayment and a finish floor over or a combination subfloor-underlayment.

Plywood: APA-rated sheathing. Various span ratings are available, but normally a 32/16 span-rated plywood 1/2 in. (13 mm) thick may be used over joists spaced 16 in. (406 mm) on center.

Particleboard: 1/2 in. (13 mm) 2-M-W grade may be used over joists spaced 16 in. (406 mm) on center. Three-quarter inch (19 mm) particleboard is used over joists 24 in. (610 mm) on center.

7-28   WOOD STRIP FLOORING ON WOOD FRAMING

Description

Figure 7-28 shows a typical installation of strip flooring on wood joist construction. This is the traditional application using full-thickness tongue-and-groove pieces blind nailed to the subfloor.

Limitations of Use

- This installation is intended for above-grade use only.
- Wood flooring should not be used in damp locations.

Detailing Considerations

- Provide a minimum of $3/4$ in. (19 mm) expansion space at wall lines.
- The base must be detailed to conceal the floor expansion space.
- Areas larger than 20 ft by 20 ft (6 m by 6 m) may require additional provisions for expansion.
- Fifteen pound asphalt felt or building paper should be installed prior to flooring installation.

Coordination Required

- The subfloor must be sound and firmly attached to joists.
- Provide air circulation below the structure. Cover crawl spaces with 6 mil (0.15 mm) polyethylene.

Figure 7-28 Wood strip flooring on wood framing 09 64 29.1

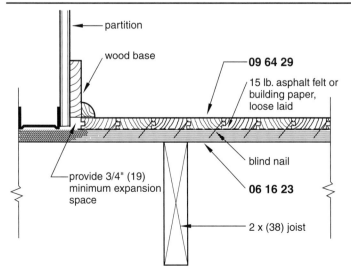

Likely Failure Points

- Warping of the finish floor due to the presence of moisture
- Buckling of the floor because of insufficient expansion space

Materials

06 16 23 SUBFLOORING

Plywood or oriented strand board (OSB) conforming to PS 2 and PRP-108 published by APA—The Engineered Wood Association.

Plywood: APA-rated exterior sheathing grade. Minimum $5/8$ in. ($19/32$ in.) (16 mm) or $3/4$ in. ($23/32$ in.) (19 mm).

OSB: APA-rated sheathing, $3/4$ in. ($23/32$ in.) (19 mm).

Plywood is laid with the long dimension perpendicular to the joists.

Provide a $1/8$ in. (3 mm) space between panels with end joints staggered 4 ft (1220 mm).

Install paneling according to the panel manufacturer's instructions, nailing every panel 6 in. (152 mm) on center. Panels may also be glue-nailed to the floor framing.

One-half inch (13 mm) strip flooring requires $3/4$ in. (19 mm) subflooring.

09 64 29 WOOD STRIP FLOORING

$3/4$ in. by $2\ 1/4$ in. (19 mm by 57 mm) or another standard size, tongue-and-groove strip flooring of oak, maple, beech, pecan, or other available species.

Install according to recommendations of NOFMA: The Wood Flooring Manufacturers Association.

7-29   WOOD STRIP FLOORING ON CONCRETE FRAMING

Description

When strip flooring must be laid on concrete subfloors and the total thickness of the construction must be kept to a minimum, the detail shown in Fig. 7-29 may be used. However, this should only be used on slabs above grade where sufficient air circulation is provided below the concrete. Strip flooring installed on grade should be laid over wood sleepers with a vapor barrier.

Limitations of Use

- This installation is intended for above-grade use only.
- The concrete slab must be thoroughly cured prior to installation of the wood flooring. The concrete should be tested for excess moisture prior to installation.

Figure 7-29 Wood strip flooring on concrete framing 09 64 29.2

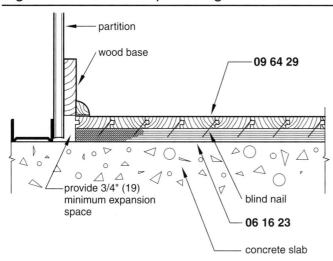

Detailing Considerations

- Provide a minimum of ³/₄ in. (19 mm) expansion space at wall lines.
- The base must be detailed to conceal the floor expansion space.
- Areas larger than 20 ft by 20 ft (6 m by 6 m) may require additional provisions for expansion.
- If flooring is installed on a properly prepared slab-on-grade, a 6 mil (0.15 mm) sheet of polyethylene or two layers of 15 lb asphalt felt must be laid over the slab prior to subfloor installation.

Likely Failure Points

- Warping of the finish floor due to the presence of moisture
- Uneven floor due to an improperly prepared slab (The slab should be level to within ¹/₄ in. in 10 ft [20 mm in 1 m], with no high spots or depressions.)
- Buckling of the floor because of insufficient expansion space

Materials

06 16 23 SUBFLOORING

Materials

Plywood conforming to PS 2 and PRP-108 published by APA—The Engineered Wood Association.

Plywood: APA-rated exterior sheathing grade; ³/₄ in. (²³/₃₂ in.) (19 mm).

Execution

Provide a ¹/₈ in. (3 mm) space between panels, with end joints staggered 4 ft (1220 mm).

Plywood should be laid loose, with a ¹/₄ in. (6 mm) to ¹/₂ in. (13 mm) gap between panels. The long dimension should be parallel to the long dimension of the room, with end joints staggered.

Panels may also be laid on a diagonal to the direction of the finished floor to help prevent the cracks associated with panel edges.

Plywood is then fastened to the slab with power-actuated fasteners.

09 64 29 WOOD STRIP FLOORING

$3/4$ in. by $2^{1}/4$ in. (19 mm by 57 mm) or other standard-size tongue-and-groove strip flooring of oak, maple, beech, pecan, or other available species.

Install according to the recommendations of NOFMA: The Wood Flooring Manufacturers Association.

7-30   LAMINATE FLOORING

Description

Laminate flooring is a layered rigid floor covering consisting of a core of high-density fiberboard impregnated with thermosetting resins, typically melamine, overlaid with an image layer and a surface wear layer. The image layer contains the actual photographic reproduction of wood, stone, or other material. A backing layer of resin-saturated paper or other material is applied to act as a balancing sheet and to protect the floor from warping caused by moisture. Laminate flooring is available in thicknesses from about $1/4$ in. (6 mm) to $1/2$ in. (12 mm) in plank form.

Figure 7-30 shows a typical installation of laminate flooring for either residential or commercial construction. Laminate flooring is typically applied over a foam underlayment as a floating floor, that is, without being attached to the subfloor or the existing flooring. Individual pieces with tongue-and-groove edges are snapped together to create a smooth, monolithic floor.

Figure 7-30 Laminate flooring 09 62 19

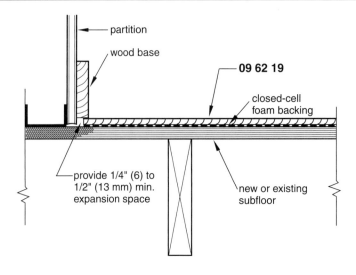

partition

wood base

09 62 19

closed-cell foam backing

provide 1/4" (6) to 1/2" (13 mm) min. expansion space

new or existing subfloor

Limitations of Use

- Laminate flooring cannot be installed directly over carpet or other fabric floor coverings.
- While some products have an integral foam backing, a separate foam underlayment is preferred. The seams can be taped together to form a vapor barrier if approved by the manufacturer.
- Laminate flooring must not be installed over floors that are damp or subject to wetting or that may become damp from below.

Detailing Considerations

- Laminate flooring may be installed over new subfloors or existing flooring (except carpeting), but the subfloor must be flat, dry (maximum moisture of 14 percent), and clean of debris.
- A space ranging from $1/4$ in. (6 mm) to $1/2$ in. (13 mm) must be maintained between the floor and vertical surfaces such as walls, cabinets, and construction.
- If laminate flooring is installed in bathrooms, laundry rooms, or kitchens, the expansion space should be filled with silicone sealant.

Coordination Required

- When laminate flooring is used over a crawl space, the crawl space must be adequately ventilated with at least 1.5 ft^2 per 100 ft^2 (0.14 m^2 per 9.3 m^2) of floor area.
- Concrete slabs must be dry and may need a vapor barrier. New concrete should cure for at least 60 days. Concrete should be tested for moisture content and compared with the manufacturer's recommendations.
- Any existing wood flooring that is glued to concrete must be removed.

Materials

09 62 19 LAMINATE FLOORING

Manufacturers' standards meeting the requirements of NALFA LF 01-2008, published by the North American Laminate Flooring Association.

Install according to the manufacturer's recommendations.

7-31 RESILIENT WOOD FLOORING SYSTEM

Description

Figure 7-31 shows a flooring system that is used when extra resilience is required in applications such as dance floors or gymnasium floors. The flooring may be installed directly on the sleepers, as shown in this detail, or applied to plywood placed over the sleepers.

Limitations of Use

- Wood flooring should not be used in damp locations or areas subject to water contact.
- Narrow-faced flooring should be used in areas of high or changing humidity.

Figure 7-31 Resilient wood flooring system 09 64 53

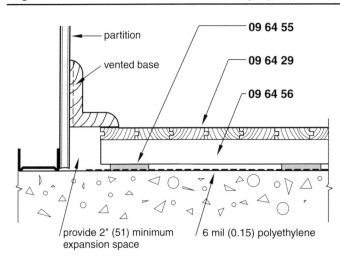

Detailing Considerations

- Slabs-on-grade should be dampproofed below the slab as well as above the slab.
- Dampproof above the slab with 6 mil (1.5 mm) polyethylene or as recommended by the manufacturer.
- A vented base must be provided to conceal the expansion space and provide ventilation.

Coordination Required

- The concrete slab must be level to within $1/8$ in. in 10 ft (3 mm in 3 m).
- The slab must have a troweled finish with high spots ground and low areas filled in.

Materials

09 64 29 WOOD STRIP FLOORING

$25/32$ in. or $33/32$ in. (19.8 mm or 26.2 mm) by $2^1/4$ in. (57 mm) or another standard-face width tongue-and-groove strip flooring of maple or other suitable species.

Install according to recommendations of NOFMA: The Wood Flooring Manufacturers Association.

09 64 55 RESILIENT PAD

2 in. by 3 in. (51 mm by 76 mm) rubber pads spaced 12 in. (305 mm) on center.

Install according to the manufacturers' recommendations.

09 64 56 SLEEPER

2 in. by 4 in. by 4 ft 0 in. (51 mm by 102 mm by 1220 mm) pressure-treated wood.

Laid 9 in. (229 mm) on center for $25/32$ in. (19.8 mm) flooring and 12 in. (305 mm) on center for $33/32$ in. (26.2 mm) flooring.

Laid end to end with approximately a $1/4$ in. (6 mm) gap between and with joints staggered a minimum of 2 ft 0 in. (610 mm).

Figure 7-32 Portland cement terrazzo, sand cushion 09 66 13.13

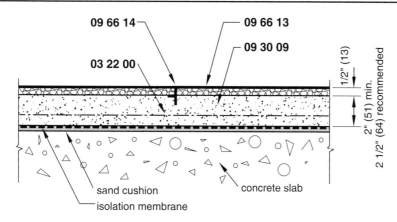

7-32 PORTLAND CEMENT TERRAZZO, SAND CUSHION

Description

Figure 7-32 shows the preferred method of terrazzo installation in which the finish floor is structurally separated from the subfloor. This allows the two surfaces to move independently, thereby minimizing cracking of the terrazzo. A reinforcing mesh must be used to make the finish layer a structural element. This is the heaviest of the terrazzo installations, weighing about 27 psf (132 kg/m^2). The National Terrazzo and Mosaic Association (NTMA) recommendations should be followed.

Limitations of Use

- A sand cushion is the most expensive type of terrazzo installation.
- White portland cement should be used. Gray portland cement should generally not be used because of the difficulty of maintaining a consistent color appearance.
- When chemical resistance is required, use an epoxy, polyester, or polyacrylate matrix.
- Conductive floors require chip sizes no larger than No. 1 with a black matrix and must meet the requirements of the National Fire Protection Association (NFPA).

Detailing Considerations

- Expansion divider strips should be located to provide areas of approximately 9 ft^2 to 36 ft^2 (0.84 m^2 to 3.34 m^2). The length of each area should not exceed twice the width.
- Because of the isolation membrane, divider strips do not have to be located over any expansion joints in the concrete slab.
- Angle or T-type divider strips may be used to provide decorative separations.
- The finish layer should be 1/2 in. (13 mm) for standard topping and 3/4 in. (19 mm) for Venetian topping.

- Minimum 6 in. by 6 in. (152 mm by 152 mm) samples should be submitted to the architect for review.
- The isolation membrane may be 4 mil (0.1 mm) polyethylene or 15 lb unperforated roofing felt.

Coordination Required

- The design and installation of joints in the concrete should coincide with the desired joint locations in the terrazzo.
- The concrete slab should be level to within $1/4$ in. in 10 ft (6 mm in 3 m) and have a floated finish.

Likely Failure Points

- Cracking of the surface if divider strips are not placed directly above any expansion joints in the concrete slab and if they do not extend the full depth of the underbed
- Dislodged aggregate in rustic terrazzo if aggregate smaller than No. 1 size is used
- Aggregate dislodged during grinding due to improper curing

Materials

03 22 00 WELDED WIRE FABRIC

ASTM A185.

Galvanized welded wire mesh, 2 in. by 2 in. × W0.3 × W0.3 (51 × 51 − MW2 × MW2) or 2 in. by 3 in. × W0.2 × W0.2 (51 × 76 − MW1 × MW1). (16 or 18 gauge).

Overlap the fabric a minimum of two squares at the ends and edges.

Stop the fabric a minimum of 1 in. (51 mm) from expansion joints.

09 30 09 PORTLAND CEMENT MORTAR

Materials

Portland cement, ASTM C150, Type 1.

Sand, ASTM C144.

One part portland cement to four parts sand and sufficient water to provide workability with as low a slump as possible.

Execution

Minimum 2 in. (51 mm) thick mortar bed; $2^1/2$ in. (64 mm) is recommended.

Install according to the recommendations of NTMA.

09 66 13 TERRAZZO

Materials

Chip types and sizes to produce standard, Venetian, Palladian, or rustic terrazzo as required by the design.

Marble chips in the size and color required. Size to conform to NTMA gradation standards.

Terrazzo matrix: white portland cement, ASTM C150, Type 1.

One 94 lb (43 kg) bag of portland cement per 200 lb (91 kg) of marble chips.

Pigment color as required by the design.

Execution

Install according to the recommendations of NTMA.

Allow the matrix to wet cure until the topping develops enough strength to prevent pulling of terrazzo chips during grinding.

Grind with 24 grit stones followed by grinding with 80 grit stones.

09 66 14 TERRAZZO DIVIDER STRIP

White alloy of zinc, brass, or plastic: 14, 16, or 18 B & S gage or 0.064 in., 0.050 in., or 0.040 in. (1.63 mm, 1.29 mm, or 1.02 mm).

$1\frac{1}{4}$ in. (32 mm) standard divider strip with an anchor for a $\frac{1}{2}$ in. (13 mm) topping or $1\frac{1}{2}$ in. (38 mm) for a $\frac{3}{4}$ in. (19 mm) Venetian topping.

Optional divider strips available with $\frac{1}{8}$ in. (3 mm), $\frac{1}{4}$ in. (6 mm), and $\frac{3}{8}$ in. (10 mm) wide exposed surfaces.

Locate at 5 ft 0 in. (1525 mm) or less on center.

7-33 PORTLAND CEMENT TERRAZZO, MONOLITHIC

Description

Monolithic terrazzo bonds directly to the concrete structural slab below. It provides a thin, lightweight installation, but one that is subject to cracking due to slab movement. Figure 7-33(a) shows a typical floor installation, and Fig. 7-33(b) illustrates the floor termination with a terrazzo base.

Limitations of Use

- This detail should not be used where the slab is subject to deflection.
- White portland cement should be used. Gray portland cement should generally not be used because of the difficulty of maintaining a consistent color appearance.
- When chemical resistance is required, use an epoxy, polyester, or polyacrylate matrix.
- Conductive floors require chip sizes no larger than No. 1 with a black matrix and must meet the requirements of the NFPA.

Detailing Considerations

- Areas between expansion divider strips should be between 200 ft^2 and 300 ft^2 (18.6 m^2 and 27.9 m^2) in rectangular areas, with the length no more than 50 percent longer than the width.
- Divider strips must be located over any expansion and construction joints in the concrete slab and at column centerlines.
- Angle or T-type divider strips may be used to provide decorative separations.

Figure 7-33 Portland cement terrazzo, monolithic 09 66 13.16

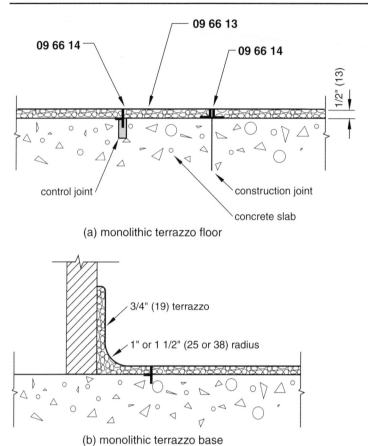

(a) monolithic terrazzo floor

(b) monolithic terrazzo base

- The horizontal flange of T strips should not be larger than 1 in. (25 mm), and it should have enough holes to allow bonding of the terrazzo to the concrete.
- The finish layer should be ½ in. (13 mm) for standard topping and ¾ in. (19 mm) for Venetian topping.
- Minimum 6 in. by 6 in. (152 mm by 152 mm) samples should be submitted to the architect for review.
- If bonding agents are used, they should be neat portland cement, epoxy, or acrylic.

Coordination Required

- Joints in the concrete should be designed and installed to coincide with desired joint locations in the terrazzo.
- The concrete slab should be level to within ¼ in. in 10 ft (6 mm in 3 m).
- The concrete slab should have a fine-textured broom finish.
- Control joints should be cut no more than one-third the depth of the slab.
- For slabs-on-grade, the soil must be thoroughly compacted.
- Slabs to receive terrazzo should be poured in alternating sections to control expansion and contraction.
- The concrete should be tamped to bring the cement to the surface.

Likely Failure Points

- Weakness or lack of bonding due to liquid curing compounds used on the concrete
- Aggregate dislodged during grinding due to improper curing
- Structural cracks telegraphed through the terrazzo if not located under divider strips

Materials

09 66 13 TERRAZZO

Materials

Chip types and sizes to produce standard, Venetian, Palladian, or rustic terrazzo as required by the design.

Marble chips in the size and color required. Size to conform to NTMA gradation standards.

Terrazzo matrix: white portland cement, ASTM C150, Type 1.

One 94 lb (43 kg) bag of portland cement per 200 lb (91 kg) to 220 lb (100 kg) of marble chips.

Pigment color as required by the design.

Execution

Install according to recommendations of NTMA.

Allow the matrix to wet cure until the topping develops enough strength to prevent pulling of terrazzo chips during grinding.

Grind with 24 grit stones followed by grinding with 80 grit stones.

09 66 14 TERRAZZO DIVIDER STRIP

White alloy of zinc, brass, or plastic: 14, 16, or 18 B & S gage or 0.064 in., 0.050 in., or 0.040 in. (1.63 mm, 1.29 mm, or 1.02 mm).

$1^1/_4$ in. (32 mm) standard divider strip with an anchor for a $^1/_2$ in. (13 mm) topping or $1^1/_2$ in. (38 mm) for a $^3/_4$ in. (19 mm) Venetian topping. Use a pair of L strips over construction joints.

Optional divider strips are available with $^1/_8$ in. (3 mm), $^1/_4$ in. (6 mm), and $^3/_8$ in. (10 mm) wide exposed surfaces.

K or L strips may be used for aesthetic reasons. Anchor them to the slab by nailing or an adhesive.

Locate strips at the positions stated in the detailing considerations above.

7-34 PORTLAND CEMENT TERRAZZO, BONDED

Description

Figures 7-34(a) and 7-34(b) illustrate a typical installation of terrazzo bonded to an intermediate layer of mortar over a concrete subfloor. As with a monolithic installation, bonded terrazzo is used where the thickness and weight of the finish must be kept to a minimum.

Figure 7-34 Portland cement terrazzo, bonded 09 66 13.19

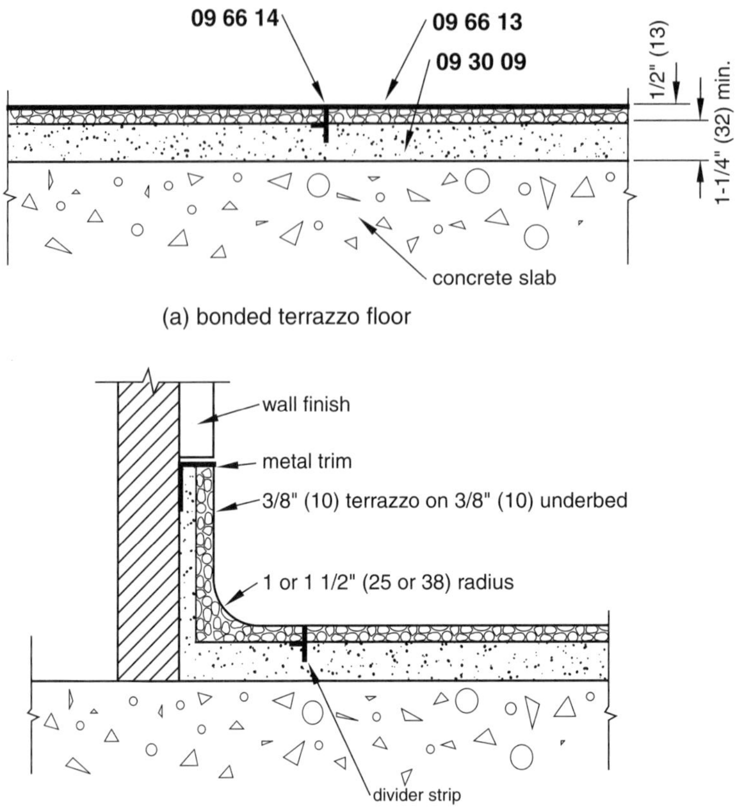

(a) bonded terrazzo floor

(b) bonded terrazzo base

However, with a bonded installation the terrazzo is less dependent on the concrete slab for flatness because of the sand–cement underbed. Like a monolithic installation, this type of installation is more likely to show telegraphing of any cracking occurring in the structural slab below than a sand cushion installation.

Limitations of Use

- This detail should not be used where the slab is subject to deflection.
- White portland cement should be used. Gray portland cement should generally not be used because of the difficulty of maintaining a consistent color appearance.
- When chemical resistance is required, use an epoxy, polyester, or polyacrylate matrix.
- Conductive floors require chip sizes no larger than No. 1 with a black matrix.

Detailing Considerations

- Expansion divider strips should be located to provide areas of approximately 16 ft^2 to 36 ft^2 (1.5 m^2 to 3.3 m^2). The length of each area should not exceed twice the width. Locate strips over subfloor expansion and construction joints.
- Angle or T-type divider strips may be used to provide decorative separations.

- The finish layer should be $\frac{1}{2}$ in. (13 mm) for standard topping and $\frac{3}{4}$ in. (19 mm) for Venetian topping.
- Minimum 6 in. by 6 in. (152 mm by 152 mm) samples should be submitted to the architect for review.

Coordination Required

- The design and installation of joints in the concrete should coincide with the desired joint locations in the terrazzo.
- The concrete slab should be level to within $\frac{1}{4}$ in. in 10 ft (6 mm in 3 m) and have a troweled finish.

Likely Failure Points

- Weakness or lack of bonding due to liquid curing compounds used on the concrete
- Structural cracks telegraphed through the terrazzo
- Dislodged aggregate in rustic terrazzo if aggregate smaller than No. 1 size is used

Materials

09 30 09 PORTLAND CEMENT MORTAR

Materials

Portland cement, ASTM C150, Type 1.

Sand, ASTM C144.

One part portland cement to four parts sand and sufficient water to provide workability with as low a slump as possible.

Execution

Minimum $1\frac{1}{4}$ in. (32 mm) thick mortar bed.

Install according to recommendations of NTMA.

09 66 13 TERRAZZO

Materials

Chip types and sizes to produce standard, Venetian, Palladian, or rustic terrazzo as required by the design.

Marble chips in the size and color required. Size to conform to NTMA gradation standards.

Terrazzo matrix: white portland cement, ASTM C150, Type 1.

One 94 lb (43 kg) bag of portland cement per 200 lb (91 kg) of marble chips.

Pigment color as required by the design.

Execution

Install according to recommendations of NTMA.

Allow the matrix to wet cure until the topping develops strength to prevent pulling of terrazzo chips during grinding.

Grind with 24 grit stones followed by grinding with 80 grit stones.

09 66 14 TERRAZZO DIVIDER STRIP

White alloy of zinc, brass, or plastic: 14, 16, or 18 B & S gage or 0.064 in., 0.050 in., or 0.040 in. (1.63 mm, 1.29 mm, or 1.02 mm).

1¼ in. (32 mm) standard divider strip with anchor for ½ in. (13 mm) topping or 1½ in. (38 mm) for ¾ in. (19 mm) Venetian topping.

Optional divider strips are available with ⅛ in. (3 mm), ¼ in. (6 mm), and ⅜ in. (10 mm) wide exposed surfaces.

Locate strips at the positions stated in detailing considerations above.

APPENDIX **A**

Standards Titles

The following list gives the full title of the industry standards that are referred to in the text by number designation only.

AMERICAN SOCIETY FOR TESTING AND MATERIALS (ASTM) (WWW.ASTM.ORG)

A 6/A 6M *Standard Specification for General Requirements for Rolled Structural Bars, Plates, Shapes, and Sheet Piling*

A 36/A 36M *Standard Specification for Carbon Structural Steel*

A 82/A 82M *Standard Specification for Steel Wire, Plain, for Concrete Reinforcement*

A 153/A 153M *Standard Specification for Zinc Coating (hot-dip) on Iron and Steel Hardware*

A 167A *Standard Specification for Stainless and Heat-resisting Chromium-Nickel Steel Plate, Sheet, and Strip*

A 185/A 185M *Standard Specification for Steel Welded Wire Reinforcement, Plain, for Concrete*

A 240/A 240M *Standard Specification for Chromium and Chromium-Nickel Stainless Steel Plate, Sheet, and Strip for Pressure Vessels and for General Applications*

A 615/A 615M *Standard Specification for Deformed and Plain Carbon-Steel Bars for Concrete Reinforcement.*

A 641/A 641M *Standard Specification for Zinc-coated (Galvanized) Carbon Steel Wire*

A 653/A 653M *Standard Specification for Sheet Steel, Zinc-coated (Galvanized) or Zinc-Iron Alloy-coated (Galvannealed) by the Hot-dip Process*

A 951/A 951M *Standard Specification for Steel Wire for Masonry Joint Reinforcement*

B 69 *Standard Specification for Rolled Zinc*

B 209 *Standard Specification for Aluminum and Aluminum-Alloy Sheet and Plate*

B 221 *Standard Specification for Aluminum and Aluminum-Alloy Extruded Bars, Rods, Wire, Profiles and Tubes*

B370 *Standard Specification for Copper Sheet and Strip for Building Construction*

C 33 *Standard Specification for Concrete Aggregates*

C 62 *Standard Specification for Building Brick (Solid masonry units made from clay or shale)*

C 90 *Standard Specification for Load Bearing Concrete Masonry Units*

C 144 *Standard Specification for Aggregate for Masonry Mortar*

C 150 *Standard Specification for Portland Cement*

C 171 *Standard Specification for Sheet Materials for Curing Concrete*

C 206 *Standard Specification for Finishing Hydrated Lime*

C 207 *Standard Specification for Hydrated Lime for Masonry Purposes*

C 208 *Standard Specification for Cellulosic Fiber Insulating Board*

C 216 *Standard Specification for Facing Brick (Solid masonry units made from clay or shale)*

C 270 *Standard Specification for Mortar for Unit Masonry*

C 475/A 475M *Standard Specification for Joint Compound and Joint Tape for Finishing Gypsum Board*

C 476 *Standard Specification for Grout for Masonry*

C 503 *Standard Specification for Marble Dimension Stone*

C 514 *Standard Specification for Nails for the Application of Gypsum Wallboard*

C 516 *Standard Specification for Vermiculite Loose Fill Thermal Insulation*

C 549 *Standard Specification for Perlite Loose Fill Insulation*

C 553 *Standard Specification for Mineral Fiber Blanket Thermal Insulation for Commercial and Industrial Applications*

C 568 *Standard Specification for Limestone Dimension Stone*

C 578 *Standard Specification for Rigid, Cellular Polystyrene Thermal Insulation*

C 591 *Standard Specification for Unfaced Preformed Rigid Cellular Polyisocyanurate Thermal Insulation*

C 612 *Standard Specification for Mineral Fiber Block and Board Thermal Insulation*

C 615 *Standard Specification for Granite Dimension Stone*

C629 *Standard Specification for Slate Dimension Stone*

C 635/C 635M *Standard Specification for the Manufacture, Performance, and Testing of Metal Suspension Systems for Acoustical Tile and Lay-in Panel Ceilings*

C 636/C 636M *Standard Practice for Installation of Metal Ceiling Suspension Systems for Acoustical Tile and Lay-In Panels*

C 645 *Standard Specification for Nonstructural Steel Framing Members*

C 652 *Standard Specification for Hollow Brick (Hollow masonry units made from clay or shale)*

C 661 *Standard Test Method for Indentation Hardness of Elastomeric-Type Sealants by Means of a Durometer*

C 665 *Standard Specification for Mineral-Fiber Blanket Thermal Insulation for Light Frame Construction and Manufactured Housing*

C 726 *Standard Specification for Mineral Fiber Roof Insulation Board*

C 728 *Standard Specification for Perlite Thermal Insulation Board*

C 739 *Standard Specification for Cellulosic Fiber Loose-Fill Thermal Insulation*

C 754 *Standard Specification for Installation of Steel Framing Members to Receive Screw-attached Gypsum Wallboard Products*

C 755 *Standard Practice for Selection of Water Vapor Retarders for Thermal Insulation*

C 764 *Standard Specification for Mineral Fiber Loose-Fill Thermal Insulation*

C 834 *Standard Specification for Latex Sealants*

C 836 *Standard Specification for High Solids Content, Cold Liquid-applied Elastomeric Waterproofing Membrane for Use with Separate Wearing Course*

C 840 *Standard Specification for Application and Finishing of Gypsum Board*

C 847 *Standard Specification for Metal Lath*

C 920 *Standard Specification for Elastomeric Joint Sealants*

C 926 *Application of Portland Cement-Based Plaster*

C 955 *Standard Specification for Load-Bearing (Transverse and Axial) Steel Studs, Runners (Tracks), and Bracing or Bridging for Screw Application of Gypsum Panel Products and Metal Plaster Bases*

C 991 *Standard Specification for Flexible Glass Fiber Insulation for Metal Buildings*

C 1002 *Standard Specification for Steel Self-piercing Tapping Screws for the Application of Gypsum Panel Products or Metal Plaster Bases to Wood Studs or Steel Studs*

C 1007 *Specification for the Installation of Load Bearing (Transverse and Axial) Steel Studs and Related Accessories*

C 1014 *Standard Specification for Spray-Applied Mineral Fiber Thermal and Sound Absorbing Insulation*

C 1029 *Standard Specification for Spray-Applied Rigid Cellular Polyurethane Thermal Insulation*

C 1036 *Standard Specification for Flat Glass*

C 1048 *Standard Specification for Heat Treated Flat Glass—Kind HS, Kind FT Coated and Uncoated Glass*

C 1136 *Standard Specification for Flexible, Low Permeance Vapor Retarders for Thermal Insulation*

C 1149 *Standard Specification for Self-Supported Spray Applied Cellulosic Thermal Insulation*

C 1177 *Glass Mat Gypsum Board*

C 1184 *Standard Specification for Structural Silicone Sealants*

C 1193 *Standard Guide for Use of Joint Sealants*

C 1249 *Standard Guide for Secondary Seal for Sealed Insulating Glass Units for Structural Sealant Glazing Applications*

C 1278 *Standard Specification for Fiber-Reinforced Gypsum Panel*

C 1280 *Standard Specification for Application of Gypsum Sheathing*

C 1289 *Standard Specification for Faced Rigid Cellular Polyisocyanurate Thermal Insulation*

C 1299 *Standard Guide for Use in Selection of Liquid-Applied Sealants*

C 1320 *Standard Practice for Installation of Mineral Fiber Batt and Blanket Thermal Insulation for Light Frame Construction*

C 1382 *Test Method for Determining Tensile Adhesion Properties of Sealants When Used in Exterior Insulation and Finish Systems (EIFS) Joints*

C 1386 *Standard Specification for Precast Autoclaved Aerated Concrete (PAAC) Wall Construction Units*

C 1396 *Standard Specification for Gypsum Board*

C 1397 *Standard Practice for Application of Class PB Exterior Insulation and Finish Systems*

C 1401 *Standard Guide for Structural Sealant Glazing*

C 1452 *Standard Specification for Reinforced Autoclaved Aerated Concrete Elements*

C 1472 *Standard Guide for Calculating Movement and Other Effects When Establishing Sealant Joint Width*

C 1481 *Standard Guide for Use of Joint Sealants with Exterior Insulation and Finish Systems (EIFS)*

C 1516 *Standard Practice for Application of Direct-Applied Exterior Finish Systems*

C 1535 *Standard Practice for Application of Exterior Insulation and Finish Systems Class PI*

C 1555 *Standard Practice for Autoclaved Aerated Concrete Masonry*

C 1564 *Standard Guide for Use of Silicone Sealants for Protective Glazing Systems*

D 41 *Standard Specification for Asphalt Primer Used in Roofing, Dampproofing, and Waterproofing*

D 226 *Standard Specification for Asphalt-Saturated Organic Felt Used in Roofing and Waterproofing*

D 312 *Standard Specification for Asphalt Used in Roofing*

D 1056 *Standard Specification for Flexible Cellular Materials—Sponge or Expanded Rubber*

D 1863 *Standard Specification for Mineral Aggregate Used on Built-Up Roofs*

D 1970 *Standard Specification for Self-Adhering Polymer Modified Bituminous Sheet Materials Used as Steep Roofing Underlayment for Ice Dam Protection*

D 2178 *Standard Specification for Asphalt Glass Felt Used in Roofing and Waterproofing*

D 2287 *Standard Specification for Nonrigid Vinyl Chloride Polymer and Copolymer Molding and Extrusion Compounds*

D 2626 *Standard Specification for Asphalt-Saturated and Coated Organic Felt Base Sheet Used in Roofing*

D 3737 *Standard Practice for Establishing Allowable Properties for Structural Glued Laminated Timber (Glulam)*

D 4068 *Standard Specification for Chlorinated Polyethylene (CPE) Sheeting for Concealed Water-Containment Membrane*

D 4434 *Standard Specification for Poly(Vinyl Chloride) Sheet Roofing*

D 4397 *Standard Specification for Polyethylene Sheeting for Construction, Industrial, and Agricultural Applications*

D 4551 *Standard Specification for Poly(Vinyl Chloride) (PVC) Plastic Flexible Concealed Water-Containment Membrane*

D 4601 *Standard Specification for Asphalt-Coated Glass Fiber Base Sheet Used in Roofing*

D 4637 *Standard Specification for EPDM Sheet Used In Single-Ply Roof Membrane*

D 4811 *Standard Specification for Nonvulcanized (Uncured) Rubber Sheet Used as Roof Flashing*

D 4869 *Standard Specification for Asphalt-Saturated Organic Felt Underlayment Used in Steep Slope Roofing*

D 6152 *Standard Specification for SEBS-Modified Mopping Asphalt Used in Roofing*

D 6162 *Standard Specification for Styrene Butadiene Styrene (SBS) Modified Bituminous Sheet Materials Using a Combination of Polyester and Glass Fiber Reinforcements*

D 6163 *Standard Specification for Styrene Butadiene Styrene (SBS) Modified Bituminous Sheet Materials Using Glass Fiber Reinforcements*

D 6164 *Standard Specification for Styrene Butadiene Styrene (SBS) Modified Bituminous Sheet Materials Using Polyester Reinforcements*

D 6222 *Standard Specification for Atactic Polypropylene (APP) Modified Bituminous Sheet Materials Using Polyester Reinforcements*

D 6223 *Standard Specification for Atactic Polypropylene (APP) Modified Bituminous Sheet Materials Using a Combination of Polyester and Glass Fiber Reinforcements*

D 6298 *Standard Specification for Fiberglass Reinforced Styrene-Butadiene-Styrene (SBS) Modified Bituminous Sheets with a Factory Applied Metal Surface*

D 6380 *Standard Specification for Asphalt Roll Roofing (Organic Felt)*

D 6509 *Standard Specification for Atactic Polypropylene (APP) Modified Bituminous Base Sheet Materials Using Glass Fiber Reinforcements*

D 6878 *Standard Specification for Thermoplastic Polyolefin Based Sheet Roofing*

E 96/E 96M *Standard Test Methods for Water Vapor Transmission of Materials*

E 108 *Standard Test Methods for Fire Tests of Roof Coverings*

E 119 *Standard Methods of Fire Tests of Building Construction and Materials*

E 283 *Standard Test Method for Determining Rate of Air Leakage Through Exterior Windows, Curtain Walls, and Doors Under Specified Pressure Differences Across the Specimen*

E 330 *Standard Test Method for Structural Performance of Exterior Windows, Doors, Skylights and Curtain Walls by Uniform Static Air Pressure Difference*

E 331 *Standard Test Method for Water Penetration of Exterior Windows, Skylights, Doors, and Curtain Walls by Uniform Static Air Pressure Difference*

E 547 *Standard Test Method for Water Penetration of Exterior Windows, Skylights, Doors, and Curtain Walls by Cyclic Static Air Pressure Difference*

E 580/E 580M *Standard Practice for Installation of Ceiling Suspension Systems for Acoustical Tile and Lay-in Panels in Areas Subject to Earthquake Ground Motions*

E 773 *Standard Test Method for Accelerated Weathering of Sealed Insulating Glass Units*

E 779 *Standard Test Method for Determining Air Leakage Rate by Fan Pressurization*

E 936 *Standard Practice for Roof System Assemblies Employing Steel Deck, Preformed Roof Insulation, and Bituminous Built-Up-Roofing*

E 1155 *Standard Test Method for Determining F_F Floor Flatness and F_L Floor Levelness Numbers*

E 1667 *Standard Specification for an Air Retarder (AR) Material or System for Low-Rise Framed Building Walls*

E 1966 *Standard Test Method for Fire-Resistive Joint Systems*

E 2112 *Standard Practice for Installation of Exterior Windows, Doors and Skylights*

E 2178 *Standard Test Method for Air Permeance of Building Materials*

E 2190 *Standard Specification for Insulating Glass Unit Performance and Evaluation*

E 2430 *Standard Specification for Expanded Polystyrene ("EPS") Thermal Insulation Boards for Use in Exterior Insulation and Finish Systems ("EIFS")*

AMERICAN NATIONAL STANDARDS INSTITUTE (ANSI) (WWW.ANSI.ORG)

A 17.1 *Safety Code for Elevators and Escalators*

A108/A118/A136.1 *Specifications for the Installation of Ceramic Tile*

American National Standard Specifications **A108**. .1A, .1B, .1C, .4, .5, .6, .8, .9, .10, .11, .12, and .13 define the installation of ceramic tile. **A118.1**, .3, .4, .5, .6, .7, .8, .9, .10, and **A136.1** define the test methods and physical properties for ceramic tile installation materials.

A 108.1A *Ceramic Tile Installed in the Wet-Set Method with Portland Cement Mortar*

A 108.1B *Ceramic Tile Installed on a Cured Portland Cement Mortar Setting Bed with Dry-Set or Latex-Portland Cement Mortar*

A 108.5 *Installation of Ceramic Tile with Dry-Set Portland Cement Mortar or Latex-Portland Cement Mortar*

A 108.10 *Installation of Grout in Tilework*

A 118.1 *Specifications for Dry-set Portland Cement Mortar*

A 118.4 *Specifications for Latex-Portland Cement Mortar*

A 118.6 *Specifications for Standard Ceramic Tile Grouts for Tile Installation*

A 118.10 *Load Bearing, Bonded, Waterproof Membranes for Thin-Set Ceramic Tile and Dimension Stone Installation*

A 118.12 *Specifications for Crack Isolation Membranes for Thin-Set Ceramic Tile and Dimension Stone Installations*

A 137.1 *Ceramic Tile*

A156.115 *Hardware Preparation in Steel Doors and Steel Frames*

A156.115W *Hardware Preparation in Wood Doors with Wood or Steel Frames*

A 190.1 *Structural Glued Laminated Timber—Production Requirements for Glulam*

Z 97.1 *Safety Glazing Materials Used in Buildings—Safety Performance Specifications and Methods of Test*

AMERICAN ARCHITECTURAL MANUFACTURERS ASSOCIATION (AAMA) (WWW.AAMANET.ORG)

AAMA/WDMA/CSA 101/I.S. 2/A440 *North American Fenestration Standard/Specification for Windows, Doors, and Skylights*

AAMA 303 *Voluntary Specification for Rigid Polyvinyl Chloride (PVC) Exterior Profiles*

AAMA 308 *Voluntary Specification for Cellular Polyvinyl Chloride (PVC) Exterior Profiles*

AAMA 501.4 *Recommended Static Test Method for Evaluating Curtain Wall and Storefront Systems Subjected to Seismic and Wind Induced Interstory Drifts*

AAMA 508 *Voluntary Test Method and Specification for Pressure-Equalized Rain-Screen Wall Cladding Systems*

AAMA 611 *Voluntary Standards for Anodized Architectural Aluminum*

AAMA 701/702 *Voluntary Specification for Pile Weatherstrip and Replaceable Fenestration Weatherseals*

AAMA 711 *Guideline for Application of Self-Adhering Flashing Used for the Installation of Fenestration Products*

AAMA 800 *Voluntary Specifications and Test Methods for Sealants*

AAMA 910-XX *Voluntary "Life Cycle" Specifications and Test Methods for Architectural Aluminum Storefront and Entrance Manual (under development)*

AAMA 2603 *Voluntary Specification, Performance Requirements and Test Procedures for Pigmented Organic Coatings on Aluminum Extrusions and Panels*

AAMA 2605 *Voluntary Specification, Performance Requirements and Test Procedures for Superior Performing Organic Coatings on Aluminum Extrusions and Panels*

AMERICAN CONCRETE INSTITUTE (ACI) (WWW.CONCRETE.ORG)

ACI 117 *Specifications for Tolerances for Concrete Construction and Materials and Commentary*

ACI 301 *Specifications for Structural Concrete*

ACI 318 *Building Code Requirements for Structural Concrete*

ACI 530/530.1 *Building Code Requirements & Specification for Masonry Structures and Related Commentaries*

ACI 530.1/ASCE 6/TMS 602 *Specification for Masonry Structures*

AMERICAN INSTITUTE OF TIMBER CONSTRUCTION (AITC) (WWW.AITC-GLULAM.ORG)

AITC 112 *Standard for Tongue-and-Groove Heavy Timber Roof Decking*

AITC 113 *Standard for Dimensions of Structural Glued Laminated Timber*

AITC 117 *Standard Specifications for Structural Glued Laminated Timber of Softwood Species—Design Requirements*

ANSI/AITC A190.1 *Structural Glued Laminated Timber—Production Requirements for Glulam*

APA—THE ENGINEERED WOOD ASSOCIATION (WWW.APAWOOD.ORG)

PRP-108 *Performance Standards and Qualification Policy for Structural-Use Panels*

PS 2 *Performance Standard for Wood-Based Structural-Use Panels*

CONSUMER PRODUCTS SAFETY COMMISSION (CPSC) (WWW.CPSC.GOV)

16 CFR 1201 *Safety Standard for Architectural Glazing Materials*

FACTORY MUTUAL (WWW.FMGLOBAL.COM)

FM 4450 *Approval Standard for Class 1 Insulated Steel Roof Decks*

FM 4470 *Approval Standard for Class 1 Roof Covers*

GLASS ASSOCIATION OF NORTH AMERICA (WWW.GLASSWEBSITE.COM)

GANA *Engineering Standards Manual*

GANA *Fully Tempered Heavy Glass Door and Entrance Systems Design Guide*

GANA *Glazing Manual*

FGMA *Sealant Manual*

GYPSUM ASSOCIATION (GA) (WWW.GYPSUM.ORG)

GA-214 *Recommended Levels of Gypsum Board Finish*

GA-216 *Specifications for the Application and Finishing of Gypsum Panel Products*

GA-226 *Application of Gypsum Board to Form Curved Surfaces*

GA-600 *Fire Resistance Design Manual*

NATIONAL FIRE PROTECTION ASSOCIATION (NFPA) (WWW.NFPA.ORG)

80 *Standard for Fire Doors and Windows*

252 *Standard Methods of Fire Tests of Door Assemblies (Same as UL 10B)*

257 *Standard on Fire Test for Window and Glass Block Assemblies*

SINGLE-PLY ROOFING INSTITUTE (SPRI) (WWW.SPRI.ORG)

ANSI/SPRI RP-4 *Wind Design Standard for Ballasted Single-ply Roofing Systems*

ANSI/SPRI WD-1 *ANSI/SPRI Wind Design Standard Practice for Roofing Assemblies*

Application Guidelines for Self Adhered Thermoplastic and Thermoset Roofing Systems

STEEL DOOR INSTITUTE (SDI) (WWW.STEELDOOR.ORG)

ANSI/SDI A250.8 *Recommended Specifications for Standard Steel Doors & Frames*

SDI 108 *Recommended Selection & Usage Guide for Standard Steel Doors*

SDI 111 *Recommended Selection & Usage Guide for Standard Details, Steel Doors, Frames, and Accessories*

SDI 122 *Installation & Troubleshooting Guide for Standard Steel Doors & Frames*

UNDERWRITERS LABORATORIES (UL) (WWW.UL.COM)

UL 10B *Standard for Safety for Fire Tests of Door Assemblies (Same as NFPA 252)*

UL 10C *Standard for Safety for Positive-Pressure Fire Tests of Door Assemblies*

UL 580 *Test for Uplift Resistance of Roof Assemblies*

UL 790 *Tests for Fire Resistance of Roof Covering Materials*

UL 1256 *Fire Test of Roof Deck Construction*

UL 1784 *Standard for Safety for Air Leakage Tests for Door Assemblies*

UL 1897 *Uplift Tests for Roof Covering Systems*

UL 2079 *Standard for Safety for Tests for Fire Resistance of Building Joint Systems*

WINDOW AND DOOR MANUFACTURERS ASSOCIATION (WDMA) (WWW.WDMA.COM)

ANSI/WDMA I.S.1-A *Architectural Wood Flush Doors*

AAMA/WDMA/CSA 101/I.S.2/A440 *Standard/Specification for Windows, Doors and Unit Skylights*

I.S. 6 *Industry Standard for Wood Stile and Rail Doors*

I.S. 6A *Industry Standard for Architectural Stile and Rail Doors*

APPENDIX **B**

Sources for More Information

CHAPTER 1 CONCRETE DETAILS

American Concrete Institute (www.concrete.org)

Formwork for Concrete, ACI SP-4

Guide to Formwork for Concrete, ACI 347

Guide to Cast-in-Place Architectural Concrete Practice, ACI 303R.

Guide for Concrete Floor and Slab Construction, ACI 302.1R–89

Guide to Joint Sealants for Concrete Structures, ACI 504R

Guide to the Use of Waterproofing, Dampproofing, Protective, and Decorative Barrier Systems for Concrete, ACI 515.1R

Specifications for Tolerances for Concrete Construction and Materials and Commentary, ACI 117

Precast/Prestressed Concrete Institute (www.pci.org)

Architectural Precast Concrete, 3rd ed.

MNL 135–00, *Tolerance Manual for Precast and Prestressed Concrete Construction*

MNL-128–01, *Recommended Practice for Glass Fiber Reinforced Concrete Panels*

Portland Cement Association (www.cement.org)

Concrete Masonry Handbook for Architects, Engineers, Builders, 6th ed.

Plastic Forms for Architectural Concrete

Trade Associations

Autoclaved Aerated Concrete Products Association, www.aacpa.org

Cast Stone Institute, www.caststone.org

Tilt-Up Concrete Association, www.tilt-up.org

CHAPTER 2 MASONRY DETAILS

National Concrete Masonry Association (www.ncma.org)

Annotated Design and Construction Details for Concrete Masonry

Control of Wall Movement with Concrete Masonry, NCMA-TEK 3. Herndon, VA: National Concrete Masonry Association, 1972.

Design of Concrete Masonry for Crack Control, NCMA-TEK 53. Herndon, VA: National Concrete Masonry Association, 1973.

Masonry Institute of America (www.masonryinstitute.org)

Design Guide for Anchored Brick Veneer Over Steel Studs

Marble and Stone Slab Veneer, 3rd ed.

Masonry Design Manual, 4th ed.

Masonry Veneer, 3rd ed.

The Masonry Society (www.masonrysociety.org)

Masonry Designers' Guide, 5th ed., MDG-5, 2007

Brick Industry Association (www.gobrick.com)

Water Penetration Resistance—Design and Detailing, Technical Note 7

Volume Changes—Analysis and Effects of Movement, Technical Note 18

Accommodating Expansion of Brickwork, Technical Note 18A

Brick Masonry Cavity Walls—Introduction, Technical Note 21 Rev.

Brick Masonry Cavity Walls—Selection of Materials, Technical Note 21A Rev.

Brick Masonry Cavity Walls—Detailing, Technical Note 21B

Brick Masonry Rain Screen Walls, Technical Note 27 Rev.

Anchored Brick Veneer, Wood Frame Construction, Technical Note 28 Rev.

Brick Veneer/Steel Stud Walls, Technical Note 28B

Brick Masonry Details, Caps and Copings, Corbels and Racking, Technical Note 36A

Wall Ties for Brick Masonry, Technical Note 44B Rev.

Books

Amrhein, James E., and Merrigan, Michael W. *Marble and Stone Slab Veneer*. Los Angeles: Masonry Institute of America, 1989.

Beall, Christine. *Masonry Design and Detailing*, 4th ed. New York: McGraw-Hill, 1997.

Loughran, Patrick. *Failed Stone: Problems and Solutions with Concrete and Masonry*. Basel, Switzerland: Birkhäuser, 2006.

Other Publications

ACI 530.1–02/ASCE 6–02/TMS 602–02, *Specifications for Masonry Structures*. Farmington Hills, MI: American Concrete Institute, 2005.

Donaldson, B., ed. *New Stone Technology, Design, and Construction for Exterior Wall Systems*. Philadelphia: American Society for Testing and Materials, 1988.

Indiana Limestone Institute of America. *Limestone Handbook*. Bedford, IN: Indiana Limestone Institute of America, Inc.

The Masonry Institute of America. *Marble Design Manual*. Farmington, MI: Marble Institute of America.

CHAPTER 3 METAL DETAILS

American Institute of Steel Construction. *Code of Standard Practice for Steel Buildings and Bridges, 302*. Chicago: American Institute of Steel Construction.

American Institute of Steel Construction. *Detailing for Steel Construction*, 2nd ed. Chicago: American Institute of Steel Construction, 2002.

Copper Development Association. *Copper in Architecture Handbook*. Greenwich, CT: Copper Development Association, Inc. n.d.

North American Steel Framing Alliance. *Low-Rise Residential Construction Details*, Publication NT6–00. Washington, DC: Steel Framing Alliance, n.d.

Steel Joist Institute. *Standard Specifications, Load Tables and Weight Tables for Steel Joists and Joist Girders*, 42nd ed. Forest, VA: Steel Joist Institute, 2005.

Zahner, L. William. *Architectural Metals*. New York: John Wiley & Sons, 1995.

Specialty Steel Industry of North America (www.ssina.com)

Design Guidelines for the Selection and Use of Stainless Steel

Stainless Steel Architectural Facts

Stainless Steel for Handrails, Railings & Barrier Applications

Standard Practices for: Stainless Steel Roofing, Flashing, Copings

Trade Associations

The Aluminum Association, www.aluminum.org

American Institute of Steel Construction, www.aisc.org

American Iron and Steel Institute, www.steel.org

Copper Development Association, www.copper.org

Industrial Perforators Association, www.iperf.org

National Association of Architectural Metal Manufacturers, www.naamm.org

CHAPTER 4 WOOD DETAILS

American Institute of Timber Construction. *Timber Construction Manual*, 5th ed. New York: John Wiley & Sons, 2004.

American Institute of Timber Construction. *Typical Construction Details, AITC 104.* Englewood, CO: American Institute of Timber Construction.

Architectural Woodwork Institute. *Architectural Woodwork Quality Standards Illustrated,* 8th ed. Reston, VA: Architectural Woodwork Institute.

Newman, Morton. *Design and Construction of Wood Framed Buildings.* New York: McGraw-Hill, 1994.

Thallon, Rob. *Graphic Guide to Frame Construction: Details for Builders and Designers,* 2nd ed. Newtown, CT: Taunton, 2000.

Trade Associations

American Institute of Timber Construction, www.aitc-glulam.org

American Wood Council, www.awc.org

Architectural Woodwork Institute, www.awinet.org

Forest Stewardship Council, www.fscus.org

Hardwood Plywood & Veneer Association, www.hpva.org

Structural Insulated Panel Association, www.sips.org

Wood I-Joist Manufacturers Association, www.i-joist.org

Wood Moulding and Millwork Producers Association, www.wmmpa.com

Wood Truss Council of America, www.wtcatko.com

CHAPTER 5 THERMAL AND MOISTURE PROTECTION DETAILS

National Roofing Contractors Association (www.nrca.net)

NRCA Construction Details (on CD-ROM)

NRCA Green Roof Systems Manual (on CD-ROM)

NRCA Metal Panel and SPF Roof Systems

NRCA Roofing Manual: Membrane Roof Systems

NRCA Roofing Manual: Metal Panel and SPF Roof Systems

NRCA Steep-Slope Roof Systems

NRCA Waterproofing Manual

Sealant Waterproofing and Restoration Institute (www.swrionline.org)

Below Grade Waterproofing Manual

Practical Guide to Waterproofing Exterior Walls

Sealants: The Professionals' Guide

Books

American Architectural Manufacturers Association. *Joint Sealants,* JS-91. Schaumburg, IL: AAMA, 1991.

American Architectural Manufacturers Association. *Rain Penetration Control—Applying Current Knowledge* (CD-ROM), RPC-00. Schaumburg, IL: AAMA, 2000.

Amstock, Joseph S. *Handbook of Adhesives and Sealants in Construction.* New York: McGraw-Hill Professional, 2000.

Asphalt Roofing Manufacturers Association. *Built-Up Roofing Systems Design Guide.* Washington, DC: Asphalt Roofing Manufacturers Association.

Brock, Linda. *Designing the Exterior Wall: An Architectural Guide to the Vertical Envelope.* Hoboken, NJ: John Wiley & Sons, 2005.

EIFS Industry Members Association. *Guide to Exterior Insulation and Finish System Construction.* Morrow, GA: EIFS Industry Members Association.

Gish, L. E., ed. *Building Deck Waterproofing,* STP 1084. Philadelphia: American Society for Testing and Materials, 1990.

Henshell, Justin, and Griffin, C.W. *The Manual of Below-Grade Waterproofing Systems.* New York: John Wiley & Sons, 1999.

Lstiburek, Joseph W., and Carmody, John. *Moisture Control Handbook: Principles and Practices for Residential and Small Commercial Buildings.* New York: John Wiley & Sons, 1996.

Rose, William B. *Water in Buildings: An Architect's Guide to Moisture and Mold.* New York: John Wiley & Sons, 2005.

Sheet Metal and Air Conditioning Contractors National Association. SMACNA Architectural Sheet Metal Manual. Vienna, VA: SMACNA.

Trade Associations

Asphalt Roofing Manufacturers Association, www.asphaltroofing.org

Building Environment and Thermal Envelope Council, www.nibs.org/betec.html

Cedar Shake and Shingle Bureau, www.cedarbureau.org

Cellulose Insulation Manufacturers Association, www.cellulose.org

EIFS Industry Members Association, www.eima.com

EPDM Roofing Association, www.epdmroofs.org

EPS Molders Association, www.epsmolders.org

Extruded Polystyrene Foam Association, www.xpsa.com

National Roof Deck Contractors Association, www.nrdca.org

National Roofing Contractors Association, www.nrca.net

North American Insulation Manufacturers Association, www.naima.org

Perlite Institute, www.perlite.org

Polyisocyanurate Insulation Manufacturers Association, www.polyiso.org

Reflective Insulation Manufacturers Association Intl., www.rimainternational.org

Sealant Waterproofing and Restoration Institute, www.swrionline.org

Sheet Metal and Air Conditioning Contractors Nat. Association, www.smacna.org

Single Ply Roofing Institute, www.spri.org

Spray Polyurethane Foam Alliance, www.sprayfoam.org

National Institute of Building Sciences, Whole Building Design Guide, Building Envelope Design Guide,www.wbdg.org/design/envelope.php

CHAPTER 6 DOOR AND WINDOW DETAILS

American Architectural Manufacturers Association (www.aamanet.org)

Aluminum Curtain Wall Design Guide Manual, CW-DG-1–96

Aluminum Store Front and Entrance Manual, SFM-1

Design Windloads for Buildings and Boundary Layer Wind Tunnel Testing, CW-11

Fenestration Sealants Guide Manual, 850

Glass and Glazing, GAG-1

Installation of Aluminum Curtain Walls, CWG-1–89

Metal Curtain Wall Manual, MCWM-1

Methods of Tests for Exterior Walls, 501–05

Sound Control for Fenestration Products, TIR-A1–04

Structural Sealant Glazing Systems, CW-13

Glass Association of North America (www.glasswebsite.com)

GANA Glazing Manual

GANA Sealant Manual

Fully Tempered Heavy Glass Door and Entrance Systems Design Guide

Insulating Glass Manufacturers Alliance (www.igmaonline.org)

Guidelines for Sloped Glazing, TB-3001

Voluntary Test Methods for Chemical Effects of Glazing Compounds on Elastomeric Edge Seals, TR-1000

Voluntary Test Methods and Voluntary Performance Quality Assurance Criteria for Spacers for Sealed Insulating Glass Units, A-2000

Steel Door Institute (www.steeldoor.org)

Guidelines for Acoustical Performance of Standard Steel Doors and Frames, SDI-128

Installation & Troubleshooting Guide for Standard Steel Doors and Frames, SDI-122

Recommended Selection and Usage Guide for Standard Steel Doors, SDI-108

Recommended Standard Steel Door Details, SDI-111-A

Standard Steel Doors and Frames for Modular Masonry Construction, SDI-110

Trade Associations

Door and Hardware Institute, www.dhi.org

Hollow Metal Manufacturers Association, www.naamm.org/hmma

Steel Window Institute, www.steelwindows.com

Window and Door Manufacturers Association, www.wdma.com

CHAPTER 7 FINISH DETAILS

Ceilings and Interior Systems Construction Association (www.cisca.org)

Ceiling Systems Handbook

Glass Fiber Custom Acoustical Wall Panel

Glass Reinforced Gypsum Guides

Guidelines for Seismic Restraint for Direct-hung Suspended Ceiling Assemblies (zones 3–4)

Metal Security Ceilings

Recommendations for Direct-hung Acoustical Tile and Lay-in Panel Ceilings (zones 0–2)

Gypsum Association (www.gypsum.org)

Application and Finishing of Gypsum Panel Products, GA-216

Application of Gypsum Board to Form Curved Surfaces, GA-226

Fire Resistance Manual, GA-600

Recommended Levels of Gypsum Board Finish, GA-214

Books

National Terrazzo & Mosaic Association. *Handbook.* Des Plaines, IL: The National Terrazzo & Mosaic Association, Inc.

Tile Council of North America. *TCA Handbook for Ceramic Tile Installation.* Anderson, SC: Tile Council of North America.

USG Corporation. *The Gypsum Construction Handbook.* Chicago: USG Corporation.

Trade Associations

NOFMA, The Wood Flooring Manufacturers Association, www.nofma.org

The National Terrazzo & Mosaic Association, Inc., www.ntma.com

Tile Council of North America, www.tileusa.com

MISCELLANEOUS

Allen, Edward, and Iano, Joseph. *Fundamentals of Building Construction: Materials and Methods,* 4th ed. Hoboken, NJ: John Wiley & Sons, 2004.

Allen, Edward, and Rand, Patrick. *Architectural Detailing, Function, Constructibility, Aesthetics,* 2nd ed. Hoboken, NJ: John Wiley & Sons, 2007.

Ballast, David Kent. *Interior Construction and Detailing for Designers and Architects,* 4th ed. Belmont, CA: Professional Publications, Inc., 2007.

Ballast, David Kent. *Handbook of Construction Tolerances,* 2nd ed. Hoboken, NJ: John Wiley & Sons, 2007.

Campbell, Peter, ed. *Learning from Construction Failures: Applied Forensic Engineering.* Hoboken, NJ: John Wiley & Sons, 2001.

Killory, Christine, ed. *Details in Contemporary Architecture: As Built.* New York: Princeton Architectural Press, 2007.

Spiegel, Ross, and Meadows, Dru. *Green Building Materials, A Guide to Product Selection and Specifications*, 2nd ed. Hoboken, NJ: John Wiley & Sons, 2006.

Wakita, Osamu, and Linde, Richard. *The Professional Practice of Architectural Detailing,* 3rd ed. Hoboken, NJ: John Wiley & Sons, 1999.

Wakita, Osamu, and Linde, Richard. *The Professional Practice of Architectural Working Drawings,* 3rd ed. Hoboken, NJ: John Wiley & Sons, 2002.

Wilson, Alex, et al., eds. *Greenspec* [R] *Directory: Product Listing & Guideline Specifications.* Brattleboro, VT: Building Green, Inc.

CSI SIX-DIGIT NUMBER INDEX

Division 3, Concrete

Division 4, Masonry

Division 5, Metals

Division 6, Wood, Plastics, and Composites

CSI Number	Section Title	Section No.
06 11 00.1	Platform framing at foundation	4-1
06 11 00.2	Platform framing at stepped foundation	4-2
06 11 00.3	Platform framing at roof	4-3
06 11 00.4	Multistory framing at foundation	4-4
06 11 00.5	Multistory framing at floor line	4-5
06 11 00.6	Multistory framing at roof	4-6
06 12 00.1	Structural insulated panel at foundation	4-7
06 12 00.2	Structural insulated panel at roof	4-8
06 18 13.1	Glulam beam at foundation wall	4-9
06 18 13.2	Glulam beam at column	4-10
06 18 13.3	Glulam purlins at beam	4-11
06 18 13.4	Glulam roof beam	4-12
06 18 16	Glulam column at base	4-13
06 41 00.1	Base cabinet	4-14
06 41 00.2	Upper cabinet	4-15
06 41 00.3	Countertops	4-16
06 41 00.4	Shelving	4-17
06 42 16	Flush wood paneling	4-18

Division 7, Thermal and Moisture Protection

CSI Number	Section Title	Section No.
07 13 00	Foundation waterproofing	5-1
07 14 00.1	Cold, liquid-applied membrane deck waterproofing	5-2
07 14 00.2	Closed joint deck waterproofing	5-2.1
07 21 13	Slab-on-grade foundation insulation	5-4
07 22 00.1	Roofing systems on steel deck	5-14
07 22 00.2	Roofing systems on concrete deck	5-15
07 24 00.1	Exterior insulation and finish system at base	5-6
07 24 00.2	Exterior insulation and finish system at parapet	5-7
07 24 00.3	Exterior insulation and finish system openings	5-8
07 25 01	Weather barrier concepts	5-5.1
07 25 01.2	Climate zones	5-5.2
07 25 01.3	Rain screen weather barrier concepts	5-5.3
07 31 13	Asphalt/glass fiber shingles at eaves	5-9
07 31 29	Wood shingles at eaves	5-10
07 32 00	Roofing tiles at eaves	5-11
07 42 13.1	Preformed metal wall panel at base	5-12
07 42 13.2	Preformed metal wall panel at parapet	5-13
07 51 00.1	Built-up roof at supported deck	5-16
07 51 00.2	Built-up roof at non-supported deck	5-17
07 51 00.3	Built-up roof at expansion joint	5-18

Division 8, Openings

Division 9, Finishes

Division 22, Plumbing

Index

NOTES

NOTES

NOTES

NOTES

NOTES

NOTES

NOTES

NOTES

NOTES

NOTES

NOTES